LADY ECLECTE

LADY ECLECTE

THE LOST WOMAN OF THE NEW TESTAMENT

LINCOLN H. BLUMELL

FORTRESS PRESS
Minneapolis

LADY ECLECTE
The Lost Woman of the New Testament

30 29 28 27 26 25 2 3 4 5 6 7 8 9 10

Library of Congress Control Number: 2025003272 (print)

Cover image: An Egyptian painted wood mummy portrait of a woman. Roman period, circa 150 CE.
Cover design: Kris E. Miller

Print ISBN: 979-8-8898-3424-3
eBook ISBN: 979-8-8898-3425-0

Λίνκολος Μαρκίᾳ τῇ συμβίῳ
μου γλυκυτάτῃ ἣν ἐγὼ ἀγαπῶ
ἐν ἀληθείᾳ, ἐν κ(υρί)ῳ πλεῖστα
χαίρειν. περὶ μὲν παντὸς εὔχομαί σε ὑγιαίνειν καὶ εὐοδοῦσθαι
καὶ τὰ μεγάλα πράττειν. τὸ προσ-
κύνημα σου ποιῶ καθ' ἑκάστην
ἡμέραν παρὰ τῷ κ(υρί)ῳ θ(ε)ῷ.
εὐχαριστῆσαι σε θέλω περὶ πάσης ἀγάπης καὶ εὐνοίας καὶ ὑπο-
στάσεως σου· τὸ βιβλίον τοῦτο
χωρὶς σοῦ οὐκ ἂν δυναίμην γράψαι, σοι ἀφιερῶ αὐτό. πολλὰ ἄλλα εἶχον γράψαι σοι ἀλλ' οὐ θέλω διὰ ταύτην ἐπιστολήν, ἀλλά
σοι στόμα πρὸς στόμα λαλήσω
ταῦτα.

ἐρρῶσθαί σε εὔχομαι
πολλοῖς χρόνοις
ἐν κ(υρί)ῳ.

πολλὰ τὰ ἔτη ἡμῖν

CONTENTS

ABBREVIATIONS AND CONVENTIONS

For abbreviations, I have followed *The SBL Handbook of Style: For Biblical Studies and Related Disciplines*, 2nd ed. (Scholars Press, 2014). For abbreviations of classical works not in *The SBL Handbook of Style*, I have followed those given in S. Hornblower, A. Spawforth, and E. Eidinow, eds., *The Oxford Classical Dictionary*, 4th ed. (Oxford University Press, 2012). For editions of papyri and ostraca, I have followed the abbreviations given in the online edition of the *Checklist of Editions of Greek, Latin, Demotic, and Coptic Papyri, Ostraca, and Tablets* available online at https://papyri.info/docs/checklist. For abbreviations of inscriptions, I have used those provided by the *Association Internationale d'Épigraphie Grecque et Latine*, available online at https://aiegl.org/grepiabbr.html. Abbreviations not appearing in the resources mentioned above or those that occur frequently are as follows:

ANF	*Ante-Nicene Fathers*. Edited by A. Roberts and J. Donaldson. 1885–87. 10 vols. Repr., Hendrickson, 1994.
APF	*Archiv für Papyrusforschung und verwandte Gebiete*
BDAG	F. W. Danker, W. Bauer, W. F. Arndt, and F. W. Gingrich. *Greek-English Lexicon of the New Testament and Other Early Christian Literature*, 3rd ed. University of Chicago Press, 2000.
CCSL	Corpus Christianorum: Series Latina
CPG	*Clavis Patrum Graecorum*. Edited by M. Geerard. 5 vols. Brepols, 1974–1987.
CPL	*Clavis Patrum Latinorum*. Edited by E. Dekkers. 2nd ed. Abbatia Sancti Petri, 1961.
CSEL	Corpus Scriptorum Ecclesiasticorum Latinorum
DELG	P. Chantraine, *Dictionanaire étymologique de la langue grecque: Histoire des mots*. New Edition. Librairie Klincksieck série linguistique 20. Klincksieck, 2009.

DRV	Douay–Rheims Version (Bible)
ECM	*Novum Testamentum Graecum: Editio Critica Maior.* Deutsche Bibelgesellschaft, 1997–.
EDC	R. Beekes, *Etymological Dictionary of Greek.* Leiden Indo-European Etymological Dictionary Series 10. 2 vols. Brill, 2013.
GA	This abbreviation indicates the Gregory-Aland numbering system used for identifying manuscripts of the New Testament. The abbreviation GA is always followed by a number referencing the manuscript.
κτλ	This Greek abbreviation stands for καὶ τὰ λοιπά ("and so on") and will be used in places where I only quote part of a passage or phrase in Greek to indicate that more properly follows.
LDAB	*Leuven Database of Ancient Books,* http://www.trismegistos.org/ldab/.
LGPN	*Lexicon of Greek Personal Names,* https://www.lgpn.ox.ac.uk.
LSJ	H. G. Liddell, R. Scott and H. S. Jones. *A Greek-English Lexicon,* 9th ed. with revised supplement. Clarendon, 1996.
Montanari	F. Montanari. *The Brill Dictionary of Ancient Greek.* Brill, 2015.
NA[28]	*Novum Testamentum Graece,* Nestle-Aland, 28th ed. Deutsche Bibelgesellschaft, 2012.
NPNF[2]	*Nicene and Post-Nicene Fathers,* Series 2
NRSVue	New Revised Standard Version Updated Edition
𝔓	Papyrus number; a superscript number will always follow it.
PGL	G. W. H. Lampe. *Patristic Greek Lexicon.* Clarendon, 1961.
SBLGNT	*Society of Biblical Literature Greek New Testament.* Edited by M. W. Holmes. Society of Biblical Literature, 2010.
SC	Sources chrétiennes. Cerf, 1943–.
TM no.	*Trismegistos Number,* http://www.trismegistos.org/.
TUGAL	*Texte und Untersuchungen zur Geschichte der altchristlichen Literatur*
TYNGNT	*The Greek New Testament.* Produced at Tyndale House Cambridge. Edited by D. Jongkind. Cambridge University Press, 2017.

I have used Latin terminations for English transliterations of Greek personal and place names; thus, Isodorus, not Isodoros, and Oxyrhynchus, not

Oxyrhynchos. Along the same lines, I have preferred the Roman transliteration c for the Greek kappa; thus, Lucius, not Lukius, and Crete, not Krete. With some Egyptian names, I deliberately left out accents because of uncertainties about accent placement and emphasis. Misspelled words in documentary papyri and inscriptions are spelled as is but corrected in notes, parentheses, or apparatus. Greek text appearing in the work is typically accented, although there are occasions when the text is deliberately unaccented. This occurs when I am reproducing a text diplomatically by only showing the letter string as it would have appeared in an ancient manuscript, inscription, or papyrus, or when I am following an established editorial convention where Greek accents are typically not included. I generally use minuscule Greek script, but at times I use majuscule script in order to approximate how the original text looked. Additionally, I periodically use the undifferentiated lunate sigma (c) instead of the medial and terminal sigma (σ, ς). Unless otherwise noted, the Greek text of the New Testament appearing in the volume is taken from the *Novum Testamentum Graece*, Nestle-Aland, 28th ed.

For convenience, some dates are listed as "I" or "II" instead of spelling out "first century" or "second century." Dates listed as "II/III" or "III/IV" should not be interpreted as meaning that the text in question dates to the "late second / early third century" or "late third / early fourth century," unless noted, but instead that it dates to the "second or third century" or "third or fourth century." This broad latitude in dating is sometimes required owing to paleographic uncertainties concerning the dating of papyri and inscriptions. Unless noted otherwise, all translations of biblical texts are taken from the *New Revised Standard Version Updated Edition* (NRSVue). All other translations appearing in the work are my own unless otherwise noted.

PREFACE

The first papyrus I edited and published was a Greek petition from Oxyrhynchus that carried a date corresponding to March 17, 291 CE.[1] It was submitted to the "police chief" of the city and was filed by a woman named Aurelia Hermanoubiaina. In the petition, she reports that her husband, Cyril, had left on business six weeks earlier in the company of a sailor named Ischyrion. She alleges that since then, she had heard nothing from her husband and that on the day she submitted the petition, she found Ischyrion back in the city wearing her husband's clothes! Fearing that the worst had befallen Cyril at the hands of the sailor, she had Ischyrion swiftly detained and was demanding that justice be exacted. At this point, the petition abruptly ended. What happened to Cyril, we may never know.

Working on this papyrus was both painfully frustrating and incredibly exciting. Decipherment of the text was complicated not only by the lacunose condition of the 1,700-year-old papyrus but also because it contained various orthographical and grammatical errors that initially frustrated the correct interpretation. Despite these challenges, piecing together each successive line of the story was exhilarating as the plot developed. Since publishing that papyrus, I have edited many other texts, from tax receipts, medical prescriptions, mummy labels, name lists, and leases to amulets, love spells, classroom lectures, and biblical fragments. I have also worked on several ancient letters, either editing previously unpublished pieces or reediting pieces previously published and adding some new insight that was lacking in an earlier edition. I have edited letters preserved on papyrus from the Ptolemaic period through the Byzantine period (ca. 323 BCE–642 CE). Letters are among my favorite texts to edit. They are highly formulaic in places but also exceptionally diverse in other places as each letter contains its own story. I think one of the reasons I am particularly drawn to ancient letters is that they often focus on people and reveal something about their daily lives and interpersonal relations. After reading someone's letter, I get to know them in a small sense.

This monograph, which primarily deals with the address in 2 John 1, is directly informed by my work in papyrology. On many fronts, 2 John shares similarities with the various epistolary papyri I have edited over the years. This should not be surprising as the underlying Greek of 2 John 12 states that the letter was written on *χάρτης* (papyrus). As such, it is the only letter in the entire New Testament canon that explicitly states the medium on which it was written. While this letter is traditionally thought to contain a metaphorical address to a church personified as an "elect lady," using the insights I have developed and honed editing and reediting ancient letters, I will demonstrate that the prevailing interpretation of the address in the letter is incorrect. Instead, the letter is addressed to a woman bearing the Greek name Eclecte (Ἐκλέκτη). Though she has been lost for nearly two millennia due to the omission of two reduplicated letters, she dramatically reemerges when the correct address is restored to 2 John 1. Just as I have sought to bring to light the lives of ancient men and women who reside in the documents they have left behind, I hope to properly bring to light Lady Eclecte of 2 John.

Lincoln H. Blumell
January 2025

ACKNOWLEDGMENTS

This work could not have been accomplished without the help and support of various students, colleagues, and friends. They carefully read drafts of chapters, discussed the ideas contained therein, and provided constant encouragement and assistance that proved indispensable to the completion of this project. Spencer Kraus, who worked as my TA during the first part of this project, was invaluable; he tracked down references, checked sources and citations, and helped at every stage of the work. Even after graduation, he continued to offer his services. Grace Blumell, Robert Flores, Richard Jarvis, and Annie Spach worked as TAs during the later stages of this project and provided much valuable help with notes, bibliography, and editorial items. I thank the graduate cohorts in Religious Education and Chaplaincy at Brigham Young University who read chapters and provided valuable feedback on different parts of the book in two graduate seminars. I also benefited greatly from colleagues in the Department of Ancient Scripture, who showed a genuine interest in my work from an early stage and provided much valuable feedback and direction. I sincerely thank Philip Abbott, Jason Combs, Kerry Hull, and Frank Judd Jr. I also genuinely thank my department chair, Shon Hopkin, for all his support during this project. Additionally, I want to thank my colleague Ross Baron, who helped me facilitate a teaching reduction so that I could get the manuscript over the finish line. I also want to thank Stephen Ehat and Bruce Griffin for reading all the chapters and providing valuable insights. Several others who deserve thanks include Charlotte Blumell, Claire Blumell, Luke Blumell, Christy Fleck, Kristian Heal, Wendy Gubler, Larry Horchata, Michael Rutter, and John Stiegl. Finally, I could not have finished this book without the constant encouragement, support, and love of my wife, Marcie. It is to her that this book is dedicated.

CHAPTER ONE

A Most Unusual Claim in Clement of Alexandria

Therefore, first read carefully and correct the errors of the scribes in such a way that you do not deserve criticism for trying to correct others without due deliberation; this kind of correction is, in my opinion, the most beautiful and glorious task of learned men.

—Cassiodorus, *Institutes of Divine and Secular Learning* (ca. 560 CE), 1.15.1[1]

IN THE LATE spring of 2023, I found myself unexpectedly immersed in the writings of Clement of Alexandria (ca. 150–215 CE). I was working on an archaeological dig in Egypt, editing a collection of Greek texts (papyri, ostraca, and inscriptions), and noticed some parallels to certain words and short phrases used by Clement. I soon found myself spending more time with Clement than I did working on the texts I had intended to edit. Before this, I only had a passing acquaintance with Clement. Though I had never read from cover to cover his *magnum opus*, *Miscellanies*, I had read large portions. I was interested in the vast array of subjects he treated and his curious, yet often perceptive, insights on select scriptural passages. When I had read his *Exhortation to the Greeks* some years earlier as a doctoral student, I was impressed with his engagement with classical sources, and it struck me that he was at the forefront of ancient Christian intellectualism. My interest in Clement has also been piqued over the last twenty years following the recurring debate over an alleged letter he wrote that references another recension of the Gospel of Mark, or Secret Mark, as it has come to be known.[2]

On my return from Egypt, I invested myself more seriously in the works of Clement. I began to peruse the three-volume critical edition of his collected works, first edited and published between 1905 and 1909 by Otto Stählin of the University of Munich.[3] The third volume eventually caught my attention. The last section consists of a collection of fragments from later Christian authors through the early Middle Ages (until the tenth century) who either remarked on Clement and provided some biographical detail about his life or referenced and quoted some fragment from a work attributed to him but that is now lost. Six principal works of Clement have come down to us in the manuscript tradition: the aforementioned *Miscellanies* and *Exhortation to the Greeks*, as well as *Christ the Educator, Salvation of the Rich, Excerpts from Theodotus*, and *Extracts from the Prophets*.[4] From the fragments, it is clear there were at least seven other works of Clement, not to mention other lost letters known only through excerpts.[5] Among these lost works, the most important in the ancient church was one titled *Hypotyposes*,[6] where Clement sketched out an abridged commentary on the books of the Old and New Testaments and other early Christian writings.[7] The earliest surviving description of this important text comes from Eusebius of Caesarea's (ca. 260/65–339 CE) *Ecclesiastical History*, published almost a century (ca. 320s CE) after Clement died. In Eusebius's history, he gives the following description of the work: "And of equal number with these are his [Clement's] books entitled *Hypotyposes*, in which he mentions Pantaenus by name as his teacher, and has set forth his interpretations of the Scriptures and his traditions. . . . And in the *Hypotyposes*, to speak briefly, he has given concise explanations of all the Canonical Scriptures, not passing over even the disputed writings, I mean the Epistle of Jude and the remaining Catholic Epistles, and the Epistle of Barnabas, and the Apocalypse known as Peter's."[8] Eusebius refers to the treatise a few other times and provides short excerpts, and overall his description helps provide the general scope of the work.[9]

As I continued to make my way through the fragments, I encountered the longest surviving excerpts of Clement. These were preserved in the writings of Cassiodorus (ca. 490–585 CE), a statesman and scholar from Squillace, Italy.[10] Cassiodorus had a flourishing political career in Ravenna but was exiled to Constantinople in the late 530s CE as part of the Justinianic war of reconquest.[11] In exile, he devoted himself to deeper theological reflection so that on his return to Italy in 554, he attracted a group of monks and grammarians and established a center of Christian learning on his family's estate.[12] Accordingly, Cassiodorus amassed an extensive collection of Christian texts to elucidate the Old and New Testaments. In his *Institutes of Divine and Secular Learning*, published circa 560 CE for the instruction of those who were tasked with the work of copying, translating, and annotating the scriptures and commentaries on them, he discusses the works of Clement of Alexandria: "On the canonical epistles Clement of Alexandria, a priest (who is called [the writer of] *Miscellanies*), has written some things in excellent Greek—i.e., on 1 Peter, on 1 and 2 John, and on James. In these works he discusses many subjects carefully but some things incautiously. I have had these translated into Latin and cleaned up by the removal of some of their errors, so that his teaching can be drawn on more safely."[13]

Given that Cassiodorus had some of Clement's works translated into Latin, it is not surprising that one of the works from his collection that has come to us is titled *Sketches of Clement of Alexandria on the Canonical Epistles*.[14] It preserves Clement's commentary from *Hypotyposes* on 1 Peter, 1 and 2 John, and Jude, although the order it preserves is 1 Peter, Jude, 1 John, and then 2 John.

As I was previously unacquainted with these fragments, I eagerly began reading them to see what interpretation and insights Clement brought to bear on these New Testament letters.[15] In Clement's commentary on 1 Peter, he proceeds sequentially through the letter. However, he does not touch on every passage, and after citing some part of the letter, he provides exposition and interpretation and often cross-references other passages of Scripture for elucidation. Besides a short digression on 1 Peter 5:13, wherein he claims that the Mark mentioned in this verse was the same person who authored the Gospel bearing this name and was Peter's companion in Rome, nothing of note stuck out to me in his brief commentary.[16] I drew a similar conclusion after reading Clement's commentary on Jude and 1 John; there were some interesting expositions, and Clement put forward some novel ideas that later Christian authors would develop, but nothing really jumped off the page.[17] This changed when I read his brief remarks on 2 John.

Clement's *Sketches* on this letter occupy only two paragraphs, and his terse summation is straightforward: The letter enjoins believers to love one another and focuses on the person of Christ by warning against those who are out to deceive.[18] In the second paragraph, Clement focuses on 2 John 10, taking the elder's counsel about not receiving heterodox persons and applying it to his own day.[19] None of this is especially noteworthy, except for the striking way Clement prefaces his short commentary: "The Second Epistle of John, which is written to virgins, is very straightforward. In fact, it was written to a certain Babylonian woman, by name Eclecte,[20] but signifies the election of the holy church."[21]

I remember chuckling in disbelief when I read Clement's opening claims about the background and addressee of 2 John 1. How could Clement have thought the letter was addressed to "virgins" and, even more unbelievable, to "a certain Babylonian woman, by name Eclecte"? Convinced that all of these claims were nonsense, I initially wondered how Cassiodorus could have permitted this into his Latin translation, especially after he had explicitly stated that in the translation, certain "errors" in Clement's work were expunged.[22] After my initial disbelief, I turned to 2 John 1 in my Greek New Testament (NA[28]) to see if I had missed something. I had never heard of such an exposition and was at a complete loss as to where he found all these references. It read:

> 2 John 1
> ὁ πρεσβύτερος ἐκλεκτῇ κυρίᾳ καὶ τοῖς τέκνοις αὐτῆς, οὓς ἐγὼ ἀγαπῶ ἐν ἀληθείᾳ, καὶ οὐκ ἐγὼ μόνος ἀλλὰ καὶ πάντες οἱ ἐγνωκότες τὴν ἀλήθειαν.
>
> NRSVue
> The elder to the elect lady and her children, whom I love in the truth, and not only I but also all who know the truth.

There is no mention of "virgins" or "Babylon/Babylonian" in the first verse—nor anywhere else in the remainder of the letter. Furthermore, the reference in 2 John 1 to a "lady and her children" seemed to run contrary to the whole idea of "virgins"! Additionally, the personal name Eclecte (Ἐκλέκτη) never appears in the text. However, the third word of the epistle, "elect" (ἐκλεκτῄ), articulated as the feminine adjective modifying the title "lady" (κυρία) that follows (i.e., "elect lady"), takes an identical form. After I examined the first verse and then perused the remainder of the epistle, my initial feeling that Clement's assertions were unsubstantiated seemed justified. I concluded that Clement had committed a serious blunder in making such baseless claims, but I was at a loss as to what he was possibly seeing in the text or which traditions he may have been relying on that led him to them.

After a few days passed, I returned to these questions. I began by searching the New Testament (in both Greek and Latin) for any reference to "virgin(s)."[23] This term is absent in the Johannine Letters, and none of its fifteen occurrences in the New Testament clarified Clement's assertion that the letter was addressed to "virgins."[24] I then searched the New Testament for any reference to "Babylon."[25] I found twelve references.[26] This search proved more helpful in shedding some light on Clement's statement about "a certain Babylonian woman." The Greek text of 1 Peter 5:13, with which Clement was familiar based on his *Sketches* on 1 Peter (discussed above), reads:

1 Peter 5:13
ἀσπάζεται ὑμᾶς ἡ ἐν Βαβυλῶνι συνεκλεκτὴ καὶ Μᾶρκος ὁ υἱός μου.[27]

NRSVue
Your sister church in Babylon, chosen together with you, sends you greetings, and so does my son Mark.

The phrase in 1 Peter 5:13, "your sister church in Babylon," has a loose parallel with Clement and may provide some basis for his statement about "a certain Babylonian woman" in 2 John. While the NRSVue—and many modern translations—renders this phrase "your sister church in Babylon," the words "your sister church" are not in the Greek text. Neither the word for "church" nor the word for "sister" is used anywhere in 1 Peter.[28] The literal rendering of this phrase is something like "she who is joint-elect in Babylon."[29] Given the reference to Babylon and the female subject, it seems that Clement could have been influenced by 1 Peter 5:13 when he mentions "a certain Babylonian woman."[30] Furthermore, as this phrase employs the feminine adjective "joint-elect" (συνεκλεκτή),[31] which is related to the feminine adjective "elect" (ἐκλεκτή) appearing in the Greek New Testament in 2 John 1, it seemed reasonable to conclude that 1 Peter 5:13 was exerting some influence on Clement. While this passage provides some explanatory help, it does not address Clement's assertion that the letter is written to virgins. Likewise, it does not adequately account for his statement that the letter's recipient is named Eclecte. For this claim, Clement was surely reading as a proper name what critical editions of the Greek text take as the feminine adjective "elect" in 2 John 1. The "joint-elect" of 1 Peter 5:13 is a different (but related) word that cannot be read in this way, and in Clement's discussion of 1 Peter 5:13, he says nothing about it, although he spends much time talking about the name Mark.

By now, I was hooked, and was determined to investigate these claims more deeply (if only to disprove them to myself). I expanded my search to see what other early Christian writers said about the opening address and context of 2 John. I initially expected to find much early commentary, but to my surprise, there was little discussion in Christian literature during the first millennium.[32] The relatively limited discussion of 2 John in Christian literature was dominated by one or both of two issues that were sometimes intertwined: the identity of the enigmatic "elder" mentioned at the beginning of v. 1 and the scriptural status of the letter.[33] Some early Christians believed the anonymous "elder" who wrote 2 John was none other than John "the Apostle,"[34] while others maintained that the "elder" was a different figure altogether.[35] How one approached authorship tended to influence one's view of the letter's "canonical" status.[36]

After Clement, the next Christian to comment on the letter's recipient was Jerome (ca. 347–419 CE), writing two hundred years later.[37] In his *Epistle* 123, written circa 409 CE, he briefly broaches the subject to an aristocratic woman named Geruchia.[38] In the letter, Jerome exhorts Geruchia, who recently found herself a widow, to reject her many suitors and take up a life of celibacy. As part of Jerome's persuasive strategy, he frequently gives scriptural examples of why this action should be pursued. In one section of the letter, he uses the example of Adam and Eve to promote monogamy. He follows it with the negative example of Lamech, who took two wives,[39] which Jerome effectively equates with a second marriage. At this point, he then digresses to point out how, in like manner, heretics split the one church into two and then multiply the division. This discussion leads Jerome to discuss Song of Solomon 6:8–9, which mentions various women ("queens," "concubines," and "virgins") but focuses on the "perfect" (*perfecta*) one who is "choice" (*electa*). Playing on the meaning of this word ("choice/elect"), Jerome states, "It is to this choice (*electa*) one that the same John addresses an epistle in these words," after which the opening of 2 John 1 is quoted verbatim.[40] As 2 John 1 is invoked in Jerome's discussion of the church, he seems to imply that "elect lady" is a metaphorical way of referencing the church, but it is not altogether clear.

As I continued with this diachronic search, I discovered that Cosmas the Monk (VI CE), known by the epithet "Indicopleustes"[41] since he sailed to India sometime circa 550 CE, discussed at some length the opening verse of 2 John. However, on closer investigation, his discussion focused solely on the identity of "the elder" and not the recipient.[42] Following Cosmas, the next Christian author to consider the context of 2 John and provide a brief statement about the recipients of the letter was Cassiodorus (mentioned above). Sometime circa 575 CE, he began publishing his own *Explanations on the Letters of the Apostles*.[43] While his explanation of 2 John is terse, he briefly speaks about the identity of the "lady and her children." He claims that "John (the Apostle)," who authored the letter under the title "elder," "writes to the chosen lady of the church and her children, whom he had begotten by the sacred font."[44] Cassiodorus, therefore, takes the "elect lady and her children" as actual people whom John had baptized.[45]

After Cassiodorus, I next came across a commentator typically referred to as *Scottus Anonymus*, who wrote a commentary on the Catholic Epistles in the latter part of the seventh century (ca. 680 CE).[46] The commentary on 2 John is short, and the first three verses occupy just a few lines. After asserting that the word "elder" (*senior*) at the beginning of the letter denotes the "dignity" of the author's spiritual maturity,[47] the commentary then turns to the recipient of the letter and states, "*To an elect lady*: it is not to be affirmed nor denied as pertaining to some bodily lady; but it should be understood as pertaining to the church."[48] Though the commentary initially equivocates and suggests that the "elect lady" might or might not be an actual woman, it immediately affirms that she "should be understood as pertaining to the church." This interpretation is reinforced because immediately after this, the commentator says that the "children" are to be understood as those of the "faith," and these even include "elders" (*seniores*) in the church.[49] Thus, this anonymous commentator seems to suggest, without being committed to the notion, that the "elect lady" perhaps refers to an individual woman who, in any event, real or not, personifies the corporate body of the church.

Another Latin commentary from around the same period, which was once thought to have originated with Hilary of Arles (d. ca. 449 CE) but is now believed to come from an anonymous eighth-century author, contains a short explanation on the Johannine Epistles.[50] In the brief exposition of 2 John, the author clearly states that the letter is addressed to the church and not to an individual: "This elect church is the one to which the letter is written."[51] At about the same time, the "Venerable" Bede (ca. 672/3–735 CE) issued a commentary on the Catholic Epistles (ca. 708/09).[52] In his exposition of 2 John, he says little about the recipient of the letter; his treatment of the first verse mainly concerns his attempt to prove "the elder" is to be taken as John the apostle and merely asserts that the addressees were those who abided "in the truth."[53]

Up to this point, all the presently extant commentary that had said anything at all about the recipient of the letter was preserved only in Latin: Clement, Jerome, Cassiodorus, *Scottus Anonymus,* and an anonymous eighth-century commentator. Among the first pieces of Greek commentary that broached this subject came from a *catena*, or "chain" of commentary preserved on 2 John.[54] When it was first published, it was thought to be based on commentary given by John Chrysostom (ca. 347–407 CE),[55] but it is best to regard its authorship as unknown and coming from a later period (ca. VI/VII CE).[56] In the commentary given on 2 John 1–3, two *catenae* are preserved side by side. Both include commentary on the recipient of the letter, although they take different but overlapping approaches:

> 1) "The [elder] is either writing to a church or to a certain woman who spiritually manages her household according to the gospel commandments."[57]
>
> 2) "The [elder] writes this epistle to one of the women who has received the proclamation of the gospel. He gives her two directives: one, to walk in love; second, to turn away heretics, and to turn them away to such an extent that she does not even give the salutation 'greetings.'"[58]

In the first catena, the writer points out that the principal recipient of the letter could be "a church,"[59] so that the phrase "elect lady" is a metaphor, or that the reference could be taken to be an unnamed woman. In the second catena, the commentator does not equivocate but states that the letter's recipient is a woman and that she is being given individual directives in the letter.

From the period shortly after these two *catenae*, some manuscripts of 2 John (in both Greek and Latin) preface the letter with a "summary."[60] While they can vary, where they converge is that they suppose the recipient is an actual woman.[61] On the other hand, in an unattributed *scholium*, or marginal note, found in one ninth-century manuscript of 2 John, the author equates the "elect lady" with "the church."[62] As one approaches the end of the first millennium, a commentary on the Catholic Epistles compiled by Ps.-Oecumenius (ca. 995 CE) gives a somewhat detailed treatment of 2 John.[63] The discussion of the opening address of 2 John 1 focuses first on the identity of "the elder," who is taken to be John the apostle, before it turns to the identity of the recipient.[64] Since the commentary supposes the letter was written to an individual woman, it compares it to 3 John and to the epistles of Titus, Timothy, and Philemon that were written to individuals. It notes that in these cases, such letters afford general benefit because of their edificatory content that can be broadly applied.[65] Then, speaking of the female addressee, it states, "To this elect person he [John] bears witness of two things: one, to go about in love; and the other, to avoid heretics. He calls her 'Elect' either because of her name (i.e., Eclecte) or because of her zeal for virtue."[66] The author of the commentary assumes the recipient of 2 John is an actual woman and admits two possibilities for the interpretation of the Greek εκλεκτη at the start of the letter: (1) It could be understood as the personal name of the woman, in which case her name would literally be Eclecte (Ἐκλέκτη), synonymous with the Greek adjective for "elect" (ἐκλεκτή), or (2) it is simply the adjective "elect" and was used because of her status and character.

From a survey of the extant commentary (in both Greek and Latin) from the first millennium, there is no consensus.[67] Some Christians believed the letter was addressed to an actual woman, but others thought the reference was best understood as a metaphor for the church.[68] Of those commentators like Clement who believed the letter was written to a woman, no one repeated the claim that it was addressed to a Babylonian woman. While Ps.-Oecumenius allows for the possibility that a woman named Eclecte (Ἐκλέκτη) may have been addressed, another interpretation is also provided. Clement was, therefore, the only author to emphatically state that the woman's name is Eclecte. Outside of Clement, none explicitly connected the letter with "virgins."

Seeing that Clement's prefatory comments on 2 John appear to have exerted little to no discernible influence on later Christian commentary,[69] I decided to dig deeper into the manuscript evidence to see what it might reveal. In addition to my survey of Greek and Latin "summaries" that prefaced the letter, I wanted to see if any manuscripts contained other interpretative or paratextual features that might shed some light on Clement's assertions.[70] Remarkably, it was here that I found some noteworthy parallels.

Chronologically, the earliest manuscript I found that contained a parallel to Clement's claim that 2 John was written to "virgins" was in a Coptic manuscript from Egypt from the sixth or seventh century CE. The subscription to 2 John read, "The Epistle of John written to the virgins."[71] As I continued my search, I found that some Greek minuscule manuscripts included a similar designation either in the inscription or in the subscription:[72] "The Second Epistle of John to the virgins."[73] However, I also found that a handful instead read, "The Second Epistle of John written to the Parthians."[74] As Parthia included the territory of Babylon in Mesopotamia, it appeared that these partially echoed Clement's assertion about a "Babylonian woman."[75] As I continued this search, I found that that some Western Christians like Cassiodorus,[76] Augustine (354–430 CE),[77] the anonymous author of *Against Varimadus* (ca. 439–484 CE),[78] and Bede[79] referred to 1 John, but not 2 John, as the letter "to the Parthians."[80] But in none of these sources was there any additional discussion of this designation, and as I turned to the manuscripts, there was no evidence that 1 John bore this designation either in the inscription or in the subscription.[81] Thus, a few manuscripts of 2 John beginning in the sixth or seventh century betrayed knowledge of traditions for which Clement is the earliest extant purveyor.[82]

Looking broadly at all Christian commentary up through the tenth century and the accompanying interpretive evidence preserved in manuscripts beginning in the sixth century and beyond, a few things became evident: (1) Clement was the only commentator to emphatically assert that the addressee in 2 John was a woman named Eclecte.[83] (2) Clement's claim that 2 John was addressed "to virgins" can only be found in the paratext of some later Coptic and Greek manuscripts but is otherwise absent in later Christian commentary.[84] (3) Clement's claim that the woman to whom 2 John was addressed was "a certain Babylonian," which can be accounted for in part via the influence of 1 Peter 5:13, appears only in the paratext of select manuscripts of 2 John that include the inscription/subscription "to the Parthians."[85] Considering all of this evidence, it became apparent that Clement's assertions that 2 John was addressed "to virgins" and that it was addressed to "a certain Babylonian woman" were clearly eisegetical and not exegetical.[86] While these claims were interesting in their own right, they say nothing about the text of 2 John and have everything to do with Clement and the hermeneutical presuppositions he brought to the text. On the other hand, the only exegetical claim Clement makes about 2 John is that the recipient's name is Eclecte. Even if it is somewhat veiled since we only have his *Sketches* on 2 John via a Latin translation, it is evident that Clement was reading the third word in 2 John, which modern editions of the Greek text universally render as the adjective "elect" (ἐκλεκτῇ), as a proper name. In the Latin translation of Clement, her name is rendered "Eclecta," which is a Latin Greekism for Eclecte (Ἐκλέκτῃ). This name is identical in form (but not articulation) to the Greek feminine adjective "elect" (ἐκλεκτῇ).[87] The Latin word Eclecta is otherwise unattested in Latin literary texts, and proper Latin would just read the name Electa if it were directly based on the Latin feminine adjective *electa* that occurs in 2 John 1.

Unlike the other two claims,[88] this assertion continued to vex me. Clement was a native Greek speaker and the only extant ancient Christian commentator on this subject in close temporal proximity to 2 John.[89] I could not, therefore, shake the feeling that Clement was seeing something in the Greek text that none of his successors writing many centuries later had seen. Once again, I returned to the Greek text of 2 John 1, but this time, instead of returning to the standard critical edition of the Greek text found in NA[28], I decided to look at the Greek in another way to see if I were missing anything. As one who works with Greek papyri of the Hellenistic, Roman, and Byzantine periods (ca. 323 BCE–642 CE), I am aware that the way Greek was written anciently and how it appears in a modern edition of the New Testament (or any modern edition of an ancient Greek author) is quite different.[90] Beyond standardizing the spelling, modern printed editions of the Greek New Testament (beginning in the sixteenth century) have added punctuation, capitalized proper nouns, and generally presented the text in a way that is conducive to the literary conventions of the modern reader. The most significant of these conventions is that modern editions are printed with word division. By contrast, ancient Greek was generally written continuously with no word breaks (*scriptio continua*) and with an undifferentiated script where there were no upper- or lowercase letters or medial and terminal letterforms. Beyond the fact that the *mise-en-page* of our modern editions can look quite different from the originals they attempt to reproduce, all modernizing of the text is, at a fundamental level, an initial interpretation of the text—in fact, in some instances, it forces us to read the text in one way when an alternative exists.[91] I therefore thought to myself that if I disposed of the initial layer of interpretation and looked at the text as it would have been written anciently, would I see something different?

With this in mind, I wrote out 2 John 1 as it may have looked in an early Christian manuscript:

> ΟΠΡΕϹΒΥΤΕΡΟϹΕΚΛΕΚΤΗΚΥΡΙΑΚΑΙΤΟΙϹΤΕΚ
> ΝΟΙϹΑΥΤΗϹΟΥϹΕΓѠΑΓΑΠѠΕΝΑΛΗΘΕΙΑΚΑΙΟΥΚ
> ΕΓѠΜΟΝΟϹΑΛΛΑΚΑΙΠΑΝΤΕϹΟΙΕΓΝѠΚΟΤΕϹΤΗΝ
> ΑΛΗΘΕΙΑΝ[92]

To conceptualize this in English, imagine if 2 John 1 were printed as follows in a modern Bible:

> THEELDERTOTHEELECTLADYANDHERCHIL
> DRENWHOMILOVEINTHETRUTHANDNOTON
> LYIBUTALLWHOKNOWTHETRUTH

Despite the initial disorientation with the Greek text, I saw nothing different than what was printed in modern critical editions. The initial letter string ΟΠΡΕϹΒΥΤΕΡΟϹ could not be intelligibly read any other way than ὁ πρεσβύτερος ("the elder"). Furthermore, as 3 John opens in the same way and gives every indication that it is written by the same "elder" who writes 2 John, this reading is secure.[93] Turning to the ΕΚΛΕΚΤΗΚΥΡΙΑ that follows, the received articulated rendering, ἐκλεκτῇ κυρίᾳ, where ἐκλεκτῇ ("elect") is the feminine singular adjective in the dative case followed by the feminine noun κυρίᾳ ("lady") in the dative case, lends itself as a reading. But looking longer at the letter string, alternatives popped into my mind. The term ΚΥΡΙΑ, which only appears twice in the New Testament (here and again in v. 5), in form could also be read as a feminine adjective (either κυρία or κυρίᾳ) that means "authority" or "power" or, in some cases, might even denote "appointed," "regular," or "supreme."[94] After considering these definitions within the immediate context of the letter, I ruled them out. It then occurred to me that KYRIA could be read as a substantive (i.e., an adjective that functions as a noun); the meaning would still be *lady*, but the problem here is that substantivized adjectives in Greek require the definite article. ΚΥΡΙΑ did not have a definite article. But when I looked back at the text, the article TH jumped out at me when the letter string was divided differently: ΕΚΛΕΚ ΤΗ ΚΥΡΙΑ. At this point, I became convinced I was on to something, even though the preceding ΕΚΛΕΚ was now problematic because it no longer had a proper Greek termination.

At a seeming impasse, but believing there was something here worth pursuing, I decided to turn to the large corpus of Greek letters preserved in the papyrological remains of Roman Egypt to see if they might prove helpful in getting a better sense of the letter string ΕΚΛΕΚΤΗΚΥΡΙΑ and if there were anything to the division ΕΚΛΕΚ ΤΗ ΚΥΡΙΑ. Having for some time worked on letters from Ptolemaic, Roman, and Byzantine Egypt, both editing previously unpublished letters and reediting published letters, I had noticed that 2 John (and 3 John) was remarkably similar in terms of format, structure, length, and even phraseology to these letters. Additionally, the author of 2 John states that the letter is written on "papyrus" (v. 12);[95] it is the only New Testament letter to explicitly state this, suggesting that a study of the papyri might provide some insight.

As I began my search, I focused on letters dated to the first couple of centuries CE. I did this since they would be temporally proximate to 2 John and because the form and structure of the address in Greek letters began to shift and change in the third century CE.[96] In these letters, I focused on the opening address and looked at the use of the substantive τῇ κυρίᾳ to see if it might provide any way forward with ΕΚΛΕΚ ΤΗ ΚΥΡΙΑ. Before long, I noticed a consistent pattern in the epistolary address where this substantive was employed: It always followed the woman's name, which was also in the dative case, and a definite article never accompanied the name.[97] To give one example, in P.Oxy. 2.300, a short letter from the first century found among the papyri from the city of Oxyrhynchus (Middle Egypt), the opening address reads as follows: Ἰνδικὴ Θαεισοῦτι τῇ κυρίᾳ χαίρειν ("Indike to the lady Thaisous, greetings").[98] As I considered this and similar epistolary addresses, I realized that the same collocation is found in 3 John 1. The sender appears first in the nominative case, followed by the name of the addressee in the dative case, but without the definite article, and then the modifying adjective appears with the article: ὁ πρεσβύτερος Γαΐῳ τῷ ἀγαπητῷ ("The elder to Gaius the beloved"). When I recognized this parallel, I wondered if 2 John 1 could have also followed the same pattern in its opening address. If this were the case, the letter string EKLEK preceding ΤΗ ΚΥΡΙΑ would have to be a personal name.

By now, I was feeling more confident that there was real promise in the reading EKLEK TH KΥPIA. Accordingly, I spent considerable time with the letter string EKΛEK, trying to figure out how it might be read as a proper name—or at least the basis of a proper name. The major problem was that as it stood, EKΛEK was still nonsensical as it did not have a proper termination and did not constitute a name, even if it sounded like the name Eclecte that Clement had proposed. For a time, I even considered whether it might be a foreign name. Such names are not always terminated according to the Greek declension system but could be left undeclined, and so context would dictate how they should be read.[99] While I tried to convince myself this was the case, I knew this was not so: The letter string EKΛEK was definitely Greek in origin.[100]

Struggling to make sense of how to divide and read the string EKLEKTHKΥPIA, since my understanding of the possible word division EKLEK TH KYPIA was not progressing, I decided as a last effort to cast as wide a net as possible and read any letter preserved on papyrus from any century (ca. 300 BCE–700 CE) that shared parallels with the opening address in 2 John 1. Based on electronic searches, I found that upward of nine hundred letters shared parallels. While this sounds like a lot, as I was only looking at the opening address, I was able to sift through the evidence rather quickly. Not long into this search, I came across SB 20.15069, a letter between two women from the Hermopolite Nome (Upper Egypt).[101] The letter is dated to the second half of the third century CE and contains an address structured like those just discussed. It opens as follows: Ἰσιδώρα Ἄνιτι <τῇ> φιλτάτ̣[η] πλεῖστα χαίρειν ("Isidora to the dearest Anis, very many greetings"). I quickly read through the address and was about to move on since there was nothing out of the ordinary, but I paused for a moment to study the article τῇ restored by the editor <τῇ>.[102] The restoration was obviously correct as the original writer of the letter had mistakenly not included it before the adjective. As I paused to think about the restoration, it seemed apparent that it was mistakenly omitted because the name of the woman being addressed ended with the syllable -τι that phonetically sounded similar, or nearly identical, to the τῇ that should have immediately followed.[103] Thus, the writer skipped the τῇ due to a simple case of haplography—the inadvertent omission of repeated letters.[104]

When the full realization of this simple mistake finally set in, the reading of 2 John 1 became clear to me in an instant. The letter was addressed to a named woman, and the Greek text should read as follows:

> ὁ πρεσβύτερος Ἐκλέκτῃ τῇ κυρίᾳ . . .
> "The elder to the lady Eclecte . . ."
> (cf. NA^{28}: ὁ πρεσβύτερος ἐκλεκτῇ κυρίᾳ . . .)[105]

2 John was addressed to a woman named Eclecte! At this point, I let out another laugh, not unlike my initial chuckle of disbelief when I first came across the proposal in Clement. This reading made perfect sense in light of the papyrological parallels and now structurally mirrored the opening address found in 3 John 1: ὁ πρεσβύτερος Γαΐῳ τῷ ἀγαπητῷ ("The elder to Gaius the beloved"). When the euphoria of the discovery finally wore off, I knew this must be the reading, but I still had many questions. Was this reading simply a conjectural emendation—a proposed reading that brought clarity to an otherwise opaque phrase but lacked any textual witnesses? Or did it have any manuscript support? Is the name Eclecte, rendered in the Latin text of Clement as Eclecta (a *hapax legomenon* in Latin literary texts), ever attested elsewhere? Furthermore, as modern commentary on 2 John has deemed it to have been written to a church, metaphorically personified as an "elect lady," could the letter be compellingly read as addressed to an actual woman?

In the following chapters, these and other questions will be explored. At this point, it suffices to say that this reading does appear in some manuscripts, although no one has ever recognized its significance. As for the female name Eclecte, it is attested elsewhere in both Greek and Latin and is more widely attested than nearly a quarter of the women's names appearing in the New Testament. Finally, 2 John reads far better as a letter addressed to a woman who held a position of authority among a group of Christians than it does as a letter addressed to some personified church that is only obtained via a feminine metaphor. This study, therefore, has far-reaching implications for the printed text of the New Testament and the role of women in the early church. It will demonstrate that there has always been a book in the New Testament whose principal recipient is a named woman, but that she has been lost in history due to the omission of two reduplicated Greek letters.

CHAPTER TWO

When a Lady Is Not a Lady

Modern Hermeneutics and the Interpretation of 2 John 1

> *2 John is addressed to "the elect lady" (v. 1), a poetic reference to a sister church.*
>
> —S. Brown and F. J. Moloney, *Interpreting the Gospel and Letters of John*[1]

> *ἐκλεκτῇ κυρίᾳ . . . The rendering of the phrase is beset by the greatest difficulties. No interpretation can be accepted as satisfactory.*
>
> —Brooke F. Westcott, *The Epistles of St. John*[2]

THE GREEK TEXT of the New Testament underwent a dramatic shift in 1881. In that year, Brooke F. Westcott, Regius Professor of Divinity at Cambridge University, and his colleague, Fenton J. A. Hort, Hulsean Professor of Divinity at Cambridge University, published a monumental edition of the Greek New Testament.[3] The work was ambitiously called *The New Testament in the Original Greek*.[4] While the title gives the impression that the "original" text was being pristinely restored, Westcott and Hort were more modest in their objectives.[5] Drawing on the best New Testament manuscripts of the day, principally the fourth-century Codex Vaticanus,[6] and refining earlier text-critical approaches of Johann J. Griesbach and Karl K. Lachmann, Westcott and Hort produced an eclectic text of the New Testament (i.e., a text derived from the synthesis of various manuscripts) in an attempt to reproduce the most ancient version. The text, despite inflaming a few vocal detractors when it was initially published,[7] revolutionized the study of the New Testament as it effectively overturned the "Received Text" (*textus receptus*) that had prevailed since the sixteenth and seventeenth centuries. Whether or not one agrees with every textual decision made by Westcott and Hort, virtually all scholars now agree that their judgments and painstaking attention to detail laid the foundation for all future textual scholarship on the New Testament.

Westcott and Hort's edition of 2 John includes only three notes in the marginal apparatus. In v. 12, they print the received reading "your joy" (ἡ χαρὰ ὑμῶν) but include a note citing the secondary reading "our joy" (ἡ χαρὰ ἡμῶν).[8] In v. 11, they refer the reader to the appendix, which includes an unusual interpolation that appears in some Latin manuscripts at the end of the verse.[9] Both of these notes are straightforward and deal with text-critical issues. Their marginal note on 2 John 1 is somewhat different. In the Greek text, they print the reading ἐκλεκτῇ κυρίᾳ ("to an elect lady"), but in the margin, they provide a secondary reading: Ἐκλέκτῃ Κυρίᾳ. The capitalization of both words is an editorial decision by Westcott and Hort signifying that they could be read as proper names: "to Electa Kyria"[10] or, correctly, "to Eclecte Kyria"—a single woman bearing a double name. That two of the best Greek scholars of the New Testament gave such a rendering shows that the phrase εκλεκτη κυρια poses problems and is amenable to an alternate reading.

Late Nineteenth Century: No Clear Consensus

Two years after Westcott and Hort's Greek New Testament appeared, Westcott published the first edition of his lengthy commentary *The Epistles of St. John: The Greek Text with Notes and Essays.*[11] The commentary is marked by meticulous attention to the Greek text: A typical page is headed by a line or two of Greek with the remainder of the page containing copious notes and discussion in smaller font. Westcott begins his detailed discussion of the phrase εκλεκτη κυρια with the claim, which prefaces this chapter, that "no interpretation can be accepted as satisfactory." Halfway through his prolonged discussion, he returns to the secondary reading he and Hort proposed in their edition of the New Testament and states, "It has also been supposed that the two words form a compound proper name ('to Electa Kyria'). This view removes the difficulty of the construction; but the combination is at least very strange."[12] Grammatically speaking, Westcott is correct. If the phrase were taken as a double name, it would remove any grammatical difficulty—names are definite by nature and in address do not require the definite article—but the presence of a double name in a text like 2 John 1 would certainly be "very strange."[13] After discussing various other possibilities, but then pointing out their shortcomings, Westcott concludes that the "general tenour of the letter favours the opinion that it was sent to a community and not to one believer" and also gives a remarkably prescient statement: "On the whole it is best to recognize that the problem of the address is insoluble with our present knowledge."[14] Whether Westcott believed that some vital piece of data lost in the ancient past held the key to unlocking the precise meaning of the address or felt some new piece of data might shed light on the passage, he does not say. It was clear, however, that he felt that no interpretation adequately explained the peculiarity of the articulated ἐκλεκτῇ κυρίᾳ.

As will be demonstrated in the next chapter, one of the keys to restoring the correct opening address to 2 John 1—Ἐκλέκτῃ τῇ κυρίᾳ ("to the lady Eclecte")—resides in the epistolary evidence provided by the Greek papyri of Roman Egypt. At the time Westcott made the statement that the proper interpretation of the address was "insoluble with our present knowledge," the rich sands of Egypt had barely begun to yield papyri of the Greek, Roman, and Byzantine periods. What became the *Egypt Exploration Fund* (EEF), the flagship archaeological society of Egyptian antiquities in the English-speaking world, had only been created in 1882, a year before the publication of Westcott's commentary on the Johannine Epistles. It was not until 1889, when W. M. Flinders Petrie, the "father of archaeology," excavated the Ptolemaic cemetery at Gurob (Fayum), that large amounts of Greek papyri became generally known. Furthermore, it was not until 1897 when the ancient "rubbish heaps" of Oxyrhynchus began to produce Greek papyri from the excavations by Bernard P. Grenfell and Arthur S. Hunt under the auspices of the EEF.[15]

A few years after Westcott's commentary appeared, Alfred Plummer, senior proctor of University College, Durham, published the next significant study on the Johannine Epistles titled *The Epistles of St. John*.[16] It was not as detailed as Westcott's earlier study, at least as it pertained to technical discussions of the Greek text, but it nonetheless made significant contributions. In an early section of the commentary, Plummer considers the opening address, ἐκλεκτῇ κυρίᾳ. Like Westcott, he points out that there are various ways it could be rendered: "to the elect lady"; "to an elect lady"; "to the elect Kyria"; and "to the lady Electa." He then notes that the first two options permit two distinct possibilities: (1) The letter is either addressed to an unnamed woman with an "elect" status, or (2) it is addressed to a larger community like a church and employs a female metaphor.[17] After laying out these interpretive possibilities, Plummer immediately disposes of the final option—"to the lady Electa"—asserting that v. 13 precludes this reading because "it is incredible that there were two sisters each bearing the very unusual name of Electa."[18] To explain and clarify this argument, 2 John 13 needs to be cited: ἀσπάζεταί σε τὰ τέκνα τῆς ἀδελφῆς σου τῆς ἐκλεκτῆς ("The children of your elect sister send you their greetings"). Plummer reasoned that if you granted that the letter string εκλεκτη in v. 1 was to be rendered as a proper name (i.e., Ἐκλέκτῃ), then you were also obligated to take the της εκλεκτης at the end of the letter in v. 13 as a proper name (i.e., τῆς Ἐκλέκτης). Thus, two sisters would bear the name "Electa." For the last 150 years, this argument, or minor variations, has been repeatedly invoked to dismiss taking εκλεκτη as a woman's name in the first verse. Since it has become so pervasive, it will be addressed in more detail at the end of this chapter and again in chapter 5. For the time being, it is simply worth noting that in v. 13, εκλεκτης cannot be read as a proper name since it has the definite article τῆς; thus, it can only be taken as an adjective of the accompanying noun "sister" (i.e., τῆς ἀδελφῆς). Plummer's argument and the iterations by others that have followed are grammatically flawed.

Plummer ultimately argues that the most likely interpretation of the opening address is "unto the elect lady,"[19] and he believes it is best understood as a reference to an actual woman who is unnamed: "That 'the elect Lady' may be a figurative name for a Church, or for the Church, must at once be admitted: and perhaps we may go further and say that such a figure would not be unlikely in the case of a writer so fond of symbolism as S. John. But is a sustained allegory of this kind likely in the case of so slight a letter?"[20] He argues that the most literal reading of 2 John is preferred—it is a personal letter, much like 3 John, but is addressed to an elect "Christian lady."[21]

Moving into the last decade of the nineteenth century, two German works on the Johannine Epistles stand out.[22] In 1896, Heinrich Poggel published *Der zweite und dritte Brief des Apostels Johannes geprüft auf ihren kanonischen Charakter*, which includes a substantial treatment of 2 John.[23] Poggel's examination primarily focuses on issues surrounding the canonicity of 2 and 3 John, but his treatment of the address in 2 John 1 is surprisingly detailed. Like previous studies, he considers whether it could refer to an actual woman or should be taken as a metaphor for a church.[24] After considering the interpretative options, in a way similar to what Westcott and Plummer had previously done,

Poggel favors the view that the letter was addressed to a woman identified only as an "elect lady" who was quite close to the sender of the letter, whom he took to be the Apostle John.[25] But not stopping there, Poggel argues that the "elect lady" was probably a widow because her husband is not mentioned in the letter, yet she had "children." Further, her actual nieces and nephews (i.e., the children of her sister) were the ones sending greetings in v. 13.[26] Thus, Poggel thought the context of the letter was thoroughly familial and had reference to two related Christian families: an "elect lady" and "her (literal) children" in v. 1 and her (literal) "sister" along with her (literal) "children" in v. 13.

The other notable German study of the time, Bernhard Weiss's *Die drei Briefe des Apostel Johannes*, published in 1899, takes a markedly different approach.[27] Like some of his predecessors, he summarily dismisses the reading "to the lady Electa" because of how he reads v. 13.[28] He then argues that the best interpretation of the address is to a specific congregation, metaphorically personified as a woman. Weiss speculates that the congregation might have been in Ephesus but also mentions other possibilities and is ultimately undecided on its precise location.[29] While Weiss's work does not advance any novel reading of the address and frequently repeats arguments previously made, a singular strength of the work is that Weiss offers an expansive bibliography on the subject that stretches back to the 1600s.

At the close of the nineteenth century, there was no clear consensus on the interpretation of εκλεκτη κυρια. Leading commentators conceded that multiple readings were possible, and the two most popular interpretations were that it contained an address to an unnamed Christian woman, only known as the "elect lady," or that it was a metaphorical reference for a church. As one charts the scholarly contours of the first few decades of the twentieth century, two trends emerge: (1) Scholars begin to use the epistolary papyri to consider the address in 2 John, and (2) a consensus begins to build around a specific interpretation—namely, that it is a metaphor for a church.

The Twentieth Century and the Dominant Consensus: 1900–1970

At the start of the twentieth century, the most noteworthy study to appear on 2 John 1 was by J. Rendel Harris.[30] In a 1901 article, Harris was the first to note the similarities 2 John (and 3 John) shared with the epistolary papyri that had just begun to be published.[31] When his article appeared, just over 150 such letters were in print. While Harris's study marshals a handful of relevant papyrological parallels, his work was largely overshadowed by his attempt to prove that 2 John was tantamount to a "love letter."[32] He argues that in 2 John, κυρία should not merely be translated as "lady" but rather "dear lady," and that when this title occurs in v. 5 it is closely connected to the last phrase of the verse: "let us love one another."[33] Noting the unconventionality of Harris's proposal, a later scholar quipped that "verse 6, which is meant to interpret 'love' in v. 5, would make this one of the most chaste love letters of all time!"[34] If this were not enough, Harris went on to argue that the lady addressed in 2 John was a gentile convert who was a widow and explicitly calls her "a second Ruth."[35] Near the end of the article, Harris briefly considers whether the woman addressed in 2 John 1 had a name. Noting the collocation of the address when compared with those that appear in certain papyri, Harris surmises that "perhaps she may be called Electa," but he provides no further discussion.[36] Given the amount of speculation in the article, it was roundly criticized and largely dismissed shortly after publication.[37] This is regrettable since Harris did marshal a few insightful papyrological parallels for the use of the title κυρία (and κύριος, "lord"), even if some of his other conclusions went well beyond the evidence.

A few years after Harris's article appeared, H. J. Gibbins published two seminal articles on the address in 2 John 1.[38] In the first one, Gibbins argues that 2 John is not addressed to a woman but rather to a community of believers metaphorically personified as an "elect lady." He claims that a conceptual precedent for this kind of interpretation resides in select prophetic texts of the Old Testament like Isaiah 54 and 55, Jeremiah 4, Ezekiel 16 and 23, and Baruch 4 and 5, where Israel, or Zion, is personified as a mother, bride, or daughter.[39] He therefore argues that 2 John is best understood as a "prophetic epistle" written by someone who believed he was a successor to the prophets of Israel in the Old Testament.[40] In the second article, Gibbins refines some of his earlier arguments and draws on more parallels from the Old Testament (Zeph 3:14 and Zech 2:7 *inter alia*), where Israel is personified as a female. He maintains that the best interpretation of "elect lady" is "not to an individual Christian matron, but to a Christian Church, personified—after the prophetic manner—as a mother with children."[41]

Gibbins's work proved significant because it was among the first to argue that the metaphorical interpretation of "elect lady" as a personification of a church was analogically similar to the metaphorical personification of Israel or Zion as a woman in select Old Testament passages. Since the publication of his two articles, those who have advocated for this interpretation have drawn on many of the passages Gibbins cited, alleging that there is biblical precedent for a metaphorical reading of the phrase "elect lady." Due to the pervasiveness of this line of reasoning, it will be considered in more detail at the end of the chapter. At this point, a question worth considering is whether clearly metaphorical sections in Isaiah, Jeremiah, or Ezekiel provide acceptable conceptual "parallels" for 2 John—a short letter that betrays no obvious signs of the use of extended metaphor.

A short time later, in 1906, a notable German study appeared by Bennona Bresky, *Das Verhältnis des zweiten Johannesbriefes zum dritten*.[42] Her treatment of the address in 2 John represents one of the more detailed examinations in the twentieth century. She considers various factors and includes a discussion, albeit flawed, of the epistolary papyri.[43] From the start, Bresky's examination is skewed by the foregone conclusion that the address εκλεκτη κυρια has to be understood as a metaphor for a church since she assumes 2 John is the letter mentioned in 3 John 9 that is written "to the church."[44] As this argument is periodically invoked in discussions of the address in 2 John 1, it will be treated at the end of this chapter, but for the time being, it is enough to say that there is nothing in 3 John 9 that necessarily connects it to 2 John.

Despite this preconceived bias, Bresky still considers whether the phrase εκλεκτη κυρια could be read "to the lady Electa." She cites two papyrological examples in her discussion: The first comes from P.Oxy. 1.112 and the second from P.Oxy. 1.123, both drawn from Harris's study and dated to the third or fourth century CE. The first address reads: χαίροις, κυρία μου Σẹρηνịạ [-ca.?-] π(αρὰ) Πετοσείριος ("Greetings, my lady Serenia [. . .], from Petosiris") and the second: κυρίῳ μου υἱῷ Διονυσοθέωνι ὁ πατὴρ χαίρειν ("To my son, master Dionysotheon, greetings from your father"). Focusing on the placement of the titles κυρία and κύριος, she notes that in both cases, they precede rather than follow the names they modify. She therefore argues that if the letter string εκλεκτη genuinely constitutes a name, then κυρία would need to precede it for it to be "to the lady Electa" (i.e., κυρίᾳ Ἐκλέκτῃ). While her reasoning flows from the two papyri she cites, as shown in the next chapter, these two papyri begin with a different address formula than the one appearing in 2 John (and in 3 John). They come from a later period, the third or fourth centuries, when Greek epistolary convention was in the habit of placing substantives and adjectives before the name and not after it, as was the convention in the first and second centuries.[45] On top of this, P.Oxy. 1.112 is not even a letter but an invitation with a totally different address formula. Bresky then provides two additional reasons why "Electa" cannot be read. Following Plummer, she contends that if εκλεκτη were taken as a name in v. 1, then one would be compelled to take της εκλεκτης in v. 13 as a name; thus, two sisters would bear the same name. Her final reason, which is similarly not without problems, is that the earliest Christians were incredibly humble and would not have employed such an exalted title of address like "lady" (κυρία) for an individual member of the church.[46]

The remainder of Bresky's examination is devoted to her foregone conclusion that the phrase εκλεκτη κυρια, which she renders ἐκλεκτῇ κυρίᾳ, represents a church. To make this argument, she notes that the letter was written to multiple recipients since it employs plural forms in vv. 4, 5, 8, and 10 and argues that these references are better understood in the context of a congregation than they are to a large family, as Poggel had suggested a decade earlier.[47] Finally, drawing on the two recent articles by Gibbins, Bresky argues that "elect lady" was simply the apostle's way of addressing a Christian congregation. She asserts that John the Revelator, whom she believes authored the letter and was endowed with a "mystical" understanding of the church, preferred to metaphorically convey information about the church.[48] Seeing the church maternally, she highlights passages in the Old Testament where female imagery is figuratively used for a community.[49]

Two years after Bresky's monograph appeared, Adolf Deissmann published his 1908 classic, *Licht vom Osten: Das Neue Testament und die neuentdeckten Texte der hellenistisch-römischen Welt.*[50] In this lengthy study, Deissmann principally uses papyri to elucidate a wide variety of topics related to the texts of the New Testament. In a lengthy discussion of ancient letter writing, wherein he draws heavily on the evidence from the papyri, Deissmann considers the corpus of letters found in the New Testament. Creating a somewhat artificial distinction between an epistle (literary) and a letter (nonliterary), Deissmann works his way through all the epistles/letters in the New Testament by assigning them to one category or the other and offers brief commentary. His discussion of 2 John is short and reads as follows:

> The second Epistle of St. John is not so full of letter-like detail as the third [3 John], but it too has a quite definite purpose as a letter, although we cannot say with complete certainty who the lady was to whom it was addressed. That it was addressed to the whole church seems to me quite impossible. The two letters [2 and 3 John] are of especial interest because they clearly betray in several instances the epistolary style of their age, and it is to be hoped that, with the aid of the papyri, we shall some day be able to determine the date of that style more exactly.[51]

While Deissmann believes 2 John is written to a woman, he provides no details about whether the letter supplies her name or if she is addressed as "elect lady." When he briefly references the address in 2 John 1 at another point in his work and compares it to one appearing at the beginning of P.Oxy. 4.477,[52] he only notes that both share parallel grammatical structures.

Two important commentaries in English that appeared not long after the work of Deissmann were George G. Findlay's *Fellowship in the Life Eternal: An Exposition of the Epistles of St. John*, published in 1909, and Alan. E. Brooke's *A Critical and Exegetical Commentary on the Johannine Epistles*, published three years later in 1912.[53] As a testament to the influence of these two commentaries, even though they are over one hundred years old, they are still periodically cited in contemporary discussions of the Johannine Letters.[54] Findlay devotes an entire chapter to the interpretation of the phrase εκλεκτη κυρια.[55] From the outset, he is emphatic that it should be understood as a metaphorical personification of a church.[56] He summarily dismisses the reading "to Electa the lady" since he declares that the name appears "nowhere else in Greek."[57] Despite this claim, which is periodically echoed in contemporary studies, chapter 5 demonstrates that this female name is attested in Greek and was already known when Findlay made this erroneous statement.[58]

Brooke's discussion of the address in 2 John overlaps with Findlay's as he makes some of the same points and "favors the view that a Church is addressed."[59] But where Brooke's commentary contributes most to the discussion is in his grammatical analysis. He argues that for the name "Electa" to be compellingly read in 2 John 1, it should have an accompanying definite article (i.e., Ἐκλέκτῃ τῇ κυρίᾳ) and that the lack of such made this reading "improbable."[60] He then cites examples from other New Testament letters like 3 John 1, Romans 16:13, and Philemon 1, noting that the definite article comes after the name and precedes the following modifier. Brooke's grammatical analysis is spot on; without the definite article intervening εκλεκτη and κυρια, the reading "Electa" is not certain. On the other hand, if the definite article is included, the name Ἐκλέκτη, correctly rendered Eclecte, is the only option for 2 John 1.[61]

Moving into the 1920s, various studies treated the address in 2 John 1, but none offered anything especially new. Charles Gore's 1920 commentary, *The Epistles of St. John*, declares that the address refers to a "Church personified" but provides no in-depth discussion.[62] A 1925 French article by Jacques Marty acknowledges the difficulty of properly interpreting the phrase εκλεκτη κυρια and points out that it might contain a proper name but ultimately contends that it is a metaphorical reference to a particular Christian congregation.[63] In the same year, Hans H. Wendt published *Die Johannesbriefe und das johanneische Christentum*.[64] In his treatment of 2 John 1, he casually dismisses the possibility that the letter could have been written to a woman, named or unnamed. He asserts that εκλεκτη κυρια refers to a particular congregation that was metaphorically styled "an elect lady" because of its "honorable Christian character."[65] In 1929, well-known New Testament scholar Martin Dibelius wrote an entry titled "Johannesbriefe" in *Religion in Geschichte und Gegenwart*.[66] In the short piece, Dibelius pronounces that the address in 2 John 1 must be taken metaphorically to refer to "a community" since 2 John is the letter mentioned in 3 John 9 that was addressed "to the church."[67]

Two German studies from the 1930s deserve mention. The first is D. Friedrich Büchsel's *Die Johannesbriefe*, published in 1933.[68] While his treatment of 2 John is detailed, and the same holds for his discussion of the interpretation of "elect lady" at the start of the letter, nothing new is brought to bear on the interpretation of 2 John 1.[69] At the outset, he asserts that the letter is addressed to a Christian community allegorized as a woman, which is apparently "obvious," and that the allegory entirely pervades 2 John even though it has all the trappings of a "personal letter."[70] The other 1930s study is a 1936 article by Franz J. Dölger that is devoted entirely to the address in 2 John 1.[71] Dölger does not even consider the name Eclecte as an interpretive option but focuses primarily on the interpretation of κυρία. He argues that it should not be read as the name Kyria but is simply the polite form of address "lady." He then adduces a few epigraphic examples where κυρία is employed as part of the phrase κυρίᾳ πατρίδι, which he renders "to the lady homeland" ("der Herrin Heimatstadt"), to show that it was used to denote a communal body.[72] From there, he argues that Christians could have similarly employed the term to refer to a religious body like a congregation or church. He concludes the article with a reference to Tertullian's (ca. 155–220 CE) work *To the Martyrs*, written at the end of the second / beginning of the third century, which begins with a reference to the "lady mother church" (*domina mater ecclesia*).[73] He then takes this phrase as an analog for the opening address in 2 John 1.[74] Since the publication of Dölger's work, this reference has often been cited by those arguing for a metaphorical reading of the address in 2 John 1.

Moving into the 1940s, the preeminent work on the Letters of John was Charles H. Dodd's *The Johannine Epistles*.[75] At the outset of his treatment of 2 John, he notes that the opening address of the letter could be interpreted in various ways and admits that an address to a named woman is among the interpretive possibilities. But he is then quick to dismiss the reading "Electa" because it is "on all grounds improbable," although no reason is ever given for the summary dismissal.[76] He then asserts that "elect lady" is a simple "disguise for a community."[77] Noting that some cities and more significant regions were periodically personified as women—Rome in Revelation 17:4 and Israel in the Old Testament—Dodd asserts that the same metaphorical personification is occurring in 2 John 1.[78] However, as Dodd prolongs his treatment of the phrase, it becomes evident that he is sensing a disconnect between the letter's straightforward presentation, on the one hand, and the metaphorical cover for the letter he is alleging on the other. To account for the disconnect, he raises the specter of persecution and "the unfavorable situation of Christianity at the time" as a potential reason why the address to an apparently well-known church is so cryptic.[79] He then ironically concludes that 2 John gives every impression it is written to a woman but that the "fiction is kept up all through . . . it is a thin disguise for a pastoral epistle to a Christian congregation."[80]

The 1950s and 1960s witnessed a significant increase in the number of publications on the Johannine Letters.[81] The studies of Hans Windish (1951),[82] Joseph Bonsirven (1954),[83] Joseph A. Wilder (1957),[84] Greville P. Lewis (1961),[85] Neil Alexander (1962),[86] John R. W. Stott (1964),[87] Ronald

A. Ward (1965),[88] Raymond R. Williams (1965),[89] and J. W. Roberts (1968)[90] provide little original discussion of the issue. While they acknowledge that 2 John could have been addressed to a woman, they all default to the position that εκλεκτη κυρια is best taken in reference to an "elect lady" who is a metaphorical personification of a church. Two additional studies from this period that take this approach but deserve more discussion since they have proven influential are Rudolf Schnackenburg's *Die Johannesbriefe*, published in 1953,[91] and Rudolph Bultmann's *Die drei Johannesbriefe*, published in 1967.[92]

Unlike Bultmann, Schnackenburg argues that 2 John represents a genuine letter. In his treatment of the address, he quickly asserts that it is a metaphor and dismissively treats any other option. Speaking of the name "Electa," he asserts that it can be safely excluded because of the final greetings in v. 13, although he never clarifies exactly how v. 13 precludes it.[93] Then, citing the work of Dölger, he argues that a metaphorical precedent for the term "lady" can be found in its use as an honorific designation for political communities.[94] Bultmann, on the other hand, argues that 2 John is an "epistolary fiction" framed as a letter to exert authority; the metaphorical personification of the church as an "elect lady" is simply part of the narrative fiction.[95] His claim that the address contains a metaphor for the church is mostly declarative, so he spends little time entertaining other possibilities. The chief piece of evidence he invokes to dismiss the possibility that 2 John could have been written to a woman named Eclecte is that it was customary in the New Testament for εκλεκτη to be read as an adjective (i.e. ἐκλεκτῄ).[96] Despite the circularity of such reasoning and the fact that aside from 2 John 13, it never occurs anywhere else in the Johannine corpus,[97] Bultmann felt compelled to not even entertain the possibility that the addressee might be an actual woman. After all, his overarching theory of the letter rested entirely on it being a fiction.

Despite the clear consensus at this time, a handful of studies took the opposite approach and argued that the address in 2 John 1 referred to a woman and not a church. In Alexander Ross's *The Epistles of James and John*, published in 1954, he argues that the phrase εκλεκτη κυρια, which he renders "to an elect lady," is best taken literally:[98] "To read into this simple letter a mystic meaning seems quite unnecessary. The elect lady is spoken of throughout as a person; her children are mentioned and are described, some of them, as walking in the truth; the Apostle promises her a visit in the near future, when he will speak to her face to face."[99]

Along similar lines, D. Hans Asmussen's *Wahrheit und Liebe. Eine Einführung in die Johannesbriefe*[100] and Walter T. Conner's *The Epistles of John*,[101] both published in 1957, as well as Ernst Gaugler's *Die Johannesbriefe*,[102] published in 1964, argue that the principal recipient of the letter is a woman. All of these studies accept the received reading "to an elect lady" (ἐκλεκτῇ κυρίᾳ) and contend that it should be taken literally. A shared feature of their respective approaches is that the letter as a whole is more comprehensible when the primary addressee is understood to be a woman.

The Last Half Century of Scholarship

If the 1950s and 1960s witnessed a proliferation in studies on the Johannine Epistles, then the 1970s to the present has seen an explosion.[103] Numerous commentaries have appeared in the last half century, and there has been a steady flow of monographs, articles, and encyclopedia entries.[104] Trying to sift through all this material is almost overwhelming. Nevertheless, it is not quite as daunting as the burgeoning bibliography on the Johannine Epistles initially appears. Studies on 2 and 3 John are dwarfed by those on 1 John, and in commentaries, the attention given to the former is only a fraction of what is devoted to the latter.[105] Therefore, while it is possible to navigate the current state of the question on the address in 2 John 1, only a handful of studies can be meaningfully discussed here, and these will be limited to the most influential of the last half century.

In the 1970s, notable commentaries on the Johannine Epistles were published by Frederick F. Bruce (1970),[106] James L. Houlden (1974),[107] I. Howard Marshall (1978),[108] Klaus Wengst (1978),[109] and Pheme Perkins (1979).[110] Without wading into the details, all of them hold that the phrase εκλεκτη κυρια does not contain a woman's name and is best understood as a reference "to an elect lady" (ἐκλεκτῇ κυρίᾳ) who is a female metaphor for a church. Moving into the 1980s, the same interpretive trend appears in commentaries by Fred D. Howard (1982),[111] Pierre Bonnard (1983),[112] Kenneth Grayston (1984),[113] Stephen Smalley (1984),[114] Robert Kysar (1986),[115] David Jackman (1988),[116] and R. Alan Culpepper (1988).[117] The most influential commentary during this period, as it is cited more than any other, is Raymond E. Brown's *The Epistles of John: A New Translation with Introduction and Commentary* (1982).[118]

Brown's work is remarkably thorough, and this is true for his treatment of the address in 2 John 1, as it is one of the most in-depth analyses of the last 150 years.[119] In line with the overwhelming majority of contemporary scholarship, Brown takes εκλεκτη κυρια as ἐκλεκτῇ κυρίᾳ and argues that the "elect lady" is a metaphorical reference to a church.[120] Notwithstanding his position, he concedes that there are five interpretive options for the phrase: In three options, it can be taken as a reference to an actual woman (named or unnamed) while in the other two, to a metaphorically personified church—either the universal "Church" or a particular "church."[121]

Brown grants that the phrase εκλεκτη κυρια could be interpreted as "to the lady Electa" (Ἐκλέκτῃ κυρίᾳ) but is then quick to point out that such an interpretation has grammatical problems, "for in Greek as in the English this construction would require the definite article, which is lacking" (i.e., Ἐκλέκτῃ τῇ κυρίᾳ).[122] He is correct, and this goes to the heart of the problem; without the definite article between the two words, the letter string εκλεκτη does not have to be read as a proper name. Brown briefly defers to the papyrological evidence in this discussion, citing two papyri (P.Oxy. 1.112 and 123) previously mentioned in Harris's 1901 article and Bresky's 1906 monograph. He notes that in similar constructions of address, the possessive pronoun "my" (μου) is typically used, but this is not the case in 2 John 1.[123] The comment adds little to the discussion, as there are many cases like 2 John 1 where μου is not used, but Brown seemingly mentions this to show how the address in 2 John 1 is unlike what appears in the papyrological examples. On one level, he is correct; as noted above, P.Oxy. 1.112 and 123 begin with different forms of address than the one appearing in 2 John 1.[124]

Brown then casts additional doubt on this reading by stating that the "evidence is insufficient for eklektē as a personal name at this time" and then notes that the name is lacking in F. Preisigke's 1922 *Namenbuch* of extant names appearing in Greek papyri, ostraca, and inscriptions from Egypt.[125] While the female name Ἐκλέκτη does not appear in Preisigke, it should be noted that this work—now over one hundred years old—preserves less than half of the names, and name variants, that are presently attested in the Greek papyri, ostraca, and inscriptions from Egypt.[126] Furthermore, Preisigke's work takes no account of attested names outside of Egypt. Even though Eclecte does not appear in Preisigke's work, it says little about the lack of "evidence" for this name.[127] Finally, Brown states that since ἐκλεκτή ("elect") is used in v.

13 as an adjective with "your sister," it "increases the likelihood that in v. 1 it is an adjective describing *kyria* 'lady.'"[128] But here, he fails to mention the key distinction between the two: In v. 13, it is accompanied by a definite article (τῆς ἐκλεκτῆς) and therefore has to be an adjective based on the construction, but in v. 1, there is no definite article, which signifies something is different.[129]

Moving on from the name Eclecte, Brown then considers whether the address might include the female name Kyria or whether the phrase "elect lady" might refer to an unnamed woman. He argues that neither interpretation is compelling.[130] He then considers whether the reading "to an Elect Lady" could refer to a church. One vein of this interpretation would be "the church at large" so that 2 John would be a "Catholic Epistle"; the other vein is that it refers to a specific church (or churches) in a region. Brown discounts the former possibility, noting "a greeting from 'the children of your Elect Sister' [v. 13] to an Elect Lady who is the universal church is implausible."[131]

To buttress his metaphorical reading of the address, Brown cites various examples, many drawn from Gibbins's 1902 and 1905 studies, where female imagery is employed to personify Israel and Zion. He cites Isaiah 54:1 and 13, where female imagery is used for Zion, and notes that in Galatians 4:25–26, Sinai and Jerusalem are personified as women. He similarly notes that in the *Shepherd of Hermas* at *Vision* 3.1.3, the church is addressed as a "lady" (κυρία). To bolster this argument, Brown cites the Greek phrase κυρία ἡ ἐκκλησία (*vel sim.*), which appears a handful of times in pre-Christian literary sources and which he renders "the lady congregation."[132] For Brown, the phrase proves that there is an established (pre-Christian) metaphorical connection between κυρία ("lady") and ἐκκλησία ("congregation"), which demonstrates that "lady" in 2 John 1 is simply a figurative expression for a "church."

A few years after the publication of Brown's commentary, Judith Lieu published *The Second and Third Epistles of John: History and Background* (1986),[133] followed some years later by *The Theology of the Johannine Epistles* (1991)[134] and then *I, II, and III John: A Commentary* (2008).[135] With these three books, Lieu has published more on the Johannine Letters than any other modern author. To a greater or lesser extent, in all of these works, she considers the address in 2 John 1 since it is essential for her understanding of the letter. Given the near-universal trend in modern scholarship to read εκλεκτη κυρια as "elect lady" and, in turn, take it as a metaphorical personification of a church, it is not surprising to see Lieu also take this approach.[136]

In her treatment of the address in 2 John 1, Lieu is typically quick to point out that the reference to the "elect lady" is best understood as a personification for a church and refers to the phrase as a "semifictional cover" for the letter.[137] She is also relatively quick to dismiss alternate interpretations: She summarily dismisses "Electa," noting that v. 13 "prohibits" the reading, but, like Schnackenburg, says nothing about precisely how v. 13 precludes the reading in v. 1.[138] However, she also concedes that the meaning of this address is "elusive" and "obscure"[139] and finds it unusual that it is not more descript: "The Second Epistle also presupposes a gathered community; as we have seen, it remains most probable that the 'elect lady' of the address (1, 5 and the elect sister of 13) represents a church rather than a particular individual with her children. Does this largely unparalleled form of address point to a particular understanding of the church? Certainly it is hard to find any purely historical reason for this 'cover'—there is no sense that persecution is necessitating code names."[140]

The curious address leads Lieu to see an "uneasy relationship" between 2 John and 3 John: While both letters share several explicit similarities, her interpretation of the address leads her to think of 2 John as a more "artificial construction" given its peculiar opening.[141] By taking "lady" as a personification of a church, she claims that it is "giving 'lady' its full weight."[142] But her meaning of "full weight" is not altogether clear. Since she contends that such a personification "is part of a rich conceptual tradition with firm biblical roots but also with pagan parallels," for Lieu "full weight" seems to imply a broader metaphorical usage of the term.[143]

This leads Lieu to reference biblical and nonbiblical passages from antiquity where a communal body is personified as a woman.[144] Like Brown, she cites Isaiah 54, Baruch 4–5, and Galatians 4:21–25, where Zion/Jerusalem or some communal body is personified as a woman. She adds Ephesians 5:29–32, where the church represents the wife of Christ, and Revelation 21, where the New Jerusalem is personified as a bride. But sensing the analogical problems of these comparisons with 2 John, Lieu admits that "the use of this imagery in the address of a letter is without parallel"[145] and later notes that such "personifications belong in contexts or in literary genres where one expects a degree of symbolism, and none fully explains such imagery in a letter."[146] This glaring problem cannot be understated; 2 John is a short letter, and to propose such a metaphorical cover belies the content of the letter and the genre to which it belongs. To Lieu's credit, however, she is the only commentator arguing for a metaphorical interpretation of the address who perceives this glaring tension. To resolve it, she is forced to question whether 2 John is an actual letter or "an artificial construction," where the author self-consciously employed the letter form.[147]

The final modern study to be considered here is Hans-Josef Klauck's *Der zweite und dritte Johannesbrief*, published in 1992.[148] Klauck's commentary stands out, not only because it represents the most significant commentary in German published in the last fifty years but also because it is the only commentary on the Johannine Epistles where 2 and 3 John are treated in a separate volume.[149] In this study, Klauck devotes an excursus to the meaning of the phrase εκλεκτη κυρια in 2 John 1.[150] Klauck reads the address ἐκλεκτῇ κυρίᾳ and, in line with Brown, Lieu, and almost all modern scholarship, argues that the "elect lady" is a female personification for a church.[151] While he considers the possibility that it might include the name "Electa," he quickly casts doubt on the reading because he questions whether the name is "supported as a given name, especially in Greek."[152] Then, noting the collocation of the address in 3 John 1 (Γαΐῳ τῷ ἀγαπητῷ), Klauck argues that for "Electa" to be the correct reading, the address would have to be Ἐκλέκτῃ τῇ κυρίᾳ but notes that the intervening article is missing.[153] Like Brooke and Brown, who also made this perceptive observation before, Klauck is correct; with the definite article, the name "Electa" (properly Eclecte) can be the only reading. But instead of considering this option in any detail, he immediately transitions to the papyrological evidence. He cites three papyri (P.Oxy. 1.112, 300, and 744) where κυρία appears in the address and notes that the definite article τῇ accompanies it and that the pronoun μου ("my") sometimes follows it, and then warns that the use of these modifiers should not be connected to extravagant theories.[154] The warning is abrupt and is directly aimed at J. Rendel Harris, who (as previously noted) had argued from certain papyri that the term κυρία denotes something more than "lady" and that in 2 John 1 (and 5), it was a title of intimate affection.[155] To conclude his discussion of the name "Electa," Klauck then argues that v. 13 effectively prohibits this reading because one would then have to suppose that the name also appears in v. 13 and that two sisters bear the same name.[156]

Moving on from Eclecte, Klauck briefly considers the name Kyria. He notes that of the two names, it is the more likely option but argues that the word order would need to be reversed, and there would have to be a definite article so that it would instead read Κυρίᾳ τῇ ἐκλεκτῇ. Curiously, he adds that if the reading were "to the elect Kyria," it would not be especially befitting of a Christian address, as it would be "really cold." However, the reasoning for this statement is never provided.[157] He then briefly considers whether it might be addressed to an unnamed woman known only by the address "elect lady." He argues that the use of both the singular and the plural in the letter militate against it being addressed to an individual and he casts doubt on the reading by citing and disparaging a couple of wild theories—none of which has been taken seriously for well over a hundred years—that the identity of the unnamed "elect lady" might be Mary the mother of Jesus or Martha the sister of Lazarus and Mary.[158]

From here, Klauck argues that "elect lady" is best understood as a metaphorical personification for a particular congregation and notes that this is the consensus view in contemporary scholarship. He then posits that the ancient rhetorical device of *fictio personae*, where a fictive persona could stand in for a larger communal body like a city or homeland, is the best way to read the ambiguous address.[159] Alleging that this rhetorical practice was widespread in ancient Near Eastern Jewish culture and that it exerted influence on early Christian traditions, Klauck proceeds to give various examples where Zion, Israel, and Jerusalem are personified with the feminine or where familial language is used for a collective. But he cites no examples that had not been previously noted.[160]

Moving beyond Brown, Lieu, and Klauck to the dozens of commentaries published in the last 30 years, the trend to render εκλεκτη κυρια as ἐκλεκτῇ κυρίᾳ and in turn take the "elect lady" as a metaphorical personification for a church widely persists. Some commentaries go so far in this interpretation that they even render the phrase "elect assembly" instead of "elect lady."[161] A survey of the literature reveals that in most cases, the arguments used to bolster this reading have remained essentially unchanged for over a century and, conversely, that the arguments invoked to discount any other interpretative option are the same ones that have been used for over a century. In fact, with few exceptions, recent treatments tend to rehash the same talking points of the last 150 years and have added little original or fresh discussion.[162] This has resulted in a status quo where prevailing opinions have gone largely unchallenged outside of minor differences contested within a framework of general agreement.[163]

Questioning the Consensus

As this chapter concludes, the validity of the principal arguments upon which the prevailing consensus has been established is worth considering. In the last

150 years, no one has questioned the received reading ἐκλεκτῇ κυρίᾳ that is typically translated "to the elect lady." This has been the printed text for over 150 years with no variation. Outside of Westcott and Hort, who proffered Ἐκλέκτῃ Κυρίᾳ as an alternative reading because it made better grammatical sense, no one else has argued for any kind of textual emendation.[164] The result is that one is left with a nondescript and highly unusual epistolary address. The opacity of the phrase is mainly responsible for the dominant metaphorical interpretation where it is understood as a reference to a personified church. From the time of Gibbins's two studies at the start of the twentieth century, it has been repeatedly claimed that there are conceptual precedents in biblical texts for this kind of interpretation, and beginning with Dölger's study in the 1930s, it has been alleged that such precedents extend to extrabiblical texts.

Starting with the Old Testament examples where Israel, Jerusalem, and Zion are periodically personified as a woman, it is repeatedly asserted that these provide the conceptual framework for 2 John to similarly personify a church as an "elect lady." This leap, however, poses significant methodological issues. In the passages from the Old Testament where the metaphorical "parallels" are typically drawn, principally Isaiah but also in other books like Jeremiah and Ezekiel, metaphor is an uncontested literary device with various explicit examples. Along the same lines, Revelation is sometimes cited as a closer contemporary example where feminine personifications are employed. But this raises the question of genre: At a structural, thematic, and literary level, 2 John is completely unlike Isaiah, Jeremiah, Ezekiel, or Revelation. Metaphor is a central component of prophetic and apocalyptic literature but hardly figures in a short letter like 2 John.[165] To bridge this gap, Gibbins argues that 2 John is best understood as a "prophetic epistle" composed by one who believed "he was a successor of the prophets or the Old Covenant, and who framed his message after their manner."[166] Modern studies have not followed Gibbins's lead in framing 2 John as a "prophetic epistle," yet the same studies draw freely on the examples he cites from the Old Testament. But can these be considered appropriate conceptual precedents, or even parallels, unless 2 John is genuinely a "prophetic epistle" written in the same manner as Isaiah or Ezekiel?

Another significant problem with these proposed "parallels," whether they are drawn from the Old or New Testament, is that in the biblical examples cited, the subject of the metaphor is typically stated. In 2 John 1, on the other hand, if one reads the address as a metaphorical cover for the letter, the alleged subject of the metaphor—a church—is altogether lacking, and it is left to the reader's discretion to figure it out. When examples like "Virgin Israel" and "Daughter Zion" are cited as parallels, the subject, either "Israel" or "Zion," is explicitly named alongside the female imagery. Additionally, in the expanded female metaphors typically drawn from Isaiah, Ezekiel, and Baruch, the personified subject is expressly mentioned in the section—either "Israel," "Zion," or "Jerusalem." The same holds for the various New Testament examples often cited from Galatians 4, Ephesians 5, and Revelation 17 and 21—in every instance, the subject of the metaphor is made explicit in the text.[167] These are not conceptual parallels nor precedents for what is being claimed in 2 John 1, as this letter never makes explicit the subject of the alleged metaphor. The same problem persists in the extrabiblical examples that are frequently marshaled. In the case of the *Shepherd of Hermas*, where in *Vision* 3.1.3, "lady" (κυρία) is used for "church" (ἐκκλησία), this only occurs after the subject ("church") is already made explicit in *Vision* 2.4.1. Likewise, although many reference the phrase "lady mother church" (*domina mater ecclesia*) that appears in Tertullian's *To the Martyrs* as an analogical parallel to what occurs in 2 John 1, it is not the same. Unlike 2 John 1, the subject of "lady mother," the "church," is made explicit in the address.[168] Furthermore, as 3 John mentions "church" three times (vv. 6, 9–10), "the elder" did not have any aversion to this term.[169] Therefore, despite the attention all these conceptual "parallels" and "precedents" are given in discussions of 2 John 1, they are not compelling and do not account for the address in the letter.

Turning to extrabiblical sources, various scholars have continued to cite Dölger's work wherein he claims that the phrase κυρίᾳ πατρίδι, which appears exclusively in inscriptions, provides another precedent for metaphorically taking κυρία in reference to a congregation or church: "to the lady homeland" ("der Herrin Heimatstadt").[170] However, there are significant problems with this line of reasoning and Dölger's rendering of the phrase. Not only is the subject, πατρίς ("hometown/homeland," etc.), made explicit, but in these epigraphical examples, κυρία is operating as an adjective. In contrast, those arguing for a metaphorical reading in 2 John 1 take κυρία as a noun that is modified by the adjective ἐκλεκτῇ. In these epigraphic examples, the proper meaning of the adjective κυρία is not "lady," as Dölger and others have assumed; instead, in these instances, the adjectival meaning is properly "honored," "principal," or even "sovereign" since it is functioning as an honorific.[171] Therefore, this epigraphical phrase does not provide a parallel to what is stated in 2 John 1.

Along the same lines, Brown and a few others have also cited the Greek phrase κυρία ἡ ἐκκλησία (*vel sim.*), which appears in pre-Christian literary sources and inscriptions and that they render "the lady congregation."[172] The phrase apparently proves that there was an established (pre-Christian) metaphorical connection between κυρία ("lady") and ἐκκλησία ("congregation"). But this argument is simply incorrect; the phrase κυρία ἡ ἐκκλησία cannot mean "the lady congregation" as Brown and others have contended. In these instances, the adjectival meaning of κυρία is "scheduled/appointed" or "principal/supreme"—not "lady"—and has nothing to do with the apparent "feminine" qualities of the feminine noun ἐκκλησία ("church") it is modifying.[173] This can be readily established from the context of the earliest usages of this phrase. It first appears in the comedy *The Acharnians* by Aristophanes (ca. 446–386 BCE) from ca. 425 BCE. In the opening scene, the protagonist, Dicaeopolis, arrives at the empty Pnyx, the traditional gathering place in Athens, for the "scheduled assembly" (not "lady assembly").[174] When it appears in Aristotle's *Politics*, it typically means "the supreme assembly."[175] Furthermore, when the renowned grammarian Harpocration (II CE ?) discusses the meaning of the phrase κυρία ἐκκλησία in his *Lexicon of the Ten Attic Orators*, it is clear that he understands it as "principal assembly."[176] The phrase, therefore, offers nothing for the imputed metaphorical reading of 2 John 1, as it contains no metaphorical usage.[177]

Another argument, occasionally invoked, is that the phrase ἐκλεκτῇ κυρίᾳ must contain a metaphor for a church since 2 John is the letter addressed "to the church" mentioned in 3 John 9. This argument was first made in an 1848 article published by Ferdinand C. Baur and has been repeated on and off for the last 180 years.[178] Baur argues that since 2 and 3 John were very similar and both were written by "the elder," the letter mentioned in 3 John 9 must have been 2 John.[179] Despite the similarities between 2 and 3 John, however, only pure conjecture can lead one to the conclusion that 2 John must be the letter mentioned in 3 John 9.[180] In much the same way, some modern commentaries have tried to identify 1 John with the letter mentioned in 3 John 9.[181] Once again, this is speculative, as there are no explicit reasons it has to be 1 John. An unstated but often underlying assumption in such arguments is the problem of lost books of scripture (i.e., the assumption that 3 John 9 can only refer to a letter we already have in the canon). While 1 or 2 John cannot be completely ruled out as the document mentioned in 3 John 9, that letter might be lost. Elsewhere in the New Testament, there is clear evidence for lost letters.[182] Here, it is also worth noting that in several manuscripts, the reading in 3 John 9 has been changed from "I have written something to the church" to "I would have written to the church."[183] This textual change was surely done to avoid the implication of a lost letter and demonstrates that the scribes who altered it did not think 3 John 9 referred to either 2 John or 1 John.[184]

Another argument that appears with some frequency, albeit as a secondary reason for why the address in 2 John 1 is best understood as a metaphorical reference to a church, is that the author of 2 John fluctuates between the use of the singular and the plural in addressing the recipient(s).

Verse	**Singular**	**Plural**
1		οὕς ("whom")
4	σου ("your")	
5	σε ("you") σοι ("to you")	
6		ἠκούσατε ("you have heard") περιπατῆτε ("you should walk")
8		βλέπετε ἑαυτούς ("be on your guard") μὴ ἀπολέσητε ("do not lose") ἀπολάβητε ("may receive")
10		ὑμᾶς ("you") μὴ λαμβάνετε ("do not receive") μὴ λέγετε ("do not say")
12		ὑμῖν ("to you") ὑμᾶς ("you")
13	σε ("you")	

Commentators claim that the personified church is being addressed when the singular is being used, but when the plural is being used, the congregants are being addressed.[185] But this argument has no bearing on the interpretation of εκλεκτη κυρια as a church. The full address in 2 John 1 clarifies that there are two addressed entities—a "lady" and "her children."[186] The most straightforward reading of the interchange of the singular and plural in 2 John is to apply the singular to the "lady," who is an actual woman, and the plural to the "lady" and "her children" collectively. This begs the question of who these "children" were. They could be taken literally as the actual children of the lady, as Poggel argued in 1896,[187] or metaphorically, as her fictive children. The latter metaphorical meaning is well attested elsewhere in the New Testament letters[188] and is the most likely interpretation of the term "children" when it appears in 3 John 4.[189] Keeping the two addressed parties in mind, the "lady" and "her children," readily accounts for the interchange of the singular and plural in 2 John.

Over the last 150 years, only one argument has consistently been directed against reading the name Eclecte in v .1. In the foregoing survey, it was Alfred Plummer who first raised this point near the close of the nineteenth century. The argument runs as follows: If one reads the name Eclecte (Ἐκλέκτη) in v. 1 instead of the adjective "elect" (ἐκλεκτή), then instead of reading τῆς ἐκλεκτῆς as an adjective in v. 13, one is obligated to take it as a name, τῆς Ἐκλέκτης. The alleged consequence is that you would have two sisters sharing the same name, and the unlikelihood of such a scenario precludes this reading. As Karen Jobes recently put it, "The thought that it is the name of an individual woman, 'Eklekte' (Ἐκλεκτή), can be eliminated in light of v. 13, for it is improbable that she would have a living sister of the same name."[190] Much more will be said about this in chapter 5,[191] as well as the fact that the name Eclecte is properly accented Ἐκλέκτη and not Ἐκλεκτή (which is the accentuation for the adjective);[192] those who have invoked this argument have not given sufficient attention to the Greek text. In v. 1, there is no definite article before the letter string εκλεκτη, whereas in v. 13, the definite article τῆς fronts εκλεκτης; the latter can only be read as an adjective that modifies the noun sister (ἀδελφή) and grammatically cannot be read as a name. It is, therefore, correctly τῆς ἐκλεκτῆς, which is the rendering in NA[28] (and all prior editions). It is remarkable that not a single advocate of this position has ever noted the absence of the article in v. 1 and the presence of the article in v. 13 and questioned its significance.[193] Thus, one can take the letter string εκλεκτη in v. 1 as a name and not be compelled to read της εκλεκτης as a name.

Furthermore, in the context of this question, no one has ever examined the conclusion of letters where the "greetings" verb (ἀσπάζομαι) that appears in 2 John 13 is used to see if the names of third parties appear with or without a definite article, as this would prove definitive. The best comparanda are the epistolary papyri since valedictory greetings employing this verb appear in nearly seven hundred letters from the first two centuries CE. In chapter 5, it will be shown from the use of this formula in the epistolary papyri, as well as other sources, that the phrase της εκλεκτης in 2 John 13 can only be read as an adjective. Thus, this oft-cited argument to discount the reading Eclecte is erroneous and premised on a faulty understanding of Greek grammar and a flawed juxtaposition of vv. 1 and 13.

To their credit, both Bultmann and Brown, who invoke v. 13 in their discussion of the proper interpretation of v. 1, correctly note that in v. 13, της εκλεκτης can only be read as an adjective (τῆς ἐκλεκτῆς).[194] Consequently, they argue that in v. 1, it is most likely an adjective that appears and not a name. Beyond the flawed circularity of this argument, one then must explain why there is no definite article before ἐκλεκτῇ in v. 1 as there is in v. 13. Bultmann never really addresses this issue;[195] and Brown argues that it is because 2 John is a "circular letter" intended for multiple recipients (i.e., congregations) so that it is deliberately addressed "to *an* elect lady" (ἐκλεκτῇ κυρίᾳ) instead of "to *the* elect lady" (τῇ ἐκλεκτῇ κυρίᾳ).[196] Besides smacking of special pleading, if this were the case, it would appear that the plural should have been used rather than the singular. In Galatians, a genuinely "circular letter," the opening address is in the plural: ταῖς ἐκκλησίαις τῆς Γαλατίας ("to the churches of Galatia").[197]

Once this argument is removed, only two other arguments against reading Eclecte in v. 1 remain. The first, which has only been periodically invoked and has gradations, is that either the name Eclecte does not exist, or there is insufficient evidence for it in Greek. Therefore, it can be discounted outright as an interpretive option in 2 John 1. As will be shown in chapter 5, the female name Eclecte (Ἐκλέκτη) does exist and is more widely attested than almost a quarter of the female names that appear in the New Testament. Accordingly, the various onomastic objections used to discount this reading have no basis. The final argument, which has only been occasionally raised by a handful of perceptive commentators, is that if the reading were genuinely Eclecte, one should expect the definite article to follow the name so that it would read Ἐκλέκτη τῇ κυρίᾳ instead of just Ἐκλέκτη κυρίᾳ. This argument is correct; the addition of the τῇ secures the reading of Eclecte as the only option.[198] Though this reading would exactly parallel the collocation of the address found in 3 John 1 (Γαΐῳ τῷ ἀγαπητῷ) and is differentiated from the received address by the reduplication of two terminal letters, no study of the last 150 years has ever considered it as an option. In part, this is because the received articulated reading ἐκλεκτῇ κυρίᾳ has been universally accepted and never been textually questioned, even though, as Lieu has observed, it is a "largely unparalleled form of address."[199]

The next chapter will show that the correct reading and articulation of the address in 2 John 1 is not ἐκλεκτῇ κυρίᾳ but rather Ἐκλέκτη τῇ κυρίᾳ. In the chapter, this restoration will be established via an examination of the epistolary papyri, which provide the best parallels for the type of opening address appearing in 2 John 1 (and 3 John 1). Though a handful of studies beginning with Harris at the start of the twentieth century employ the epistolary papyri in investigations of the address in 2 John 1, they are perfunctory and, in some cases, fail to properly differentiate the various epistolary prescripts (i.e., opening addresses) that are attested and the type of prescript appearing in 2 John (and 3 John).[200] In chapter 4, it will be shown that the reading Ἐκλέκτη τῇ κυρίᾳ even appears in the manuscript evidence, but remarkably, no one has ever recognized its significance. Furthermore, no study has examined the text-critical basis of the received reading ἐκλεκτῇ κυρίᾳ and its accompanying articulation in printed editions of the Greek New Testament. While NA^{28} gives the impression that the received reading is secure, the manuscript evidence and the printed editions of the Greek New Testament before the ascension of NA^{28} provide a different story.

CHAPTER THREE

The Answer Is in the Papyri

> *The Second Epistle of John is a shadowy, faceless little work, and if it were necessary to declare redundant one item in the New Testament canon, it would be highly eligible.*
>
> —James L. Houlden, *A Commentary on the Johannine Epistles*[1]

James L. Houlden's assessment of 2 John as "a shadowy, faceless little work" in his acclaimed commentary highlights the problem of its address.[2] For Houlden, as well as most commentators of the last fifty years, the curious address εκλεκτη κυρια only becomes intelligible as a cipher for a Christian congregation personified as an "elect lady" (ἐκλεκτὴ κυρία).[3] This reading of the address is essentially the only interpretive option taken seriously in contemporary scholarship.[4] Scholars will quarry the biblical canon or scour classical literature to find any kind of precedent for a female personification of a corporate body to show that by analogy, the unparalleled address in 2 John 1 contains a metaphorical circumlocution for a church. A consequence of the fixation is that it results in the most fundamental question being overlooked: Is the articulated reading ἐκλεκτῇ κυρίᾳ the only way to resolve the address? In the last half century of scholarship, this reading has not been questioned. In fact, one must go back to 1881 when Westcott and Hort reservedly put forth Ἐκλέκτῃ Κυρίᾳ ("to Eclecte Kyria") as a secondary alternative since it made better grammatical sense.

This chapter will reconsider the address in 2 John 1. It will show that the letter preserves a personal form of address that is well attested and structurally mirrors the address in 3 John 1. Instead of the obscure and unparalleled ἐκλεκτῇ κυρίᾳ, it will be argued that the correct rendering of the address is Ἐκλέκτῃ τῇ κυρίᾳ so that the principal addressee of 2 John is a woman named Eclecte. This reading will primarily be established by examining the epistolary papyri of Roman Egypt since (aside from 3 John, which will also figure in the examination) they provide the closest parallels to 2 John in terms of structure, style, format, and genre.

Papyri, Letters, and 2 John

The first epistolary papyrus ever edited and published was in 1833.[5] It is part of a small collection in the Vatican Library that was purchased at the start of the nineteenth century.[6] Sometime between 1815 and 1825, locals in Memphis (so the story goes) unearthed a clay vessel and on finding that it contained multiple texts written on papyrus, decided to market the pieces separately. The result was that the collection ended up in museums all over Europe.[7] The letter, now known as UPZ 1.60, was written sometime around the year 179 BCE or, alternatively, 168 BCE and was sent by a man named Dionysius to his brother Hephaistion.[8] The letter preserves a request to Hephaistion asking him to return to his family since he had been away and was needed at home. According to the dominant interpretation, Hephaistion had sequestered himself in the Serapeum at Memphis to obtain divine healing.[9] The letter is reproduced here:[10]

→ Διονύσιος Ἡφαιστίωνι τῶι ἀδελφῶι χαίρειν.
εἰ ἐρρωμένωι σοι τἆλλα κατὰ λόγον ἀπαντᾶι,
εἴη ἂν ὡς βούλομαι, καὶ αὐτὸς δ' ὑγίαινον καὶ
Εὐδαιμονὶς καὶ τὰ παιδία καὶ Ἰσιὰς καὶ τὸ παιδίον σου
καὶ οἱ ἐν οἴκωι πάντες. κομισάμενος τὴν
παρὰ σοῦ ἐπιστολήν, ἐν ἧι διεσάφεις διασεσῶισθαι
ἐγ μεγάλων κινδύνων καὶ εἶναι ἐν κατοχῆι,
ἐπὶ μὲν τῶι ἐρρῶσθαί σε \⟦ε...αι..⟧/ τοῖς θεοῖς ἐπευχαρίστουν,
ἠβουλόμην δὲ καὶ σὲ παραγεγονέναι εἰς τὴν
πόλιν, καθάπερ καὶ Κόνων καὶ οἱ ἄλλοι οἱ ἀπει-
λη[μμέν]οι π[ά]ντες, ὅπ[ω]ς καὶ ἡ Ἰσιὰς τοῦ
παιδίου σου εἰς τὰ ἔσχατα ἐληλυθότος διασεσωι-
κυῖα αὐτὸν ἐκ παντὸς τρόπου, ἔτι δὲ καὶ τοιούτους
καιροὺς ἀνηντληκυῖα νῦγ γε \ἰδοῦσά σε/ τύχηι τινὸς
ἀναψυχῆς. οὐ γὰρ πάντως δεῖ στενῶς ἐπανά-
γοντά \σε/ προσμένειν ἕως τοῦ πορίσαι τι καὶ κατε-
νεγκεῖν, ἀλλὰ πᾶς τις πειρᾶται, ὁπηνίκ' ἂν

ἐκ κινδύνων διασωθῆι, ταχέως παραγίνεσθαι καὶ ἀσπάζεσθαι τήν τε γυναῖκα καὶ τὰ παιδία καὶ τοὺς φίλους. καλῶς οὖν ποιήσεις, εἴπερ μὴ καί σε ἀναγκαιότερόν \τι/ περισπᾶι, συντόμως πειραθεὶς παραγενέσθαι, ⟦. .⟧ καὶ τοῦ σώματος ἐπιμελόμενος, ἵν' ὑγιαίνηις, ἔρρωσο. (ἔτους) β Ἐπεὶφ λ.

↓ Ἡφαιστίωνι.

---

2. *l.* τὰ ἄλλα. 6. *l.* διασεσῶσθαι. 12–13. *l.* διασεσωκυῖα. 14. *l.* νῦν.

Dionysius to Hephaistion his brother, greetings. If you are well and if your other affairs turn out in a like manner, it would be as I wish; I, myself, am also well, as are Eudaimones and the children, and Isias and your child, and the entire household. When I received your letter in which you made it clear that you had come safely through great danger and that you were being held fast (or "in the possession" [of the god]), for this, that you are well, I gave thanks to the gods. But I wish that you would come back to the city, just as Konon and all the others who had been detained (by the god), in order also that Isias, who, when your child had passed through the most extreme (circumstances), preserved him from every manner of difficulty, and even yet patiently endured such crises, would now, at least, on seeing you, meet some relief. For, it is not at all necessary that you postpone your return until you have earned something to bring home, but anyone would try, at the very moment he has been rescued from danger, to return speedily and greet wife and children and friends. Therefore, unless something more urgent detains you, please try to return immediately, . . . and take care of yourself to stay well. Good-bye. (Year) 2, Epeiph 30. (On the back of the papyrus, an address) To Hephaistion.

When considering 2 John, this letter is informative for several reasons. It is just under 200 words and is written on a single sheet of papyrus measuring 32.9 × 18.2 (cm).[11] 2 John is a little longer at 245 words but could have easily fit on a single sheet of papyrus with the same dimensions.[12] The opening address in line 1 follows the same basic pattern as is found in 2 John 1: sender (first position nominative) to addressee (second position dative with no article) followed by a salutation (third position). Both letters express hope that the receiving party is doing well (2 John 3 and UPZ 1.60.2–5) and express joy at receiving good news (2 John 4 and UPZ 1.60.5–8). Likewise, both letters make requests to the receiving parties (2 John 5 and UPZ 1.60.9–11) and express hope that a personal meeting will soon take place (2 John 12 and UPZ 1.60.20–22). Finally, greetings using the same Greek verb are mentioned near the end of each letter (2 John 13 and UPZ 1.60.19–20). Thus, there are several shared features between UPZ 1.60 and 2 John so that the relevance of the epistolary papyri for a study of 2 John is readily apparent.[13]

In 1881, when Westcott and Hort published their new edition of the Greek New Testament, only a dozen or so epistolary papyri were published and were only available in obscure venues. The first papyrological volume to contain letters was still a decade away.[14] At the start of the twentieth century, when J. Rendel Harris was the first to incorporate the epistolary papyri into a study of the address in 2 John 1, only a little over 150 epistolary papyri had been published.[15] Nearly a century and a quarter later, there are now over 4,500 published letters in Greek that range in date from the early Ptolemaic period through the Arab conquest of Egypt (ca. 323 BCE–642 CE)—and if one counts documents that include "epistolary features," the number is more than doubled and grows to near 10,000.[16] Given this large body of evidence, one gets a comprehensive view of Greek letter writing during this period. Beyond the obvious advantages of having the original letters, the sheer size of this growing corpus ensures confidence regarding Greek epistolary habits and chronological trends.

Before delving into a papyrological investigation, it is necessary to address two issues that have a bearing on the correct rendering of the address in 2 John 1. To make a compelling case that the original reading of 2 John 1 is not the received reading ἐκλεκτῇ κυρίᾳ but rather Ἐκλέκτῃ τῇ κυρίᾳ, two related claims should be convincingly established. First, it needs to be demonstrated that the evidence decidedly favors the position that 2 John and 3 John have common authorship (i.e., the author of 2 John also authored 3 John). While this may appear to be arguing the obvious, a small but influential vein of scholarship has argued the opposite—namely, that different authors wrote 2 John and 3 John. The common authorship of both letters is important to the overall argument of this chapter since one would then expect natural parallels between 2 John and 3 John, in terms of structure, style, and phraseology, that are typical of letters composed by a single author. For example, if 3 John 1 includes the address "to Gaius the beloved" (Γαΐῳ τῷ ἀγαπητῷ), a structure that is widely attested in letters of the Roman period, whereas 2 John 1 uses "to an elect lady" (ἐκλεκτῇ κυρίᾳ) that is obscure and without parallel, one could see how the reading "to the lady Eclecte" (Ἐκλέκτῃ τῇ κυρίᾳ) would be more likely since it would structurally mirror the collocation of 3 John 1.

A second related claim that needs to be convincingly established is that 2 John is a genuine letter with its closest parallels (aside from 3 John) to be found in the epistolary papyri. If 2 John is an authentic letter and not a "literary fiction" (i.e., a purely literary production without a specific recipient that only takes the form of a letter to endow it with an air of authenticity), then one would expect it to possess standard epistolary features found in other letters. This would particularly be the case with the opening address, which would be expected to adhere to customary patterns found in letters to actual recipients. On the other hand, if 2 John is a mere "fiction" and only incorporates certain epistolary features for rhetorical convenience, significant deviations in its letter form could be possible.

2 John and 3 John: Two Letters, One Author

Of all the letters in the New Testament, one would be hard-pressed to find two with more in common than 2 John and 3 John. Stylistically and structurally, they are remarkably similar and are the two shortest letters in the New Testament: 2 John consists of 245 words, while 3 John has 218 words.[17] In both letters, the author self-identifies as "the elder" at the beginning. However one chooses to take the address in 2 John 1, like 3 John 1, it immediately follows the mention of "the elder" in the dative case without the definite article. Additionally, as part of the opening salutation in both letters, the recipients are informed of the sender's "love" for them "in the truth" using nearly identical phraseology. As they transition into their respective thanksgivings, the same phraseology is employed, and in both letters, these are immediately followed by requests. While the main body of each letter is unique and serves a different purpose, which can be expected in letters written to different recipients dealing with various sets of issues, they once again converge as they conclude. Using nearly identical phraseology, they express hope to see the recipients in person and close with a final "greeting" that employs the same verb. Given these stylistic, structural, and phraseological commonalities, the letters give every indication they have common authorship. From these parallels, which are unique to 2 John and 3 John, most scholars conclude the same author wrote them.[18]

Parallels Between 2 and 3 John[19]	
2 John	**3 John**
2 John 1a	3 John 1a
ὁ πρεσβύτερος . . . ("The elder . . .")	ὁ πρεσβύτερος . . . ("The elder . . .")
2 John 1b	3 John 1b
οὓς ἐγὼ ἀγαπῶ ἐν ἀληθείᾳ ("whom I love in the truth")	ὃν ἐγὼ ἀγαπῶ ἐν ἀληθείᾳ ("whom I love in the truth")
2 John 4	3 John 3
ἐχάρην λίαν ὅτι . . . ("I was overjoyed that . . .")	ἐχάρην γὰρ λίαν . . . ("For I was overjoyed . . .")
2 John 4	3 John 4
εὕρηκα ἐκ τῶν τέκνων σου περιπατοῦντας ἐν ἀληθείᾳ, . . . ("I found some of your children walking in the truth, . . .")	ἀκούω τὰ ἐμὰ τέκνα ἐν ἀληθείᾳ περιπατοῦντα. ("I hear that my children are walking in the truth.")
2 John 5	3 John 5
καὶ νῦν ἐρωτῶ σε, κυρία, . . . ("and now I ask you, lady . . .")	Ἀγαπητέ, πιστὸν ποιεῖς . . . ("beloved, you do faithfully . . .")

Parallels Between 2 and 3 John[19]	
2 John	**3 John**
2 John 12–13	3 John 13–15
[12]πολλὰ ἔχων ὑμῖν γράφειν οὐκ ἐβουλήθην διὰ χάρτου καὶ μέλανος, ("I have much to write to you, I would rather not use papyrus and ink,")	[13]πολλὰ εἶχον γράψαι σοι ἀλλ᾽ οὐ θέλω διὰ μέλανος καὶ καλάμου σοι γράφειν· ("I have much to write to you, but I would rather not write to you with pen and ink.")
ἀλλ᾽ ἐλπίζω γενέσθαι πρὸς ὑμᾶς καὶ στόμα πρὸς στόμα λαλῆσαι, . . . ("But I hope to come to you and to speak face to face, . . .")	[14]ἐλπίζω δὲ εὐθέως σε ἰδεῖν, καὶ στόμα πρὸς στόμα λαλήσομεν. ("But I hope to see you soon, and we will speak face to face.")
[13]ἀσπάζεταί σε τὰ τέκνα τῆς ἀδελφῆς σου τῆς ἐκλεκτῆς. ("The children of your elect sister greet you.")	[15] . . . ἀσπάζονταί σε οἱ φίλοι. ἀσπάζου τοὺς φίλους κατ᾽ ὄνομα. (". . . The friends greet you. Greet the friends, each by name.")

Notwithstanding this evidence, a small but influential group of scholars argue that different authors wrote 2 John and 3 John. Since 1900, the first to advocate for this position was Carl Clemen.[20] In a 1905 article, he sought to shed light on the authorship of the Johannine Epistles and the identity of the "heretics" of the letters. Within the context of this discussion, he also considers the recipients of the respective letters. He argues that because 2 John is written to "an ideal(ized) congregation," which he derives from a metaphorical reading of the address ἐκλεκτῇ κυρίᾳ, and 3 John is written to an individual named "Gaius," they could not have been written by the same person. He concludes that 2 John is composed by an apparent forger who had access to 3 John.[21] For Clemen, the author of 2 John had conscripted 3 John to compose a letter that was meant to be "catholic" in outlook, as it was addressed to "an ideal(ized) congregation" that could be read in every congregation.[22] The problems with Clemen's proposal are myriad. The whole scenario he advocates is more declared than proven, as he never engages with the stylistic, structural, and phraseological parallels between 2 John and 3 John beyond defaulting to a general theory of plagiarism. Likewise, he never provides compelling reasons why an apparent forger would want to plagiarize 3 John to fabricate a "catholic" letter to "an ideal(ized) community." The central argument he puts forth for this tenuous scenario is the unusual address in 2 John 1 (ἐκλεκτῇ κυρίᾳ); since he assumes it can only be taken as a metaphorical personification for "an ideal(ized) community," whereas 3 John 1 is addressed to a named individual, he concludes that both letters could not have been written by the same person. This point is crucial because it shows that the fundamental plank in Clemen's proposal—and in the subsequent iterations of this argument that have appeared in the twentieth and twenty-first centuries—is the obscure address in 2 John 1 and attempts to reconcile it with the remainder of the letter, which seems relatively straightforward, and with 3 John 1, which is written to an individual.

A remarkably similar approach was echoed years later in Rudolph Bultmann's influential commentary *Die drei Johannesbriefe*. There, Bultmann argues that 2 John and 3 John were authored by two different individuals and that the author of 2 John, again an apparent forger, pilfers from 1 John and 3 John. Bultmann even identifies some of the verses he believes are plagiarized, declaring that the attribution to "the elder" in 2 John 1 is lifted directly from 3 John 1 and that 2 John 12–13 is taken over from 3 John 13–14.[23] According to Bultmann, 3 John 9 emboldened the author of 2 John since it references a letter sent to a church and established that it was customary to deliver letters to individual churches.[24] For Bultmann, this whole scenario is buttressed by the generic address ἐκλεκτῇ κυρίᾳ, which he takes as a metaphorical personification of a Christian community. Since no specific community is identified, he contends that the forger is promoting "early catholicism" ("Frühkatholizismus").[25] But since 2 John 12, copied from 3 John 13–14, gives the impression that the letter was directed to a specific community, the tension within the letter reveals its literary fissures and apparently permits Bultmann to spot a forger creating an epistolary fiction.[26]

The scenario proposed by Bultmann is highly speculative. He does not establish his contentions by marshaling compelling evidence but mainly states them declaratively. Furthermore, the convoluted scenario he proposes is not persuasive. Lacking in Bultmann's argument is a convincing narrative for why the author of 2 John, who was seeking to compose a "catholic" epistle, would decide to model it primarily on 3 John, an explicitly personal letter. But at a more fundamental level, Bultmann consistently rejects the most obvious implications of the evidence. Instead of starting from the premise that the multiple overlaps between 2 John and 3 John point to the common authorship of the two letters, he casually dismisses them as "proof" that the author of 2 John copies 3 John. Besides being incredibly disingenuous with his handling of this evidence, it is more than curious that less than a decade before Bultmann put forth this convoluted theory, he takes the opposite view in his entry on the Johannine Epistles in the third edition of *Religion in Geschichte und Gegenwart*. There, he claims that the same author writes 2 John and 3 John because of their commonalities![27] Ultimately, Bultmann's form-critical approach—wherein he proposes that he has identified conflicting elements in 2 John, which he then interprets as evidence that 2 John is a literary fabrication by a different author than 3 John—is based on the acceptance of a concocted scenario. There are, therefore, compelling reasons to doubt his circular argument regarding the authorship of 2 and 3 John.

At about the same time Bultmann made this argument, another scholar, Jürgen Heise, put forth a similar proposal.[28] Like Bultmann, he contends that 2 John is written by a forger who has access to 3 John. For Heise, the most important indicator that something is different about 2 John is that it is not addressed to an individual and does not contain any personal names.[29] Specifically, Heise sees the opening address "to an elect lady" as a metaphor for any and every Christian community.[30] Therefore, despite any similarities 2 John shares with 3 John, the former is "catholic," while the latter is strictly personal, so the two letters are fundamentally different. On top of this, Heise alleges that the term "children" (τέκνα), appearing in 2 John 1, 4, and 13, is "peculiarly elaborated" and is different from how it appears in 3 John 4. Further, the injunction given in 2 John 10–11 not to admit heretics into the church cannot be easily reconciled with Diotrephes carrying out the same kinds of actions in 3 John 9–11.[31] He, therefore, concludes that the letters are incompatible.

Heise's reasoning for rejecting the common authorship of both letters is rooted more in a presumed scenario behind each letter than in the actual contents of the letters themselves. His argument that the two letters are incompatible based on his reading of 2 John 10–11 and 3 John 9–11 is mainly informed by Ernst Käsemann's thesis about the context behind 3 John, which has largely been rejected given its highly speculative nature.[32] At face value, nothing about 2 John 10–11 and 3 John 9–11 is mutually exclusive. Furthermore, Heise's contention that the usage of "children" in 2 John is somehow different from its usage in 3 John is not compelling. In 2 John, the term "children" appears in the address (v. 1) and the closing greeting (v. 13), and when it appears in the letter (v. 4), it occurs with nearly identical phraseology to its use in 3 John 4.[33]

While the argument that 2 John and 3 John are composed by different authors, with 2 John being written in imitation of 3 John, has not been perpetuated in any significant way in more recent scholarship, it is still pervasive in certain quarters. Gerd Schunack's commentary *Die Briefe des Johannes* argues that the most economical way to understand the relationship between 2 John and 3 John is to see 2 John as a later composition by an apparent forger who mimics 3 John.[34] Citing the earlier work of Bultmann, he argues that the reference to "the elder" at the start of the letter could have been taken directly from 3 John 1 and that the same may have been the case with the closing formulae appearing in 2 John 12–13 and 3 John 13–14.[35] Notably, he also argues that the nondescript address in 2 John 1 suggests that the same author does not write 3 John, which he takes as the "only real private letter" in the entire New Testament.[36] For Schunack, the address in 2 John 1, which he takes metaphorically to refer to the "Church," suggests that the author has attempted to craft a "catholic" letter in contradistinction to 3 John, which is a personal letter.[37] He, therefore, argues that 2 John is composed by a different author than 3 John. At the same time that Schunack's work appeared, Horst Balz published a lengthy article titled "Die Johannesbriefe," where he raises the possibility that 2 John and 3 John do not share common authorship.[38] While he concedes that the letters are remarkably similar on a number of fronts and that common authorship is a distinct possibility, he also feels that two different authors could have written the letters.[39] In particular, he claims that there are certain "antithetical" elements between the two letters and specifically cites 2 John 9 and 3 John 11b.[40] But it is hard to see anything in these two passages that is "antithetical" unless one reads them through the lenses of a preconceived theory.

More recently, in Hans-Josef Klauck's commentary, he suggests that the many similarities between 2 John and 3 John indicate they share a common authorship and warns of speculative theories that have been previously proposed.[41] But he also grants the possibility they could have been authored by two different persons, with one simply imitating the other.[42] Along the same lines, Judith Lieu does not preclude the possibility that 2 John and 3 John are written by different authors. She argues that since the identity of the "elect lady" in 2 John 1 is "obscure," from which she then claims that 2 John has a "high degree of artificiality when compared with 3 John," she is open to the possibility that 2 John is composed by someone other than the author of 3 John.[43] While she avoids the convoluted scenarios proposed earlier, she aligns with them in principle. If 2 John is written by a different author than 3 John, then 3 John was the original text: "A consequence is that any reconstruction should give priority to 3 John as to what appears to be a genuine letter from someone who could identify himself only as 'the elder,' an epithet whose potential 2 John then exploits."[44] But she is quick to backtrack and states that 2 John and 3 John do not necessarily have to be written by different authors. While she leaves the door open to the possibility that the letters could have been composed by different authors, she equivocates on the matter. She concludes that "the letters are too short to make stylistic arguments for or against common authorship decisive."[45] On this point, I disagree entirely. There are plenty of distinct points of contact between 2 John and 3 John to make a compelling case for common authorship, and this becomes even more evident when the correct form of address is restored to 2 John 1.

Laying aside the far-fetched scenarios and theories that have sometimes served as the basis from which to contest the common authorship of 2 John and 3 John, the principal basis used by proponents of this view boils down to the received address ἐκλεκτῇ κυρίᾳ. Seeing in this address a metaphorical cover for not just "a church" but rather "the Church," it is often alleged that 2 John aspires to be "catholic." Turning to 3 John, despite the salient parallels it shares with 2 John, it contains an unambiguous personal address. The received address of 2 John 1 is therefore critical to this argument. But if it is not the opaque ἐκλεκτῇ κυρίᾳ and is instead the personal Ἐκλέκτῃ τῇ κυρίᾳ that structurally mirrors the pattern of 3 John 1, the principal basis on which this tenuous argument stands is removed and left in its place is yet another distinct parallel between 2 John and 3 John, reinforcing their common authorship.

2 John: "Literary Fiction," "Semifiction," or Genuine Letter?

It has been periodically claimed—typically but not exclusively by those who argue that 2 John and 3 John are written by different authors—that 2 John is not a "real letter" but a "literary fiction." Though it is not altogether clear what proponents of this view mean by "literary fiction," the basis of this claim seems to be that, in some significant sense, 2 John is artificial and only took the form of a letter to vest it with a sense of authenticity and authority. It was not composed to address a historically present situation detailed in the letter, nor to be sent to one or more actual recipients physically removed from the sender. An early iteration of this view goes back to Adolf Jülicher in the last decade of the nineteenth century. Jülicher claimed that both 2 John and 3 John were the works of a forger who had access to the Gospel of John and 1 John.[46] He then claims that both letters were fabricated to regulate church discipline and asserts that the scenarios they present are wholly fictitious. Accordingly, he belives the names Gaius, Diotrephes, and Demetrius, which appear in 3 John, do not belong to actual people but are simply pseudonyms for fictional characters generated by the author to create a plausible narrative and advance theological claims.

A few decades later, in an entry on the Johannine Letters in the second edition of *Religion in Geschichte und Gegenwart*, Martin Dibelius raises the possibility that 2 John and 3 John are literary fictions and refers to them as "Literary Letters" ("Kunstebriefe").[47] Dibelius provides no evidence for this claim nor furnishes any motive for why the author behind 2 and 3 John would have created such fictions. He simply raises this possibility and notes that almost nothing can be established with certainty about the two letters. But even if there were little that could be ascertained with certainty about the backgrounds of 2 John and 3 John, it hardly follows that they should be relegated to the realm of "literary fiction." A few years later, in his study of the Johannine corpus, Emanuel Hirsch goes well beyond what Dibelius suggests and unequivocally pronounces 2 and 3 John to be epistolary fictions.[48] Claiming that the final version of 1 John was a composite work with a primary and a secondary hand, he argues that the second hand later composed 2 and 3 John to ramp up the fight against the heresy of Cerinthus.[49] Hirsch is vague regarding the contexts behind 2 and 3 John but treats the letters like literary fictions. He claims that in 3 John, Diotrephes and Demetrius are likely literary inventions and not actual people or, if they were real, are ghosts of an earlier generation that the author conjures to combat present heresies.[50] Thus, he believes there was nothing genuine about either letter. Along similar lines, but a few decades later, in a short but influential article on 2 and 3 John, Roland Bergmeier argues that both 2 and 3 John are essentially fictions.[51] Though he believes both are composed by the same author, he contends that in relation to the earlier Gospel of John and 1 John, they are tantamount to the "Pastoral Epistles" but in the Johannine tradition.[52]

Shortly thereafter, Bultmann followed with his argument that 2 John is nothing more than a literary fiction. He differs from Jülicher, Dibelius, Hirsch, and, to some extent, Bergmeier because he regards 3 John to be a genuine letter, as he believes it addresses an actual interpersonal situation in the early church.[53] His argument that 2 John is a literary fiction is directly tied to his contention that it is composed by a different author than 3 John. Bultmann argues that since 2 John displays evidence of an "early catholicism," which he sees in the opening address, ἐκλεκτῇ κυρίᾳ, that he takes metaphorically and could refer to every church, 2 John is a crafted fiction based on 3 John.[54] Since 2 John is impersonal, he argues that it suggests an artificiality, and that parallels between 2 John and 3 John result from the former copying the latter. As noted previously, Bultmann's declaration that the parallels between 2 John and 3 John are best taken as evidence of the dependence of 2 John on 3 John by a different author smack of special pleading.[55] A central pillar in Bultmann's claim that the letter is a fiction is the nondescript address ἐκλεκτῇ κυρίᾳ. But if this is not the correct address, and it is rather Ἐκλέκτῃ τῇ κυρίᾳ, the letter suddenly becomes personal and a significant plank on which Bultmann builds his theory vanishes. It should be noted that for Bultmann, the main criterion by which he judges 3 John to be a genuine letter is that it is a personal letter addressed to an individual named Gaius, and he could find no compelling reason why someone would fabricate it.

Over the decades, others have put forth iterations of Bultmann's literary theory about 2 John. In his lengthy commentary on the Johannine Letters, Dutch scholar Marinus de Jonge argues that 2 John is "hardly a real letter."[56]

De Jonge views the letter as a literary work written to address a particular set of theological circumstances and that the epistolary form is just a cover for the entire treatise. Central to his argument that 2 John is not a genuine letter is the address to an "elect lady," which he finds perplexing. He wonders why the author metaphorically addresses a congregation in such a way when the letter is so brief and otherwise straightforward.[57] Another study that takes the same approach with 2 John is Ulrich Körtner's work on Papias of Hierapolis.[58] Though Körtner's work is devoted to an in-depth study of Papias and his works, in an extended discussion of the enigmatic "John the elder" mentioned by Papias, whom some have taken as "the elder" of 2 John, he considers the letter.[59] Körtner almost entirely subscribes to the view of Bultmann and declares 2 John to be a literary fiction, although outside of citing Bultmann, he provides no additional evidence for this claim.[60] In a remarkably ironic statement, Körtner acknowledges that 2 John conforms in every way to the structure and style of a "Hellenistic letter" but that these features only attest to the quality of the literary fiction.[61] Here, Körtner's reasoning is undoubtedly colored by his preconceived ideas about the alleged context of 2 John. Surely, if 2 John bears the structure and style of a genuine letter, the most obvious conclusion is that it is an actual letter and not an exquisitely executed fiction taking a letter in form only. Interestingly, the only feature that Körtner notes in his summary of 2 John that is an exception to the general epistolary pattern is the unusual address that does not mention a named recipient and that he takes as a metaphorical reference to a community personified as an "elect lady."[62]

While such theories, in their excess, are not as commonplace in contemporary scholarship, iterations persist. Johannes Beutler's more recent commentary on the Johannine Epistles argues that some compelling reasons exist to view 2 John as a literary fiction primarily based on 3 John.[63] He contends that in 2 John, there is almost a complete absence of specific features, as the letter does not contain any names, and the metaphorical address to a personified church at the start of the letter gives it a general outlook that is very different from 3 John. While Beutler takes these features as evidence for a kind of fictionality with the letter, he concedes that 2 John lacks literary and theological terms that one would expect in a purely literary fiction.[64] He, therefore, suggests that its fictional components are tempered. Similarly, while Judith Lieu avoids calling 2 John a "literary fiction," she contends that it contains "semifictional" elements.[65] In particular, she argues that the phrase ἐκλεκτῇ κυρίᾳ carries with it an "artificiality" that covers the whole letter:

> [2 John] is using the letter format as a cloak, a strategy that is not unusual in the ancient world. . . . The anonymity of the sender is matched by that of the recipient, "the elect lady," and is sustained throughout the letter. This introduces an artificial note, which could suggest that the contrast between "the elder" and "the lady" is deliberately chosen as appropriate to a letter of concern and direction; the letter format was commonly used in antiquity as a fictional device and as a vehicle for teaching, for example of a philosophical nature, although the recipient is often named even in these.[66]

Here, she asserts that the author of 2 John wanted to broach various ecclesiastical issues and that the form of a letter was the best medium for doing so. That she invokes examples of "fictional" letters from antiquity to compare with 2 John shows that for Lieu, it is somewhere on a trajectory approaching one of these "literary fictions." She then states that 3 John "represents a more normal letter style and perhaps provided the model that 2 John has imitated."[67] Thus, for Lieu as for Beutler, there is a clear degree of fictionality in 2 John that goes back to the curious opening address, ἐκλεκτῇ κυρίᾳ.

One of the best ways to judge whether 2 John should be regarded as a "genuine" letter, as opposed to a "literary fiction" or even "semifiction," is to compare it with the epistolary papyri, or "Hellenistic letters," as they have sometimes been called. As one would be hard-pressed to argue that the epistolary papyri do not represent "genuine" letters, if 2 John shares points of contact with these letters, it surely increases the likelihood that 2 John is what it appears to be—an actual letter and not an artificially contrived fiction only taking the form of a letter to endow it with authority. Even though 2 John lends itself to a comparison with the epistolary papyri, it is stunning how the same studies that have dismissively relegated it to the realm of "literary fiction" are seemingly oblivious to these sources and their overlaps with 2 John. Only one of these studies includes the epistolary papyri in its discussion of 2 John.[68]

Epistolary Papyri

The first to employ the epistolary papyri in a study of 2 John was J. Rendel Harris at the start of the nineteenth century. As noted in the previous chapter, Harris utilized the papyri to consider the address in 2 John 1, but his study was largely derailed trying to prove that 2 John was tantamount to a love letter.[69] Brenna Bresky's study that followed a few years later considered a few papyri, but as the papyri came from a later period (III and IV CE) and the prescripts contained therein contained different formulae than the one appearing in 2 John (and 3 John), her papyrological conclusions are misleading.[70] Adolf Deissmann used the papyri to illuminate the texts of the New Testament in his 1908 classic but never conducted a thorough study of 2 John and only made a few passing comparisons.[71] In Jacques Marty's 1925 article on 2 and 3 John, he briefly referenced the epistolary papyri in his discussion of the address in 2 John 1 but never provided any kind of examination.[72]

Among the first to provide a cursory overview of some of the parallels 2 John (and 3 John) shared with the epistolary papyri (although without a discussion of the address in 2 John 1) is Robert W. Funk in a 1967 article published in the *Journal of Biblical Literature*.[73] Funk sets out to demonstrate that 2 John (and 3 John) shares "points of contact with the common Hellenistic letter" and notes two phraseological parallels as well as some general structural parallels.[74] The article is mostly insightful, despite some factual errors, as it highlights some specific overlaps.[75] But a notable shortcoming of the work is Funk's reluctance to acknowledge any implications of these parallels. Writing the article in the wake of a specifically German trend to declare 2 John, and in some circles 3 John, "literary fictions," Funk sidesteps the whole issue and states that he does not intend to wade into the debate over whether it is an "actual" or a "fictive" letter.[76] But his analysis that demonstrates that 2 John (and 3 John) shares distinct points of contact with the epistolary papyri has bearing on this question. Such points of contact surely suggest we are unlikely to be dealing with a "literary fiction" conjured by a forger to rhetorically foist an ecclesiastical agenda. Rather, they should suggest that 2 John is a genuine letter dealing with historically present circumstances.[77]

In the last fifty years, commentaries on the Johannine Epistles have generally contained little to no discussion of the epistolary papyri and parallels between 2 John (and 3 John). For example, Brown and Klauck cite a few papyri in their general treatment of 2 John, but it is so perfunctory that it offers very little.

Furthermore, the texts they cite had previously been noted so that nothing new is brought to bear.[78] The one notable exception is Judith Lieu's *The Second and Third Epistles of John: History and Background* in which she devotes a chapter to considering these letters in light of the epistolary papyri.[79] She begins the chapter with a concise introduction to the "classical letter," wherein she notes a few hallmarks and then turns directly to the epistolary papyri for the remainder. The chapter is generally insightful, and to Lieu's credit, she cites specific papyri and examples where parallels can be found.[80] However, she never explicitly treats the address in 2 John 1, and throughout the chapter, there is an overt push to treat 2 John and 3 John differently. She asserts that there is a distinct "contrast" between the two letters and that they "defy treatment as a 'pair of inseparable twins.'"[81] She argues that of the two letters, 3 John is a "genuine letter according to the conventions of the age" but that "2 John is more consciously constructed than 3 John and, in a sense, more artificial; even if a letter, it is more than just a letter."[82] This characterization is informed by her metaphorical reading of the received address in 2 John 1.[83]

Turning to 2 John, it is time to consider this text in light of the epistolary papyri. As will be seen, 2 John accords remarkably well with the structure, style, and phraseology of these letters. A notable feature of 2 John that invites a specific comparison with the epistolary papyri is that it discloses the material on which it was written. In this regard, it is unique among all the letters preserved in the New Testament. Near the end of the letter in 2 John 12, it reads: πολλὰ ἔχων ὑμῖν γράφειν οὐκ ἐβουλήθην διὰ χάρτου καὶ μέλανος ("Although I have much to write to you, I would rather not use paper and ink."). The translation in the NRSVue of "paper and ink" is idiomatic, and the word "paper" is anachronistic; the Greek word underlying the translation "paper" is actually "papyrus."[84] The beginning of 2 John 12 should properly read, "Although I have much to write to you, I would rather not use *papyrus* and ink." It is clear, therefore, that 2 John was originally inscribed on a sheet of papyrus. Though the papyrus plant is native to the shores of the Nile, from which the writing medium papyrus was made, Pliny the Elder (23/24–79 CE) notes that it was widely available outside of Egypt during his lifetime.[85] Thus, wherever 2 John may have been written, it seems reasonable to conclude that the author could have readily acquired it.

Beyond the medium of the letter, a feature of 2 John that aligns well with the epistolary papyri is its overall length. Only reading the letters in the

New Testament, one might get the impression that it was not uncommon for letters to be quite lengthy so that they might span many chapters. But as evidenced by the papyri and other examples of the Hellenistic/Classical letter, a general hallmark of such letters was brevity. Writing on the subject of style, Ps.-Demetrius (ca. 200 BCE–300 CE) notes that a letter is to represent half a conversation; thus, most letters tend to be just that and are succinct.[86] By and large, the epistolary papyri are to the point and relatively brief. Most are written on one side of a sheet of papyrus, and estimations based on extant papyri in the Roman period (ca. 30 BCE–284 CE) suggest that an average letter was around 100 words from start to finish.[87] By comparison, Cicero's (106–43 BCE) letters average 331 words per letter, Pliny the Younger's (ca. 61–113 CE) 175 words, and Cornelius Fronto's (ca. 100–60 CE) 235 words.[88] 2 John comes in at 245 words and is the second shortest letter in the New Testament after 3 John, which contains 218 words.[89] 2 John could have easily fit on one side of a single sheet of papyrus.[90]

Besides their general brevity, another characteristic of the epistolary papyri is that they tend to be highly structured and typically consist of an ordered set of components. Additionally, they tend to be highly formulaic at certain junctures and employ customary or stereotyped vocabulary and phraseology. But as the epistolary papyri span about a one-thousand-year period, from the fourth century BCE through the seventh century CE, they attest to evolving epistolary features. In terms of structure, phraseology, and vocabulary, letters from the Ptolemaic period (ca. 323–30 BCE) can possess some unique characteristics that can differentiate them from letters written during the Roman period (ca. 30 BCE–284 CE);[91] likewise, letters from the Roman period can be differentiated from letters from the later Byzantine period (ca. 284–642 CE).[92] Epistolary changes do not appear to have taken place suddenly but seem to have evolved over about a century, with the third and fourth centuries CE witnessing some of the most significant structural and phraseological changes in Greek epistolarity.[93] For the present examination, focus will be given to epistolary features of letters from the Roman period with a further focus on the first two centuries since this is the general period in which 2 John was authored.[94]

During the Roman period, the typical epistolary papyrus, whether it was a personal/familial, business, administrative, or official letter, tended to consist of the following components: (1) a prescript (i.e., opening address);[95] (2) a proem (i.e., preface); (3) the body of the letter that might contain different components like a petition, request, or appeal; and (4) a conclusion that often included a greeting and valediction.[96] The most structured and formulaic parts of a letter were sections 1, 2, and 4, which regularly followed a set pattern and used a limited set of vocabulary in a limited set of epistolary phrases. Alternatively, while the letter's body might contain some stock phrases and epistolary clichés, this was the most diverse part of the letter, as every letter contained its own narrative.

The epistolary prescript (*praescriptio*) in the Roman period was tripartite and consisted of a superscription (*superscriptio*), an adscription (*adscriptio*), and a salutation (*salutatio*).[97] The superscription was the first element of the letter and consisted of the name of the sender, or names of the senders if more than one was involved, in the nominative case. This was directly followed by the adscription that contained the name, or names if more than one person was being addressed, of the recipient(s) of the letter. A definite article did not accompany the name, which was always in the dative case, as it was regarded as inherently definite in epistolary address. It was then customary to have a proper salutation. This was typically communicated through the infinitive verb "to rejoice/greet" (χαίρειν) that followed the name of the addressed party.[98] Thus, the basic opening address in a Roman-period letter looked like the following: "Pisais to Heracleus, greetings" (Πισάις Ἡρακλήῳ χαίρειν).[99] This kind of address, which takes the form "A [to] B, greetings," is the most widely attested form of address with over 2,300 attestations in the epistolary papyri from the Ptolemaic through Byzantine periods.

Following the epistolary prescript, it was customary for the sender to include a proem. In this section, the sender expressed hope that the receiving party was doing well.[100] It often contained stereotyped language where the basic form included a phrase like "before all else, I pray that you are well."[101] It could, however, be expanded, employ other verbs for health, and might also include a disclosure about the health of the sender.[102] While it was common in Roman-period letters, it gradually faded away by the Byzantine period.[103] A secondary formula that often followed was the *proskynesis* formula.[104] Here, the sender expressed hope that the health and prosperity of the addressee would continue, and so they inform them they are making their "obeisance" (προσκύνησις) before a deity.[105] This formula is attested over 250 times in letters of the first four centuries CE.[106]

The body, which followed, typically marked the longest section, as the sender narrated the circumstances that necessitated the letter.[107] At the most essential level, the body served two functions: (1) to disclose or seek information and/or (2) to make requests or demands.[108] Many letters belong to the realm of everyday life, as they address quotidian matters and pressing concerns.[109] Nevertheless, letters could be exceptionally diverse and broach various subjects, from business or work-related matters to family or personal issues. Notwithstanding the diversity of topics broached within the body, like the opening and closing sections of a letter that were replete with formulaic language, the body also tended to employ a good deal of stereotyped phraseology and clichés.[110]

As the letter transitioned to the conclusion, two features stand out. The first is that it was common for the author to "greet" (ἀσπάζομαι) persons in perceived proximity to the recipient of the letter. Similarly, it was common for the immediate family of the sender, or mutual friends or associates, to pass along greetings at the end of the letter to the recipient, extended family, or mutual friends. After the final greeting, many letters contained a proper "farewell" (ἔρρωσο/ἐρρῶσθαί),[111] but a less common alternative was "may you prosper" (διευτύχει/εὐτύχει).[112]

2 John

Several points of contact exist between 2 John and the epistolary papyri. Cumulatively, these suggest that 2 John is a genuine letter and not a contrived "epistolary fiction." Considerably more will be said about the prescript in 2 John 1 later in this chapter. For now, it is sufficient to note that the superscription ("the elder"; ὁ πρεσβύτερος) contains the standard pattern appearing in letters of the Roman period where it is the first element of the letter and appears in the nominative case. Similarly, the adscription follows the pattern typical in Roman-period letters where it immediately follows the superscription in the dative case and is devoid of the definite article. Therefore, the epistolary address in 2 John takes the form "A [to] B." In the epistolary papyri, the most common form is "A [to] B, greetings," where "greetings" (as noted above) are made through the verb χαίρειν.[113] While this verb is the most popular form of salutation, other greetings like "be well" (εὐ πράττειν), "be of good courage" (εὐψυχεῖν), or "be of good cheer" (εὐθυμεῖν) are occasionally attested. Their usage appears to relate to the context of the letter.[114] Occasionally, letters might not contain any greeting and might simply include the name of the sender followed immediately by the addressee's name.[115]

In Paul's Letters, the salutation takes the basic form "grace to you and peace"[116] but is periodically expanded: "Grace to you and peace from God our Father and the Lord Jesus Christ."[117] Like Paul's salutation, the one appearing in 2 John 3 incorporates grace and peace but adds other elements: "Grace, mercy, and peace will be with us from God the Father and from Jesus Christ, the Father's Son, in truth and love."[118] Therefore, although the style of the salutation in 2 John is unique, the overall prescript follows the structure found in the epistolary papyri of the Roman period.[119]

Superscript (first position)	**Adscript (second position)**	**Salutation (third position)**
ὁ πρεσβύτερος (v. 1)	ἐκλεκτῇ κυρίᾳ . . . but properly restored Ἐκλέκτῃ τῇ κυρίᾳ . . . (v. 1)	ἔσται μεθ' ἡμῶν χάρις ἔλεος εἰρήνη κτλ . . . (v. 3)

The proem follows the prescript. Here, the sender might include a health wish for the recipient and offer a prayer for their well-being. Unlike 3 John 2, where there is a health wish for the recipient, 2 John contains no such formula.[120] This is not entirely surprising since 3 John is sent to a single individual, so it is more personal, whereas 2 John is sent to a collective—a named "lady" and "her children." Nonetheless, in 2 John 4, one finds an element of the proem in the expression of joy where the elder praises some of the "children" of the addressee for "walking in the truth." A common motif found in epistolary papyri is the exclamation of gladness or joy that news about the addressed party has reached the sender in advance of the letter being sent, and so this news is then echoed in the proem of the letter. As John L. White notes, the "expression of joy in the letter opening is, or usually is, a variant or surrogate statement of the sender's concern about the recipient's welfare."[121] At another level, it is used by the sender to obtain the goodwill of the recipient by flattering them with complimentary language that is shortly followed by a request, as is the case in 2 John 5.[122] The expression of joy in 2 John 4 is communicated via the Greek phrase "I was overjoyed" (ἐχάρην λίαν), which is also used in 3 John 3. It finds parallels in various epistolary papyri where the sender not only "rejoices" but "exceedingly rejoices" on hearing good news about the recipient. Furthermore, as in 2 John 4, the phrase is typically positioned in the proem of the letter.

2 John 4 ἐχάρην λίαν ("I was overjoyed")[123]	
SB 12.11125.1–4 (51 or 57 CE)	Νῖλος Νεμεσίωνι τῶι ἀδελφῶι χ[α]ίρειν. ἐχάρην λίαν ἀκούσας ὅ̣[τι] ἐλύθης. "Nilus to Nemesion his brother, greetings. I was overjoyed upon hearing that you were freed."
P.Oxy. 85.5523.1–4 (I/II CE)	Ἀμμώνιος Ἀπολλωνίωι τῶι ἀδελφῶι χαίρειν. ἔλαβόν σου ἐπιστολὴν δι' ἧς ἔγνων ἐρρῶσθαι καὶ λειαν (*l.* λίαν) ἐχάρην. "Ammonius to Apollonius his brother, greetings. I received your epistle through which I learned you do well and I was overjoyed."
P.Giss. 1.21.1–3 (ca. 113–115 CE)	Εὐδα[ι]μονὶς Ἀπολλωνίωι τῶι υἱῶι πλεῖστα χαίρε̣ι̣ν. λίαν ἐχάρην ἀκούσασα ὅτ̣ι . . . "Eudaimonis to her son Apollonius, very many greetings. I was overjoyed when I heard that . . ."

2 John 4 ἐχάρην λίαν (“I was overjoyed”)[123]	
P.Mich. 8.474.2 (II CE)	[Ταβεθεῦς(?) Κλαυδίῳ Τιβ]εριανῷ τῷ ἀ[δε]λφ[ῷ] πλεῖστα χαίρειν. [πυθομένη ὅτι παρ]εγένου ε[ἰ]ς Ἀλεξάνδρ[ει]αν λίαν ἐχάρην [μ]ετὰ [τῶ]ν ἐμ[ῶν] πάντων. “[Tabetheus(?) to Claudius Tib]erianus, her brother, very many greetings. [When I learned that] you had come to Alexandria, I was overjoyed together with my entire family.”
P.Oxy. 59.3991.1–5 (II/III CE)	Σαραπιὰς Ἰσχυρίωνι τῷ ἀδελφῷ χαίρε(ιν). λείαν (*l.* λίαν) ἐχάρην κομισθέντων σου τῶν γραμμάτων. “Sarapias to his brother Ischyrion, greetings. I was overjoyed when your letter was received.”
SB 14.12177 (early III CE)	χαῖρε κύριέ μου τέκνον Ἀπολλώνιε· Σαραπίων σε προσαγορεύωι (*l.* προσαγορεύω) κομισάμενοί σου γράμματα σήμερον ἥτις (*l.* ἥ) ἐστὶν κ λείαν (*l.* λίαν) ἐχάρημεν. “Greetings, my lord and son Apollonius. I, Sarapion, salute you. When we received your letter today, which is the 20th, we were overjoyed.”

2 John 5–11 effectively represents the body of the letter. Given the wide variety of subjects treated in letters, it is unsurprising to find that there could be great diversity within this section; as there is no conventional format for a letter's body—situation or necessity dictates this section. Nevertheless, this section is bracketed by the use of various formulae, and these signal to the addressee that the primary purpose of the letter is now being introduced since the introductory matters (prescript, proem, etc.) have been conveyed. Likewise, certain formulae appearing at the end of the body point to the reader the central message had been communicated, and now the letter is coming to a close. While various phrases are employed to introduce the main

purpose of the letter—and these vary depending on that purpose—in letters where an overarching request is being made, it is common for the body of the letter to begin with a verb of request.[124] Though various verbs of "asking/requesting" could be used, the verb "I ask" (ἐρωτάω), used in 2 John 5, is common in this formula.

2 John 5 καὶ νῦν ἐρωτῶ σε, κυρία . . . ("But now, dear lady, I ask you . . .")[125]	
P.Oxy. 38.2861.6–7 (II CE)	καὶ νῦν σε ἐρωτῶ . . .[126] "and now I ask you . . ."
BACPS 27 (2010) p. 56, no. 2 l. 6 (II CE)	καὶ [ν]ῦν ἐρωτῶ "and now I ask you . . ."
W.Chr. 480.11 (II CE)	ἐρωτῶ σε οὖν, κύριέ μου πάτηρ(*l.* πάτερ) . . . "I therefore ask you, my lord father . . ."
P.Coll. Youtie 1.53.3–4 (II CE)	ἐρωτῶ σε οὖν, μῆ[τε]ρ . . . "I therefore ask you, mother . . ."
P.Mich. 8.475.10 (II CE)	ἐρωτῶ σε οὖν, ἄδελφε "I therefore ask you, brother . . ."
P.Mich. 8.491.9 (II CE)	ἐρωτῶ σε οὖν, μῆτηρ "I therefore ask you, mother . . ."
BGU 3.814.26 (III CE)	ἐρωτῶ σε οὖν, μῆτηρ . . . "I therefore ask you, mother . . ."

A secondary parallel between 2 John and the epistolary papyri is worth noting. After introducing the request, the elder employs the vocative κυρία ("lady"). In the epistolary papyri, persons are not typically referred to by their name in the body of the letter when a request is made but most often by the title they are given in the address. In 2 John 1, κυρία is clearly the title "lady," so when a personal request is made, the title is repeated. For example, the prescript in W.Chr. 480 (see table above) reads "Apion to Epimachus, his lord and father, very many greetings."[127] When the request is employed later in the letter, the sender defaults to addressing his father by the titles used in the address: "I therefore ask you, my lord father."[128] 2 John, therefore, shares yet another stylistic parallel with the request formula appearing in the epistolary papyri.[129]

2 John 5–6, which opens the body of the letter, contains the request/petition section. 2 John 7 provides more information about the basis of the request and is governed by it. 2 John 8–11 is a new unit where final exhortation and instructions/recommendations are given before the letter closes. The opening of this section uses vocabulary and syntax found in the epistolary papyri in the same manner. 2 John 8 uses the imperative "pay attention! / be on guard!" (βλέπετε) to warn the addressed parties, followed by the construction *μή* plus the subjunctive, not to let something happen. This same construction is found in the epistolary papyri with some regularity when the sender wants to exhort the recipient to be careful not to perform an activity. As in 2 John 8, this construction typically marks a discrete unit within a letter.[130]

2 John 8 βλέπετε ἑαυτούς, ἵνα μὴ . . . ("Be on your guard, so that you do not . . . ")[131]	
P.Berl.Zill. 9.13–14 (Oct. 6, 68 CE)	βλέπε οὖν, μὴ ἄλλως ποιήσῃς. "Therefore, pay attention so that you do not do otherwise."
SB 24.16337.7 (ca. 98–102 CE)	βλ̣έπ̣ε̣ μὴ ἐκβάλῃς σου τὰ ἔργα. "Pay attention, lest you cast off your work."
P.Graux. 2.23.13–14 (II CE)	βλέπε οὖν μὴ ἀφῇς αὐτὴν. "Therefore, pay attention that you do not lose it."

(*Continued*)

2 John 8 βλέπετε ἑαυτούς, ἵνα μὴ . . . ("Be on your guard, so that you do not . . .")[131]	
P.Mil.Vogl. 2.77.8–10 (II CE)	βλέ[πε δ]ὲ μὴ ἔλθω καὶ εὕρω [τὸν] τοῖχ[ο]ν [ἀν] - οικοδόμητον. "But pay attention lest I come and find the wall not built."
P.Oslo 2.56.7–8 (II CE)	βλέπε οὖν μὴ ἀμελήσῃς . . . "Therefore, pay attention that you do not neglect . . ."
SB 4.7354.8 (II CE)	λοιπὸν οὖν βλέπε, μὴ πισθῇς (*l.* πεισθῇς) . . . "In the future, then, pay attention that you are not persuaded . . ."
SB 28.17144.7–9 (II CE)	βλέπε Δωνάτῳ (*l.* Δονάτῳ) μὴ δοῖς (*l.* δῷς). "Pay attention so that you do not give it to Donatus."
P.Iand. 6.96V.10 (II/III CE)	βλέπετε δὲ μὴ π[ο]ιήσητε ἀηδίαν πρὸς ἀλλήλους, . . . "But pay attention so that you do not perpetrate unpleasantness with one another, . . ."
P.Oxy. 14.1773.33–35 (III CE)	βλέπε δαὶ (*l.* δὲ) μὴ ἀμαρ[τ]ά̣ν̣ῃς κ̣[αὶ ἐνε]δρεύσῃς τοὺς ἀν̣[θρώπους εὐ]πυεῖαν (*l.* εὐποιίαν) μοι πυή[σαντας] (*l.* ποιήσαντας). "Pay attention that you do not blunder and hinder the men who have benefited me."

2 John 12–13 marks the concluding section of the letter. Here, the elder declares his intention regarding a coming visit.[132] It is not unusual for letters to contain a phrase, typically near the end, where the sender informs the addressee of their desire to come and visit.[133] While this expression can be conveyed through various verbs, the verb "I hope" (ἐλπίζω) is periodically used and appears in the same way as it does in 2 John 12 (and 3 John 14).[134]

2 John 12 . . . ἀλλ' ἐλπίζω γενέσθαι πρὸς ὑμᾶς . . . (". . . ; instead, I hope to come to you . . .")[135]	
P.Mich. 8.481.14–15 (II CE)	κἀγ[ὼ] γὰρ ἐλπίζω ταχ[έ]ως πρὸς ὑμᾶς ἀν[ε] - λθεῖ[ν]. "For I soon hope to come up to you."
P.Mich. 3.211.5–7 (II/III CE)	ἐλπίζω τάχιον ἐκπλέκσε (*l.* ἐκπλέξαι) καὶ ἀναπλεῦσε (*l.* ἀναπλεῦσαι) πρὸς ὑμᾶς. "I soon hope to straighten matters out and sail up to you."
P.Oxy. 14.1681.20–24 (III CE)	ἐλπίζω οὖν μετὰ τρεῖς καὶ ἐγὼ πρὸς ὑμᾶς ἐλθεῖν καὶ τὰ περὶ ἐμοῦ ὑμῖν ἐξηγήσασθαι. "I hope then after three days I too will come to you and tell you my news."

2 John concludes with a third-party "greeting" (ἀσπάζομαι) employing the verb typically used to extend such greetings at the end of a letter. Similar greetings are attested in over seven hundred letters from the Roman period alone. Those included in the table below are a small sample but instructive because of the parallels they share with 2 John 13.

2 John 13 ἀσπάζεταί σε τὰ τέκνα τῆς ἀδελφῆς σου τῆς ἐκλεκτῆς. ("The children of your elect sister send you their greetings.")[136]	
BASP 47.76.9–10 (I/II CE)	ἀσπάζεται σαι (*l.* σε) πολλὰ ἡ ἀδελφή σου καὶ τὰ τέκνα αὐτῆς. "Your sister and her children greet you much."
P.Mich. 8.481.26 (II CE)	ἀσπ[άζεταί σ]ε τὰ τέ[κν]α ἡμῶν. "Our children greet you."
P.Mich. 8.510.37 (II/III CE)	ἀ[σπάζεταί σε] ἡ ἀδελφή σου καὶ τὰ τέκνα αὐτῆς. "Your sister and her children greet you."
PSI 12.1247V.12–13 (III CE)	ἀσπάζεται ὑμᾶς τὰ τέκνα ὑμῶν. "Your children greet you."

The foregoing comparison of 2 John with the epistolary papyri reveals significant points of contact regarding structure, style, and phraseology. In the entire epistolary corpus preserved in the New Testament, the only other letter that shares such a degree of overlap with the epistolary papyri is 3 John. From the epistolary prescript to the epistolary phraseology and formulae employed at various junctures in the letter to the concluding section where the elder makes known that the letter was inscribed on papyrus, 2 John contains multiple parallels. In fact, in the places where one expects epistolary formula and clichés to appear in the epistolary papyri, at the beginning and end of the letter and at various junctures, 2 John possesses these features. In light of these points of contact, the most obvious implication is that 2 John is a genuine letter sent to address a historically present situation to an addressee who is physically removed from the sender. To claim otherwise and declare that the letter is a "literary fiction" in the face of such evidence is to ignore this evidence—and remarkably, in many instances, this appears to have been the case.

The Adscript is Not ἐκλεκτῇ κυρίᾳ; It Is 'Εκλέκτῃ τῇ κυρίᾳ

The obscure address ἐκλεκτῇ κυρίᾳ in 2 John 1 is unusual in its own right but is especially strange in light of the remainder of the letter that shares several parallels with the epistolary papyri. Outside of this address, the letter otherwise indicates that it is a conventional letter that adheres to established norms. In this section, it will be shown that the proper rendering of the adscript is 'Εκλέκτῃ τῇ κυρίᾳ, which conforms to the typical pattern of address in Roman-period letters that is also attested in 3 John 1. As previously noted, 2 John attests the tripartite prescript in the usual order: superscription (*superscriptio*), adscription (*adscriptio*), and then salutation (*salutatio*). The prescript of 2 John only differs from those typically appearing in the epistolary papyri in that it contains a more elaborate salutation akin to the salutation appearing in Paul's Letters.[137] The superscript and adscript in 2 John 1 parallel the most common address "A [to] B," where the first two words in a letter are respectively the name (or title) of the sender in the nominative case followed immediately by the name of the addressee in the dative case without the definite article.

This ubiquitous pattern of address has nearly two thousand attestations in letters of the Roman period.[138] The following examples illustrate the basic structure of this address that opens a letter.

Greeting Type: A [to] B	
BGU 4.1079.1 (Aug. 4, 41 CE)	Σαραπίων Ἡρακλείδῃ "Sarapion to Heraclides"
O.Ber. 3.348.1 (I CE)	Ἀντώνιος Ζανέῳ "Antonius to Zaneus"
P.Oxy. 2.296.1–2 (I CE)	Ἡρακλείδης Ἀσκλατᾶι "Heraclides to Asclatas"
P.Fay. 109 (late I CE)	Πισάις Ἡρακλήῳ "Pisais to Heracleus"
P.Col. 8.216.1 (I/II CE)	Σευηριανὸς Ἀμ[μ]ῳνιανῷ "Severianus to Ammonianus"
BGU 3.794.1 (II CE)	Ῥοῦφος Ἡρακλειανῷ "Rufus to Heraclianus"
P.Fay. 124 (II CE)	Θεογίτων Ἀπολλωνίῳ "Theogiton to Apollonius"

This structure of address is attested in a diverse array of correspondence. It appears in personal letters (between one sender and addressee), group letters (sent and/or received by multiple parties), private letters (dealing with personal matters between sender and addressee), and administrative/official letters (dealing with issues of governance and sent by officials).[139] Furthermore, it appears in letters between persons of all ranks and social status without any negative connotations.[140] Finally, it is the same form of address that is used in 3 John 1: ὁ πρεσβύτερος Γαΐῳ . . . ("The elder to Gaius . . .").

It is not uncommon for this pattern of address to be expanded and for the sender to provide additional description of the addressee through the use of kinship terminology, titles of address, or both. The most common modifiers attached to the adscript are kinship terms. The two most common to appear are "brother" or "sister" (ἀδελφός/ἀδελφή), which occur around eight hundred times in epistolary papyri between the third century BCE and the sixth/seventh century CE.[141] When they are employed, it is not always clear whether they are being used literally for blood relations—an actual brother or sister—or being used figuratively.[142] In official documents (e.g., census records, contracts, petitions, wills, etc.), it is typically best to assume that when familial terms appear, it is literal,[143] but in personal/private correspondence, it is more difficult to determine. When this terminology modifies the adscript, it always appears after the name of the addressee in the dative case, as it is in agreement with the case of the name, and the accompanying definite article appears between the name and the kinship term. The following examples illustrate this paradigm.

Examples of the Use of "Brother"/"Sister" (ἀδελφός/ἀδελφή) in the Adscript	
SB 18.13226.1 (late I BCE)	Παμμένης Ἀλκίμωι τῶι ἀδελφῶι "Pammenes to Alcimus his brother"
P.Wash.Univ. 2.106.1 (Jan. 13, 18 BCE)	Διονυσία Πανεχώτῃ τῷ ἀδελφῷ "Dionysia to Panechotes her brother"
P.Oxy. 8.1154.1 (I CE)	Θέ[ω]ν Σαραποῦτι τῇ ἀδελφῇ "Theon to Sarapous his sister"
O.Ber. 3.459.1–2 (late I CE)	Ἰούλιος Σαταβῷ τῷ ἀδελφῷ "Julius to Satabus his brother"
SB 3.6265.1–2 (late I CE)	Ἀσκλῆς Σερήνῳ τῷ ἀδελφῷ "Ascles to Serenus his brother"
BGU 2.602.1 (II CE)	Τασουχάριν Νίλῳ τῷ ἀδελφῷ "Tasoucharion to Nilus his brother"
SB 14.12032.1–2 (II CE)	Κέλερ Πλουτίωνι τῷ ἀδελφῷ "Celer to Ploution his brother"

Various other kinship terms appear in the epistolary papyri, albeit not with the same frequency, and the pattern and collocation in the adscript are the same.[144] Likewise, the sender of a letter might apply various titles of respect to the recipient, and when this is done, the pattern and collocation are the same.[145] One notable title that appears with some frequency in the adscript is "lord" or "lady" (κύριος/κυρία).[146] These titles conventionally functioned as a polite form of address in the early Roman period and are a Latinism related to the use of *dominus* ("lord") and *domina* ("lady").[147] Though it has been thought that they are inherently hierarchical and are predominantly used when a subordinate addresses a superior, it has been shown that they are often a courteous form of address irrespective of status. As Eleanor Dickey points out in her work on Greek forms of address:

> In papyrus documents of the first century AD κύριε is found as a general polite address usable even between close relatives, and in the second century it seems often to be simply a standard neutral address, usable even between parents and children. . . . κυρία "mistress, lady" is also extremely common in papyri and appears to function in the same way as its masculine κύριε. It must have been current in spoken late Greek, given its dialect survival and its position in modern Greek as the standard equivalent of "Mrs."[148]

Dickey shows that κύριος and κυρία were often used for family, friends, and social equals and not just for superiors but that δεσπότης ("master") and δέσποινα ("mistress") tended to be used hierarchically.[149]

In the epistolary papyri, "lord" (κύριος) and "lady" (κυρία) appear in the same position as the other modifiers and titles just mentioned—immediately following the name of the addressee in the same case and marked with the definite article. It is essential to point out that they act substantively, as do the kinship terms "brother" (ἀδελφός) and "sister" (ἀδελφή), and like these kinship terms may be the only extension in the opening address or may appear with additional modifiers. Given that they are a predominantly polite form of address and most often occur without distinct hierarchical overtones, it is not unusual to see them in conjunction with "brother" or "sister": thus, "lord brother" or "lady sister," or less frequently with other familial terms. The examples provided below illustrate this paradigm.

Examples of the Use of "Lord"/"Lady" (κύριος/κυρία) in the Adscript	
P.Oxy. 2.300.1–2 (I CE)	Ἰνδικὴ Θαεισοῦτι τῇ κυρίᾳ "Indike to the lady Thaisous"
P.Giss. 1.13.1–2 (ca. 116–20 CE)	Ἐπαφρόδειτος Ἀπολλωνίωι τῶι κυρίωι "Epaphrodeitus to his lord Apollonius"
P.Oslo 3.152.1–2 (I/II CE)	Διονύσιος Φιλονίκωι τῶι κυρίωι πατρὶ "Dionysius to his lord father Philonicus"
O.Claud. 1.138.1–2 (ca. 110)	Μάξιμος Σεραπειάδει τῇ ἀδελφῇ κυρ̣ί̣ᾳ "Maximus to his lady sister Sarapias"
SB 8.9903.1–2 (II CE)	Διογένης Ἡλιοδώρᾳ τῆι κυρίᾳ ἀδελφῇ "Diogenes to his lady sister Heliodora"
P.Bastianini 22.1–2 (II CE)	[Σαρ]απᾶς Θρακίδᾳ τῶι κυρίῳ ἀδελφῷ "Sarapas to his lord brother Thacidas"

While the address "A [to] B" was by far the most common form in the first two centuries CE, beginning in the third century, one sees the positions of the sender and addressee inverted in epistolary address so that it began to take the form "to B, (from) A." While this form is rarely attested in the first two centuries, in the third century, it becomes distinctly more prominent so that it becomes the most popular form of address in the fourth century. As observed by Delphine Nachtergaele in her study of the epistolary papyri, "In the letters dated to the 3rd century AD, 361 have the formula ὁ δεῖνα τῷ δεῖνι χαίρειν, whereas only 34 address the receiver with the phrase τῷ δεῖνι ὁ δεῖνα χαίρειν. In the letters dated to the 4th century AD, the relationship is inverse: 55 have the formula ὁ δεῖνα τῷ δεῖνι χαίρειν, whereas the phrase τῷ δεῖνι ὁ δεῖνα χαίρειν is found in 165 private letters."[150]

What caused this change is debated and ultimately lies outside the scope of the present investigation.[151] But this epistolary change is worth noting because, in the address, we see a change in the position of kinship terms, titles of address, and other modifiers as they relate to the adscript. In the address "A [to] B," which is ubiquitous in the first two centuries, modifiers always appear after the name of the addressee and are accompanied by a definite article, but in the latter address, "to B, (from) A," they are positioned before the name of the addressee, and a definite article is not typically present. The following examples illustrate this paradigm.

Greeting Type: "to B, (from) A"	
P.Oxy. 14.1671 (III CE)	κυρίῳ μου Ζωΐλῳ Διονύστος "To my lord brother Zoilus, (from) Dionysius"
SB 3.6222.1 (III CE)	[κυρίᾳ μ]ου [ἀδ]ελφῇ Σοφρ[όν]η Δῖος "To my lady sister Sophrone, (from) Dios"
O.Douch 4.368.1–2 (IV CE)	κυρ(ίῳ) ἀδελφῷ Ἀρυώτει Ὄλβιος "To my lord brother Haryotes, (from) Olbius"
P.Oxy. 12.1495 (IV CE)	κυρίῳ ἀδελφῷ Ἀπολλωνίῳ Νεῖλος "To my lord brother Apollonius, (from) Neilus"
P.Kellis 1.12 (IV CE)	τῶι κυρίωι μου πατρὶ [Τιθοῆτι] Σαμοῦν "To my lord father Totoes, (from) Samoun"
O.Douch 5.547.1–2 (IV/V CE)	[τῇ κυρί]ᾳ μου μητρὶ Ταπᾶφι [Σαρα]πάμμων "To my lady mother Tapaphis, (from) Sarapammon"

The change in the collocation of the superscription and adscription is essential to note for the present discussion, as the order of the typical address attested in the Roman period becomes reversed: "A [to] B" became "to B, (from) A." Remarkably, some who argue that the phrase εκλεκτη κυρια could not contain the personal name Ἐκλέκτη, and citing papyrus letters of the third and fourth centuries CE that contain this latter form of address, also claim that one expects the title to precede the name, and so εκλεκτη can only be a modifier and not a name.[152] However, the type of address appearing in 2 John 1 (and 3 John 1) clearly follows the pattern "A [to] B" that is most common in the Roman period. Therefore, based on the form of address used in 2 John 1, in the phrase εκλεκτη κυρια, only Ἐκλέκτη ("Eclecte") could properly be considered a name and not Κυρία ("Kyria").[153] Furthermore, in the form of address "A [to] B," the adscript (name of the addressee) always directly follows the superscription (name of the sender) with no intervening text—articles, titles, or modifiers follow the name and do not precede it.

Turning to 3 John 1, this is precisely the pattern of address attested: ὁ πρεσβύτερος Γαΐῳ τῷ ἀγαπητῷ ("the elder to Gaius the beloved"). The superscription (ὁ πρεσβύτερος) appears first, the adscription immediately follows (Γαΐῳ) with no definite article, and the modifier with the definite article (τῷ ἀγαπητῷ) directly follows the adscript. Looking at the tables above, the pattern in 3 John 1 is well attested. As 3 John and 2 John contain numerous structural, stylistic, and phraseological parallels, it makes sense for the two letters, if they share common authorship, to likewise share the same pattern of address. Immediately after the opening address, both letters share a nearly identical phrase: "whom I love in the truth."[154]

Returning to the epistolary papyri, it can be observed that there is a tendency for authors of more than one letter to employ similar, if not identical, patterns of address in the prescript across their respective letters. The names of addressed individuals and titles or modifiers might be uniquely personal, but the structure and format remain constant. Though various examples can be given, a couple of notable examples will suffice.[155] In 1903, in Volume III of *Aegyptische Urkunden aus den Königlichen Museen zu Berlin*, a famous letter was published: BGU 846.[156] The letter is dated to the second century CE and was written by a young man named Antonius Longus. He wrote the letter to his mother, Nilous, who had apparently disowned him, hoping to be reconciled with her. He begins the rather pathetic letter by explaining that he "goes about in filth" and even claims that he is "naked." A little later in the letter, he informs his mother that he is in debt and elsewhere begs her to "be reconciled" and states that he has "been chastised" and has "sinned."[157] The contrition on the part of Longus and the vocabulary he employs led several early commentators to draw parallels to the parable of the prodigal son in Luke 15:11–32.[158] The opening address and proem of the letter read as follows:

> Ἀντῶνις Λόνγος Νειλοῦτι
> [τ]ῇ μητρὶ π[λ]ῖστα χαίρειν. καὶ δι-
> ὰ πάντω[ν] εὔχομαί σαι ὑγειαίνειν. τὸ προσκύνη-
> μά σου [ποι]ῶ κατ' αἰκάστην ἡμαίραν παρὰ τῷ

κυρίῳ [Σαρ]άπειδει. κτλ

2. *l.* πλεῖστα 3. *l.* σε *l.* ὑγιαίνειν 4. *l.* ἑκάστην ἡμέραν 5. *l.* Σαράπιδι

Antonius Longus to his mother Nilous, very many greetings. I continually pray that you are well. Your obeisance I make every day before the lord Sarapis.

A quick look at the prescript reveals that it contains, in order, the typical elements one expects in a Roman-period letter. The letter begins with the superscript, followed by the adscript, then the modifier, and finally the salutation. Additionally, the proem that follows contains the health wish formula followed by epistolary *proskynesis* to Sarapis.

A little over three decades after the letter was published, papyrologist Eric G. Turner published the first and only volume of papyri in the Aberdeen University collection: *Catalogue of Greek and Latin Papyri and Ostraca in the Possession of the University of Aberdeen.*[159] Among the Greek texts he published was P.Aberd. 187. It is a small scrap measuring about 6 cm^2 with the vestiges of four fragmentary lines of Greek text that are so severely damaged that the left margin of the text is completely lost, as well as portions of the right margin. On the first line, only two words are extant in full: Λόνγος Νιλοῦτ̣ι̣. After some searching, Turner realized he had found the top part of another letter Antonius Longus wrote to his mother, Nilous. He was able to completely reconstruct the opening of the letter, despite its very fragmentary nature, because it contains a nearly identical opening to what appears in BGU 3.846. In fact, some of the same spelling errors in BGU 3.846 are repeated in P.Aberd. 187.

[Ἀντώνι]ς Λόνγος Νιλοῦτ̣ι̣
[τῇ μ]ητρεὶ πλε̣ί̣στα χα̣ί̣ρ̣ι̣ν [καὶ διὰ]
[παν]τὸς εὔχομα̣ί̣ σα[ι ὑγιαίνειν.]
4 [τὸ προ]σ̣κ[ύνημά σο]υ π̣ο[ιῶ] κ[ατ']
-- -- -- -- -- -- -- -- -- -- -- -- -- -- -- --

2. *l.* μητρί *l.* χαίρειν 3. *l.* σε

> Antonius Longus to his mother Nilous, very many greetings. I continually pray that you are well. Your obeisance I make every [day before the lord Sarapis.]

Seventy years after the publication of P.Aberd. 187, a fragment from a third letter from Antonius Longus to his mother was discovered. In 2010, a joint expedition of the University of California, Los Angeles; the Rijksuniversiteit Groningen; and the University of Auckland worked as part of the URU Fayum Project, surveying and conducting fieldwork at the site of Karanis—a prominent village in the Fayum from the Pharaonic through Byzantine periods.[160] While excavating a street on the east edge of town, a small scrap of papyrus was discovered. It measures 10.5 × 6.5 cm and preserves 13 very partial lines of text; only 9–13 letters are still extant at the start of each line.

After its discovery, I was asked to examine the piece since I was working at a nearby dig in the Fayum at Fag el-Gamous ("The way of the water Buffalo").[161] The text was initially difficult to read since I could only make out some letters and a few syllables, but after getting a feel for the script, I noticed that a complete word could be read at the beginning of l. 3: "I pray" (εὔχομαι). I then noticed on l. 2 that some letters had been written and then crossed out by the writer, and then the word "mother" was written, although it was misspelled (μητρεί; *l.* μητρί). At this point, I suspected that it might be the remnant of an ancient letter. As it was customary for letters to carry an address on the back side of the papyrus, I removed the fragment from the backing it was mounted on and turned it over. Though it was damaged, there was an address, and I was able to read the name of the addressee, who was identified on the front side as the mother, as well as the name of her son. Once I could obtain internet access, I began searching for these names on a papyrological database and, after about five minutes, came across BGU 3.846. Before long, I was able to completely reconstruct the first four lines of the text even though there were only a handful of letters at the start of each line; this was because it paralleled the text of the previous two letters written by Antonius Longus. Some of the same spelling errors that occur in BGU 3.846 and P.Aberd. 187 are likewise repeated.[162]

> Ἀντῶ[νις Λόνγος Νειλοῦτι τῇ]
> [[μο καὶ]] μητρεὶ [πλεῖστα χαίρειν καὶ διὰ πάντων]
> εὔχομαί σαι ὑγ[ιαίνειν. τὸ προσκύνημά σου ποιῶ]
> κατ' αἰκάστην ἡ[μέραν παρὰ τῷ κυρίῳ Σαρά-]

πειδει. κτλ

2. *l.* μητρὶ 3. *l.* σε 4. *l.* ἑκάστην 5. *l.* Σαράπιδι

Antonius Longus to his mother Nilous, very many greetings. I continually pray that you are well. Your obeisance I make every [day before the lord Sara]pis.

The remains of the three letters Antonius Longus wrote to his mother attest that authors of letters tend to be remarkably consistent across letters in the crafting of the epistolary prescript. The example provided by these three letters is not an isolated case.[163] Outside of letters written by the same author to the same recipient, the evidence is such that letters by the same author to different recipients tend to employ the same pattern of address. Such letters are harder to come by since, in collections like ancient archives, we typically find incoming mail to a single recipient from different authors and rarely find outgoing mail from the same author to different recipients.[164] Nevertheless, the evidence we do have shows that when the same author is writing letters to different individuals, they tend to employ the same pattern of address. For example, there is a collection of ten letters in the Archive of Nemesion of Philadelphia (Fayum) from the middle of the first century CE.[165] While most are sent by different individuals to Nemesion, we possess copies of two letters Nemesion sent to two different individuals. Even though the content of the respective letters is quite different, the epistolary prescript in each letter follows exactly the same pattern.[166]

Two Letters of Nemesion	
P.Mich. 12.656.1–2	Νεμεσίων Τρύφωνι τῶι ἀδελφῶι χαίριν (*l.* χαίρειν). "Nemesion to Tryphon, his brother, greetings."
P.Princ. 2.65.1–2	Νεμεσίων Διονυ[σ]ίωι τῶ[ι] ἀδελφῶι χαίρειν. "Nemesion to Dionysius, his brother, greetings."

Returning to 2 and 3 John with this in mind, these letters share common authorship and are structurally, stylistically, and formulaically similar. The opening of 3 John 1 follows a well-attested pattern of address: ὁ πρεσβύτερος Γαΐῳ τῷ ἀγαπητῷ. 2 John 1 likewise begins with ὁ πρεσβύτερος but is then followed by an unparalleled adscript ἐκλεκτῇ κυρίᾳ. The reading ἐκλεκτῇ, which is articulated as the adjective ἐκλεκτή, fits the conventional epistolary pattern if the adscript immediately following the superscription is not articulated as the adjective but as the female name Ἐκλέκτη. In form, ἐκλεκτή and Ἐκλέκτη are identical aside from articulation and capitalization, both of which are interpretive elements added later. When εκλεκτη becomes Ἐκλέκτη, the adscript in 2 John 1 mirrors the adscript in 3 John 1 that also contains a name: Γαΐῳ. As with ἀγαπητῷ that follows the name in 3 John 1, the κυρίᾳ that follows Ἐκλέκτη would modify it in the same way. A survey of some of the attestations of κυρία appearing in the adscript shows that it always follows the name it modifies.

Examples of the Use of "Lady" (*κυρία*) in the Adscript	
P.Oxy. 2.300.1–2 (I CE)	Ἰνδικὴ Θαεισοῦτι τῇ κυρίᾳ "Indike to the lady Thaisous"
P.Giss. 1.77.1 (116–20 CE)	Τεεὺς [Ἀ]λινῇ τῇ κυρίᾳ "Teeus to the lady Aline"
O.Krok. 319.1–2 (98–117 CE)	Ἰσχυρᾶς Ζωσίμ[η] τῇ κυρίᾳ "Ischyras to the lady Zosime"
O.Did. 426.1–2 (early II CE)	Εἰσιδώρα (*l.* Ἰσιδώρα) Θαεισοῦτι (*l.* Θαϊσοῦτι) τῇ κυρίᾳ "Isidora to the lady Thaisous"
P.Tebt. 2.413.1 (II CE)	Ἀφοδίτη (*l.* Ἀφροδίτη) Ἀρσινοῆτι τῇ κυρίᾳ "Aphrodite to the lady Arsinoe"
BGU 4.1081.1 (II/III CE)	Δίδυμο[ς] Ἑρμιόνῃ τῇ κυρίᾳ "Didymus to the lady Hermione"
P.Oxy. 14.1761.1–2 (II/III CE)	Κα[λ]λιρώη Σαραπάδι (*l.* Σαραπιάδι) τῇ γυρίᾳ (*l.* κυρίᾳ) "Kalliroe to the lady Sarapas"
P.Oxy. 55.3810.1–2 (II/III CE)	Καλλίας Κυρίλλῃ τῇ κυρίᾳ . . "Kallias to the lady Kyrilla"

The problem with the reading in 2 John 1 is the missing definite article τῇ between the name (Ἐκλέκτῃ) and the modifier (κυρίᾳ); all the papyrological examples in the table above contain the definite article. Likewise, 3 John 1 similarly includes the expected article τῷ after the name (Γαΐῳ) and before the modifier (ἀγαπητῷ).

As noted in the first chapter, it was not until I came across the address in SB 20.15069, a late third-century letter CE between two women, that the proper rendering of the opening address in 2 John 1 became apparent. SB 20.15069 was first published in 1938 by G. A. Gerhard in *Veröffentlichungen aus den badischen Papyrus-Sammlungen. Vol. VI: Griechische Papyri* and, until its reedition, was referred to as P.Bad. 6.171.[167] In this edition of the text, Gerhard misread parts of the address and rendered it Ἰσιδώρα Ἄπιτι φιλτάτ[ῳ] πλεῖστα χαίρειν ("Isodora to the dearest Apis, very many greetings"). He supposed the sender, a woman named Isidora, was writing to her husband, a man named Apis. In a reedition of the papyrus, it was shown that the recipient's name was not the masculine Apis but rather the female name Anis (Ἄνις): Initially, the ν had been mistaken for a π. Furthermore, there was an error in the original address that was never corrected in the edition by Gerhard. Between the name of the addressee, now rendered Ἄνιτι, and the following modifier, now rendered φιλτάτῃ ("dearest") to correspond with the feminine name, the definite article τῇ needed to be added since the phrase is not grammatically complete without it. As noted by the editors of the reedition, the definite article was likely omitted due to haplography as a result of the terminating -τι at the end of the name Ἄνιτι.[168] The address was properly restored: Ἰσιδώρα Ἄνιτι <τῇ> φιλτάτ̣[ῃ] πλεῖστα χαίρειν ("Isidora to the dearest Anis, very many greetings").

The insertion of the definite article does not represent an editorial imposition, but rather a restoration of a reading implied by the original context but lost through a grammatical error. The sender was clearly intending "to the dearest Anis" with the phrase Ἄνιτι φιλτάτ̣[ῃ] but failed to supply the definite article. To give an analogy in English, take the following sentence as an example: "The mom picked up the shirt to clothe the child." Now, suppose that on one occasion, you came across this sentence, and it was rendered: "The mom picked up the shirt to clothe child." Immediately, you would recognize something was amiss; the definite article "the" before "child" is missing. It is not grammatically correct without it. Since "the" is immediately preceded by "clothe," a compelling argument could be that the writer of the sentence mistakenly dropped it due to haplography—they wrote "clothe child" and mentally thought/saw "clothe the child." By restoring "the," you have not given the sentence a new meaning but have restored the grammatically correct reading intended from the start.

The example of the address in SB 20.15069 and the lack of a definite article is not an isolated case. When one starts reading the epistolary papyri, one finds all kinds of grammatical errors. To help deal with this, a whole system of sigla has been created so that ancient mistakes can be both preserved and corrected at the same time.[169] The absence of an article when one otherwise needs to be present to make a short phrase or a sentence grammatically correct is not uncommon.[170] In the specific case of epistolary address, there are two additional examples exactly like the one found in SB 20.15069, where the article is dropped in the address and where restoration is made in the edition.[171]

Loss of the Definite Article in the Adscript	
O. Claud. 4.893.1–2 (ca. 150–54 CE)	Ἀπολλώνιος Ἀθηνοδώρῳ <τῷ> τιμιωτάτῳ χαίρειν. "Apollonius to the most esteemed Athenodorus, greetings."
P.Stras. 6.518.1 (ca. 300 CE)	Ἀμμώνιος Γεροντίῳ <τῷ> υἱῷ χαίρειν. "Ammonius to his son Gerontius, greetings."

There are more examples of this phenomenon in other epistolary papyri, but the editors neglect to restore the article in the text.[172] BGU 4.1080, a personal letter from the second or third century CE, begins as follows: Ἡρακλείδης Ἡρᾷ υἱῷ χαίρειν. The meaning of the address is clear: "Heraclides to his son Heras, greetings." But the Greek grammar is not correct, and the editor should have restored the definite article so that it is properly transcribed: Ἡρακλείδης Ἡρᾷ <τῷ> υἱῷ χαίρειν.[173] Similarly, in PSI 15.1560 from the third century CE, the letter opens as follows: Θεωνᾶς Μησουρίῳ ἀγαπητῷ ἀδελφῷ ἐν κ(υρί)ῳ χαίρειν. The address obviously reads "Theonas to Mensurius a beloved brother, in the Lord greetings" but should correctly be transcribed with the addition of the definite article: Θεωνᾶς Μησουρίῳ <τῷ> ἀγαπητῷ ἀδελφῷ ἐν κ(υρί)ῳ χαίρειν.[174] There are similarly other examples in epistolary address where a letter, or string of letters, is erroneously omitted due to haplography.

To give another epistolary example, CPR 5.10 is an official letter issued sometime during the first half of the fourth century CE by a man named Aurelius Dioscourides, who functioned as the *strategus* and *exactor* of the Hermopolite nome.[175] The letter opens with his name and titles as follows: Α[ὐρ]ήλιος Διοσκουρίδης τραγηγὸς ἤτοι ἐξ(άκτωρ) Ἑρμοπολ(ίτου) κτλ. The third word, τραγηγος, is nonsensical; among other things, it requires an initial sigma so that it should read στρατηγός ("*strategus*").[176] The initial sigma is omitted due to haplography because his name, which immediately precedes it, terminates with a sigma. The writer of the letter wrote ΔΙΟCΚΟΥΡΙΔΗCΤΡΑΓΗΓΟC with one sigma but intended ΔΙΟCΚΟΥΡΙΔΗCCΤΡΑΤΗΓΟC with two sigmas (i.e., Διοσκουρίδης στρατηγός).

Returning to 2 John 1, the reading Ἐκλεκτῇ τῇ κυρίᾳ becomes obvious. Not only does it now mirror the collocation of epistolary address in papyri of the Roman period, but more importantly, it mirrors Γαΐῳ τῷ ἀγαπητῷ in 3 John 1. The most likely reason for the loss of the definite article τῇ at some point was due to haplography. Ancient Greek was typically written *scriptio continua*, so it is easy to see how in the letter string εκλεκτητηκυρια, which contains the substring -τητη-, the second -τη- could have been mistakenly omitted. The result would be εκλεκτηκυρια, which has now been articulated ἐκλεκτῇ κυρίᾳ. If 2 John did not have an interpretive tradition that promoted the received reading ἐκλεκτῇ κυρίᾳ, which sees in this unattested form of address a metaphorical personification of a church, and this letter had been discovered in the last century among the papyri, this traditional reading and interpretation would have never emerged. Instead, the letter string ΟΠΡΕCΒΥΤΕΡΟCΕΚΛΕΚΤΗΚΥΡΙΑ would have been restored and articulated as ὁ πρεσβύτερος Ἐκλέκτῃ <τῇ> κυρίᾳ ("The elder to the lady Eclecte") because of all the papyrological parallels for this form of address and because the loss of the definite article immediately following a word terminating with the same two letters is a well-attested phenomenon.[177]

The restoration of two reduplicated letters creates a seismic shift in the interpretation of 2 John 1. In light of this reading, it can no longer be maintained that the letter contains a metaphorical address to a church personified as an "elect lady." Accordingly, any notion that the letter is a "fiction," or even a "semifiction," based on what was thought to be a peculiar form of address in 2 John 1, is no longer tenable. The principal recipient of the letter is a lady bearing the name Eclecte. The address mirrors the pattern appearing in 3 John 1, which is the most common pattern in the epistolary papyri of the Roman period. Whereas grammars and handbooks of New Testament Greek have universally reported that εκλεκτη in 2 John 1 is an adjective and the κυρια that follows is a noun, this is not correct.[178] Rather, εκλεκτη is a proper noun because it is a personal name (Ἐκλέκτη), and this is why there is no article preceding it. The κυρια that follows is not a noun but rather a substantive, and the correct rendering is τῇ κυρίᾳ. The opening address in 2 John 1 properly reads Ἐκλέκτη τῇ κυρίᾳ—"to the lady Eclecte."

CHAPTER FOUR

The Reading Is Even in Some Manuscripts

There are discussable variants in John's second epistle . . . All are interesting but none critical for interpretation.

—Robert W. Yarborough, *1–3 John*[1]

ROBERT W. YARBOROUGH'S sentiments are indicative of most text-critical assessments of 2 John. A handful of principal variants appear in the letter, but in each case, the correct reading is either readily established or if some ambiguity does exist, it is not "critical for interpretation." For example, in v. 3, where the readings "from Jesus Christ" or "from the Lord Jesus Christ" appear, the former is preferred based on the nature of the manuscript evidence where it seems that the addition of "Lord" is a scribal expansion.[2] In v. 8, where "what we worked for" and "what you worked for" are both attested, and there is less consensus due to the nature of the manuscript evidence, the general sense is that neither reading substantially changes the meaning of the overall passage.[3] The same is also the case in v. 12, where both "our joy" and "your joy" can be found and where the manuscript evidence is split rather evenly.[4] A handful of secondary variants appear in vv. 9, 11, and 13 that are potentially more significant, but it is agreed that they are not original (or early) but arose at various times in the textual life of 2 John.[5] Beyond these principal sets of variants that affect less than half the verses in the letter (vv. 3, 8, 9, 11, 12, 13), there are hundreds of additional variants in the diverse witnesses of 2 John that affect every verse. These include the addition, omission, or alteration of articles, conjunctions, particles, and prepositions; can occasionally include the use of different synonyms; and attest various syntactical, grammatical, and orthographical alterations.[6] Given the number of these variants and, in most cases, their inconsequential effect, it is no wonder they are rarely discussed in commentaries. Even in as useful a resource as the NA[28], only the most significant variants are brought to the reader's attention in the apparatus. In the case of 2 John 1, not a single note appears.[7] It is, therefore, understandable that many have the impression there is no textual discussion to be had on this verse.

Examining every variant that appears in a short letter like 2 John is hard enough. Turning to the text of the entire New Testament, where it has been estimated that there are upward of half a million variants (not including differences in spelling), is nigh impossible.[8] In light of the sheer number of variants, it is no surprise that only the more obvious get much attention where a distinct word, phrase, or entire passage possesses a different rendering that changes the meaning of a passage. On the other hand, the vast majority of variants that are rather slight and concern a couple of letters, like an article, are rarely, if ever, treated in any detail. The general thinking is that in the vast majority of cases, these "insignificant" differences have little or no impact on the text and its interpretation, so they merit little or no attention. While I am generally inclined to agree with such sentiments, the textual evidence of 2 John 1 suggests otherwise. Hiding among the hundreds of thousands of seemingly "insignificant" variants in the New Testament is the most significant variant in 2 John, where the difference is the addition of two reduplicated letters that results in the formation of a definite article. In fact, it may well turn out to be one of the most significant articular variants in the entire New Testament. When the address in 2 John 1 goes from εκλεκτη κυρια to εκλεκτη τη κυρια, the only way to read it is as a personal address to a lady named Eclecte.

Despite the implications of this variant, it has never been examined. While this variant is listed in the detailed apparatus of the *Novum Testamentum Graecum Editio Critica Maior*, although the apparatus fails to include every manuscript attestation, no one has hitherto recognized its importance.[9] To give a personal example illustrating this point, when I first discovered the reading εκλεκτη τη κυρια and found that the article τη was attested in some manuscript witnesses of 2 John, I decided to run it by a colleague who was well established in New Testament textual criticism. Before I went down this road too far, I wanted to see if I was really on to something. As I began email correspondence, I stated that I wanted to get their opinion on a potentially significant variant I had discovered and in a subsequent email, mentioned 2 John 1 but without specifying the reading I was proposing. In the return email, I was informed that they had looked and that there were no significant variants in 2 John 1; they then wondered if I had misstated the reference and had a different verse from 2 John in mind. After clarifying that the variant was indeed in 2 John 1 and consisted of the mere addition of the two-letter article τῇ and that its incorporation meant the principal addressee of 2 John was a named woman, my colleague immediately recognized the import of the reading. In a return email, they conceded that it was a significant variant "hiding in plain sight." In what follows, I intend to show that the received reading and articulation ἐκλεκτῇ κυρίᾳ, which is taken for granted and never questioned in contemporary scholarship, is less secure than is presently assumed in the textual tradition. Furthermore, a case for Ἐκλέκτῃ τῇ κυρίᾳ can be made on textual grounds, and not just papyrological grounds, as this reading is evinced in multiple manuscripts.

The Printed Address in 2 John 1: Erasmus to Mace

The first printed text of the Greek New Testament appeared in 1516.[10] It was produced by Desiderius Erasmus of Rotterdam (1467(?)–1536) and carried the title *Novum Instrumentum Omne* (later titled *Novum Testamentum Omne*).[11] It was a diglot edition of the New Testament that included the Latin Vulgate in one column and Erasmus's Greek text in the other. At 2 John 1, the printed address read ἐκλεκτῇ κυρΐᾳ. This rendering was based on two twelfth-century manuscripts that Erasmus had at his disposal and only differs from the rendering appearing in the NA[28] with the use of the *diaeresis* (*trema*) that is printed over the iota in κυρΐᾳ.[12] In Erasmus's *Annotationes in Novum Testamentum*, an appendix to the text that discusses various readings, and appeared in the first and subsequent editions, contains no discussion of this section of 2 John 1. When the Complutensian Polyglot Bible was issued, bound, and printed in 1522, the reading was the same for the opening of 2 John 1, with the only difference being that κυρίᾳ was printed without the *diaeresis*.[13] Parisian printer Simon de Colines (ca. 1480–1546) issued an edition of the Greek New Testament in 1534, but as his printed text was based on the earlier editions of Erasmus and the Complutensian Polyglot, he had the same reading for the address in 2 John 1.[14]

The next significant publication of the Greek New Testament occurred a little over a decade later when the notable Parisian printer Robert Estienne (1503–1559; aka Robertus Stephanus) began publishing editions of the Greek New Testament. In his first two editions, published respectively in 1546 and 1549, the address in 2 John 1 appeared as it was printed previously: ἐκλεκτῇ κυρίᾳ.[15] But in his famous third edition published in 1550, commonly known as the *Editio Regia* ("Royal Edition") since it was published for King Henri II of France, and with the distinction of being the first "critical edition" of the New Testament ever printed since it displayed textual variants, the address in 2 John 1 had a distinctly different rendering.[16] Instead of ἐκλεκτῇ κυρίᾳ, Estienne now rendered it Ἐκλεκτῇ κυρίᾳ. By capitalizing Ἐκλεκτῇ (although his articulation was incorrect and should have been Ἐκλέκτῃ), Estienne was making it clear that it was to be read as a proper name and not as an adjective. The translation would have to be "to the lady Eclecte." Estienne provides no commentary for this significant change. He does, however, print a brief Greek summary that dates to the eighth or ninth century to preface his edition of 2 John. Since it implies that the letter was written to a woman, it seems to have influenced his rendering.[17] In the fourth and final version of the Greek New Testament issued by Estienne in 1551, which has the distinction of being the first New Testament that includes versification, the reading is kept.[18]

Despite the importance of Estienne's Greek New Testament, it was largely eclipsed by another sixteenth-century edition produced by French reformer and biblical scholar Theodore Beza (1519–1605). In 1565, Beza published the first edition of his Greek New Testament, which was accompanied in parallel columns by his own Latin translation of the Greek as well as the text of the Latin Vulgate.[19] While the basis of his Greek text was the 1551 edition by Estienne, he did make changes to the text where he saw fit. With regard to the address in 2 John 1, instead of following Estienne, Beza renders the text ἐκλεκτῇ κυρίᾳ. In a Latin note accompanying the phrase, Beza argues against reading a personal name in the address and states, "Some believe that Electa is a proper name, which I do not approve. For it would have been said κυρίᾳ Ἐκλεκτῇ, 'to the lady Electa.'"[20] He then asserts in the note that the address is best understood as a reference to a prominent yet unnamed early Christian woman. In total, ten editions and reprints of Beza's Greek New Testament appeared, with the final edition appearing posthumously in 1611.[21] In every edition, the address is rendered ἐκλεκτῇ κυρίᾳ, and the same commentary that appeared in the first edition appears in the apparatus below explaining how the phrase could not contain the name "Electa."

Like the sixteenth century, the seventeenth century also witnessed distinct trends in how the address in 2 John 1 was treated. Beginning in 1624, Abraham Elzevir (1592–1652) and Bonaventure Elzevir (1583–1652), two

Dutch printers, are credited with issuing three editions of the Greek New Testament: 1624, 1633, and 1641.[22] Though the Greek text appearing in all three editions was a near reprint of the 1565 edition of Beza so that the address in 2 John 1 was rendered ἐκλεκτῇ κυρίᾳ, the 1633 edition was notable because it was here that the designation *textus receptus*, or "Received Text," emerged.[23] About the same time that the third Elzevir edition appeared, the first known textual emendation was proposed by Patrick Young (1584–1652; aka Patricius Junius) for the opening address in 2 John 1.[24] Young had served as the royal librarian to King James I and King Charles I and was an accomplished biblical scholar. During his tenure as librarian, he had spent considerable time cataloging manuscripts. When Codex Alexandrinus was given to King Charles I in 1627, Young was entrusted with a revision of the Septuagint. While working on biblical manuscripts, he came up with various conjectural readings and circulated these with the likes of Hugo Grotius (1583–1645) and Archbishop James Ussher (1581–1656). Though he never published any of his biblical conjectures, a manuscript in the Library at the University of Amsterdam titled *Secundae stricturae Patricii Junii* and dated to about 1642 contains a number of them.[25] For 2 John, Young only had two related conjectures that concerned vv. 1 and 5. He noted that 2 John 1 began with ὁ πρεσβύτερος ἐκλεκτῇ κυρίᾳ and alleged that the κυρίᾳ should instead be substituted with ἐν κυρίῳ so that the opening of the letter would read ὁ πρεσβύτερος ἐκλεκτῇ ἐν κυρίῳ ("The elder to an elect [church] in the Lord"). Similarly, for the beginning of v. 5, which reads καὶ νῦν ἐρωτῶ σε, κυρία, he argued for the same emendation: καὶ νῦν ἐρωτῶ σε, ἐν κυρίῳ ("And now I ask you in the Lord"). No manuscript has emerged to support either conjecture; the phrase ἐν κυρίῳ does not appear in any of the Johannine Letters or the Gospel of John, and presumably, Junius derived the phrase from Paul's letters, where it appears frequently.[26] In the few Latin notes accompanying this conjecture, he remarks that the change made sense as it clarifies that the "church," and not an actual lady, was being addressed in the letter.[27] While this conjectural reading periodically appeared in textual discussions of 2 John 1, no one has taken it seriously since the middle of the nineteenth century.[28]

Another important work that appeared in the middle of the seventeenth century that left a lasting impact, at least through the nineteenth century, on the interpretation of the opening address in 2 John 1 was Hugo Grotius's nine-volume *Annotationes in Novum Testamentum* (1641–1650).[29] Grotius, a Dutch polymath who published influential works in philosophy, political theory, and law, also produced a massive commentary, largely philological, on the text of the New Testament. His discussion of 2 John 1 occupies about half a page, and much of this treatment has to do with the address in the letter. At the outset, he renders the Greek "Ἐκλεκτῇ κυρίᾳ,"[30] thereby making it clear that he took εκλεκτη as a proper name.[31] He begins his discussion by noting that the related συνεκλεκτή ("joint-elect"), which appears in 1 Peter 5:13, refers to a church. Then, turning to 2 John 1, he states, "But here, one person is entirely indicated, as we see below in [verse] 13. And ἐκλεκτῇ, I believe, has become a proper name."[32] Grotius also believed that ἐκλεκτῆς in 2 John 13 was a name but argued that it read better as the name Εὐδέκτης ("Eudecte"), and so the letter mentioned the name Eclecte at the start and Eudecte at the end. Despite Grotius's conjecture about the latter, where he even alleged it appeared in some manuscripts, no such reading has been attested, and at present, this name is not attested anywhere else in Greek.[33]

Shortly after the publication of Grotius's tome on the New Testament, Brian Walton (1600–1661) oversaw the publication of the six-volume *Biblia Sacra Polyglotta*, or London Polyglot Bible.[34] The work contained the biblical text side by side in nine languages for the Old Testament (vols. 1–4) and five languages for the New Testament (vol. 5).[35] The New Testament languages included Greek, Latin, Syriac, Ethiopic, and Arabic, with an accompanying Latin translation for the latter three. The printed Greek text was based on Estienne's 1550 edition. But whereas Estienne had printed εκλεκτη as a name (e.g., "Ἐκλεκτῇ") in 2 John 1, Walton printed it ἐκλεκτῇ, taking it as an adjective. Where the London Polyglot most impacted the reading of 2 John 1 was in the rendering given in the Syriac and Ethiopic versions.[36] In the Ethiopic, it was noted that 2 John 1 opened with "From an Elder to an elect and a lady and her children."[37] Thus, "elect" and "lady" were now separated by a conjunction, and it was implied these were either two different persons or perhaps an entity (i.e., "elect [church]") and a "lady." Though this reading was periodically noted in text-critical discussions of 2 John 1 into the nineteenth century, it never impacted the rendering of the verse and was eventually dropped.[38] To date, no Greek manuscript evinces the reading with the conjunction *και* separating εκλεκτη and κυρια. On the other hand, the Syriac reading had a more significant impact on the rendering of 2 John 1 that can still be felt in certain quarters to the present day. In the Syriac translation printed in the London

Polyglot, the Greek word κυρία ("lady") is rendered with the Syriac transliteration *quriya* (Syr. ܩܘܪܝܐ) so that the Syriac translation was thought to have taken it as a female name (i.e., Quriya). In the Latin translation accompanying the Syriac, the name Kyria is given.[39] While there is some ambiguity about whether or not the Syriac translation is taking κυρια as a name—and in the earliest extant Syriac commentary on 2 John from the twelfth century, it is understood simply as "lady"—the impression from the London Polyglot is that it is a proper name.[40] When this became more generally known among New Testament scholars traditionally trained in Latin and Greek, within a century, it began to directly impact the Greek rendering of 2 John 1, as it periodically started to be printed Κυρία ("Kyria") instead of κυρία ("lady").[41]

The last quarter of the seventeenth century saw the publication of John Fell's (1625–1686) Greek New Testament in 1675.[42] As it largely followed the Elzevir edition of 1633, the address in 2 John 1 was rendered ἐκλεκτῇ κυρίᾳ.[43] A younger friend and colleague of Fell's, John Mill (1645–1707), published an edition of the Greek New Testament in 1707.[44] In many ways, Mill's critical work paved the way for future editions. It included an extensive apparatus that contained readings from Greek and Latin manuscripts as well as Syriac, Coptic, and Ethiopic sources.[45] In his rendering of the address in 2 John 1, he printed "Ἐκλεκτῇ κυρίᾳ," signaling that it contained the name Eclecte, but as he essentially reprinted the 1550 text of Estienne, the reading just reflects the earlier edition. In the apparatus, Mill notes that the capitalization signaled Estienne took it as a proper name, but Mill himself thought it referred to one who was "elect" or "converted to the faith in Christ" and did not take it as a personal name.[46]

Four years after the publication of Mill's edition, Gerhard von Maestricht (Mästricht; 1639–1721) issued a Greek text that reprinted the text of Fell but with an apparatus that supplemented the one produced by Mill.[47] The address in 2 John 1 was thus rendered ἐκλεκτῇ κυρίᾳ.[48] A couple of decades later, in 1729, Daniel Mace (d. ca. 1753), a relatively unknown English scholar, anonymously published a Greek and English diglot titled *The New Testament in Greek and English: Containing the Original Text Corrected from the Authority of the Most Authentic Manuscripts*.[49] Using the *textus receptus* as his textual base, he made several alterations selected from the apparatus provided in Mill's 1707 edition or from personal conjecture.[50] For the opening address in 2 John 1, he rendered the Greek "Ἐκλεκτῇ κυρίᾳ." He translated it "to the lady Electa."[51] Presumably, the capitalization of "'Εκλεκτῇ" was taken directly from the text of Mill, whose edition he extensively quarried.

The Printed Address in 2 John 1: Bengel to Weiss

With the work of Johann Albrecht Bengel (1687–1752), the rendering of the address in 2 John 1 took a distinct shift. Bengel, a Lutheran schoolmaster from Württemberg, initiated a "new era" in the Greek text of the New Testament with the publication of his edition in 1734.[52] While he printed the *textus receptus*, he included variant readings and introduced critical symbols to designate manuscripts. In this edition, he renders the address in 2 John 1 as ἐκλεκτῇ κυρίᾳ.[53] But he changed his position on this reading a few years later. In 1742, he published his famous *Gnomon Novi Testamenti*, where he provides extensive commentary on the Greek text of the New Testament and discusses variant readings at length.[54] In several instances, he revises readings he had previously included in his 1734 edition of the Greek New Testament. For the address in 2 John 1, he now argues that it should be rendered ἐκλεκτῇ Κυρίᾳ so that it should be translated "to the elect Kyria."[55] Bengel's principal reason for changing it is that the Syriac translation from the London Polyglot took κυρία as a proper name.[56] In his *Apparatus Criticus*, which was expanded and updated from the apparatus appearing in the 1734 edition of his Greek New Testament and was published posthumously by his son-in-law in 1763, a note on 2 John 1 (and 5) is added that states that κυρια is to be taken as a "proper name."[57]

Bengel's commentary on the address in 2 John 1 profoundly impacted subsequent renderings. In Edward Harwood's (1729–1794) edition of the Greek New Testament, published in 1776, he renders the opening address by capitalizing κυρία and taking it as a proper name: "ἐκλεκτῇ Κυρίᾳ" ("to the elect Kyria").[58] The same reading also appears in Georg Christian Knapp's (1753–1825) Greek New Testament, published in 1797.[59] Bengel's rendering became so prominent in the latter part of the eighteenth century that it was promoted in John Wesley's (1703–1791) enormously popular *Explanatory Notes on the New Testament*, first published in 1755.[60] The work consisted of Wesley's translation of the New Testament with various textual notes and commentary. Wesley translated the opening address in 2 John 1 as "The elder unto the elect Kuria" and includes a note, which is entirely specious, about why the female name "Kuria" is the only way to read the address: "*Kuria* is undoubtedly a proper name, here and in v. 5. For it was not then usual to apply the title of *lady* to any but the Roman empress; nor would such a way of speaking have been suitable to the simplicity and dignity of the apostle."[61]

Two additional eighteenth-century Greek New Testaments are worth mentioning due to their treatment of the address in 2 John 1. The first is the two-volume New Testament published by Johann Jakob Wettstein (1693–1754) in 1751–1752.[62] The printed Greek text largely followed the 1624 Elzevir text; consequently, the address was rendered ἐκλεκτῇ κυρίᾳ. But in the critical notes at the bottom of the page, he noted that the printed reading ἐκλεκτῇ had been taken by some of his predecessors as a proper name and was rendered "Ἐκλεκτῇ."[63] The other eighteenth-century edition, which proved to be the most significant of them all, was published in the last quarter of the century by Johann Jakob Griesbach (1745–1812). The first edition of his *Novum Testamentum Graece* was published between 1775 and 1777, and for the address in 2 John 1, he prints the received reading ἐκλεκτῇ κυρίᾳ without any critical notes on the verse.[64] In his second edition (1796–1806), the printed reading remained unchanged, but he expanded the critical apparatus so that variant readings were now included for this verse.[65] Griesbach notes the conjectural emendation proposed by Young (κυρίᾳ > ἐν κυρίῳ), which he neutrally cites, and includes a reference to the Ethiopic, where he provides the Greek translation καὶ κυρίᾳ since the Ethiopic included a conjugation in the opening address. He also notes that two Greek manuscripts include the reading "τῇ κυρίᾳ" so that the definite article is attested (i.e., εκλεκτη τη κυρια).[66] In his final edition (1805–1807), a manual edition for students that was a shortened version of his second edition, he made a few additional changes to the Greek text.[67] At 2 John 1, the address was changed from ἐκλεκτῇ κυρίᾳ to ἐκλεκτῇ Κυρίᾳ.[68] The capitalizing of Κυρια shows that Griesbach ultimately took it as a proper name: "to the elect Kyria." In the apparatus at the bottom of the page, Griesbach also notes that the reading "Ἐκλεκτῇ τῇ" is attested in some manuscripts, although he does not cite them. Griesbach, therefore, was the first to point out the reading (properly articulated) Ἐκλέκτῃ τῇ κυρίᾳ, but neither he nor anyone else ever pursued it![69]

Following on the heels of Griesbach's late eighteenth- and early nineteenth-century editions of the Greek New Testament, Karl Lachmann (1793–1851) published his monumental 1831 edition that made a break with the *textus receptus*.[70] The printed Greek text occupies the entirety of each page, and an apparatus appears at the end of the volume, although it is limited. Lachmann prints the address in 2 John 1 as ἐκλεκτῇ Κυρίᾳ, and as Griesbach had done previously, capitalizes κυρια, signifying that it was to be read as a proper name. In the apparatus appearing at the end of the volume, there are no notes on 2 John 1. In the second edition of his Greek New Testament (1842–1850), this rendering did not change, and while he now included a lengthy apparatus at the bottom of each page, no textual notes appear on 2 John 1.

After the revolutionary edition of Lachmann and before the culminating edition of Westcott and Hort in 1881, there were two other important nineteenth-century editions of the Greek New Testament. Constantin von Tischendorf (1815–1874) profoundly impacted the text of the New Testament in the nineteenth century with his discovery and incorporation of various manuscripts, not least of which was his discovery of Codex Sinaiticus at St. Catherine's Monastery in 1844. In total, he published eight different editions of the Greek New Testament between 1841 and 1872. In his monumental *Editio Octava Critica Maior* (1869–1872), Tischendorf prints the address in 2 John 1 as both Griesbach and Lachmann had done before him and capitalizes κυρια, taking it as a proper name: ἐκλεκτῇ Κυρίᾳ.[71] In the apparatus that accompanies the reading "εκλεκτη," Tischendorf noted a Greek variant that had "εκλ. τη," but unlike Griesbach, he never explicitly noted that with this reading, εκλεκτη had to be taken as a proper name. Then, for κυρια, which he rendered "Κυρίᾳ," he remarked that the Syriac translation took it as a name but admitted that the Greek, as well as the Coptic and Latin, was ambiguous.[72] A contemporary of Tischendorf, Samuel Prideaux Tregelles (1813–1875), published a single edition of the Greek New Testament between 1857 and 1872.[73] The edition printed the Greek in the interior center of the page with a Latin translation in the outer margin and with the entire bottom of the page devoted to a critical apparatus. He printed the address of 2 John 1 without any capitalization as it appeared in the received reading: ἐκλεκτῇ κυρίᾳ. But in the lone text-critical note on the phrase, Tregelles points out the attested variant reading "εκλ. τῇ κυριᾳ" that had been first noted by Griesbach, but as with Tischendorf, he does not make it explicit that εκλεκτη then had to be taken as a name.[74]

The culminating edition of the Greek New Testament in the nineteenth century was Westcott and Hort's *The New Testament in the Original Greek*, published in 1881 and discussed in chapter 2.[75] As noted there, the reading given for the address is ἐκλεκτῇ κυρίᾳ, but in the marginal apparatus, the secondary reading Westcott and Hort provide is Ἐκλέκτῃ Κυρίᾳ, a double name. In the appendix to the edition that appeared the following year and provided rationale for various readings, only a variant at the end of v. 11 of 2 John is mentioned. Eleven years after the publication of Westcott and Hort's monumental edition, lay scholar Richard F. Weymouth (1822–1902) published an edition of the Greek New Testament called *The Resultant Greek Testament*.[76] Here, Weymouth produced an eclectic text by collating the editions of previous scholars from Estienne (1550) through Westcott and Hort (1881) and printing the "consensus" readings while noting variants in the apparatus. For the address in 2 John 1, he printed ἐκλεκτῇ κυρίᾳ,[77] but noted the different readings that had previously been proposed and included the articulated reading "Ἐκλεκτῇ" as well as "Κυρίᾳ."[78] Within a couple of years of Weymouth's edition, German theologian Bernhard Weiss (1827–1918) began publishing a three-volume critical edition of the Greek New Testament (1894–1900).[79] Weiss, who was primarily an exegete and was a professor of New Testament exegesis at Kiel and then Berlin, text critically determined readings not only by recourse to manuscripts but also by an approach that discriminated readings based on what he felt was the most appropriate meaning based on context. Accordingly, several of his readings were based on "intrinsic probability." For the address in 2 John 1, he prints ἐκλεκτῇ κυρίᾳ and in the apparatus gives as the primary justification his belief that the letter is addressed to a congregation instead of a named woman.[80]

The Printed Address in 2 John 1: Twentieth and Twenty-First Centuries

Today, the dominant Greek text of the New Testament is most directly indebted to an edition published at the end of the nineteenth century. In 1898, Eberhard Nestle (1851–1913) produced the first of many editions of his *Novum Testamentum Graece*.[81] The text was based on the most important editions of his day and consisted of the majority reading from Tischendorf, Westcott and Hort, Weymouth, and Weiss (Acts to Revelation). In a "double apparatus" appearing underneath the text, he printed the differences between the modern editions in the upper apparatus and the manuscript variants in the lower apparatus. For the address in 2 John 1, he printed ἐκλεκτῇ κυρίᾳ, but he does note in the upper apparatus that both Ἐκλέκτη and Κυρία are attested marginal readings and that the latter is printed in Tischendorf's edition. In the lower apparatus, no textual variants are cited.[82] Nestle produced eight more editions, with the ninth appearing in 1912. In all of these, the printed reading and apparatus on this passage remain unchanged.[83] When he died in 1913, his son Erwin Nestle (1883–1972) took over editorial duties and was responsible for additions made to the apparatus in the tenth (1914), eleventh (1920), and twelfth (1923) editions. None of these editions made any change to 2 John 1. In the thirteenth edition, published in 1927, Nestle unified the apparatus so that there was no longer a double apparatus. However, nothing changed concerning 2 John 1: The printed text remained the same, and in the apparatus, it still noted both Ἐκλέκτη and Κυρία as marginal readings and that the latter was the printed text of Tischendorf.

When Kurt Aland (1915–94) joined the project, he first served as editor of the apparatus for the twenty-first edition (1952) and then became coeditor with Nestle for editions twenty-two (1956) through twenty-five (1963). In these editions, nothing changed either in the text or in the apparatus regarding 2 John 1. When Aland succeeded Nestle as the project's executive director and issued the twenty-sixth edition (1979; commonly now called "Nestle-Aland"), significant changes occurred.[84] Aland replaced the Greek text of Nestle with the Greek text of the third edition of *The Greek New Testament* of the United Bible Society (UBS³; 1975), but the only difference was some punctuation changes.[85] Therefore, the text of 2 John 1 remained unchanged. But Aland overhauled and redesigned the apparatus. Where there was any doubt about the text or where it was thought to be helpful for a better understanding of the manuscript tradition, only the most important textual witnesses were presented. Additionally, Aland dropped from the apparatus all dissenting readings of modern editions. This resulted in the disappearance of any alternate articulation for the address in 2 John 1.[86] In these respects, the twenty-seventh edition (1993) and the most recent twenty-eighth edition (2012) are identical.

Here, two changes to the marginal notes that appeared in the twenty-sixth edition are worth noting. Beginning with this edition and followed in the two subsequent editions, a new marginal note is affixed to 2 John 1. A cross-reference is now provided to 1 Peter 5:13, and the note is surely added to influence the interpretation of the address. It equates the "elect" (ἐκλεκτή) in 2 John

1 with the "joint-elect" (συνεκλεκτή) in 1 Peter 5:13 that has been taken as a reference to a "sister church" (NRSV and NRSVue). The other significant marginal change in 2 John 1 is the removal, beginning with the twenty-sixth edition, of the cross-reference to 3 John 1. In every edition of Nestle, starting in the first (1898) through the twenty-fifth (1963), the first marginal cross-reference in 2 John 1 always starts with 3 John 1. The cross-reference connects "the elder" of 2 John 1 and "the elder" of 3 John 1, who have been taken as the same figure. The curious removal of this reference, which even continues in the twenty-seventh edition, is ostensibly to sever the common authorship of both letters, as "the elder" of 2 John 1 does not have any relationship to "the elder" of 3 John 1. As it was in vogue, particularly in German scholarship of the time, to assert that 2 and 3 John were the work of different authors, the reasons for removing this cross-reference are readily apparent. Though these two marginal alternations are seemingly minor and subtle, it is nonetheless clear that they were (and are) promoting a particular reading of the address in 2 John 1 that extends to the remainder of the letter.

As this overview of the printed text of the Greek New Testament has shown, although the articulated reading ἐκλεκτῇ κυρίᾳ prevailed in most editions starting at the beginning of the sixteenth century and for the last 150 years has gone unchallenged, historically, other articulations have exerted considerable sway. Starting with Estienne's third edition in 1550, the phrase was rendered "Ἐκλεκτῇ κυρίᾳ," signaling that the letter string εκλεκτη should be taken as the proper name Eclecte. This reading was periodically picked up and reprinted in various editions of the Greek New Testament in both the seventeenth and eighteenth centuries. Remarkably, in the apparatus to Griesbach's 1805–07 edition of the Greek New Testament, he notes that some manuscripts contain the reading Ἐκλέκτη τῇ κυρίᾳ. However, neither he nor anyone else ever pursued it. Instead, Griesbach became convinced that the best rendering was ἐκλεκτῇ Κυρίᾳ, and so this reading appears in the final edition of his Greek New Testament. This reading gained support with the publication of the London Polyglot in the middle of the seventeenth century, and Bengel popularized it in the eighteenth century. Following Griesbach in the nineteenth century, the two other proponents of it were Lachmann and Tischendorf.

In printed editions of the Greek New Testament, only the letter string εκλεκτη κυρια, articulated ἐκλεκτῇ κυρίᾳ, Ἐκλεκτῇ κυρίᾳ (*sic*), or ἐκλεκτῇ Κυρίᾳ, has ever appeared in print.[87] But all of these renderings have serious problems. The reading ἐκλεκτῇ Κυρίᾳ cannot work because the collocation of the name and modifier is in the wrong position.[88] As noted in chapter 3, the address appearing in 3 John 1 follows the typical pattern of address widely appearing in letters of the Roman period where the name always precedes the modifier, so for κυρια even to be considered a name, the letter string would have to be at least reversed and read κυρια εκλεκτη. But even if this were the case, another significant problem is introduced that also plagues the reading Ἐκλέκτῃ κυρίᾳ. Without an intervening definite article, the grammar does not work. For the name to be either "Kyria" or "Eclecte," the grammar would have to be either Ἐκλέκτῃ τῇ κυρίᾳ or Κυρίᾳ τῇ ἐκλεκτῇ, which is how the address is collocated in 3 John 1 with Γαΐῳ τῷ ἀγαπητῷ. Simply capitalizing one or the other of the words to signify that it should be a name does not solve the complexity of the address.[89] Lest it be thought that ἐκλεκτῇ κυρίᾳ is the only option of the three without complications, it is also plagued by problems. It is an unparalleled form of epistolary address consisting of just an anarthrous adjective fronting a noun, and to account for its unusualness, an elaborate metaphorical reading is typically invoked. Given the inherent problems with all three renderings, it is time to turn to the manuscripts to see if they provide another way forward.

The Address in 2 John 1: The Manuscript Witnesses

The manuscript evidence for the text of the New Testament is diverse and spans about 1,500 years—from the second century to the sixteenth century. The earliest extant remains of the New Testament that date to the second century consist of a handful of small fragments.[90] These all come from Egypt, where the dry sands and arid conditions have been conducive to the preservation of a variety of ancient texts written on papyrus. As one moves chronologically into the third century, the extant remains of the New Testament expand. While these remains also come from Egypt and are dominated by fragments where typically no more than a mutilated page, or just a section of a page, is preserved, there are a few notable examples from this century where more significant portions of the text of the New Testament have survived.[91] Thus, until circa 300 CE, the extant New Testament remains are rather haphazard and entirely of Egyptian provenance.[92] As one moves to the remains from the fourth century, the situation begins to distinctly shift. The geographic distribution of the extant manuscript evidence expands to include areas outside of Egypt, and the nature of the extant manuscript evidence also rapidly expands in terms of the preserved content. While there continue to be small, scattered fragments, evincing passages from the New Testament from the fourth and subsequent centuries, more significant New Testament remains including pandect Bibles appear beginning in the fourth century. As one moves into the fifth century, the extant textual evidence continues to grow, and by the ninth and subsequent centuries, there are significant numbers of extant New Testament manuscripts.

This temporally and geographically diverse body of evidence for the Greek text of the New Testament may be categorized and summarized as follows:[93]

1) Papyri[94]

   At present, nearly 150 known Greek papyri of Egyptian provenance preserve the text of the New Testament and range in date from the second through eighth centuries. Many are small fragments attesting only a handful of verses, but some include full books or even bound collections. Owing to their general antiquity, these are regarded as among the most important witnesses to the text of the New Testament.

2) Majuscules[95]

   Currently, there are just over 325 known majuscule (or uncial) manuscripts evidencing the Greek text of the New Testament. These manuscripts date from the third through the eleventh centuries and are almost exclusively written on parchment.[96] Some majuscule witnesses are fragments consisting of only a few verses, while others contain complete bound copies of the New Testament. Majuscules are important witnesses, but their individual value for the text of the New Testament may vary somewhat depending on various factors (such as age, provenance, text-type, etc).

3) Minuscules[97]

   To date, there are nearly three thousand known minuscule manuscripts of the Greek New Testament. They range in date from the ninth century through the sixteenth century.[98] Many include large sections of the New Testament, while some include complete

> bound copies of the New Testament. They are written on both parchment and paper but from the twelfth century on, mostly on paper. Despite their late date, minuscules can still help establish the text of the New Testament.

To this principal body of evidence, other kinds of witnesses can be added. However, they are different since they do not attest "continuous-text" (i.e., text from a book belonging to the New Testament) but only evince a verse or a more extended passage embedded within another kind of text. This evidence includes a quotation or a citation from the New Testament by an ancient church father or might consist of the use of a New Testament passage in an ancient inscription, epitaph, amulet, or some other "non-continuous" text.[99] Similarly, documents like lectionaries that preserve "non-continuous" text blocks from the New Testament that are to be read during the liturgical course of the church calendar are also of use in text-critical matters.[100]

With this body of evidence in mind, let us turn to the manuscript evidence itself to see what it reveals about the address in 2 John 1. Beginning first with the papyri, at present, there is only one extant papyrus witness of 2 John 1. It is 𝔓[74], also known as P. Bodmer XVII, a sixth- or seventh-century papyrus codex containing Acts and the Catholic Epistles.[101] The codex consists of 124 leaves (of the 132 original) and is written in one column per page. While some pages are mostly intact, many are badly damaged and fragmentary, especially in the last half of the codex. Unfortunately, this is the case with the page containing 2 John 1.[102] The sole fragment from this page, which begins with 2 John 1, only preserves three very partial lines of text. The transcription of this fragment, as it is rendered by Rudolphe Kasser, the editor of the codex, reads as follows:[103]

> ο πρεϲβυτεροϲ εκ]λ[εκ
> τη κυρια και] τ̣ο̣ιϲ
> τεκνοιϲ αυτηϲ]· ουϲ
> εγω αγαπω εν αλη] [
> [θεια..................]

Having examined an image of the fragment, there are some issues I have with Kasser's transcription, but overall, they are minor.[104] The main point I wish to make about this fragment is that while Kasser reconstructs the address spanning lines 1 and 2 as εκλεκτη κυρια, and here I do not fault him since this is the conventional reading, the fragment could have just as easily accommodated the reading εκλεκτη τη κυρια within the spacing. Having edited fragmentary New Testament papyri and parchments where most of the line is missing, one most often resorts to the conventional text for the reconstruction, and if there were a two-letter variant in a significant lacuna in a line, as is the case here where over half of the line is lost, it could not be readily detected.[105] In Kasser's reconstruction of the text of 2 John, which consists of two fragments, lines range from thirteen to seventeen letters per line. So if line 2, for example, had an extra τη, it would have sixteen letters instead of fourteen and would still fit within the typical range.[106] The main point I am trying to make here is this: $\mathfrak{P}^{74}$ is not evidence against the reading εκλεκτη τη κυρια. Given the minuteness of the fragment combined with the little extant text of 2 John 1, it is not definitive whether or not it contained the definite article τη.[107]

Proceeding to the majuscule evidence, there are five principal witnesses attesting 2 John 1 before the ninth century, but on closer examination, only two of these five witnesses are diagnostic for the present investigation. The first of the majuscules to evince the address in 2 John 1 is Codex Vaticanus, dated to the fourth century.[108] This pandect Bible, of which 759 leaves (of an original 830) survive, includes large sections of the Septuagint and New Testament written in three columns per page.[109] It is rightly regarded as one of the most important witnesses of the Greek text of the New Testament and was used extensively by Westcott and Hort in their 1881 edition. The entirety of 2 John occupies two columns on page 1142 of this codex, and the letter begins at the top of the middle column.[110] The opening of 2 John 1 reads ο πρεcβυτεροc εκλε|κτη κυρια κτλ.[111] Though the address is split between two lines, it is εκλεκτη κυρια. Therefore, the earliest majuscule witness for this verse evinces the shorter reading without the definite article.

The next majuscule witness of 2 John 1 appears in Codex Sinaiticus of the fourth century.[112] This majuscule was brought to light in 1844 by Constantine von Tischendorf during a visit to Saint Catherine's Monastery, and so it did not begin to play a role in text-critical studies of the New Testament until the latter half of the nineteenth century.[113] Like Vaticanus, it is a pandect Bible that includes both the Septuagint and New Testament and even the Epistle of Barnabas and Shepherd of Hermas.[114] But whereas Vaticanus is written with three columns per page, Sinaiticus contains four. 2 John occupies the last outside column on folio 324 and the first outside column on folio 324b.[115]

The opening of the letter reads ο πρεcβυτεροc | εκλεκτη κυρια κτλ.[116] As with Codex Vaticanus, Sinaiticus also evinces the shorter reading.

A third majuscule witness of 2 John 1 from roughly the same period as Vaticanus and Sinaiticus is the fifth-century Codex Alexandrinus.[117] Like Vaticanus and Sinaiticus, Alexandrinus is a pandect Bible that contains the Septuagint and New Testament, although it also adds 1 and 2 Clement. But whereas the former two bibles were written in three and four columns per page, Alexandrinus contains two columns per page. The text of 2 John fits entirely in the outside column of fol. 109b. In 1860, the transcription of the Greek New Testament, which has been subsequently reprinted and reused, was made by Benjamin H. Cowper (1822–1904) from a facsimile produced nearly a century earlier by Charles G. Woide (1725–1790).[118] The opening of 2 John 1 is transcribed as follows by Cowper: ὁ πρεσβύτερος Ἐκλε[κτῇ] κυρίᾳ κτλ.[119] The capitalization of "Ἐκλε[κτῇ]" in the transcription is purely interpretive, as Alexandrinus—as with all ancient manuscripts—does not distinguish proper nouns with the use of uppercase and lowercase letters. In subsequent editions of the transcription, the capitalization (and accentuation) has been dropped, and it is transcribed "εκλε[κτη]." Having examined an image of the page, I would transcribe the opening of 2 John 1 as follows: ο πρεcβυτεροc εκλεκ̣[±3]| κυρια κτλ.[120] In Alexandrinus, 2 John 1 starts at the very top of the outside column, but due to wear and tear, the top right corner of the page has been torn off with the result that the ends of the first five lines are broken off. While every transcription assumes the reading is εκλε[κτη] since it is directly followed at the beginning of the next line by κυρια, it could just as easily have been εκλεκ̣[τη τη] | κυρια as there is plenty of room in the lacuna at the end of the line to accommodate two additional letters. It is worth noting that in the line just below that also suffers from the same damage, the transcription given by Cowper assumes that four letters are lost at the end of the line: τέκνοις α[ὐτῆς] | οὓς κτλ.[121] Therefore, despite transcriptions that assume the reading εκλεκτη κυρια, as with 𝔓[74], Codex Alexandrinus is not evidence against the longer reading.

Beyond the "big three" majuscule witnesses for 2 John 1,[122] there are two additional witnesses of this verse before the ninth century. One is GA 048, a fifth-century parchment manuscript that preserves portions of Acts, the Catholic Epistles, and the Pauline Epistles written in three columns per page.[123] But the manuscript is badly damaged because it is a palimpsest: The

New Testament text was largely erased some five hundred years after it was written so that homilies of Gregory Nazianzen (ca. 329–90 CE) could be overwritten.[124] In the manuscript, the text of 2 John spans all three columns on folio 307r and is badly effaced in places so that it is riddled with lacunae. While the title of the letter can be easily read, "+ ϊωαννου β̅," since it is only partially effaced and appears in the upper margin where there is no overwritten text, 2 John 1 does not become legible until nearly three-quarters of the way through the verse.[125] Thus, GA 048 offers no insight into the rendering of the address in 2 John 1.

The other majuscule witness that attests 2 John 1 is GA 0232 (=P.Ant. 1.12), which has also been dated to the fifth century.[126] It consists of a single sheet of parchment discovered in Antinoopolis (Sheikh Abâda; Egypt) by the EEF during a 1913–14 excavation and was subsequently published in 1950 by C. H. Roberts.[127] The sheet preserves 2 John 1–5 on the front side and 2 John 6–9 on the back side and bears the page numbers 164 and 165.[128] The most curious aspect of the fragment is that the first line that is fully intact begins with κυρια, and the few words that preceded and opened 2 John were presumably written at the end of the previous page that is no longer extant. Roberts was perplexed trying to ascertain why a scribe did not simply begin 2 John at the top of the page since there was plenty of space above the first line in the upper margin, but decided to write the first few words on the last line of the previous page.[129] Thus, GA 0232 tells us nothing about the address in 2 John 1 before κυρια.

To summarize the manuscript evidence as it presently stands, for the first nine centuries, only two extant witnesses preserve in full the address in 2 John 1. The first is Codex Vaticanus, and the second is Codex Sinaiticus, and both evince the shorter reading εκλεκτη κυρια. In the remaining four witnesses that attest 2 John 1, Codex Alexandrinus, GA 048, and GA 0232, all from the fifth century, and 𝔓[74] from the sixth or seventh century, in each of these manuscripts some part of the address is lost, so one cannot conclusively determine the exact reading of the address. As the Greek text of 2 John 1 is not evinced in another manuscript until the ninth and subsequent centuries, one must now deal primarily with the evidence provided by the minuscules. As previously noted, there are nearly three thousand known minuscule manuscripts attesting the text of the New Testament, and approximately six hundred of these contain all or part of the Johannine Epistles.[130] There is no way this study could treat every such manuscript or even cursorily mention and list each one. But as the vast majority of these manuscripts contain the reading εκλεκτη κυρια, there is no need to rehearse all such evidence. Furthermore, as most minuscules reflect the "Byzantine text"—a carefully controlled, standardized, and uniform text of the New Testament that emerged through a long process and was widely attested in the Byzantine Empire—many do not evince any other readings beyond what became "standardized." While the address εκλεκτη κυρια is attested in both Vaticanus and Sinaiticus, it also became the received reading in the Byzantine text.

The focus here will be on manuscripts that exhibit the reading εκλεκτη τη κυρια. The purpose will be to show that it appears in some important manuscripts, which are otherwise known to preserve early readings, and that there is even a distinct relationship among most (or all) of them. This last point is significant. If the addition of the article τη in the address in 2 John 1 just appeared in a handful of unrelated manuscripts, one might wonder whether this two-letter addition was a random scribal insertion where two letters were accidentally reduplicated through dittography. On the other hand, if the manuscripts that evince this reading are related and form some kind of relationship where they are being copied and recopied, and the article τη persists across multiple manuscript copies from multiple centuries, it is not a random scribal addition. Instead, the reading is being deliberately perpetuated by each successive copy because the reading is regarded as legitimate. It, therefore, considerably strengthens the case that we are dealing with an authentic variant reading.

The earliest minuscule that evinces the reading εκλεκτη τη κυρια at 2 John 1 is GA 1243. This eleventh-century manuscript is housed in the library of St. Catherine's Monastery and contains the text of the Gospels, followed by the Apostolos (i.e., Acts and the Catholic Epistles), and finally the Pauline Letters.[131] Despite the eleventh-century date, the textual importance of sections of the manuscript has long been recognized. In Kurt and Barbara Aland's discussion of Greek New Testament manuscripts and their import for its textual history, they divide them into five categories.[132] In their judgment, manuscripts belonging to Category I contained text that possessed "a very special quality which should always be considered in establishing the original text . . . The papyri and uncials up to the third/fourth century belong here almost automatically because they represent the text of the early period."[133] By contrast, manuscripts assigned to Category V were judged to be much less helpful in text-critical matters because they contained "a purely or predominantly Byzantine text."[134] With each gradation from categories I through V, a manuscript's value becomes less helpful for text-critical purposes. In the case of GA 1243, they consider the Greek text of the Catholic Letters to firmly belong to Category I so that readings preserved in this portion of the manuscript should be regarded with roughly the same textual status as our earliest Christian manuscripts written centuries earlier.[135]

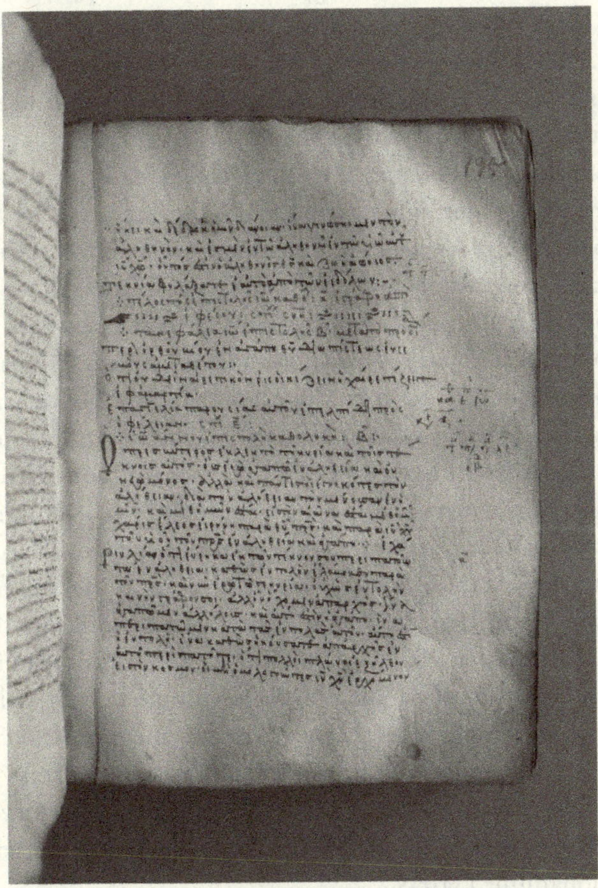

Figure 4.1. GA 1243: Opening of 2 John. Sinai Greek 262, f. 195r. Image reproduced with permission from St. Catherine's Monastery in the Sinai. Photo taken by Father Justin Sinaites.

Speaking specifically of the pedigree and antiquity of the Greek text of the Catholic Epistles in GA 1243, various studies have shown that it preserves several readings with an ancient pedigree. Murial M. Carder's work on the manuscript has shown that its text "is certainly not a late Byzantine text in the Catholic corpus, in spite of its late date."[136] She adds that "although written in the eleventh century, [it] provides a link with antiquity that can be gathered from its plain, simple superscriptions at the head of each book."[137] She, therefore, judges it to be one of the "valuable texts . . . hidden among the minuscules" that preserves several ancient readings in the Catholic corpus.[138] More recently, in Klaus Wachtel's *Der byzantinische Text der katholischen Briefe*, the textual value of GA 1243 is recognized.[139] He points out that 1243 possesses a text type that is generally distinct from the late Byzantine text and has a textual profile that parallels earlier manuscripts.[140]

W. Larry Richards's detailed work on the manuscript witnesses of the Johannine Epistles highlights the textual importance of GA 1243. In his study, Richards compares eighty-one manuscripts that preserve the Johannine Epistles—these range from Codex Vaticanus and Sinaiticus down to GA 1876 from the fifteenth century. Conducting a thorough assessment of different readings that appear in most verses in the Johannine Letters—although there is no examination or discussion of 2 John 1 in the study[141]—Richards attempts to develop a classification and profile for the manuscripts. Without rehearsing all his findings and sticking with GA 1243, Richards notes that this manuscript consistently evinces readings that are found in the most ancient witnesses. Accordingly, he classifies it as an "A^3" manuscript or an "Alexandrian" manuscript, where manuscripts in Category 3 tend to "deviate from the TR (*textus receptus*) more than any of the manuscripts examined in the study."[142] Richards also notes that of all eighty-one manuscripts surveyed in his study, GA 1243 shares the most parallels in the Johannine Letters with the extant text appearing in 𝔓^{74}. He notes that it shares agreement with 𝔓^{74} 85.7 percent of the time;[143] by comparison, he notes that Vaticanus shares 71.4 percent agreement, while a text like GA 1873 from the fifteenth century only shares 35.7 percent agreement.[144] Therefore, GA 1243 is an important witness of the text of the Johannine Letters.

Another minuscule of the eleventh century that preserves the reading εκλεκτη τη κυρια is GA 451, a parchment manuscript of the Apostolos followed by the Pauline Letters that is housed in the Biblioteca Apostolica Vaticana.[145] For the text of the Catholic Epistles, the Alands judge it to belong to Category V, which contains "a purely or predominantly Byzantine text."[146] Robert B. Waltz has shown that this categorization is largely merited since in 98 sample readings from the Catholic Epistles, only eight were "non-Byzantine."[147] It is, therefore, somewhat unusual to find that this reading appears at 2 John 1. An interesting feature about GA 451 is that it closely aligns with another manuscript, GA 300, a twelfth-century manuscript that contains the Gospels, the Apostolos, and Pauline Epistles and is kept in the National Library of Russia.[148] In a study of the two manuscripts, it has been noted that they fully agree in 436 of 464 test readings, including 75 of 77 readings where both are "non-Byzantine."[149] In fact, the manuscripts are so close that it is thought that they might even be "sisters" and derive from a common exemplar or, alternatively, that 451 was an "ancestor" of 330. It is clear, therefore, that they belong to the same textual family. In GA 330, the address preserved at 2 John 1 also reads εκλεκτη τη κυρια.

A fourth minuscule manuscript that also exhibits the reading εκλεκτη τη κυρια is GA 2492. This manuscript dates to the fourteenth century and, as with GA 1243, is located in the library at St. Catherine's Monastery.[150] It contains the Gospels, Apostolos, and Pauline Letters.[151] Due in part to the date of the manuscript, but also intrinsic features, the Alands assign the text of the Catholic Epistles to Category III—"Manuscripts of a distinctive character with an independent text, usually important for establishing the original text, but particularly important for the history of the text."[152] In Wachtel's comprehensive study, he shows that in the Catholic corpus, the text possesses many agreements with the Byzantine text but that it also possesses noteworthy features.[153] Similarly, Waltz notes that in the Catholic Epistles, while it appears to be a mostly "Byzantine" text, it is "scattered with readings of all other types" so that it is still helpful for text-critical investigation.[154]

Beyond attesting the longer reading at 2 John 1, GA 2492 is important because it helps tie all four manuscripts together. As noted above, it is already established that GA 300 and GA 451 belong to the same family, given that they share several unique textual features. While GA 2492 is a little removed textually from both GA 300 and GA 451, it has been shown that it belongs within the group but that it has "a slightly more Alexandrian-influenced version of the same text."[155] A relationship, therefore, emerges among the three manuscripts in the Catholic Epistles. On top of this, it has been noted in the Catholic Epistles that GA 2492 shares various parallels with GA 1243, so there is some relationship between the two, although not as close as among GA

2492, GA 300, and GA 451.[156] Therefore, a cluster of four related manuscripts emerges that all evince the longer reading εκλεκτη τη κυρια, establishing that the addition of the τη is not random but is a genuine variant reading.

In addition to these four manuscripts, the longer reading is also attested in one other. Though the ECM neglects to note that this manuscript includes the article in the address (and the same is the case with GA 451), the fifth manuscript is GA 69.[157] Otherwise known as the Codex Leicester since it was previously held in the Leicester Library, it is a fifteenth-century codex that preserves the entire New Testament with the exception of four notable lacunae.[158] The text is written in a single column per page, and the entirety of 2 John occupies the top three-quarters of the column on folio 201r. The first line of the column contains the title of the letter, written with red ink, and the letter begins in the second line and is written with dark-brown ink. My transcription of the opening of 2 John 1 reads as follows: ο πρεσβυτεροс εκλεκτη τη[±20], after which the remainder of the line is lost in a lacuna, as the top outside corner of the page has been torn away (just like Alexandrinus). The next line begins with της ουс εγω κτλ. A likely reconstruction of the full text is ο πρεσβυτεροс εκλεκτη τη [κυρια και τοιс τεκνοιс αυ]|της ουс εγω κτλ. Even though the address breaks off right before κυρια, the manuscript evinces the longer reading with the definite article τη after εκλεκτη.

GA 69 is a curious manuscript that has met with different appraisals regarding its text of the Catholic Epistles. The Alands assigned the text to Category V, which is "a purely or predominantly Byzantine text."[159] In Carder's more detailed work on the manuscript, she recognizes the Byzantine influence on the text of the Catholic Epistles but argues it "has long been known to preserve an ancient lineage."[160] She contends that it is a distinctly mixed text that preserves some important readings. In her text-critical discussion of the Catholic Letters, she also notes that in several places, the readings that GA 69 attest accord with those found in GA 1243 so that they belong together in a group.[161] If this is the case, it would connect GA 69 with the other manuscripts that attest the longer reading εκλεκτη τη κυρια. Thus, five related manuscripts that span the eleventh through fifteenth centuries would all contain this reading. However, in a critique of Carder's work by Richards, he feels that the connection between GA 69 and GA 1243 is not as straightforward as Carder alleges. While Richards agrees with Carder that GA 69 is a mixed text that evinces some important readings, he is unconvinced that its overall profile in the Catholic Epistles suggests it has close ties with GA 1243.[162] More recently, Matthew Burks has shown that in the Catholic Epistles, GA 1243 shares some distinct agreement with GA 69, but it is not as pronounced as other manuscript witnesses.[163]

Regardless of the exact relationship between GA 69 and GA 1243, there is (at least) a group of four related manuscripts, and five total, that evince the longer address in 2 John 1. While this is a small group, these five manuscripts constitute important witnesses for the reading εκλεκτη τη κυρια. Here, it is essential to keep a couple of textual points in mind about this evidence. The first is that even though it is only attested in minuscule witnesses, it has long been recognized they can preserve ancient readings that have been hitherto lost because of the fragmentary nature of the ancient manuscript witnesses. Returning to Westcott and Hort, in the *Introduction and Appendix* to *The New Testament in the Original Greek*, a companion volume to their Greek New Testament published the following year, they discuss the manuscript evidence for the New Testament.[164] In a section devoted to the importance of the minuscule evidence, they remark that "valuable texts may lie hidden among them" and that "many of them are doubtless sprinkled with relics of valuable texts now destroyed."[165] In a similar vein, B. H. Streeter pointed out that the minuscules can be very helpful in some text-critical matters and despite their late date that "the precedence of manuscripts depends, not on their age, but on their pedigree."[166] In the case of GA 1243, we are dealing with a minuscule that gives every impression in the Catholic Epistles that it preserves an ancient lineage. Another point worth keeping in mind as we consider the longer reading εκλεκτη τη κυρια is that for the first nine centuries, we only have two extant textual witnesses for the full address in 2 John 1, Codex Vaticanus and Codex Sinaiticus. These are important witnesses, but despite such evidence, it is not inconceivable that the readings they preserve might not be the most ancient. There is a notable case, not unlike the present one before us, where both of these codices—as well as a host of other ancient witnesses—agree on a reading, but a different one, only attested in much later manuscripts of the ninth and subsequent centuries, is considered the more original. For this example, we must turn to Origen of Alexandria (ca. 185–253 CE).

Origen occupies an important place in the history of early Christianity.[167] A leading intellectual in the church in the first half of the third century, Origen was posthumously condemned and ultimately excommunicated a few centuries later for holding unorthodox views.[168] The result is that only a fraction of his voluminous output has survived and is mostly extant in fragments or via translation (in Latin). A survey of Origen's extant literary remains reveals that he was acutely aware of textual variants in both the Old and New Testaments. In fact, one of his major works was the composition of his massive *Hexapla* (*Sixfold*; completed ca. 245 CE), where he produced a comparison of the text from the Old Testament in both Hebrew and Greek in six parallel columns.[169] According to Origen, one of the principal reasons for the work was "due to discrepancies between the manuscripts of the Old Testament."[170] While Origen developed nothing of the kind for the text of the New Testament, a survey of his writings reveals he periodically commented on New Testament passages where variants existed and, on occasion, even offered reasons for his preferred reading.[171]

In his lengthy *Commentary on Matthew*, which is only partially preserved, and the latter part only exists via a later Latin translation, Origen makes various text-critical remarks.[172] For example, he notes at Matthew 16:20 that he was aware of a variant reading appearing "in some of the manuscripts."[173] A little later, at Matthew 18:1, he points out a variant where some manuscripts read "in that hour," while others read "in that day."[174] Then, at Matthew 19:19, Origen argues that the statement "Love your neighbor as yourself" was likely "added by someone who did not grasp the exact significance of the passage" and then shortly followed with "it is a recognized fact that there is much diversity in our copies, whether by the carelessness of certain scribes, or by some culpable rashness in the correction of the text, or by some people making arbitrary additions or omissions in their corrections."[175] Origen makes other text-critical comments at Matthew 21:9, 24:19, 26:63, and 27:9.[176] His last such comment, which appears at Matthew 27:17, is most interesting and occupies our attention.

After citing the lemma for Matthew 27:16–18, Origen focuses on v. 17 and Pilate's question to the crowd about whom he should release: Barabbas or Jesus. Origen then notes that in some manuscripts, Barabbas's given name is Jesus (i.e., Jesus Barabbas) but is then quick to disregard this reading by providing the specious argument that no unjust person could bear this name:

> In many copies [of the scriptures] it is not contained that "Barabbas" was also called "Jesus," and perhaps rightly [it was not contained] so that the name "Jesus" does not apply to any unjust person. For in so

> great a multitude of scriptures we know no sinner named Jesus. In the case of other names of just people we find that unjust people also have the same name. Take, for example, Judas; there was the apostle called the zealot, likewise Judas the patriarch, and Judas Maccabees, all praiseworthy people, but there was also Judas the betrayer. In Genesis, you will also find sons of Seth and sons of Cain with the same name, such as Enoch, Lamech, and Methuselah. But no such thing was appropriate with the name Jesus.[177]

Though Origen notes that "many copies" of the scriptures just read "Barabbas," his discussion shows that he is aware that the reading "Jesus Barabbas" is attested in some copies.

Turning to the earliest manuscripts that preserve Matthew 27:17 (16),[178] Vaticanus, Sinaiticus, and Alexandrinus, the reading "Jesus" is not present in any of them.[179] Similarly, this reading is missing in other important early manuscripts like Codex Bezae and Codex Washingtonianus.[180] The cumulative force of these five witnesses is exceptionally strong against reading "Jesus" in Matthew 27:17 (16). The reading "Jesus" does not appear in any Greek manuscript before the ninth century, where it first appears in Codex Koridethi.[181] It then appears in manuscripts belonging to *family*^{1}, a group of manuscripts ranging in date from the tenth to fourteenth centuries,[182] as well as GA 700 from the eleventh century.[183] Thus, the reading "Jesus Barabbas" is confined to a few late manuscripts.

Notwithstanding the nature of the manuscript evidence, many believe that the inclusion of "Jesus" is the more original reading in Matthew 27:17 (16). Consequently, it is included in the text of the NA^{28}, albeit in square brackets, and was included in the Greek text starting with the twenty-sixth edition published in 1979.[184] Commenting on the inclusion of "Jesus" in the Greek text of this verse in UBS^{3}, which is the Greek text used for NA^{26}, Bruce Metzger notes, "A majority of the Committee was of the opinion that the original text of Matthew had the double name in both verses and that Ἰησοῦν was deliberately suppressed in most witnesses for reverential considerations. In view of the relatively slender external support for Ἰησοῦν, however, it was deemed fitting to enclose the word within square brackets."[185]

Returning to 2 John 1, a similar textual scenario occurs: A reading is attested in an early church father, in this case, Clement of Alexandria; it is not attested in any of the major ancient textual witnesses but is attested much later in a small group of manuscripts. Just as Metzger (and the UBS^3 committee)[186] felt that the reading 'Ἰησοῦν is the more original based on external circumstances, so, too, the reading εκλεκτη τη κυρια is to be preferred over εκλεκτη κυρια as the more original when external factors are considered. Whereas the latter is an unparalleled form of address, the former makes far more sense in light of the evidence provided by the epistolary papyri and, most important of all, parallels exactly the collocation of the address appearing in 3 John 1. The longer reading is far superior on external grounds.

When discussing the omission of "Jesus" from Matthew 27:16–17, Metzger notes that it was the opinion of the committee that the name Jesus was suppressed for "reverential considerations." With the present case, I can find no direct evidence that the female name Eclecte was being suppressed from the address in 2 John 1 for similar reasons (i.e., that it would have been deemed inappropriate for a letter that became part of the scriptural canon to be addressed to a named woman). In much later centuries, Christians became emphatic that the principal addressee of 2 John was not a woman but the church, and in some minuscule manuscripts, the word κυρία is even given the marginal gloss "church" (ἐκκλησία),[187] but the most likely reason for the initial loss of τη is simply a scribal oversight. As noted above, Origen remarked that "the carelessness of certain scribes" had resulted in several variants being introduced into manuscripts.[188] The most likely scenario here is that at some point through a scribal "eye skip," the letter string εκλεκτητηκυρια was accidentally shortened to εκλεκτηκυρια through haplography.[189]

A growing number of studies on scribal habits and the transmission of early Christian manuscripts have shown that errors that result in textual variants tend to create shorter readings. Of these studies, the premier work is by James R. Royse, who has examined scribal habits and tendencies in an effort to make informed judgments about the origin of variant readings.[190] As he noted, "Knowing which errors are likely and which are unlikely will help one to choose among the many possible sequences of variants in the transmission of the text and thus to decide (as reasonably as possible) what the original text was."[191] Examining the major papyrological remains of the New Testament contained in $\mathfrak{P}^{45}$, $\mathfrak{P}^{46}$, $\mathfrak{P}^{47}$, $\mathfrak{P}^{66}$, $\mathfrak{P}^{72}$, and $\mathfrak{P}^{75}$,[192] Royse concludes that the manuscripts showed that in copying a text, scribes had a greater propensity to shorten text than they did to lengthen it. He found that there were more cases where scribes would omit text through an accidental "leap," especially when the omitted text was just a single word or a short passage, so variant readings were typically the shorter reading.[193] Though the conventional thinking since the time of Griesbach was that scribes tend to add to the text so that "the shorter reading is preferable" (*lectio brevior potior*), Royse demonstrably shows that in more cases, the opposite is true—namely, the longer reading is often the more original since the shorter reading can be shown to have come about through a scribal omission.[194] Royse is not alone in this finding; other studies have noted the same scribal tendency in early Christian manuscripts.[195] In fact, recent studies have been even more forceful, arguing that the evidence is such that the conventional text-critical canon *lectio brevior potior* needs some serious qualification and refinement.[196] This is not to deny this canon outright but to stress that the burden of proof has shifted so that, in many cases, the longer reading is preferred (*lectio longior potior*). While variants can be introduced into manuscripts in different ways, and scribes can undoubtedly add to the text (as Royse and others acknowledge), the more common variants are shorter readings since omission (typically accidental) is the more common scribal tendency.[197]

Returning to the address in 2 John 1, it is easy to see how the letter string -τητη- could be accidentally shorted to -τη- through a scribal slip. This omission is precisely the kind one could expect based on scribal habits and tendencies in early Christian manuscripts, where the more common variants are the direct result of omission. Not only do we see this phenomenon in early Christian manuscripts, but as noted in the discussion of the epistolary papyri in chapter 3, we also have explicit examples in epistolary address where an article is mistakenly dropped since the name that precedes terminates with the same letters as the dropped article. The received shorter reading εκλεκτη κυρια is, therefore, the result of a scribal omission of two reduplicated letters. While this is a minor omission, it has huge implications for the address in 2 John 1 and how the letter would come to be read historically. Now that the proper address in 2 John 1 has been restored, Ἐκλέκτῃ τῇ κυρίᾳ, in the next chapter, the focus will shift to an examination of the female name Eclecte.

CHAPTER FIVE

Is Eclecte Even a Name?

Onomastics, Inscriptions, and the Order of Things

The "Elect Lady" of 2 John was a personification and not a person, . . . Eklekté occurs nowhere else in Greek . . . as a woman's name.

—George G. Findlay, *An Exposition in the Epistles of St. John*[1]

IN 1909, GEORGE G. FINDLAY published one of the most detailed studies of the Johannine Letters to appear in the first half of the twentieth century: *Fellowship in the Life Eternal: An Exposition in the Epistles of St. John*. As a testament to the depth of the work, it is still periodically referenced. Findlay's exposition is such that, in several places, the reader is left with the impression that no stone remains unturned. For example, an entire chapter is devoted to the meaning of the phrase εκλεκτη κυρια in 2 John 1.[2] Findlay concludes that the best way to interpret the phrase is to the "lady church," but he briefly entertains, then quickly dismisses, the possibility that the reading could contain the personal name "Eklekté" (*sic*). His primary argument against it is that the name "occurs nowhere else in Greek." Therefore, the letter string εκλεκτη could be nothing other than the adjective "elect" (ἐκλεκτή) since "Eklekté" is nothing more than a "ghostname"—a name that does not actually exist.[3] Given the enduring nature of his work, Findlay's onomastic declaration is occasionally recited by modern commentators.[4]

While contemporary treatments of 2 John 1 generally include little or no onomastic discussion, a few maintain that one of the reasons the opening of the letter cannot be addressed to a woman named Eclecte is because there is no evidence for this name. For example, Raymond Brown rejects it in part because "the evidence is insufficient for eklektē as a personal name at this time."[5] Similarly, Donald W. Burdick's *The Letters of John the Apostle: An In-Depth Commentary*, claims that "studies have not shown it to appear elsewhere as a proper name."[6] More recently, in Hans J. Klauck's commentary on 2 and 3 John, he likewise rejects reading Eclecte because he questions whether the name even exists in Greek.[7]

While it may strike the reader as strange that some doubt the existence of this female name, especially in the face of the evidence provided by Clement of Alexandria, who mentions this name in connection with 2 John 1, most of the commentators who have made this claim tend to dismiss Clement altogether. After all, this evidence only exists in a later Latin translation (Clement originally wrote in Greek), and this claim is intermixed with other assertions by Clement that find no place in 2 John. It is addressed to "virgins" and is connected to a "Babylonian woman."[8] Therefore, everything Clement says is treated with distrust and ultimately rejected. However, as noted in chapter 1, in Clement's prefatory remarks on 2 John, he makes both eisegetical and exegetical claims. His contention about "virgins" and a "Babylonian woman" are eisegetical since they are never explicitly mentioned anywhere in the letter. On the other hand, he does make a single exegetical claim: Clement was reading the third word in 2 John, the letter string εκλεκτη, as a name. It is, therefore, essential to carefully differentiate between the two sets of statements made by Clement and not simply dismiss one because of the other.

This chapter will show that despite claims to the contrary, the female name Eclecte, correctly rendered in Greek as Ἐκλέκτη, existed in the period in which 2 John was authored. Outside of Clement, the name is attested in both Greek and Latin and is more widely attested than a number of female names appearing in the New Testament. After establishing the name's existence, this chapter will return to the principal argument marshaled against reading it in 2 John 1—namely, that the name would also have to be read in 2 John 13 so that two sisters would bear the same name. While this issue was briefly addressed at the end of chapter 2, this chapter will provide a more thorough rebuttal. From here, the chapter will conclude with a discussion of the female name Kyria (Κυρία), sometimes rendered Cyria, and why it can be excluded as an interpretive option in 2 John 1. In various studies, it is alleged that if the phrase εκλεκτη κυρια were to contain a proper name, then the most likely candidate would be Kyria. These claims often appear as bald assertions without any supporting evidence. They will sometimes cite Athanasius of Alexandria (ca. 296–373 CE) as the first commentator to propose this reading. However, as will be shown, Athanasius never made this claim.

Is Eclecte Even a Name?

To establish the existence of the female name Eclecte and how it could have been overlooked for all these years, this section will begin with a brief introduction to Greek onomastics. In formation, Greek names, regardless of whether they are masculine or feminine, are either simple or compound.[9] A compound name is derived from a combination of nouns, adjectives, or even verbs or adverbs. The well-attested Greek name Nicodemus (Νικόδημος) is an example of a compound name derived from the nouns "victory" (νίκη) and "people" (δῆμος).[10] On the other hand, a simple name is derived directly from a noun or an adjective or is one that is so derived and adds a suffix. The masculine name Stephen (Στέφανος) is a simple name based directly on the masculine noun "crown" or "wreath" (στέφανος), while the masculine name Aristius (Ἀρίστιος) is an example of a simple name derived from the adjective "excellent" (ἄριστος) but with the addition of a suffix.[11]

Simple names can pose unique challenges when deciphering ancient texts (e.g., inscriptions, papyri, etc.). These names, devoid of modern accentuation or capitalization, are ambiguous since they may be identical in form to the noun or adjective on which they are based. To give an example from a fictitious inscription, consider how one might translate the following line if found on an inscribed stone or some other medium:[12] ΜΕΤΑΤΗΝΜΑΧΗΝϹΤΕΦΑΝΟ ϹΜΕΠΕΡΙΜΕΝΕΙ. One alternative could be "after the battle, a crown awaits me" (μετὰ τὴν μάχην στέφανός με περιμένει). But another could be "after the battle, Stephen awaits me" (μετὰ τὴν μάχην Στέφανός με περιμένει). The central interpretive crux is whether ϹΤΕΦΑΝΟϹ is to be taken as the noun "crown" or "wreath" (στέφανος) or as the proper name "Stephen" (Στέφανος).[13] In such circumstances, context becomes the critical factor in deciding which rendering is best.[14] So, for example, when the letter string ϹΤΕΦΑΝΟϹ occurs in Acts 6:8, context dictates that the best reading is the proper name "Stephen", but when the same letter string occurs in Philippians 4:1, context dictates the best reading is the noun "crown" or "wreath."

Returning to 2 John 1, since the female name Ἐκλέκτη is identical to the adjective ἐκλεκτή on which it is based, context becomes the most critical factor in determining its correct interpretation: an adjective or a personal name. The contextual evidence provided by 3 John 1 is crucial, as it contains the standard form of address appearing in the epistolary papyri of the Roman period. In this address, the type "A [to] B," the name of the recipient always follows the name (or title) of the sender without any intervening text, and this is the case with the name "Gaius" in 3 John 1, as it directly follows "the elder" (ὁ πρεσβύτερος Γαΐῳ).[15] Therefore, in 2 John 1, context suggests the letter string εκλεκτη should be taken as a personal name (ὁ πρεσβύτερος Ἐκλέκτῃ). However, for this reading to be considered, it must be established that Eclecte is a genuine onomastic possibility. If the name does not exist, the only alternative is to read the adjective.

Returning to Greek onomastics, another feature of ancient Greek (and Latin) names is that they typically possessed both a masculine and feminine form. So, if there were a masculine attestation of a name, one would also expect that there would be a complimentary feminine counterpart. For example, there is the simple Greek masculine name Agathus (Ἄγαθος), directly derived from the masculine adjective "good" (ἀγαθός), and there is the feminine name Agathe (Ἀγάθη) that is directly based on the feminine form of the adjective "good" (ἀγαθή).[16] The same holds for simple Greek names based on nouns, names that include suffixes, and compound names. Turning to the Latin evidence, one finds the same phenomenon: A masculine or feminine name tends to have a corresponding counterpart for the opposite gender. Thus, the Latin masculine *gentilicium* Julius had as its feminine counterpart the name Julia, and the Latin feminine *gentilicium* Claudia had as its counterpart the masculine Claudius. Consequently, when a name is attested in one gender, it can usually be assumed that it existed in the other, at least notionally, even if it is unattested. Returning to the Greek Ἐκλέκτη and the corresponding Latin Eclecte, one would assume that if this were a genuine name, one would also find a masculine counterpart. According to the declension of the masculine Greek adjective, it would be Ἔκλεκτος, and the corresponding Latin would be Eclectus. Both the masculine and feminine Greek forms of this name are adjectival as they are directly based on the Greek adjective (masc.) ἐκλεκτός or (fem.) ἐκλεκτή and carry the inherent meaning "picked out," "select," "choice," or "elect."[17] In fact, in an articulated text, the only difference between the adjective and the proper name is the capitalization of the latter and the recension of the accent: ἐκλεκτός becomes Ἔκλεκτος, and ἐκλεκτή becomes Ἐκλέκτη.[18]

There are a wide array of ancient sources to sift in the search for the female name Ἐκλέκτη/Eclecte. The most well-known are traditional literary sources from antiquity that include works of history or literature, as they can be replete with ancient names. In such texts, one finds references to named officials, administrators, military leaders, famous and infamous persons, and noble and ignoble persons who enter and exit the flow of the narrative presentation. For example, the New Testament contains about 200 named persons across the 27 books, attesting nearly 170 different names.[19] Eusebius of Caesarea's *Ecclesiastical History* mentions just over 650 named persons and attests over 530 different names.[20] Therefore, these sources offer a good starting point for surveying ancient names to see whether the female name Eclecte is attested.

The best place to begin a search of Greek literature is the *Thesaurus Linguae Graecae* (TLG), a database of Greek literary texts from roughly the eighth century BCE through the fifteenth century CE that contains over ten thousand works associated with over four thousand authors.[21] A search for the female name Ἐκλέκτη (*vel sim.*) on the TLG reveals no attestations. In other words, a woman bearing this Greek name is not attested in any known Greek literary text in the database. On the other hand, a search for the Greek male name Ἔκλεκτος (*vel sim.*) shows that it is an attested name in literary sources. The histories of Herodian (late II / early III CE) and Lucius Cassius Dio (ca. 165–235 CE) mention that one of the coconspirators in the assassination of the emperor Commodus (d. Dec. 31, 192 CE) was a freedman named Eclectus (Ἔκλεκτος).[22] The evidence of the masculine form indicates that, in principle, the feminine form of the name could exist.

Turning to the *Library of Latin Texts* (LLT), the Latin counterpart to the TLG that includes Latin literary texts from the third century BCE through the Middle Ages, a search for the name Eclecte (*vel sim.*) reveals a single attestation.[23] As noted previously, in Clement of Alexandria's *Sketches on the Canonical Epistles*, he argues in his brief commentary on 2 John that it is written to a woman "by name Eclecte" (*Eclectam nomine*). Outside of this reference, the name Eclecte does not appear in any other literary source in Latin. Turning to the masculine counterpart Eclectus, the name is attested in the anonymous *Historia Augusta* (IV CE ?) when narrating the assassination of Commodus. Thus, the same person named Eclectus, who appears in Herodian and Dio Cassius, is also mentioned in Latin sources.[24] Therefore, in the entire Greek and Latin corpus of known literary texts that are presently available for digital searching, the female name Ἐκλέκτη is never attested in Greek and is only attested once in Latin by Clement of Alexandria. On the other hand, the male counterpart Ἔκλεκτος/Eclectus is attested in both Greek and Latin literary texts for a single individual.

While evidence for the female name Eclecte in Greek and Latin literary sources is virtually nonexistent, these sources only represent a portion of the available onomastic evidence from antiquity. The largest onomastic repository from the ancient world is found in the extant inscriptions and papyri of the Mediterranean world. Of the two, inscriptions are the single largest repository of names. They span the entire Mediterranean and attest named persons from various backgrounds and social classes, from the emperor and senatorial elites down to the artisan, farmer, and slave. For various societal reasons, named men are more attested than named women, but women still figure widely in the epigraphic data. Likewise, named children, both male and female, can prominently figure in memorial inscriptions and funerary epitaphs. Like inscriptions, documentary papyri also afford a large onomastic reservoir to draw on. They are only second to inscriptions because they are principally (but not exclusively) limited to Egypt, where the dry sands and generally arid conditions are conducive to their preservation. In the papyri, one finds tax registers, lists, census reports, and a wide variety of documents replete with onomastic data. For example, on a single broken roll of papyrus from Philadelphia (Fayum; Egypt) that records payments for a tax from roughly July to August of 33 CE, 992 different people are mentioned by name, attesting over 500 different names of Greek, Latin, Egyptian, and even Semitic origin.[25] Cumulatively, between the extant epigraphic and papyrological data, nearly three-quarters of a million named persons who lived in the Mediterranean world are known, attesting tens of thousands of different names, several of which never appear in any literary source. For these reasons, these two datasets are the most useful for locating ancient names.

Accessing this vast reservoir of onomastic data is not as easy as running a simple search on the TLG or the LLT, as the evidence is spread out over a number of different resources. The foremost tool for searching Greek names is the *Lexicon of Greek Personal Names* (LGPN), originally appearing in a printed multivolume series but now readily accessible in an online database.[26] The epigraphic record is the largest resource for the names appearing in this database. Though it is still somewhat geographically limited, and does not yet fully incorporate onomastic data in Greek from Egypt and the Near East, it is fairly comprehensive and relatively up-to-date for most other regions. At present, it contains Greek names of nearly 400,000 persons between the late eighth century BCE and 600

CE and attests almost 40,000 different names. The *Trismegistos Name* database (TM Nam) accounts for the onomastic evidence for Egypt. It attests nearly 40,000 name variants from papyri and other sources (i.e., inscriptions, ostraca, *dipiniti*, *graffiti*, etc.) between the eighth century BCE and the eighth century CE that appear in Greek, Latin, Coptic, and Demotic.[27] For the Near East, which includes the areas of Judea, Syria, and the Transjordan, at present, the best resource is the two-volume *Lexicon of Jewish Names* (LJN) that documents names appearing principally in Aramaic, Hebrew, Greek, and Latin from these regions between 330 BCE and 600 CE.[28] Notably lacking in the resources outlined thus far is the vast onomastic data only preserved via the Latin inscriptional evidence. While there is nothing in Latin akin to the LGPN, the *Epigraphik-Datenbank Clauss/Slaby* (EDCS) seeks to include all published Latin inscriptions.[29] It attests over 500,000 inscriptions with hundreds of thousands of named persons.[30] While it is more challenging to draw out onomastic data when compared to either the LGPN or TM Nam, searching for an individual name like Eclecte (*vel sim.*) is relatively straightforward. Taking all these resources together, one is provided with a massive set of personal names to survey Greek and Latin onomastics in the ancient Mediterranean world. While they surely don't include every attested name, and the digital databases are in constant need of updating as the onomastic data continues to grow with the publication of new texts, they cumulatively provide the best vantage point to assess the question at hand: Did the name Ἐκλέκτη/Eclecte exist?

Turning first to the onomastic data of Egypt contained in the TM Nam, a search for the female name Ἐκλέκτη (*vel sim.*) reveals that it is presently unattested in any published text. On the other hand, the masculine counterpart Ἔκλεκτος (*vel sim.*) is attested twelve times. All the attestations come from papyri dated to the Roman period (ca. 30 BCE–284 CE).[31] A noteworthy feature of the attestations of the name Ἔκλεκτος is that more than half of the time, it is spelled Ἔγλεκτος instead of Ἔκλεκτος, with an initial gamma instead of a kappa. While some might be tempted to suppose this is a different name, it is a common phonetic interchange (κ > γ) that is widely attested in papyri (and inscriptions).[32] Proceeding to the epigraphic evidence, the masculine name Ἔκλεκτος/Eclectus (*vel sim.*) is attested over fifty times in Greek and Latin inscriptions of the Roman period that geographically span the entire Mediterranean. Based on the occurrences of the name, it was held by slaves, citizens, soldiers, and even a few high-ranking officials.[33] Thus, the masculine counterpart to Ἐκλέκτη/Eclecte appears to have been reasonably well established throughout the ancient Mediterranean world.

In Greek and Latin inscriptions, the female name Ἐκλέκτη/Eclecte is attested eighteen times.[34] One of the earliest attestations of this female name appears in a Latin epitaph from Rome of the mid-first century (ca. 53–62 CE).[35] In it, a woman named Eclecte commemorates the loss of her husband:

> Cypaerus Octavi[ae]
> Aug(usti) f(iliae) disp(ensator) vix(it) an(nos) X[. . .].
> Eclecte sibi et coniugi s[uo]
> fecit piissimo de quo n[i(hi)l]
> uncquam doluit nisi quo[d]
> mortuus est.

---

5. *l.* umquam

> Cypaerus, steward of Octavia (who is) daughter of Augustus, lived for [. . .] years. Eclecte made this (inscription) for herself and for her most devoted spouse, about whom she never had anything to grieve except when he died.

Beyond establishing that the name Eclecte existed, this inscription, even though it is in Latin, also evinces the existence of the Greek name Ἐκλέκτη. As noted earlier, Ἐκλέκτη is directly based on the Greek feminine adjective ἐκλεκτή. In Latin, conversely, the counterpart feminine form of the adjective is *electa* (masc. *electus*). The Latin female name directly based on this Latin adjective is Electa, which is an attested female name in Latin.[36] But here, we do not have Electa but rather Eclecte, which shows that it is based on the Greek form. Thus, Eclecte is actually evidence, even if it is somewhat indirect, for the Greek female name Ἐκλέκτη.

Additional Latin inscriptions contain Eclecte or a variant form like Eglecte or Eclecta. In the former case, we have a simple c-to-g shift already noted in Greek (κ > γ); in the latter case, a terminal vowel shift to a proper Latin termination. In total, there are sixteen known Latin inscriptions attesting the name Eclecte from the Roman period. These geographically come from Spain, Britain, and Italy. For the sake of brevity and convenience, all have been included in the table below and have been arranged in chronological order.

EDCS 64900989[37] Narnia (Italy) Date: 41–100 CE	Di{i}s Manibus | Ti(beri) Claudi Privati Primigeni | Aug(usti) lib(erti), vixit annos XXXX, | Claudia Eglecte | coniunx piissima. "To the spirits of the departed (and) to Tiberius Claudius Privatus, first-born, freedman of Augustus, he lived for 40 years; Claudia Eclecte most devoted spouse (set up this inscription)."
EDCS 16100009 CIL 6.14959 (=CIL 3.23923) Rome Date: mid I CE	Ti(berio) Claudio Karo vix(it) ⟨a⟩n(nos) VIII mens(es) XII dies XI | Dis Manib(us) | Claudiae | Eglecte | Antoniae divi | Claudi f(iliae) delicio | piissimae et b(ene) m(erenti) | v(ixit) a(nnos) VI m(ensem) I d(ies) VIIII | Threptus Ecloge | parentes fec(erunt).[38] "To Tiberius Claudius Karo who lived 8 years, 12 months, and 11 days (and) to the spirits of the departed (and) to Claudia Eclecte Antonia, beloved daughter of the divine Claudius, most dutiful and well-deserving, who lived 6 years, 1 month, and 9 days; Threptus (and) Ecloge, the parents, made this (inscription)."
EDCS 12600483 CIL 6.21421 Rome Date: I CE	Livia Eglecte | fecit | M(arco) Iulio Amerimno | filio suo v(ixit) a(nnos) XV. "Livia Eclecte made this (inscription) for Marcus Julius Amerimnus, her son, who lived 15 years."

(*Continued*)

EDCS 09600270 CIL 6.15396 (1) Rome Date: c. 51–150 CE	Dis Manibus | Claudia [Ea]rine | vixit annis XXXII | mensibus III | Claudia Eglecte | filia pientissima et | Onesimus Prime | Caesaris | coniugi bene merenti. "To the spirits of the departed; Claudia Earine lived for 32 years and 3 months. Claudia Eclecte, most devoted daughter, (set up this inscription) and Onesimus Prime, (a servant) of Caesar, (also set up this inscription) to his well-deserving wife."
EDCS 07800986 CIL 7.254 Eboracum (Britain) Date: late I / early II CE	D(is) M(anibus) | Eglectae an(norum) | XXX h(ic) s(itae) sec(us) | Crescentem | f(ilium) an(norum) III Anto(nius) | St{h}ep(h)an(us) coniugi | f(aciendum) c(uravit). "To the spirits of the departed (and) to Eclecte, aged 30, here buried beside her son Crescens, aged 3; Antonius Stephanus arranged for this to be made for his wife."
EDCS 08700928 CIL 2.5044 Teba (Spain) Date: ca. 131–70 CE	Eglecte | ann(orum) XXV | h(ic) s(ita) e(st) s(it) t(ibi) t(erra) l(evis). "Eglecte, aged 25, is buried here. May the earth lie lightly upon you."
EDCS 12101113 CIL 6.19205 Rome Date: II CE	Dis Manibus | Helio | Munatia Eclecte | coniugi suo | bene merenti | posuit | cum quo | vixit annis XXIII | sine iniuria | et sibi. "To the spirits of the departed (and) to Helius; Munatia Eclecte set up this (inscription) for herself and for her husband who was well deserving, with whom she lived for 23 years without harm."
EDCS 52603065 CIL 6.39629 Rome Date: II CE	Proentae (*l.* Proeniae) C(ai) f(iliae) | Proculae | Doryphorus et | Baburia Eglecte | parentes. "For Proenia Procula, daughter of Gaius; Doryphorus and Baburia Eclecte her parents (set up this inscription)."[39]

EDCS 13800527 CIL 6.24281 Rome Date: II CE	D(is) M(anibus) | Plautiae Eglecte | filiae | M(arcus) Plautius | Eglectus. "To the spirits of the departed (and) to Plautia Eclecte; Marcus Plautius Eclectus (set up this inscription) for (his) daughter."
EDCS 14200530 CIL 6.26350 Rome Date: II CE	D(is) M(anibus) | P(ublio) Sermulio Felici et | Seiae Eglecteni[40] | P(ublius) Sermulius ⟨H⟩ermes | et P(ublius) Sermulius Bauclas | l(i)b(erti) fecerunt et sibi et | suis libe(rtis) libertabusque | posterisque eorum. "To the Spirits of the departed (and) to Publius Sermulius Felix and Seia Eclecte; Publius Sermulius Hermes and Publius Sermulius Bauclas, freedmen, made this (inscription) for themselves and for their freedmen and freedwomen and for their descendants."
EDCS 06500026 I.Ital. 1 (1) 55 Salernum (Italy) Date: II CE	D(is) M(anibus) Eclectes | vixet ann(os) X. | Fec(it) mater | filiae. "To the spirits of the departed; Eclecte lived for 10 years. Her mother made this (inscription) for her daughter."
EDCS 70900031[41] Nomentum (Italy) Date: II CE	Dis Man(ibus) | Iuliae Hygiae fil(iae) | et Iulio Fortunato | coniugi | Iulia Eglecte bene mer(entibus) | fecit. "To the spirits of the departed (and) to Julia Hygia and Julius Fortunatus; Julia Eclecte made this (inscription) for (her) daughter and for (her) husband who were well deserving."
EDCS 12001594 CIL 6.16695 Rome Date: ca. 171–200 CE	D(is) M(anibus) | Cuspia Eglecte | et Hermes Cuspio | Tychico filio | dulcissimo | vixit annis [. . .] | mensibus [. . .]. "To the spirits of the departed (and) to Cuspius Tychicus; Cuspia Eclecte and Hermes (set up this inscription) for (their) sweetest son. He lived [. . .] years (and) [. . .] months."

(*Continued*)

EDCS 15400404 CIL 6.13606 (1) Rome Date: II/III CE	D(is) M(anibus) | Blasto Eg{g}lecte | contibernali (*l.* contubernali) suo | memoriae fec(it). "To the spirits of the departed (and) to Blastus; Eclecte made this (inscription) for a memorial to her husband."
EDCS 76600124[42] Rome Date: II/III CE	D(is) M(anibus) | [.]utroniae Eglecteni[43] | – – – – – "To the spirits of the departed (and) to . . . Eclecte"

Turning to the Greek epigraphic evidence, this name is likewise attested. To date, two extant Greek inscriptions from the Roman period preserve this name. The first to be discussed is *IGUR* 2.477, which comes from Rome. The inscription contains no date but has been assigned on various internal grounds to the second or perhaps early third century CE.[44] It is a funerary inscription dedicated to a wife and mother by her surviving husband and son. The Greek text is inscribed with regularity and precision, suggesting it was the work of a skilled inscriber. The Latin influence on the inscription can be seen both in the opening formula and in the presentation of the Greek layout that employs midpoints to separate words.[45]

Θεοῖς · Καταχτθο-
νίοις·
ψυχῇ ἀγαθῇ·
Διόδωρος · ἀνὴρ
καὶ · Ἀντιγενίδας
υἱὸς· μνίας χάριν
αἰωνίας
Ἰουλίᾳ · Ἐκλέκτῃ
ἐπόησαν·
ἔζησεν · ἔτη · λ·γ·

6. *l.* μνείας 9. *l.* ἐποίησεν

To the spirits of the departed (and) to a good soul.[46] Diodorus (her) husband and Antigenidas (her) son for an eternal remembrance made this (inscription) for Julia Eclecte. She lived 33 years.

Figure 5.1. IGUR 2.477. Inscription: Epitaph of Julia Eclecte by her husband Diodorus and her son Antigenidas. Roman. 43.5 x 42.5 x 4 cm. MA180. © Musée du Louvre, Dist. RMN-Grand Palais / Daniel Lebée/Carine Deambrosis / Art Resource, NY.

The name of the deceased woman in this inscription is Julia Eclecte (Ἰουλίᾳ Ἐκλέκτῃ). The letter string ΕΚΛΕΚΤῌ can only be read as a proper name and follows the same pattern found in several Latin inscriptions cited above: Claudia Eclecte, Cuspia Eclecte, Livia Eclecte, and Munatia Eclecte.

The second Greek attestation of this name also comes from a burial stele, but it is considerably less ornate and consists of a single word—the name of the deceased etched across two lines of a headstone. The inscription was found in 1952 on the island of Lipara (modern Lipari) and was first published as I.Lipara 391.[47] It is dated to the Roman period (ca. I/II CE). The short text reads: Ἐγλέ|κτης and translates as "(The gravestone) of Eclecte."[48] One with a careful eye will quickly spot that the name in this inscription is not Eclecte but rather Eglecte. As noted previously with the masculine name Ἔκλεκτος attested in the papyri, in a number of instances, the name is rendered Ἔγλεκτος due to a well-attested interchange of kappa and gamma.[49] To give an example of this interchange from a text cited in chapter 3, P.Oxy. 14.1761, a letter of the late second or early third century CE between two women, begins as follows: Κα[λ]λιρώη Σαραπάδι τῇ γυρίᾳ χαίρεν ("Calliroe to the lady Sarapas, greetings"). There are a few misspellings in the text,[50] but the directly relevant one is the spelling γυρίᾳ —as spelled, it is not even a proper Greek word. It is evident, based on the common κ > γ interchange, as well as epistolary parallels that begin in the same way, that γυρίᾳ is simply the misspelling of κυρίᾳ ("lady"). Returning to I.Lipara 391, the spelling Ἐγλέκτη is evincing the name Ἐκλέκτη.

The onomastic statistics for the name Eclecte can be summarized as follows: of the eighteen epigraphic attestations of this name, sixteen are in Latin, and two are in Greek. If one includes Clement's Latin reference, the total is nineteen.[51] All attestations of the name fall within the first three centuries CE, with most of them falling within the first two. As the epigraphic evidence presently stands, it is mainly confined to Italy, with most of the attestations coming from Rome. However, two additional attestations come from outside of Italy: one from Spain and the other from Britain. When the evidence from Clement is brought to bear, the name is also attested from Egypt. Given the geographic distribution of the evidence, it appears that the name was more popular in the West, although any such statement is speculative given the relatively small amount of evidence.[52] Another item worth noting about the name Eclecte is that the evidence does not suggest that it was a strictly servile name (i.e., a name used principally for slaves).[53] In perhaps the earliest attestation of this name from the middle of the first century (CIL 6.8827), the female bearing the name Eclecte was a slave since she is only identified by a single name, which was a typical convention for slaves in Latin inscriptions.[54] Similarly, when the lone name Eclecte appears in CIL 6.13606, it suggests servile status. In CIL 6.14959, the Eclecte who is memorialized in this funerary inscription is a freedwoman. In the remaining Latin inscriptions containing this name and one of the Greek examples, they preserve a double name and establish that the person was a free woman.

Attestations of the Female Name Eclecte				
	Date	Language	Preserved Form	Location
1	ca. 53–62 CE	Latin	Eclecte	Rome
2	ca. 41–100 CE	Latin	Eglecte	Narnia (Italy)
3	mid I CE	Latin	Eglecte	Rome
4	I CE	Latin	Eglecte	Rome
5	ca. 51–150 CE	Latin	Eglecte	Rome
6	late I / early II CE	Latin	Eglectae	Eboracum (Britain)
7	I/II CE	Greek	Ἐγλέκτης	Lipara (Italy)
8	ca. 131–70 CE	Latin	Eglecte	Teba (Spain)
9	II CE	Latin	Eclecte	Rome
10	II CE	Latin	Eglecte	Rome
11	II CE	Latin	Eglecte	Rome
12	II CE	Latin	Eglecteni	Rome
13	II CE	Latin	Eclectes	Salernum (Italy)
14	II CE	Latin	Eglecte	Nomentum (Italy)
15	ca. 171–200 CE	Latin	Eglecte	Rome
16	II / early III CE	Greek	Ἐκλέκτη	Rome
17	II/III CE	Latin	Egglecte	Rome
18	II/III CE	Latin	Eglecteni	Rome
19	II/III CE	Latin	Eclectam	Alexandria (Egypt, from Clement)

While nineteen total attestations of the name Eclecte is a small number, it nonetheless establishes that the name existed in the general period in which 2 John was written. It is not, therefore, a ghostname, as some have implied. Furthermore, lest anyone attempt to discount this reading in 2 John 1 because of the relative infrequency of the name, the question I would ask in return is this: Can women in the New Testament only have names well attested in ancient sources? Here, it is worth contextualizing the onomastic evidence for the name Ἐκλέκτη/Eclecte in light of other women who appear in the New Testament. By my count, there are thirty-seven named women (excluding Eclecte) in the New Testament, attesting thirty-three different names.[55] In this number, I exclude the names Eve, Hagar, Rachel, Rahab, Rebekah, Ruth, Sarah, and Tamar since when these names appear, they are referencing an Old Testament figure and are not attesting a name of a contemporary woman in the New Testament.[56] Using the same resources I drew on to find the name Ἐκλέκτη/Eclecte revealed that it is better attested than close to a quarter of the female names in the New Testament.

The statistics (see table on pp. 131–35), which are admittedly provisional and provide an impressionistic portrait of onomastic practice in the ancient Mediterranean based on extant attestations, can nevertheless help to contextualize the evidence for the name Ἐκλέκτη/Eclecte. Based on the onomastic corpora surveyed, the most attested female names in the New Testament are Claudia, Julia, and Mary, by significant margins. In the EDCS database alone, each name has over five hundred attestations. This is not surprising with the names Julia and Claudia since they were common *gentilicia* and appear frequently; by the same token, their masculine counterparts, Julius and Claudius, are also exceptionally well attested. Based on the statistics, the Semitic name Mary has the broadest geographic popularity, with numerous attestations all over the Mediterranean. The rising popularity of this personal name in late antiquity—a feature not displayed in the table below—is almost certainly owed to the spread and growth of Christianity that popularized it.[67]

After these three names, the extant onomastic evidence for other female names appearing in the New Testament drops off precipitously. Statistically, the next most attested name is the Latin Prisca, with over 500 attestations, followed by another drop to Berenike, Anna, Priscilla, Junia, and Tryphaena, whose attestations range in the mid to low 200s. Of the 33 women's names attested in the New Testament, 24, or 73 percent, presently have fewer than

Named Women in the New Testament Listed Alphabetically

	Name	Origin	LGPN (Greek)	TM Nam (Egypt)	LJN (Palestine)	EDCS (Latin)	Total
1.	Ἄννα (Anna or Hannah) Luke 2:36	Semitic	58	78	16[57]	97	**249**
2.	Ἀπφία (Aphia) Philemon 2	Greek	165	0	1	56	**222**
3.	Βερνίκη (Berenice) Acts 25:13, 23, 26:30	Greek	77	127[58]	12	36	**252**
4.	Δάμαρις (Damaris) Acts 17:34	Greek	1	0	0	2	**3**
5. 6.	Δορκάς (Dorcas) / Ταβιθά (Tabitha) Acts 9:36, 39	Greek/ Semitic	37/ 1	0[59]/ 3	2/ 3	48/ 0	**87/** **7**
7.	Δρούσιλλα (Drusilla) Acts 24:24	Latin	2	22	1	10[60]	**35**
8.	Ἐλισάβετ (Elizabeth) Luke 1:5, 7, 13, 24, 36, 40–41, 57	Semitic	0	67	5[61]	0	**62**

(*Continued*)

Named Women in the New Testament Listed Alphabetically							
	Name	**Origin**	**LGPN (Greek)**	**TM Nam (Egypt)**	**LJN (Palestine)**	**EDCS (Latin)**	**Total**
9.	Εὐνίκη (Eunice) 2 Timothy 1:5	Greek	13	1	0	4	**18**
10.	Εὐοδία (Euodia) Philippians 4:2	Greek	50	4	0	98	**152**
11.	Ἡρῳδιάς (Herodias) Matthew 14:3, 6; Mark 6:17, 19, 22; Luke 3:19	Greek	1	0	3	1	**5**
12.	Ἰεζάβελ (Jezebel) Revelation 2:20	Semitic	0	0	0	0	**0**[62]
13.	Ἰουλία (Julia) Romans 16:15	Latin	216	153	6	500+	**875+**
14.	Ἰουνία (Junia) Romans 16:7	Latin	9	1	0	217	**227**
15.	Ἰωάννα (Joanna) Luke 8:3, 24:10	Semitic	6	41	15	12	**74**
16.	Κλαυδία (Claudia) 2 Timothy 4:21	Latin	52	154	2	500+	**708+**

Named Women in the New Testament Listed Alphabetically

	Name	Origin	LGPN (Greek)	TM Nam (Egypt)	LJN (Palestine)	EDCS (Latin)	Total
17.	*Λύδια* (Lydia) Acts 16:14, 40	Greek	6	0	1[63]	5	**12**
18.	*Λωΐς* (Lois) 2 Timothy 1:5	Greek	0[64]	0[65]	0	0	**0**
19.	*Μάρθα* (Martha) Luke 10:38, 40–41; John 10:1, 5, 19–21, 24, 30, 29, 12:2	Semitic	19	70	31	39	**159**
20.	*Μαρία* (Mary) Matthew 1:16, 18, 20, 2:11, 13:55, 27:56, 27:61, 28:1; Mark 6:3, 15:40, 15:47, 16:1, 9; Luke 1:27, 30, 34, 38–39, 46, 56, 2:5, 16, 19, 34, 8:2, 10:39, 42, 24:10; John 11:1–2, 19–20, 28, 31–32, 45, 12:3, 19:35, 20:1, 11, 16, 18; Acts 1:14, 12:12; Romans 16:6	Semitic	118	373	100	500+	**1,091+**
21.	*Νύμφα*[66] (Nympha) Colossian 4:15	Greek	26	15	0	67	**108**

(*Continued*)

Named Women in the New Testament Listed Alphabetically

	Name	Origin	LGPN (Greek)	TM Nam (Egypt)	LJN (Palestine)	EDCS (Latin)	Total
22.	Περσίς (Persis) Romans 16:12	Persian	13	1	0	9	**23**
23. 24.	Πρίσκα (Prisca) / Πρίσκιλλα (Priscilla) Acts 18:2, 18, 26; Romans 16:3; 1 Corinthians 16:19; 2 Timothy 4:19	Latin/ Latin	14/ 10	8/ 10	0/ 0	500+/ 211	**522+/ 231**
25.	Ῥόδη (Rhode) Acts 12:13	Greek	33	8	1	24	**66**
26.	Σαλώμη (Salome) Mark 15:40, 16:1	Semitic	0	4	84	0	**88**
27.	Σάπφιρα (Sapphira) Acts 5:1	Semitic	0	0	15	0	**15**
28.	Συντύχη (Syntyche) Philippians 4:2	Greek	43	2	0	119	**164**
29.	Συοσάννα (Susanna) Luke 8:3	Semitic	5	57	6	27	**95**

Named Women in the New Testament Listed Alphabetically							
	Name	**Origin**	**LGPN (Greek)**	**TM Nam (Egypt)**	**LJN (Palestine)**	**EDCS (Latin)**	**Total**
30.	Τρύφαινα (Tryphoena) Romans 16:12	Greek	83	44	0	78	**205**
31.	Τρυφῶσα (Tryphosa) Romans 16:12	Greek	64	1	0	62	**127**
32.	Φοίβη (Phoebe) Romans 16:5	Greek	44	1	0	135	**180**
33.	Χλόη (Chloe) 1 Corinthians 1:11	Greek	21	0	0	72	**93**

200 attestations across the onomastic databases surveyed. Euodia, Martha, Nympha, Syntyche, Tryphosa, and Phoebe fall into the range from 100 to 199, which means that 18, or 55 percent, of the women's names in the New Testament presently have fewer than 100 attestations across the surveyed onomastic corpora. Given these statistics, the name Eclecte, with 18 attestations (excluding the reference in Clement), is not unusual or an outlier. It cannot be dismissed from discussion in 2 John 1 based on some argument about the implausibility of a "rare" or "unusual" name appearing in the New Testament.

On the other side of things, on the bottom end of the spectrum are the names Jezebel, Lois, Damaris, Herodias, Lydia, Tabitha, and Sapphira. Jezebel and Lois have only one attestation each in the New Testament and are not attested in any onomastic source surveyed. The lack of other attestations of the female name Jezebel, which only occurs once in the New Testament at Revelation 2:20 (Thyatira), may be because it is an unusual Semitic name of Phoenician origin.[68] Revelation speaks about "Jezebel" as though she were a real woman: "You tolerate that woman Jezebel."[69] The lack of any other attestation of the Greek name Lois (beyond its one attestation in 2 Timothy 1:5) is more curious, and even BDAG notes that the name "is found nowhere else."[70] Since the name Lois is unisex, there are a handful of attestations of the masculine Lois (masc. Λῶις; cf. fem. Λωΐς), but the complete lack of other female attestations is unusual.[71] Along with the two names Jezebel and Lois, the name Damaris also appears only once in the New Testament but is attested only twice (and questionably a third time) in the onomastic sources surveyed. While the LGPN lists one other attestation of the name in Greek, commenting on the inscription in which it allegedly appears, BDAG notes that "the fragmentary state of SEG XI, 669 (IV–III BC) does not permit a reliable restoration in that inscription."[72] The name does, however, appear in two Latin inscriptions.[73] The paucity of attestations of the name Herodias is somewhat surprising given that its masculine counterpart, Herod (Ἡρῴδης and Ἡρωΐδης), has well over one thousand attestations.[74] While Lydia is little attested, it was common enough that both Horace and Martial mention this female name.[75] At its core, it is like the female name Eclecte, which is a simple Greek name; in form, it is no different from its adjective, λύδιος, -α, -ον, which means "of/from Lydia." Tabitha and Sapphira are Semitic names with few attestations outside of texts from Palestine.

The name Eclecte has more attestations in the onomastic sources surveyed than those seven female names that appear in the New Testament. Based on the derived statistics, the name closest to Eclecte in terms of the number of attestations is the female name Eunice. Most of its attestations are in Greek, but a handful are in Latin. With slightly more attestations is the female name Persis, which is an adjectival name like Eclecte (and Lydia above) and is derived from the common adjective περσίς, which means "Persian."

Returning to where this chapter began, George G. Findlay was incorrect when he claimed that the name Eclecte "occurs nowhere else in Greek." This statement is not just factually wrong in the twenty-first century because of the publication of new texts; it was already incorrect in 1909 when Findlay made it. Almost twenty years earlier, in 1890, Georg Kaibel published *Inscriptiones Graecae, XIV. Inscriptiones Siciliae et Italiae, additis Galliae, Hispaniae, Britanniae, Germaniae inscriptionibus.*[76] In this volume, inscription number 1543 contains a published attestation of the Greek female name Ἐκλέκτη (=*IGUR* 2.477 cited above). While Kaibel's 1890 edition of this inscription incorporated it into a specialized epigraphical publication, this was not the *editio princeps*. The piece had undergone previous editions earlier in the nineteenth century and was already known.[77] In fact, the first publication of this inscription occurred in 1650 in Giacomo Manilli's *Villa Borghese fuori di Porta Pinciana*.[78] Thus, the name Ἐκλέκτη has been attested in a published Greek text since the middle of the seventeenth century. On top of this, in 1863 in Wilhelm Pape's and Gustav Eduard Benseler's *Handwörterbuch der griechischen Sprache. 3.1: Wörterbuch der griechischen Eigennamen: A–K*, they include the female name Ἐκλέκτη.[79] Seemingly unaware of the Greek inscription that preserves the name, they deduce that it must have existed because the woman's name, Eclecte (/Eglecte), appears in Latin inscriptions. They then cite Johann Caspar von Orelli's 1828 edition of Latin inscriptions, *Inscriptionum Latinarum Selectarum Amplissima Collectio*, as the source.[80] Modern studies that insist the name lacks onomastic support are uninformed. The name is securely established with eighteen attestations (besides Clement) in the onomastic corpora surveyed and with geographic provenance from Spain, Britain, and Italy. It can no longer be summarily discounted from interpretive discussions of 2 John 1 based solely on onomastics, as it is attested with more frequency than a number of female names that appear in the New Testament.

If Her Name Is Eclecte, Does She Have a Sister with the Same Name?

Now that the name Eclecte is indisputably established, it is time to return to the principal argument marshaled against it. As noted in chapter 2, for the last 150 years, numerous commentators have claimed that if one reads "Eclecte" in 2 John 1, then one is also compelled to take the phrase της εκλεκτης in 2 John 13 as "Eclecte" (i.e., τῆς Ἐκλέκτης). The result is that two "sisters" would bear the same name.[81] The improbability of such a scenario, according to exponents of this argument, makes it untenable. However, the problems with this line of argumentation are manifold. Leaving aside the fact that "sister" could be used figuratively in 2 John 13[82] or that there are examples from antiquity where siblings bore the same name so that the scenario is not impossible on *a priori* grounds,[83] the real problem with this fallacious argument is that it forces an artificial either/or reading: Either both attestations of the letter string εκλεκτη are adjectives, or both are personal names. Furthermore, and most importantly, this argument is based on a misapprehension of the Greek grammar in each verse.

No proponent of this argument has ever pointed out that in the first instance of εκλεκτη (v. 1), it is not accompanied by a definite article, but that in the second instance (v. 13), there is a definite article signaling that something is different between the two.[84] The papyrological parallels marshaled in chapter 3 establish that names do not need a definite article in address, and this is also the case in 3 John 1: ὁ πρεσβύτερος Γαΐῳ ("the elder to Gaius"). This is why there is no definite article before εκλεκτη in v. 1: It is functioning as a proper name. Turning to 2 John 13, της εκλεκτης appears as part of the letter closing, where "greetings" are passed along by a third party via the verb ἀσπάζομαι ("I greet").[85] This is a common epistolary feature that finds parallels in other letters in the New Testament. These parallels reveal that when third parties send greetings, a definite article never accompanies their names. In Romans 16:21–23 (see the table below), where the same greeting structure appears and the names Timothy, Lucius, Jason, Sosipater, Tertius, Gaius, Erastus, and Quartus are used, the names are never introduced with a definite article in the greeting. Furthermore, as the example from Romans shows, it is only modifiers of names that receive the definite article, which further establishes that της εκλεκτης in 2 John 13 cannot be taken as a personal name. It is an adjective modifying τὰ τέκνα τῆς ἀδελφῆς σου that immediately precedes. Taken together, it properly reads "the children of your elect sister" (τὰ τέκνα τῆς ἀδελφῆς σου τῆς ἐκλεκτῆς). When the same greeting formula appears in 1 Corinthians 16:19, and Aquila and Prisca send greetings, their names are not accompanied by the definite article. The same is also the case in Colossians 4:10–12, 14, when Aristarchus, Mark, Jesus, Epaphras, and Luke send their greetings. This example is notable because in the case of Luke, not only does his name not have a definite article, but also the adjective "beloved" (ἀγαπητός) that follows contains a definite article. When a final greeting appears in Philemon 23 and 2 Timothy 4:21, the names are similarly not accompanied by the definite article.

Romans 16:21–23	21 ἀσπάζεται ὑμᾶς Τιμόθεος ὁ συνεργός μου καὶ Λούκιος καὶ Ἰάσων καὶ Σωσίπατρος οἱ συγγενεῖς μου. 22 ἀσπάζομαι ὑμᾶς ἐγὼ Τέρτιος ὁ γράψας τὴν ἐπιστολὴν ἐν κυρίῳ. 23 ἀσπάζεται ὑμᾶς Γάϊος ὁ ξένος μου καὶ ὅλης τῆς ἐκκλησίας. ἀσπάζεται ὑμᾶς Ἔραστος ὁ οἰκονόμος τῆς πόλεως καὶ Κούαρτος ὁ ἀδελφός. "21Timothy, my coworker, greets you; so do Lucius and Jason and Sosipater, my fellow Israelites. 22I Tertius, the writer of this letter, greet you in the Lord. 23Gaius, who is host to me and to the whole church, greets you. Erastus, the city treasurer, and our brother Quartus greet you."
1 Corinthians 16:19	ἀσπάζονται ὑμᾶς αἱ ἐκκλησίαι τῆς Ἀσίας. ἀσπάζεται ὑμᾶς ἐν κυρίῳ πολλὰ Ἀκύλας καὶ Πρίσκα σὺν τῇ κατ᾽ οἶκον αὐτῶν ἐκκλησίᾳ. "The churches of Asia send greetings. Aquila and Prisca, together with the church in their house, greet you warmly in the Lord."

(*Continued*)

Colossians 4:10–12, 14	[10] ἀσπάζεται ὑμᾶς Ἀρίσταρχος ὁ συναιχμάλωτός μου καὶ Μᾶρκος ὁ ἀνεψιὸς Βαρναβᾶ (περὶ οὗ ἐλάβετε ἐντολάς, ἐὰν ἔλθῃ πρὸς ὑμᾶς, δέξασθε αὐτόν) . . . [11] καὶ Ἰησοῦς ὁ λεγόμενος Ἰοῦστος, . . . [12] ἀσπάζεται ὑμᾶς Ἐπαφρᾶς ὁ ἐξ ὑμῶν, δοῦλος Χριστοῦ [Ἰησοῦ], . . . [14] ἀσπάζεται ὑμᾶς Λουκᾶς ὁ ἰατρὸς ὁ ἀγαπητὸς καὶ Δημᾶς. "[10]Aristarchus my fellow prisoner greets you, as does Mark the cousin of Barnabas, concerning whom you have received instructions; if he comes to you, welcome him. . . . [11]And Jesus who is called Justus greets you. . . . [12]Epaphras, who is one of you, a servant of Christ, greets you. . . . [14]Luke, the beloved physician, and Demas greet you."
Philemon 23	ἀσπάζεταί σε Ἐπαφρᾶς ὁ συναιχμάλωτός μου ἐν Χριστῷ Ἰησοῦ. "Epaphras, my fellow prisoner in Christ Jesus, sends greetings to you."
2 Timothy 4:21	ἀσπάζεταί σε Εὔβουλος καὶ Πούδης καὶ Λίνος καὶ Κλαυδία καὶ οἱ ἀδελφοὶ πάντες. "Eubulus sends greetings to you, as do Pudens and Linus and Claudia and all the brothers and sisters."

Turning to the epistolary papyri, there are nearly seven hundred examples where greetings by third parties are sent to the addressee using the same verb of "greeting" that appears in 2 John 13. A few examples that are structurally similar to what occurs in 2 John 13 are provided in the table directly below. They further illustrate that the letter string της εκλεκτης in 2 John 13 can only be taken as an adjective and not as a proper name.

2 John 13 Ἀσπάζεταί σε τὰ τέκνα τῆς ἀδελφῆς σου τῆς ἐκλεκτῆς. ("The children of your elect sister send you their greetings.")	
BGU 2.530.32–33 (I CE)	ἀσπάζεταί σε ἡ ἀδελφή σου Ἑλένη. "Your sister Helene greets you."
CPR 7.54.13–14 (II CE)	ἀσπάζεταί σαι (*l.* σε) πολλὰ ἡ ἀδελφή σου Ἀρσοῦς "Your sister Arsous sends you many greetings."
P.Oxy.Hels. 48.20–21 (II/III CE)	ἀσπάζεταί σε ἡ μήτηρ σου Πλουσία{ς} καὶ ἡ ἀδελφή σου Ἑρμιόνη. "Your mother Plousia greets you and your sister Hermione."
P.Berl.Cohen 15.15–16 (II/III CE)	ἀσ[π]άζεταί σε ἡ [θυ]γάτηρ σου Ἀπλωνοῦς. "Your daughter Apolonous greets you."
P.NYU 2.20.3–4 (II/III CE)	Ἀ΄σπαζεταί σ[ε] Μελίσταnος ὁ υἱὸ[ς] σου καὶ Μυρισμὸς καὶ ἡ μήτηρ σου Ἀφροδεισία. "Melistanos, your son, greets you and Murismos and your mother Aphrodisia."
P.Iand. 6.96v.8–9 (III CE)	καὶ ὁ [υἱ]ός σου Ὡρείων πολλά σε ἀσπάζεται. "And your son Horion sends you many greetings."
P.Köln 3.164.9–10 (III/IV CE)	ἀσπάζεται ὑμᾶς πολλὰ ὁ ἀδελφός μου Ἀπολλώνιος. "My brother Apollonios sends you many greetings."

In these examples, a familial epithet, whether literal or fictive, like "sister" (ἀδελφή), "brother" (ἀδελφός), "mother" (μήτηρ), or "daughter" (θυγάτηρ), is followed by a possessive pronoun, as in 2 John 13, and then the personal name. In not a single case is the name ever accompanied by the definite article in these constructions. The definite article accompanying εκλεκτης in 2 John 13 assures that we are dealing with the adjective and not a proper name. Those who insist that a name must be read in v. 13 if it is read in v. 1 have overlooked the construction of the Greek grammar in the final greeting.[86]

A variation of this argument is that the letter string εκλεκτη in 2 John 1 must be an adjective because in 2 John 13, it is an adjective. While proponents of this view at least have the grammar correct for v. 13, they fail to account for the missing article in v. 1. Without rehashing all the details regarding the significance of the missing article before εκλεκτη in v. 1 and how it shows that we are dealing with a proper name, it is curious how proponents of this view are reticent about exactly why the reading in v. 13 has to govern the reading in v. 1. Rudolf Bultmann, for example, asserts this view but never precisely explains why this has to be the case.[87] Similarly, Judith Lieu asserts that "'Your elect sister' in v. 13 prohibits reading 'Electa' as a proper name" in v. 1 but then has nothing to say to substantiate this assertion.[88] While commentators have refused to admit the possibility that in one instance we have a proper name (v. 1) but in the other an adjective (v. 13)—and yet this is the case—what are the immediate implications of this interchange?

It may initially seem awkward and redundant to employ an adjective that is textually undifferentiated from the name of the addressee, but the repetition of εκλεκτη is undoubtedly more than coincidence. Its use in v. 13 is a deliberate echo of v. 1.[89] Here, a pun on the meaning of the proper name emerges that connects the addressee "Eclecte" and her "elect sister."[90] In the next chapter, the potential meaning(s) of "sister" will be explored and whether it is best taken literally or figuratively, but in either case, the familial term is referring to an actual woman in v. 13. While some might question whether the author of 2 John would include a name play in this letter, plays on names are among the most common types of puns in Greek. Simple names, like Eclecte, especially lent themselves to such plays because they were directly based on an adjective or a noun and carried an inherent meaning. Greek literature has examples of plays on names from Homer to the comedic playwrights to Aristotle and beyond.[91] Furthermore, such plays are found in ordinary and mundane writing like tombstones, crudely cut inscriptions, and graffiti, so a simple name play is not evidence of "high literature."[92] While such wordplays often had a comedic effect, in several instances, such plays also signified an affinity, familiarity, and comfortability between the person initiating the play and the recipient.

Turning to the New Testament, two examples of plays on names are already similar to what is occurring in 2 John.[93] The most well-known example appears in Matthew 16:18. In this passage, Jesus informs Peter (Πέτρος), a "simple" Greek name indistinguishable (except for capitalization) from the noun πέτρος ("rock," "stone," "boulder"),[94] that he will build his church on this rock (πέτρα).[95] The pun on Πέτρος and πέτρα is both obvious and meaningful as it is meant to convey the principle that divinely revealed knowledge of Christ's Sonship serves as the "bedrock" of the "church."[96] Another pun revolving around a name occurs in Paul's letter to Philemon. In this letter, Paul entreats Philemon on behalf of a man named Onesimus. Like the female name Eclecte, Onesimus (Ὀνήσιμος) is a simple Greek name based directly on the adjective ὀνήσιμος, -ον, which means "useful, profitable, or beneficial."[97] Slaves often bore the name, and in the letter to Philemon, the likely interpretation is that Onesimus had servile status.[98] Immediately after mentioning Onesimus in v. 10, in v. 11, Paul notes that whereas Onesimus ("useful") was formerly "useless" (ἄχρηστος) to Philemon, he will once again become "useful" (εὔχρηστος). The wordplay between εὔχρηστος and ἄχρηστος is most apparent, but the former also plays with the meaning of the name Onesimus since it carries a comparable meaning.[99]

Simple name puns like those cited in the New Testament can also be found in the epistolary papyri in otherwise routine and mundane letters. While various examples could be given,[100] one comparable example can be found in P.Oxy. 56.3858, a personal letter from the fourth century CE between a man named Barys (Βαρύς) and his friend Diogenes (Διογένης). In this letter, Barys informs Diogenes of his plans to come and visit and then asks for a favor for a friend. Whereas the name of the addressee, Diogenes, is a compound name (theophoric) meaning "born of Zeus," Barys is a simple Greek name like Eclecte that is based directly on the adjective βαρύς, -εῖα, -ύ that means "weighty, heavy, or burdensome."[101] After the opening address, Barys informs Diogenes of his plans to visit but clarifies that he does not want to burden him by doing so. The rare verb Barys chooses when discussing his impending visit is ἐπιβαρέω, which means "to weigh down, make heavy, burden," and has the same root that appears in his name.[102] One can readily see how Barys's name, βαρύς, which means "weighty," is directly related to the verb ἐπιβαρέω, which means "to weigh down." The pun is that Barys ("weighty") does not want to "weigh down" his friend with his visit.[103] The pun on his name is probably best seen as evidence of an affectionate playfulness on the part of Barys that may even include some humorous self-deprecation and is employed to lighten a friendly request.

Returning to 2 John, given the use of the personal name Ἐκλέκτη in v. 1 and the adjective ἐκλεκτῆ in v. 13, the best way to view this play is that the author was signaling that both Eclecte and her "sister" shared a common role. The play, therefore, seeks to accentuate what they had in common by directly linking Eclecte's name with the adjective applied to her "sister." Though the play primarily connects Eclecte and her "sister" by playing off the personal name, at another level, it may be possible for it to reflect back and reciprocally highlight that Eclecte is true to her name (i.e., "elect").[104] Finally, the play should reinforce a familiarity and comfort between the elder and Eclecte so that it is neither awkward nor out of place.[105] While the novelty of this interpretation might be hard for some to accept, this simple play is far more palatable than the grand metaphor previously thought to pervade 2 John.

The Order of Things: Her Name Can't Be Kyria

For over a century, the vast majority of scholarship has accepted the received address in 2 John 1 and interpreted it as a metaphorical personification of a church. Despite this, many of the same studies have conceded that if somehow the address contained a name, the most obvious choice would be Kyria. For example, in Bruce Metzger's textual commentary, he states that the address is best understood "metaphorically of a local congregation" but then grants that the name "Kyria (or, Cyria)" is a possibility.[106] Raymond Brown similarly takes the opening address metaphorically but states that between the options Eclecte and Kyria, the latter reading would be preferred if the address were to contain a personal name.[107] In more recent studies, the same trend can be found.[108] This preference can also be seen in select translations of 2 John. For example, while the *American Standard Version* (ASV; 1901) translates the first part of the address in 2 John 1 as "unto the elect lady," in a note on "lady," it offers the alternate reading "Or, Cyria," taking it as a female name. The same note also appears on the word "lady" in 2 John 5. More recently, *The Living Bible* (TLB; 1971) reads "Cyria," so the letter opens with an address to a woman bearing this name.[109] One also finds that in more recent renderings of the

New Testament, the name Kyria is periodically mentioned as a secondary alternative to "lady."[110]

Aware of this secondary view, BDAG argues against reading Kyria in 2 John 1 (and 5) strictly on onomastic grounds because it claims that as a personal name, it is "rare and late as a proper name."[111] It then cites Friedrich Preisigke's *Namenbuch* published in 1922 and then Hermann W. Beyer's and Hans Lietzmann's *Die jüdische Katakombe der Villa Torlonia in Rom*, published in 1930, to show that the evidence for the name is "late."[112] The *Namenbuch* lists only three attestations of the name in papyri;[113] today, however, there are now 38 attestations of the name and 137 if one counts its variants.[114] In the epigraphic record, while the name appears to have become more common in the third and fourth centuries CE,[115] it is now well attested in the first two centuries. It even has multiple attestations in pre-70 CE Jerusalem.[116] This does not even include the Latin equivalent Cyria that is also attested.[117] Therefore, arguments against reading Kyria (Cyria) based solely on onomastic grounds are hardly compelling. The reasons for rejecting the reading Kyria in 2 John 1 (and subsequently in v. 5) as an interpretive possibility have nothing to do with onomastic considerations; the name is possible if one only considers the onomastic data in isolation. The name can be quickly and definitively dismissed as an interpretive option because the collocation of the address forbids it. In other words, order matters! Returning to 3 John 1, the address follows the customary pattern in the early Roman period evinced in the epistolary papyri where the name of the recipient precedes any modifiers: Γαΐῳ τῷ ἀγαπητῷ ("to Gaius the beloved"). Therefore, if Kyria were to be seriously considered as the name of the addressee, at the very least κυρια would have to appear before εκλεκτη. As the address reads, κυρια is in the wrong position to even be considered as a name.

If this were not enough, the use of κυρια in 2 John 5 also shows that κυρια in 2 John 1 is not a personal name but a modifier that means "lady." As briefly noted in chapter 3, when a recipient is referred to in the body of a letter, it is customary for the sender not to use their name but rather the modifier that appears in the address.[118] For example, the address in W.Chr. 480 (II CE) reads "Apion to Epimachus, his lord and father, very many greetings."[119] When Apion makes a request later in the letter using the same verb that appears in 2 John 5, he does not use his father's name, Epimachus, but defaults to the titles used in the address: "I, therefore, ask you, my lord father."[120] This is also the case in 3 John 5. When the elder makes a polite request to Gaius in this verse, he does not use his name but defaults to the modifier "beloved" (ἀγαπητός), used in the opening address: "To Gaius the beloved . . . Beloved, you do faithfully."[121] This is precisely what is occurring in 2 John. The elder is not calling the addressee of the letter by the name Kyria but is using the modifier κυρία ("lady") employed in the address to entreat the recipient: "Lady . . . and now I ask you, lady."[122] The papyrological examples provided in the table below reinforce this point.

2 John 1, 5 κυρίᾳ . . . καὶ νῦν ἐρωτῶ σε, κυρία. ("Lady . . . and now I ask you, lady.")[123]	
P.Tebt. 2.413.1 (II CE)	Ἀφοδίτη (*l.* Ἀφροδίτη) Ἀρσινοῆτι τῇ κυρίᾳ πολλὰ χαίρειν. . . . μὴ δόξῃς με, κυρί[α,] ἠμεληκέναι σου τῶν ἐντολῶν. "Aphrodite to the lady Arsinoe, many greetings. . . . Do not think, lady, that I am negligent of your commands."
P.Mich. 8.491.1–2, 9 (II CE)	Ἀπολινᾶρις Ταήσι (*l.* Ταήσει) τῇ μητρεὶ (*l.* μητρὶ) καὶ κυρίᾳ πολλὰ χαίρειν. . . . ἐρωτῶ σε οὖν, μήτηρ (*l.* μῆτερ), . . . "Apollinarius to Taesis, his mother and lady, many greetings. . . . I therefore ask you, mother, . . ."
W.Chr. 480.1–2, 11 (II CE)	Ἀπίων Ἐπιμάχῳ τῶι πατρὶ καὶ κυρίῳ πλεῖστα χαίρειν. . . . ἐρωτῶ σε οὖν, κύριέ μου πάτηρ (*l.* πάτερ) "Apion to Epimachos, his father and lord, very many greetings. . . . I, therefore, ask you, my lord father "
PSI 8.943.1–3, 11–12 (II CE)	Μάξιμος Κορβόλονει τῶι (*l.* τῷ) γλυκυτάτῳ ἀδελφῷ πλεῖστα χαίρειν. . . . διὸ οὖν ἐρωτῶ σε, ἄδελφε, . . . "Maximos to Korbulo his sweetest brother, very many greetings. . . . now therefore I ask you brother, . . ."

2 John 1, 5 κυρίᾳ . . . καὶ νῦν ἐρωτῶ σε, κυρία. ("Lady . . . and now I ask you, lady.")[123]	
P.Würzb. 1.21.1–3, 18–19 (II CE)	Ἀντωνία Προ[.]ịῳ τῷ πατρὶ καὶ κυριο (*l.* κυρίῳ) πλεῖστα χαίρειν. . . . ἐρωτῶ σε οὐ (*l.* οὖν), κύριέ μου πάτηρ (*l.* πάτερ) . . . "Antonia to Pro . . . her father and lord, very many greetings. . . . now I ask you my lord father . . ."
SB 22.15378.1–3 (II CE)	Κώνστας Νίγερι τῶι ἀδελφῶι χ(αίρειν). ἐρωτῶ σε ἄδελφε . . . "Constans to Niger her brother, greetings. I ask you brother . . ."

A final issue regarding the name Kyria needs to be discussed. Several commentators who ultimately reject the reading "to the elect Kyria" and favor the received reading "to an elect lady" claim that Athanasius of Alexandria was the first to propose it. For example, while discussing the possibility of the name Kyria in 2 John 1, Raymond Brown points out that it was "proposed by Athanasius."[124] Along the same lines, commentaries by D. E. Hiebert, D. L. Larkin, P. W. Comfort and W. C. Hawley, and W. H. Harris assert in their respective discussions that Athanasius claimed 2 John was addressed to a woman named "Kyria."[125] While they all reject this reading, they also note that the weight of Athanasius at least makes Kyria a reasonable alternative. Additionally, in the most recent edition of the *New English Translation* (NET; 2019) of the Bible, which contains copious notes and commentary, on 2 John 1, the following is reported in the note to this verse: "Others see the letter addressed to a Christian lady named 'Kyria' (first proposed by Athanasius) or to an unnamed Christian lady."[126]

I was stunned when I first encountered this claim—not only because I feared I had somehow overlooked it in my survey of patristic commentary on 2 John 1 but also because I genuinely value what patristic commentators have to say about the reading of a particular passage. The evidence provided by Athanasius, a larger-than-life figure in fourth-century Christianity, is undoubtedly important.[127] Accordingly, I wanted to track down the evidence myself and see precisely what Athanasius had said about the passage and why he thought the letter was addressed to a woman named Kyria. Having read several letters of Athanasius, I was perplexed how he could make such a claim when it was evident that he was aware of epistolary conventions in antiquity. After an extensive search of his corpus, I could not locate the reference anywhere in Greek or Coptic. I then returned to the commentaries where this claim was promulgated to see if they could provide a reference. Not a single commentary provided a citation. By this point, I was beginning to sense that something suspicious was happening, so I began a deep dive to find the source of this potentially significant claim.

This search took me back to the middle of the eighteenth century. As noted in the previous chapter, Johann Albrecht Bengel was highly influential in New Testament studies during that time.[128] Not only did he issue an edition of the Greek New Testament in 1734, but he also produced two influential commentaries on the New Testament that were widely cited for the next 150 years. The first was his *Gnomon Novi Testamenti*, published in 1742, and the second was published posthumously, his *Apparatus Criticus ad Novum Testamentum* in 1763.[129] In his 1734 edition of the Greek New Testament, he renders the opening of 2 John 1, following the *textus receptus*, as ὁ πρεσβύτερος ἐκλεκτῇ κυρίᾳ ("The elder to an elect lady"). But by the time his 1742 commentary appeared, he became convinced that the reading was not ἐκλεκτῇ κυρίᾳ but rather ἐκλεκτῇ Κυρίᾳ. By capitalizing κυρία, he was taking it as the female name Kyria. In the lengthy Latin note appearing on this verse in his *Gnomon*, he states that Athanasius had espoused the reading.[130] Bengel then cites a work, referred to by the title *Synopsis scripturae sacrae*, as the Athanasian source.[131]

In 1600, this work, which preserves a series of *sententiae* on the Bible, was first included by Peter Felckmann (ca. 1565–1603) among the works of Athanasius.[132] But nearly a century later in 1698, when the Benedictine monk Bernard de Montfaucon (1655–1741) published his erudite *Athanasii archiepiacopi Alexandrini opera omnia* (three volumes), he rejected the work outright as belonging to the Athanasian corpus since it was so different from the undisputed works of Athanasius.[133] Montfaucon notes that no ancient source ascribes the work to Athanasius, and no medieval manuscript attributes it to him either. On top of this, he points out that in various places, the *Synopsis scripturae sacrae* contradicts what Athanasius had stated about specific books of scripture in his thirty-ninth Festal Letter. Thus, Montfaucon argues there is no reason to believe Athanasius authored it. Following the lead of Montfaucon, when the work was republished in 1857 in the twenty-eighth volume of the *Patrologiae cursus completus (series Graeca)*, it was placed among the "*dubia*" of Athanasius. When Theodor Zahn carefully studied the text in 1890, he concluded that Athanasius could not have been the author and that the text was unlikely to have been composed any time before the sixth century.[134] Accordingly, the work is no longer included among the "*dubia*" of Athanasius but is securely placed among the "*spuria*."[135]

Athanasius, therefore, never claims that the addressee of 2 John is a woman named Kyria. But if this were not enough, the passage from the *Synopsis scripturae sacrae* that Bengel cites as the source of this reading does not take κυρία as a proper name either! The passage Bengel employs to make this argument is printed as follows in the edition of Felckmann: ταύτην ὡς πρεσβύτερος γράφει κυρίᾳ καὶ τοῖς τέκνοις αὐτῆς.[136] As κυρίᾳ is not capitalized by Felckmann, and in the accompanying Latin translation that parallels the Greek text, it is rendered "*dominae*" ("to a lady"), the Greek passage would translate "as an elder he writes this (letter) to a lady and her children." In the edition by Montfaucon, κυρίᾳ is similarly not capitalized, and in his Latin translation, it is also rendered with "*dominae*."[137] When Bengel reproduces the passage, he does not capitalize κυρίᾳ but insists that it is a proper name, although no arguments from the Greek text are used to buttress this interpretation. As he claims that the Syriac takes it as a proper name, this is likely where he is deriving his forced interpretation of this Greek text.[138]

Despite the false attribution to Athanasius by Bengel in his 1742 *Gnomon Novi Testamenti*, Bengel's posthumous 1763 work reemphasized that κυρία in 2 John 1 and 5 is a "proper name."[139] Given the popularity of his commentaries in subsequent centuries and the fact that the *Gnomon Novi Testamenti* was eventually translated into English and became quite popular in the nineteenth century, this erroneous claim gained wide circulation. This is presumably why it has persisted and even found its way into modern commentaries and study Bibles. After nearly three hundred years, it is finally time to put an end to this specious claim that Athanasius never made.

To conclude, for literally centuries, erroneous statements have circulated around the address in 2 John 1. These range from false claims imputed to Athanasius and flawed assertions about Greek grammar to ill-informed declarations about onomastics. Starting with the personal name Eclecte, despite periodic declarations that there is no evidence for this female name, this chapter has definitively shown this name existed in both Greek and Latin in the period in which 2 John was composed. In a published Greek inscription, the name first appeared in 1650, and by the first half of the nineteenth century, it was relatively well attested in published Latin inscriptions. It is not, therefore, a ghostname and is more widely attested than a number of female names appearing in the New Testament. As for the female name Kyria, those who have claimed that if the address in 2 John 1 were to contain a name, then Kyria would be the most likely candidate are misinformed. The form of address appearing in 2 John 1 is of the type "A [to] B," typical in the Roman period and evinced in 3 John 1, where modifiers follow the name of the addressee. For the name Kyria to even be considered as an option, it would have to appear before εκλεκτη. The collocation precludes it. On top of this, since κυρια appears in 2 John 5, it also establishes that it is functioning as a title of address (i.e., "lady"). In the epistolary papyri, when the recipient is referred to in the body of the letter, it is not typically by their name but by the title appearing in the address. This also occurs in 3 John 5 and 11, where Gaius is referred to as "beloved," which is the title of address that appears in 3 John 1. Finally, notwithstanding the repeated assertions of the last 150 years, one is not compelled to read εκλεκτη in the first verse of 2 John in the very same way as the εκλεκτης in the last verse. Purveyors of this reading have not given sufficient attention to the Greek text and have failed to recognize the different grammatical constructions operative in each verse. Now that the final obstacles surrounding the name Eclecte are removed, in the next chapter, 2 John will be read anew with the principal addressee restored—"lady Eclecte."

CHAPTER SIX

Rereading 2 John

The Elder, the Lady, Her Children, and a House

The papyrus letters help us catch a sound from the voice of the common Christian which has been all but lost in the glory of the great letter writers of the golden age.

—Stanley K. Stowers, *Letter Writing in Greco-Roman Antiquity*[1]

IN THIS CHAPTER, I will consider 2 John in a fresh light. How would this document be read if it had come to us via a different set of circumstances devoid of the interpretive layers of the last 1,500 years? Imagine if it were discovered during a recent excavation in Egypt and was coming to light for the first time. It is written on a papyrus (2 John 12); the text is inscribed with dark-brown ink (2 John 12); the script displays characteristics of a Roman-period hand (I/II CE).[2] The first line can be diplomatically transcribed as follows: ΟΠΡΕϹΒΥΤΕΡΟϹΕΚΛΕΚΤΗΚΥΡΙΑ. Since the line begins with an omicron, and the eleventh and twelfth letters are ΟϹ, which often terminate masculine nouns in the nominative case, the reading ὁ πρεσβύτερος ("the elder") becomes apparent. While the type of document is not yet known because the entire text has not been deciphered, a letter becomes a distinct possibility. In the Roman period, letters begin with a nominative construction where the sender appears first. Before moving on to the decipherment of the letter string that follows, an electronic search of this title in previously published papyri reveals that it occurs in various documents. One of these texts, known by the (fictitious) papyrological siglum P.3John (i.e., 3 John), jumps out since it also begins with the same title. It is a letter and dates to the Roman period (I/II CE). Perusing the transcription of that letter and then comparing it against the present document, it is apparent that both are about the same length and have a similar structure. On further investigation, it becomes evident that both texts employ identical phraseology in certain places and in other places near-identical phraseology. Two things become clear: (1) The present papyrus preserves a letter and (2) both letters are sent by the same person, who self-identifies with the title "the elder."[3]

In P.3John, the address following the title reads "to Gaius the beloved" (Γαΐῳ τῷ ἀγαπητῷ). This kind of address is typical of a Roman-period letter: The recipient's name appears immediately after the sender, without a definite article and in the dative case, and is frequently followed by a modifier accompanied by a definite article. Returning to the remainder of the first line of the unpublished papyrus, the letter string ΕΚΛΕΚΤΗΚΥΡΙΑ needs resolution. The string ΕΚΛΕΚΤΗ can be rendered Ἐκλέκτῃ ("Eclecte") since a name is expected, and this female name is attested in onomastic lexica.[4] While it would be the first attestation of this name in a Greek papyrus, previously unattested names regularly appear in papyri, and the name is otherwise attested in both Greek and Latin inscriptions. Furthermore, the male counterpart, Eclectus (Ἔκλεκτος), is attested multiple times in papyri of the first two centuries.[5] The ΚΥΡΙ̣Α that follows is initially a little more difficult to resolve; when this title appears in epistolary address, it is always a substantive and is properly rendered τῇ κυρίᾳ. Since the preceding name terminates with -τη, the correct resolution becomes obvious: Ἐκλέκτῃ <τῇ> κυρίᾳ. The accidental omission of an article is a well-attested phenomenon in Greek papyri, and the same grammatical error is attested elsewhere in epistolary addresses.[6] Additionally, the address is rendered grammatically correct in P.3John (Γαΐῳ τῷ ἀγαπητῷ), so the restoration is entirely secure and the meaning clear: "to the lady Eclecte."

Momentarily stepping away from this imagined scenario, I am not arguing that in the autograph copy of 2 John, the elder dropped the article τῇ in the address due to haplography or some grammatical oversight. It is most probable that in the transmission history of 2 John, the article got dropped in some manuscripts since minor variants caused by omission are the more common.[7] Here, the point I wish to make is that even if this "recently discovered papyrus" were to contain the reading ΕΚΛΕΚΤΗΚΥΡΙΑ, it would readily and rightly be restored Ἐκλέκτῃ <τῇ> κυρίᾳ in every modern edition of the letter. This would be done today because thousands of parallels for this form of address have come to light, the loss of an article following a word terminating with the same two letters is well attested in papyri (and inscriptions), the other letter by the elder contains the usual pattern of address that includes the article (Γαΐῳ τῷ ἀγαπητῷ), and the shorter articulated reading ἐκλεκτῇ κυρίᾳ has grammatical problems.[8] On this last point, due to all the interpretive layers that have accrued on 2 John 1, contemporary scholarship has grown oblivious to its inherent problems and most obvious resolution. The result is that this unusual and unparalleled form of address is most often resolved via a metaphorical reading.

Returning to the imagined scenario, if 2 John were discovered under the circumstances just outlined and formed part of a dossier of two letters and, despite the grammatical problems of ἐκλεκτῇ κυρίᾳ, an editor were to insist on this reading, none would then make the leap that the "elect lady" is best understood as a metaphorical personification for a "church." If such an argument were to be made, the swift response would be that in the other letter (i.e., 3 John), when the (same) elder wants to refer to a church, he uses the word ἐκκλησία (3 John 6, 9, 10). Given that both letters are written by the same author and have several shared features, why are secrecy and metaphor in one letter but transparency and directness in the other?

Moving on from this imagined scenario, but keeping its perspective in mind, this chapter will read 2 John anew. It will consider how parts of the letter properly read now that the original address to a named woman has been restored: Ἐκλέκτῃ τῇ κυρίᾳ ("to the lady Eclecte"). Treating the letter as though it were a recently discovered papyrus that forms a dossier with 3 John, this chapter will provide a kind of "edition" of 2 John that overlaps with what one would find in a papyrological treatment. Therefore, the chapter's aim is not to present a new commentary on 2 John. There is no shortage of commentaries on the letter. While most of them are colored in how they approach the letter by immediately defaulting to an overarching metaphor because of the received address that is no longer tenable (i.e., ἐκλεκτῇ κυρίᾳ), many still provide useful insights on several fronts. This chapter, therefore, will focus on those elements in 2 John that are most directly impacted by the restoration of the original form of the address and the fact that the letter represents a genuine example of personal correspondence.

The Elder

When the proper address is restored to 2 John 1, the most striking element of the opening of the letter is the identity of the sender. Instead of using a proper name, which is the most common practice in the epistolary papyri, the sender defaults to a title. While the male name Presbyterus (Πρεσβύτερος) is attested, the definite article (ὁ) indicates that we are dealing with a title and not a personal name.[9] Ancient Christians and modern commentators have devoted considerable attention to the identity of the enigmatic "elder." Is it John the apostle? A mysterious figure known as "John the elder," who is first mentioned in a fragment of Papias of Hierapolis (ca. 60–130 CE)?[10] Or someone else altogether? This investigation is not going to enter the debate on whom he might or might not have been. It will instead focus on the title "elder" and what it means that the sender of a letter would default to a title instead of a personal name.[11]

The title ὁ πρεσβύτερος is a substantive that is based on the masculine comparative adjective πρεσβύτερος, which comes from the adjective πρέσβυς.[12] The principal meaning of the adjective has to do with age and denotes "elderly" (as opposed to "younger") so that it literally means "the older man" or "the elderly man."[13] This connotation of the title is evinced in the Latin Vulgate of 2 John 1 (and 3 John 1), where instead of using *presbyter*, which would be a direct Greek carryover into Latin, the rendering is *senior*.[14] While it is unknown what exactly constituted an "elderly man," Philo of Alexandria (ca. d. 50 CE) cites the famous Greek physician Hippocrates (ca. 460–370 BCE), who notes that in the "seven ages" of a man's lifespan, "the elderly man" (πρεσβύτης) ranged from 50 to 56 years old.[15] Other ancient schema, like the one subscribed to by Irenaeus of Lyon (ca. 130–200 CE), differentiated five stages of life, where the fifth and final stage consisted of the "elderly" (*senior*) one.[16]

Despite the title's explicit association with age—whether or not it designates a specific bracket—it developed a sense apart from age, where it could denote one who possessed authority or held a position of leadership. It could, therefore, be used as a general title for a "leader."[17] For example, officials within the priesthood of certain Greek cults were designated by the title, and certain civil magistrates also held this title irrespective of "elderly" age.[18] Similarly, local officials who helped oversee various agricultural issues and acted as intermediaries between local villagers and administrators were designated "elders of the village."[19]

When πρεσβύτερος first appears in Genesis 18:11, its meaning is "elderly," and in most subsequent usages in the LXX, it carries the same meaning.[20] Nevertheless, it is clear from context that on occasion it also designates one who holds a leadership position or possesses some authority, whether by virtue of age or some other criterion (social status, financial status, education, etc.).[21] The Gospels almost exclusively refer to "the elders" as a group alongside the "chief priests" (ἀρχιερεῖς) and "scribes" (γραμματεῖς), who wield a collective authority.[22] In Acts, it frequently carries the same meaning,[23] but at 11:30, it is first used for "elders" of the church, and then at 14:23, it is noted that Paul and Barnabas "appointed elders . . . in each church."[24] It is also used alongside the title "apostles" (ἀπόστολοι) in various references, including a letter, embedded in Acts 15:23–29, that is sent by "the apostles" and "the elders."[25] The title is then principally used in the Pastorals and Revelation,[26] along with a handful of usages in Hebrews, James, and 1 Peter.[27] Looking at early Christian literature, "the elders" are periodically described as a link connecting the apostles with the next generation of Christians.[28] Along these lines, Irenaeus of Lyon calls certain "elders" of the church the "disciples of the Apostles."[29] Given that the context behind 2 John is largely unknown, it is not possible from the available evidence to infer how exactly the title is being used and what precise ecclesiastical overtones it may or may not carry.[30]

The author of 2 John (and 3 John) might self-describe as "the elder" due to his age, and in 2 John 4 (cf. 3 John 4), he writes with approval about "children" and adopts a paternal tone, but he never directly invokes age to exert authority. When he makes requests or gives imperatives, they come from authority he seemingly knows his letter's recipients will recognize and a common tradition he believes he shares with Eclecte and the others addressed in the letter. This leaves one with the impression that in 2 John 1, the title "elder" has more to do with his recognized authority, so that it conveys the principal meaning of "leader" as opposed to "elderly man."[31] In the elder's capacity, he feels he has the authority to judge those who are "walking in the truth" per the commandments (v. 4); he can emphasize a "commandment" that was "had from the beginning" (v. 5); he can give exhortation to keep a commandment (v. 6); he can weigh in on a Christological dispute and identify the parties who are in error (vv. 7–9); he can issue directives about how to engage with those who are in error (vv. 9–11); he can expect to be received by the recipients when he comes and to be able to provide further directives and explanation (v. 12); and he can communicate greetings from other parties who are known to the recipients (v. 13).

Turning to the papyri, there are various instances where the sender's self-identity includes the use of titulature in correspondence. This is typically done to highlight their capacity and to frame the communication by reference to their position of authority. In official correspondence, it is common for the sender to include their title, and this is customary for officials of all ranks—from the village scribe up to the prefect of Egypt. But there is a notable difference between how the sender regularly employs titulature in official correspondence and how it appears in 2 John 1. In the former, the custom is for the sender to identify using their personal name, followed by their title, whereas in 2 John 1, only the title appears, devoid of any other identifier. While both share the use of titulature, there is a key difference.

In the papyri, the only official correspondence where the name of the sender is routinely absent, but their title appears at the opening, is in so-called summonses.[32] In these documents, one official writes to another and petitions the other "to send" (πέμπω or some compound) for a third party.[33] Of the nearly one hundred published summonses that principally range in date from the first century through the third century CE, in the cases where the name of the sender is not present, the typical title to appear is that of the *strategus* (ὁ στρατηγός).[34] SB 18.13172, a summons that dates to the end of the first century, begins as follows: "The *strategus* to the elders and policemen of Kaine."[35] A similar summons from the second century, P.Oxy. 74.5002, begins, "The *strategus* to the policemen and chief of police of the village of Naouis."[36] In Hans-Joachim Drexhage's study of summonses, he notes that whereas the names of the addressed parties are often mentioned and the name of the individual to be summoned is always given, when the *strategus* issued the summons, his name did not regularly appear. He argues that this is because the identity of the *strategus* is known to the lower official(s) he is addressing by virtue of his office.[37] So, it was not essential to include his name; the title sufficed.

With this in mind, there are a couple of implications for 2 John. The most obvious is that the elder is known to Eclecte without using his personal name. His identity, though hidden from us, is obvious to her simply by the title. A second implication is that the title establishes the authority of the sender from the start and sets the tone for what follows. Summonses in the papyri are short and contain pointed directives and imperatives owing to the authoritative position of the sender. Similarly, in 2 John, the title "the elder" serves to highlight or reinforce the authoritative position of the sender of 2 John in relation to Eclecte and the others. It is, therefore, not surprising that in the letter, exhortations, directives, and imperatives are given in a rather straightforward manner. For the purposes of 2 John, the sender's title is more important than his name.

Commenting on the sender's use of a title instead of a personal name in 2 John (and 3 John), Judith Lieu claims that it "is unparalleled in a private letter."[38] But this is not accurate; like 2 John (and 3 John), private letters exist where the sender only identifies by a title. In the epistolary papyri, there are a handful of such letters, and these provide a comparative framework for 2 John 1. Three of these "nameless" letters open with the sender only identifying with the title "the father" (ὁ πατήρ), but a better rendering that probably captures the essence of the title is "your father." In these letters, where in some cases the internal evidence suggests that the title is used because the sender is the literal "father" of the recipient, the title is employed to highlight the authority of the sender in relation to the recipient and to frame the letter. As in 2 John, the overriding purposes of these letters have to do with the sender issuing explicit directives to the recipient. The presence of the title, instead of a name, serves as a marker of authority that prompts the recipient to carry out the instructions as they have been presented.

In P.Tebt. 3.1.752, a letter from the second century BCE, we read, "The father to Adamas, greetings."[39] While the letter ultimately breaks off due to damage, immediately after the address, it begins with an order to send information without delay so that the sender will not have to personally come and deal with certain matters.[40] The tone of the letter is direct and gives the impression that "the father" wields a position of authority over Adamas, who needs to comply with the instructions. Another letter from around the same time, BGU 6.1296, opens with "The father to Ammonius and all those in his house, greetings."[41] The pattern of address is remarkably similar to 2 John 1—the sender only identifies by a title and then addresses an individual by name, followed by an unnamed collective. In the lines following the address, the sender gives a series of directives and concludes with "the father" informing Ammonius "as for the other matters, I write nothing further to you."[42] Last, PSI 8.968, which dates to the first century BCE, reads, "The father to Hestiaius, greetings and health."[43] Like the previous two letters, it contains instructions that Hestiaius is to carry out.[44]

The title "father" is not the only one to appear at the beginning of a letter that is devoid of a personal name. In BGU 4.1205, a letter from the late first century BCE, a woman only identified as "the mother" sends a letter: "The mother to Asklas, greetings, and may you be healthy continually just as I pray."[45] But since the letter is not extant after the opening address, one cannot say how the title may have framed what followed. In another letter, P.Rein. 2.118 from the third century, the sender only self-identifies as "the daughter" (ἡ θυγάτηρ).[46] After the proem, wherein she prays that her mother be in good health, the body of the letter promptly begins with a request that her mother send linen cloth. She then tells her mother that if she makes any alterations to a tunic, it will be sent along. As she concludes the letter, greetings are then warmly exchanged: "Send greetings to my sisters and their children. My children send you their greetings."[47] Based on the general tone of the letter, which is strikingly familial, the use of "the daughter" is used to connect the sender and recipient and advance the former's purposes. While the title "daughter" does not carry overt authority, it perhaps does serve to remind her mother of the close relationship so that she might promptly fulfill her requests.

Based on these letters, a few additional observations may be applied to 2 John. The title "elder" is employed to remind the recipient of an established relationship that is then exploited as part of a rhetorical strategy to leverage and maximize influence. In the cases where letters only begin with the title "the father," one is left with the impression that the sender defaults to this familial title to establish their authority or to remind the recipient of their authority so that instructions and imperatives are carried out. As 2 John attempts to persuade Eclecte and others to follow a certain course of action and tries to dissuade them from another, the letter can be generally classified as one of exhortation that contains both directives and prohibitions.[48] Therefore, the use of a recognized title becomes clear—it establishes and enhances the authority of the sender from the very beginning. That it was important for a speaker (or letter writer) to clearly establish their authority is noted by the orator Quintilian (ca. 35–100 CE): "The most important aspect of giving advice is the speaker's own authority. Anyone who wants everybody to trust his judgement on what is expedient and honourable must be, and be thought to be, both very wise and very good."[49] Thus, for the sender of 2 John, the title "elder" encapsulates those things that are both "wise" and "good" and advances their objectives with the audience. Finally, just as the intended meaning of the title ὁ πατήρ is "your father," so, too, in 2 John, ὁ πρεσβύτερος might carry the meaning "your elder" to buttress the request. If so, the inclusive use of "us" in 2 John 2, 3, and 5 could be meant to unite Eclecte and the others to the sender since he is "your elder."

The Lady

In 2 John 1, the title "lady" (κυρία) is a substantive that follows and modifies the name Eclecte (Ἐκλέκτη τῇ κυρίᾳ). This usage is consistent with how it appears in the adscript of the epistolary papyri of the first two centuries CE.

All Epistolary Adscripts That Employ the Title κυρία: I–II CE	
P.Oxy. 2.300.1–2 (I CE)	Ἰνδικὴ Θαεισοῦτι τῇ κυρίᾳ χαίρειν. "Indike to the lady Thaisous, greetings."
P.Corn. 49.1 (I CE)	[Διογ]είνης (*l.* [Διογ]ένης) Θερμουθᾶτι [τῇ μ]ητρεὶ (*l.* [μ]ητρὶ) καὶ κυρείᾳ (*l.* κυρίᾳ) χαίρειν. "Diogenes to Thermouthas, his mother and lady, greetings."
O.Claud. 1.138.1–2 (ca. 110 CE)	Μάξιμος Σεραπειάδει τῇ ἀδελφῇ κυρίᾳ πλεῖστα χαίρειν. "Maximus to his lady sister Sarapias, very many greetings."
O.Did. 386.1–2 (early II CE)	Είουλία (*l.* Ἰουλία) Σκνὶψ (*l.* Σκνιπὶ) τῇ μη[τρὶ χαίρειν] καὶ κυρίᾳ. "Julia to Sknips, her mother and lady, greetings."
O.Did. 426.1–2 (early II CE)	Εἰσιδώρα (*l.* Ἰσιδώρα) Θạεισοῦτι (*l.* Θαϊσοῦτι) τῇ κυρίᾳ πλεῖστα χαίρειν. "Isidora to the lady Thaisous, very many greetings."
P.Giss. 77.1 (116–120 CE)	Τεεὺς [Ἀ]λ̣ινῇ τῇ κ̣υρίᾳ χ̣αίρειν. "Teeus to the lady Aline, greetings."
O.Krok. 2.204 (98–117 CE)	[. . . . . .]ạ Σκνείψῃ [τῇ μ]ητρὶ καὶ κυρίᾳ χạίρ(ειν). ". . . . . .a to Sknips, her mother and lady, greetings."

(*Continued*)

All Epistolary Adscripts That Employ the Title *κυρία*: I–II CE	
O.Krok. 2.289.1–2 (98–117 CE)	[Ἰσχυρᾶς Ζωσ]ίμῃ τῇ κυρίᾳ καὶ ἀ[δελφῇ πλεῖστα] χαί(ρειν). "Ischyras to her lady sister Zosime, very many greetings."
O.Krok. 2.291.1–2 (98–117 CE):	Ἰσχυρᾶς Ζωσίμῃ τῇ κυ[ρίᾳ] καὶ ἀδε̣λ̣φῇ χαί(ρειν). "Ischyras to her lady sister Zosime, greetings."
O.Krok. 2.319.1–2 (98–117 CE)	Ἰσχυρᾶς Ζωσίμ[ῃ] τῇ κυρίᾳ χα(ίρειν). "Ischyras to the lady Zosime, greetings."
P.Mert. 2.82.1–2 (II CE)	[Νεί]κ̣ῃ Βερενείκηι τῆι [κυ]ρίᾳ ἀδελφῆι πλεῖστα χαίρειν. "Nike to her lady sister Berenike, very many greetings."
P.Mich.8.465.1–2 (107 CE)	[Ἀπολινάρι]ο̣ς Τασουχαρίωι τῇ κυρίᾳ [μου μητ-] ρ̣ε̣ὶ (*l.* [μητ]ρὶ) πλεῖστα χαίρειν. "[Apollinarius] to Tasoucharion, [my] lady mother, very many greetings."
P.Mich. 8.491.1–2 (II CE)	Ἀπολινᾶρις Ταήσι (*l.* Ταήσει) τῇ μητρεὶ (*l.* μητρὶ) καὶ κυρίᾳ πολλὰ χαίρειν. "Apollinarius to his lady mother Taesis, many greetings."
P.Mich. 15.751.1–2 (II CE)	Σεμπρώνι[ος] Σ̣ατορνίλᾳ τῇ μητρὶ καὶ κ̣υ̣ρίᾳ [πλεῖσ]τα χαίρειν. "Sempronius to his lady mother Satornila, very many greetings."
SB 3.6263.1–2 (II CE)	Σεμπρώνιος Σατουρνίλᾳ τῇ μητρεὶ (*l.* μητρὶ) καὶ κ̣υ̣ρίᾳ πλεῖστα χαίρειν. "Sempronius to his lady mother Satornila, very many greetings."

All Epistolary Adscripts That Employ the Title κυρία: I–II CE	
P.Oxy. 3.528.1–2 (II CE)	Σερῆνος Εἰσιδώρᾳ [τῇ ἀδελ]φῇ καὶ κυρίᾳ πλαῖστ[α] (*l.* πλεῖστα) [χαίρειν]. "Serenus to his lady sister Isidora, very many greetings."
P.Oxy. 12.1481.1 (II CE)	Θεωνᾶς Τεθεῦτι τῆι μητρὶ καὶ κυρίᾳ πλεῖστα χαί(ρειν). "Theonas to his lady mother Tetheus, very many greetings."
P.Wisc. 2.72 (II CE)	Καικίλις Γέμελλος Διδυμάριο (*l.* Διδυμαρίῳ) τῇ ἀδελφῇ καὶ κυρίᾳ πλῖστα (*l.* πλεῖστα) χάριν (*l.* χαίρειν). "Caecilius Gemellus to Didymarion his sister and lady, very many greetings."
P.Tebt. 2.413.1 (II CE)	Ἀφοδίτη (*l.* Ἀφροδίτη) Ἀρσινοῆτι τῇ κυρίᾳ πολλὰ χαίρειν. "Aphrodite to the lady Arsinoe, many greetings."
P.Oxy. 14.1761.1–2 (late II/early III CE)	Κα[λ]λιρώη Σαραπάδι (*l.* Σαραπιάδι) τῇ γυρίᾳ (*l.* κυρίᾳ) χαίρεν (*l.* χαίρειν). "Kalliroe to the lady Sarapas, greetings."
BGU 4.1081.1 (II/III CE)	Δίδυμο[ς] Ἑρμιόνῃ τῇ κυρίᾳ πο[λλ]ὰ χαίρειν. "Didymus to the lady Hermione, many greetings."
P.Oxy. 55.3810.1–2 (II/III CE)	Καλλίας Κυρίλλῃ τῇ κ̣υ̣ρί̣ᾳ χαίρειν. "Kallias to the lady Kyrilla, greetings."
SB 14.12081 (II/III CE)	Φιλέας Κυρίλλῃ τῇ κυρίᾳ πλεῖστα χαίρειν. "Phileas to lady Cyrilla, very many greetings."

While this title only appears in the New Testament at 2 John 1 and 5, it is rather common outside of the New Testament.[50] Epictetus (ca. 50–135 CE) notes that the title "lady" is a common form of address for females fourteen years and older: "Immediately after they are fourteen, women are called 'ladies' (κυρίαι) by men."[51] Turning to the examples in the table above, the title is reasonably well attested in the epistolary papyri of the first two centuries. As an epistolary title of address, it appears on its own or is used alongside the modifiers "sister" (ἀδελφή) or "mother" (μήτηρ).[52] The sense one gets from its use in the epistolary papyri is that it is employed primarily as a courteous, even endearing, title of address. As noted in chapter 3, it functions as the Greek counterpart of the Latin *domina* (cf. masc. *dominus*; Grk. κύριος) that carries the colloquial meaning of "Ms./Mrs." in the early Roman period.[53]

Beyond these general observations about the title κυρία, there may be some additional insights extrapolated from its use in 2 John. In much later usage, Christian authors like John Chrysostom (ca. 347–407 CE) occasionally couple "lady" with the office of "deaconess."[54] In 2 John, there is no indication that it conveys this meaning, but given the larger context of the letter, it might shed light on ecclesial functions Eclecte could have performed. In Plutarch's (ca. 45–120 CE) *Moralia*, he has an essay titled *Roman Questions*, wherein he explores certain traditions, customs, and practices of ancient Rome.[55] As part of this survey, he devotes attention to explaining certain ceremonial practices that took place before, during, and shortly after a traditional Roman wedding. After describing how it was common for the bride to be carried over the threshold into her new matrimonial home, he then remarks that on entrance into the house, it is customary for the bride to utter a formulaic expression of solidarity with the husband.[56] Plutarch then speculates that the intended meaning of the formulaic expression is tantamount to "Wherever you [husband] are lord and master, there am I lady and mistress."[57] For the present discussion, it is noteworthy that Plutarch associates the title "lady" (κυρία) with "mistress" (οἰκοδέσποινα), which literally means "female master of the house."[58]

Focusing on the connection of these two titles, in 2 John 10–11, the elder speaks to Eclecte and her children about a "house" (οἰκία) and issues directives. The most straightforward way of taking the reference is to an actual residence of which Eclecte is a part and was likely its "mistress" (οἰκοδέσποινα). Here, the elder gives specific imperatives about admission to the "house," and they are such that it is assumed Eclecte possesses some degree of authority to act as a gatekeeper. As will be elaborated below, the directives suggest that the house is a locus of early Christian activity. Therefore, with the use of "lady," the elder may have also been subtly signaling Eclecte's authoritative position as the "female master of the house," which could extend to a position of authority among the Christians who were gathering there.

One additional way to consider the title "lady" is to compare it to the title of address used in 3 John. The gendered parallel of "lady" (κυρία) is the masculine "lord" (κύριος) that is widespread in the epistolary papyri of the first couple of centuries CE. But the elder does not use this title for Gaius. In 3 John 1 (2, 5, and 11), Gaius is addressed as "beloved" (ἀγαπητός). Unlike "lady," this adjective is well attested in the New Testament with over sixty occurrences.[59] The adjective is thought to signify a special relationship between the person so designated and the one bestowing the epithet, such that the former is regarded as especially "dear" or "valued" by the latter.[60] As an epistolary title of address, "beloved" appears first in select New Testament letters. Given the evidence, for the first few centuries, it initially appears to have been an exclusively Christian title of epistolary address.

Use of ἀγαπητός as an Epistolary Address in the New Testament	
Romans 1:7	πᾶσιν τοῖς οὖσιν ἐν Ῥώμῃ ἀγαπητοῖς θεοῦ, κλητοῖς ἁγίοις, χάρις ὑμῖν καὶ εἰρήνη ἀπὸ θεοῦ πατρὸς ἡμῶν καὶ κυρίου Ἰησοῦ Χριστοῦ. "To all God's beloved in Rome, who are called to be saints: Grace to you and peace from God our Father and the Lord Jesus Christ."
Philemon 1	Παῦλος δέσμιος Χριστοῦ Ἰησοῦ καὶ Τιμόθεος ὁ ἀδελφὸς Φιλήμονι τῷ ἀγαπητῷ καὶ συνεργῷ ἡμῶν. "Paul, a prisoner of Christ Jesus, and Timothy our brother, To our beloved coworker Philemon."
2 Timothy 1:1–2	1Παῦλος ἀπόστολος Χριστοῦ Ἰησοῦ διὰ θελήματος θεοῦ κατ' ἐπαγγελίαν ζωῆς τῆς ἐν Χριστῷ Ἰησοῦ 2Τιμοθέῳ ἀγαπητῷ τέκνῳ, χάρις, ἔλεος εἰρήνη ἀπὸ θεοῦ πατρὸς καὶ Χριστοῦ Ἰησοῦ τοῦ κυρίου ἡμῶν. "1Paul, an apostle of Christ Jesus by the will of God, for the sake of the promise of life that is in Christ Jesus, 2To Timothy, my beloved child: Grace, mercy, and peace from God the Father and Christ Jesus our Lord."

(*Continued*)

Use of ἀγαπητός as an Epistolary Address in the New Testament	
3 John 1	ὁ πρεσβύτερος Γαΐῳ τῷ ἀγαπητῷ, ὃν ἐγὼ ἀγαπῶ ἐν ἀληθείᾳ. "The elder to the beloved Gaius, whom I love in truth."
Jude 1–3	[1]Ἰούδας Ἰησοῦ Χριστοῦ δοῦλος, ἀδελφὸς δὲ Ἰακώβου, τοῖς ἐν θεῷ πατρὶ ἠγαπημένοις καὶ Ἰησοῦ Χριστῷ τετηρημένοις κλητοῖς· [2]ἔλεος ὑμῖν καὶ εἰρήνη καὶ ἀγάπη πληθυνθείη. [3]Ἀγαπητοί, πᾶσαν σπουδὴν ποιούμενος γράφειν ὑμῖν περὶ τῆς κοινῆς ἡμῶν σωτηρίας. . . "[1]Jude, a servant of Jesus Christ and brother of James, To those who are called, who are beloved in God the Father and kept safe for Jesus Christ: [2]May mercy, peace, and love be yours in abundance. [3]Beloved, while eagerly preparing to write to you about the salvation we share. . ."

Beyond establishing a genuine affection for Gaius, the title could also be employed to create and foster solidarity between both parties.[61] In the epistolary papyri, the adjective "beloved" is not used in an epistolary address until the third century and then, for a time, appears only in Christian letters. A noteworthy feature of the early letters in which this title occurs is that they are all letters of commendation where one or more individuals are recommended to a receiving party.[62] These letters vouch for the character of the recommended individual(s) and ostensibly employ the title "beloved" to create a sense of solidarity between the sender and recipient so that the former's recommendation can be trusted.[63] In total, there are nine such letters, all dated to the third or fourth century CE, and in every single one, the recipient is addressed as "beloved."[64] In light of this evidence, it is noteworthy that in 3 John 1, the title "beloved" is used since this letter also serves as a letter of commendation.[65] While various issues are addressed in the letter, a central purpose is to commend a man named Demetrius to Gaius and to assure the latter of the former's character (3 John 12): "Everyone has testified favorably about Demetrius, and so has the truth itself. We also testify for him, and you know that our testimony is true."[66]

Returning to a comparison of the titles "beloved" and "lady" that are used for Gaius and Eclecte, the former is more intimate than the latter. While this might suggest the elder and Gaius have a closer relationship than the elder and Eclecte, some of the intimate features of 3 John also appear in 2 John. In both letters, the elder expresses "love" (ἀγαπάω) for each of them and likewise hopes that a personal meeting will take place where they can speak "face to face."[67] These features suggest that despite the different titles of address, the respective relationships Eclecte and Gaius had with the elder have much in common.

The feminine parallel to the masculine title ἀγαπητός ("beloved") is ἀγαπητή ("beloved"). But whereas the masculine title of address is attested in the New Testament in certain letters and then reappears in various letters of the third and subsequent centuries, the feminine title of address does not appear in the greeting of any extant letter until the fourth century.[68] The earliest of these is SB 8.9746, which has been dated to the first quarter of the fourth century CE.[69] In this letter, a group of women writes to another woman: "[To] my beloved [lady] sister, (from) [Didyme and] the sisters, greetings in the Lord."[70] In one other letter, P.Neph. 18, which is broadly dated to the fourth century, the opening reads, "To my lord brother Eudaimon and my beloved sister Apia your wife, (from) Taouak, greetings in the Lord."[71] The sender of this second letter is also a woman, so in the two earliest usages of this epistolary address, it is women bestowing the feminine title "beloved" on other women. In the second letter, it is noteworthy that the male recipient is addressed "my lord brother" (κυρίῳ μου ἀδελφῷ) but the female "my beloved sister" (τῇ ἀγαπητῇ ἀδελφῇ μου). This is the inverse of what appears in 2 and 3 John—"lady Eclecte" (Ἐκλέκτῃ τῇ κυρίᾳ) and "beloved Gaius" (Γαΐῳ τῷ ἀγαπητῷ). With this inversion, can we subtly detect a gendered matter of decorum on the part of the elder, where it is more appropriate in epistolary address for members of the opposite sex to be addressed "Mr./Mrs." instead of "beloved"?[72]

Her Children

Up to this point, this work has focused on the restoration and significance of "lady Eclecte" as the principal recipient of 2 John. But the full address in 2 John 1 includes a second group so that it reads "to the lady Eclecte and her children" (Ἐκλέκτῃ τῇ κυρίᾳ καὶ τοῖς τέκνοις αὐτῆς). This raises a natural question: How is the term "children" to be understood? Are they Eclecte's literal children? Or are they her metaphorical children so that the reference is being used figuratively to signify a close (non-biological) relationship between them and Eclecte? If the latter is the case, then by virtue of them being designated "her children," what kind of authority did she possess over them?

In early Christian literature, familial terms like "child" (τέκνον), "son" (υἱός), "daughter" (θυγάτηρ), "sister" (ἀδελφή), "brother" (ἀδελφός), "father" (πατήρ), and "mother" (μήτηρ) could be used literally or fictively. Determining which interpretation is preferred depends on a variety of factors. In the New Testament, there are examples where familial titles are used figuratively.[73] In Matthew 12:50, for example, Jesus encourages such usage, stating that those who do "the will of my Father" are "my brother and sister and mother."[74] On the other hand, there are clear examples from the New Testament and early Christian literature where familial titles are used unambiguously for blood relations—a literal mother, father, brother, or sister.[75] There are yet other examples where familial titles are used but the precise connotation is unclear.[76]

The challenge in 2 John is determining which interpretation is the more likely for "children." As a general rule in papyri, when familial terms appear in official documents (e.g., census records, contracts, wills, petitions, etc.), they are best understood literally.[77] But when they appear in personal letters, it is more difficult to determine whether they are being employed literally or fictively. In Eleanor Dickey's study of the use of literal and extended kinship terminology, she argues that certain "rules" can help dictate how familial terms are best interpreted in personal correspondence.[78] She argues that in the absence of contextual evidence, when familial terms like "brother" and "sister" appear in the address, they can be either literal or fictive. Alternatively, when they are applied to a third party mentioned in the letter, they are more likely to be literal.[79] She also notes that with other familial terminology, the literal meaning is more common. Speaking of the term "child," she states, "It is probably not used with extended meaning before the second century AD, and its extended usage is probably confined to the vocative case."[80] This observation potentially has significant implications for 2 John. If this "rule" holds, it would suggest taking "children" as the literal offspring of Eclecte. In this case, the elder would be writing to a mother and her literal children. On the other hand, Dickey also notes that there are some exceptions and grants that in Christian letters, some of the "rules" are more difficult to apply because of the penchant for extended (i.e., metaphorical) usage of familial language.[81]

In the epistolary papyri of the first three centuries, the familial terms "child/children" (τέκνον/τέκνα) only appear in the adscripts of four letters.

In one of these (P.Athen.Xyla 15r), the letter breaks off immediately after the opening so that it cannot be surmised how it is being used, but in the other three letters, the impression from the contents is that the term is literal so that Dickey's "rule" seems to hold.

Attestations of *τέκνον/τέκνα* in the Epistolary Prescript	
P.Oxy. 38.2860 (II CE)	Ἡρακλάμμων Καλλίστῳ τῶι τιμιωτάτῳ τέκνῳ χαίρειν. "Heraclammon to Callistus his most honored child, greetings."
BGU 1.332 (II/III CE)	Σεραπιὰς τοῖς τέκνοις Πτολεμαίῳ καὶ Ἀπολιναρίᾳ καὶ Πτολεμαίῳ πλεῖστα χαίρειν. "Serapias to her children Ptolemy and Apolinaria and Ptolemy, very many greetings."
P.Oxy. 14.1768 (II/III CE)	Ἡράκλειος Θέωνι καὶ Σαραπιάδι τοῖς γλυκυτάτοις τέκνοις χαίρειν. "Heracleius to Theon and Sarapis his sweetest children, greetings."
P.Athen. Xyla 15r (III CE)	[Στ]έφανος τῇ ἀδελφῇ καὶ [τ]οῖς τέκνοις χαίρειν. "Stephen to his sister and her children, greetings."

If 2 John is written to a mother and her children, it would presuppose a thoroughly familial context where a specific family is being singled out and given a series of instructions. This reading of the letter has not been advanced in any significant way since Heinrich Poggel's monograph in 1896.[82] He argues that the "elect lady" and her children are a Christian family who are close to the elder and he is showing them paternal care since she is a widow and her children are fatherless. To arrive at the whole scenario Poggel envisions, he comes to 2 John with a set of speculative assumptions. Leaving these aside and reading the letter on its own, the term "children" could be taken literally. After all, the primary meaning of the term "children" indicates offspring in the literal sense, and this is the dominant meaning when it appears in the epistolary papyri.

But 3 John also bears on this question since it is also written by the elder and likewise employs the term "children." While Gaius is the sole recipient of the letter, the elder employs the term in 3 John 4. In the preceding verse (v. 3), the elder commends Gaius since "some brothers and sisters" have arrived and informed him that Gaius continues to "walk in the truth."[83] On receipt of this news, the elder states (v. 4), "I have no greater joy than this, to hear that my children are walking in the truth."[84] In vv. 3 and 4, "walking in truth" is in parallel so that it is clear the elder has Gaius in mind and counts him among his "children." The question is whether Gaius is to be understood as a literal or a metaphorical "child" of the elder. The tenor of the letter strongly favors the reading that Gaius is not the literal "child" of the elder but that he is a figurative "child" (i.e., a disciple because he continues to "walk in the truth" prescribed by the elder).[85]

Returning to 2 John, the elder again mentions Eclecte's "children" in 2 John 4: "I was overjoyed to find some of your children walking in the truth."[86] This verse finds a close parallel in 3 John 4, where the elder similarly expresses great joy at the news that his "children are walking in the truth."[87] The reference establishes that Eclecte has multiple "children" and may even suggest many "children," some of whom "the elder" has met and others who are still with her.[88] In 2 John 13, "children" are mentioned a final time. In this verse, "the elder" includes greetings from a third party: "The children of your elect sister send you their greetings."[89] As in v. 1, the question is whether these are literal or figurative "children." But this also raises the attendant question of whether the familial term "sister" that appears in the same verse is to be taken literally or metaphorically—a literal sister of Eclecte or a figurative sister (i.e., "sister" in the faith).

This is the only time in either 2 or 3 John that the term "sister" is employed. In 3 John, the term "brothers" (ἀδελφοί) appears in 3 John 3, 5, and 10 (although the NRSVue renders it inclusively "brothers and sisters"). In 3 John 3 (discussed above), "brothers (and sisters)" arrive and bear witness to the elder that Gaius is "walking in the truth." In 3 John 5, the elder then exhorts Gaius, "You do faithfully whatever you do for the brothers (and sisters), even though they are strangers to you."[90] In the final reference at 3 John 10, the elder reports that a man named Diotrephes (mentioned in v. 9) refuses "to welcome brothers and sisters" and even prevents others from doing so.[91] The elder writes as though he and Gaius have "brothers (and sisters)" in common, and yet he regards Gaius among his "children." In v. 5, he tells Gaius to receive "the brothers (and sisters) . . . even though they are strangers to you." These references make it certain that in 3 John the elder is using the term "brothers" metaphorically.[92]

The internal evidence provided by 3 John decidedly favors taking the familial terms "children" and "brothers" fictively. Assuming the elder is consistent with this usage across letters, which appears reasonable based on the content of 2 John and the general similarities it shares with 3 John, then the best reading is that the terms "children" and "sister" are also functioning figuratively in 2 John. If this is the case, the most natural conclusion is that just as the elder occupies a position of authority where he can refer to members of the community as "children," then he perceives that Eclecte exercises a domain of authority within that same community, where she, too, has figurative "children." Along similar lines, if "sister" is taken fictively in 2 John 13, in keeping with the metaphorical usage of "brothers" in 3 John, then Eclecte has a female counterpart—punningly deemed "elect" since she functions in a similar capacity as Eclecte and has figurative "children" of her own.[93] The implication from 2 John would be that two women are prominent within the ecclesial network of the elder and wield authority with their respective "children." In the case of Eclecte, it is evident from 2 John that the elder implicitly trusts her to appropriately influence her "children."

A House

2 John 5–11 forms the body of the letter. This section opens with a request that Eclecte and her children "love one another" and is followed with a clarification that "love" is to "walk according to his [Father's] commandments."[94] In 2 John 7–11, the elder proceeds by warning about people "who do not confess that Jesus Christ has come in the flesh" and insists that such people are "the deceiver and the antichrist."[95] Considerable attention has been given to the theological profile of these people, with a wide range of characterizations being offered. They have been identified with teachers who carry a docetic or gnostic message, Jewish Christians who reject essential Christological tenets, and Judaizers who have forsaken the Gospel covenant and have returned to the synagogue.[96] There is no need to rehash and reconsider each possibility here. For the scope of the present investigation, the most important element of this section is what follows

in 2 John 9–11: "[9]Everyone who does not abide in the teaching of Christ, but goes beyond it, does not have God; whoever abides in the teaching has both the Father and the Son. [10]If anyone comes to you and does not bring this teaching, do not receive and welcome this person into your house, [11]for to welcome is to participate in the evil deeds of such a person."[97] The elder begins this section with an elaboration of the people described in 2 John 7 and adds that they do not "abide in the teaching of Christ" and "go beyond" it.[98] He then gives a warning in 2 John 10 not to "welcome" any such person if one "comes to you." While it is not an inevitability such a person will come, the elder anticipates it is a distinct possibility. If a meeting were to take place, under what circumstance(s) could such a person encounter Eclecte and her children?

This question is typically addressed by equating such people with itinerant teachers or prophets, who, in the course of their evangelizing, might encounter the disciples of the elder.[99] The backdrop that informs this reconstruction is the larger phenomenon of wandering preachers in early Christianity who evangelize and temporarily attach themselves to a community.[100] Despite the framing of such persons as itinerants, this characterization is more assumed than proven; 2 John is not explicit on this point. Therefore, instead of defaulting to this rather nebulous characterization, this examination will proceed from the perspective of the elder himself and address two related questions that seek to elucidate the elder's imperatives about those people who should not be welcomed: (1) How might he know about them and (2) why would he anticipate contact? These questions are all the more important now that lady Eclecte has been restored to the letter. If the elder expects them to come in contact, did they know about her previously, and if so, how? Admittedly, attempts to broach these questions involve some speculation, but by focusing on these two questions, we remain within the epistolary domain of the letter, its sender, and its principal recipient.

From 2 John (as well as 3 John), it is hard to gauge the extent of the ecclesial network of the elder. In the letter, three loci emerge. One is that of the elder, who is physically removed from Eclecte and her children. Historically, some studies have assumed the locus of the elder was Ephesus or somewhere else in Asia Minor, but there is nothing within the letter that suggests where he was located when he wrote it. From 2 John, it is only evident that wherever the elder may have been at the time of writing, he can personally visit Eclecte and her children and might even encounter her children.[101] The same can be said of 3 John: Persons in close proximity to Gaius can go and meet the elder.[102] Likewise, it is assumed that a man named Demetrius, who is in the presence of the elder at the time he is writing 3 John, can go and meet Gaius.[103] Furthermore, the elder anticipates a personal visit to Gaius, just as he does with Eclecte.[104] While we have no concrete idea about the physical distances separating the elder and Eclecte or the elder and Gaius, the letters give the impression of regular, or at least intermittent, traffic back and forth. If this picture is accurate, we are unlikely to be dealing with persons traversing great distances (e.g., Jerusalem to Ephesus or Corinth to Rome) but are more probably dealing with travel within a region or even a limited part of a region so that it might be more localized. The epistolary evidence from Roman Egypt shows that, in most cases, letters were sent and received within a rather limited geographic scope and were often confined within a nome or a nearby region.[105] While there are cases of long-distance epistolary networks in the papyri, these are the exception and not the norm. Given the movement attested in 2 John, as well as in 3 John, the impression one gets is that the elder does not appear to be separated from Eclecte by a great distance.

The second locus of concern in 2 John pertains to the place where Eclecte and her children were physically situated. As with the elder, the letter gives no indication of their whereabouts. However, it appears to center them around a "house" (οἰκία) that is mentioned in 2 John 10. This is the only time this term appears in either 2 or 3 John.[106] From the immediate context, the best reading of the term "house" is as a physical residence, as opposed to some social unit like a "family" or "household" that can be encompassed by the lexical range of the term.[107] When the elder gives a specific prohibition against welcoming certain persons "into the house," the literal meaning becomes obvious. From the letter, no physical specifics about the residence, its size, or its layout are conveyed.[108] The prohibition that immediately precedes the reference is cast by the elder in the plural. Accordingly, he considers it the collective responsibility of Eclecte and her children to ensure that such visitors are not received and welcomed. But given Eclecte's prominence in the letter—she is the principal addressee and the only person mentioned by name, the elder gives her specific instructions in the singular, and she is individually greeted at the end—the larger context of the letter indicates she holds a position of prominence. From this, it can be assumed that her standing extended to the "house," where she would play a leading role in enforcing the elder's directives. Additionally, while the elder vaguely refers to the "house" without a possessive like "your house" (singular or plural) or "her house," the impression of the letter is that she could be its proprietor.[109]

From the letter, a few unique functions of the "house" emerge from the elder's perspective. In the warning in 2 John 10 about potential visitors, there is an implicit acknowledgment that the "house" has a reputation within his ecclesial network such that persons who have some affiliation, or even knowledge of it, can stop in. It, therefore, appears to have functioned as a known resting stop for those in the network and provided temporary relief to those passing through. Other important activities associated with the house can be inferred from 2 John 12: "Although I have much to write to you, I would rather not use paper and ink; instead, I hope to come to you and talk with you face to face."[110] While the intended visit would afford the elder, and Eclecte and her children, an opportunity to renew relations so that there would be personal elements involved, this is not the stated purpose of the visit. In 2 John 12, the elder begins by informing them that he has much more to write but would prefer to relay the information personally. In keeping with the purpose of 2 John, where a series of instructions and exhortations are issued, the elder's primary purpose in coming is to extend the instructions and exhortations to Eclecte and her children—the "you" in 2 John 12 is not the singular but the plural. The logical venue where these would be communicated is at the "house." This could suggest that it served as a place where teaching and/or preaching occurred and, as such, was a place where disciples within the elder's ecclesial network, and under the more direct purview of Eclecte, could congregate.[111]

The third locus in 2 John is the site of Eclecte's "elect sister" mentioned in the last verse.[112] As discussed above, the best reading of this reference is to a woman, fictively regarded as a "sister" to Eclecte, who likewise has "children" in the figurative sense: "The children of your elect sister send you their greetings."[113] While some commentators have claimed that this greeting is "strange" since there is no salutation from the sister, from which they contend the sister is a metaphorical personification of another church, there is a more natural explanation that accords with the details that emerge from 2 and 3 John.[114] From these two letters, one gets the sense of regular movement: The elder can visit Eclecte or Gaius, "brother (and sisters)" from Gaius can visit the elder, the elder might encounter children of Eclecte, and the elder can send a man named Demetrius to Gaius. In light of this evidence for the movement of multiple persons within the network of the elder, a reasonable inference is that at the time he is writing 2 John, "children" of Eclecte's "elect sister," but not the "sister," are in his company. This is why their greetings, but not the greetings of the "elect sister," are appended at the end of the letter. Studies of final greetings in the papyri have shown that persons who are in the immediate presence of the writer of a letter and who have some connection to the addressed party tend to pass along greetings.[115] Therefore, there is nothing "strange" about this greeting. On the contrary, it seems to conform to the picture that emerges where there is movement between the different loci.[116]

Within this context where movement between the loci appears regular, the prohibition is given to Eclecte and her children to not receive or welcome persons carrying what the elder considers a theological contagion. While such persons could include itinerant teachers who nebulously made their way into the ecclesial network of the elder from elsewhere, a more likely scenario is that they already have a connection to it. The fact that the elder has reasonable knowledge of them, and good reason to suspect they will come into contact with Eclecte, increases the likelihood we are not dealing with a completely foreign or unknown set of itinerant preachers. In Raymond Brown's profiling of these people, he argues that they are secessionists who have rebelled and are going about disrupting the community by spreading a message in contradistinction to the one prescribed by the elder.[117] While every feature of Brown's reconstruction is not compelling, locating such persons from within the ecclesial network of the elder has merit. It best explains how the elder knows about them and why he anticipates these people will come into contact with Eclecte and her children—they are already aware of the so-called nodes in the network, and so they could be expected.[118] In their efforts to spread their counter message, they may have actively evangelized within the network, but it might also be possible that some disseminated their message less directly. It is not inconceivable that some persons who are already attached to the network and had previously used the benefits it afforded might have attempted to share the messages more passively as they trafficked the network on routine travel that is not strictly missional.

Worried about the influence of such people, and the damage they might cause if they are able to infiltrate those who "abide" in the correct teaching, the elder gives Eclecte and her children a double imperative at the end of 2 John 10. The NRSVue renders it, "Do not receive and welcome this person into your house." A more literal reading of the passage is "Do not receive this person into the house and do not say to them, 'greetings.'" By prohibiting "greetings," does the elder mean that Eclecte and her children are not even to say a simple hello to such a person if they encounter them? Or does the prohibition entail something more? To get a better sense of the scope of this imperative, a statement made by Jesus to his apostles about missionary work in Matthew 10:11–13 may be relevant. Jesus counsels, "Whatever town or village you enter, find out who in it is worthy, and stay there until you leave. As you enter the house, greet it. If the house is worthy, let your peace come upon it, but if it is not worthy, let your peace return to you."[119] In Matthew 10, a prerequisite of the apostles entering a "house" (οἰκία) is to "greet it." This implies more than the exchange of a simple hello. A proper greeting between the host and visitor is the initial step whereby the latter gets their foot in the door. Through a greeting, the host is participating in a process that can lead to this outcome; by not participating in this process, the visitor is forced to go elsewhere. It seems, therefore, that the elder's imperative not to "greet" goes well beyond polite niceties. It is a rejection of them and, by extension, in this case, their message. The elder's charge not to "greet" might be in effect saying that Eclecte and her children are not to even recognize that such a person is a fellow disciple, and they are not welcome.

The other imperative in 2 John 10 forbids entrance "into the house." The opening of one's doors to such a person could be understood in a couple of different ways. One interpretation is that the elder is expressly prohibiting Eclecte and her children from extending hospitality to such visitors. Returning to Clement's *Sketches* on 2 John, even though they only occupy two paragraphs, Clement devotes the entirety of the second paragraph to a discussion of 2 John 10.[120] After quoting the verse, he states, "He [the elder] forbids us to greet such and to receive them to our hospitality (*in hospitium*)" before outlining other circumstances where a person should not share company with a heretic. Here the reference to "hospitality" is important, as Clement reads the letter as though this is a natural extension of the "greeting."

In the ancient Mediterranean world, "hospitality," literally translated in Greek as "love of strangers" (φιλοξενία), was extended and governed by various customs.[121] In a day before online reservations and comfortable hotels, where ancient inns and hostels were far and few between and often had notorious reputations, many a traveler had to rely on the hospitality of others for lodging. As noted in the statement from Matthew 10:11–13, Jesus expected that when the apostles went out to preach, they might be able to draw on the hospitality of strangers in opening their homes. Consequently, hospitality played an important role in the growth and spread of Christianity, and there are specific scriptural injunctions encouraging its extension.[122] Beyond opening one's doors and providing the visitor with sustenance and other necessities, hospitality also entails acting as a kind of protector so that the visitor might have some temporary standing in the community as a guest.[123] If the elder has the subject of hospitality in mind with this prohibition, Eclecte could have had a central role to play, as it was often the responsibility of the "lady of the house" to oversee and provide hospitality.[124] Further, by providing hospitality to such a visitor, not only are you establishing, or reestablishing, a personal relationship, but such acts of hospitality also tend to unite and bind larger communities with the exchange and billeting of its members. With this larger context in mind, it is easy to see how the extension of hospitality to a visitor from a heterodox group could trouble the elder, as it would be, in effect, inviting such a person back into the ecclesial network.

The other facet of the elder's charge to not permit one to enter "into the house" may have been because he feared it would have direct implications for the Christian community associated with the "house." By permitting such a person into its confines, the elder feared that they would be given a platform to propagate their teachings. As noted above, 2 John 12 suggests that the "house" could be used as a place of Christian gathering and instruction, so it could afford such a visitor a ready audience. The question this raises is whether the "house" effectively functioned as a "house church" so that by opening its doors to such a person, they were being given access to a congregation.

It is well established that early Christians often congregated in the homes of their members.[125] It was there that they often fellowshipped, worshipped, shared meals, received gospel instruction, and partook of the Eucharist, so that the "house" doubled as a "church." In the New Testament, the Letters of Paul are the principal sources of evidence for early Christian house churches. In his letters, there are four unambiguous references to houses that doubled as a church. One appears in Roman 16, where Paul concludes the letter by sending greetings to several individuals. Beginning in 16:3, he sends a lengthy greeting to "Prisca and Aquila" and concludes it in 16:5 with "greet also the church in their house."[126] The phrase Paul uses here is ἡ κατ' οἶκον ἐκκλησία, which means "the church at the house."[127] In 1 Corinthians 16:19, the "house church" of Prisca and Aquila is mentioned again, seemingly in a different location, using the same phraseology.[128] In Colossians 4:15, the phrase is used once again in a farewell salutation to a woman named Nympha: "Give my greetings to the brothers and sisters in Laodicea and to Nympha and the church in her house."[129] Last, in Philemon 1–2, Paul mentions a church in the home of Philemon and employs the same phraseology.[130]

All these references are important, but one stands out for the present investigation. The reference in Colossians 4:15 is noteworthy for a couple of reasons. First, like lady Eclecte, Nympha has been a modern "addition" of sorts to the New Testament; historically, the name was thought to be the masculine Nymphas, so the reference was taken as a "church in his house."[131] Second, and more importantly for the present purposes, the reference establishes that a church met in the house of a woman. While Nympha is the only woman in the New Testament for whom we have unambiguous evidence that her house doubles as a church, there are other examples where the houses of women are used for gathering, prayer, or as a base from which to evangelize. In Acts 12:12, the "house" (οἰκία) of Mary, the mother of John Mark, is used as a place of gathering and prayer. In Acts 16:14–15, Paul and Silas use the "house" (οἶκος) of the recent convert Lydia as a base from which to preach the Gospel. In 1 Corinthians 1:11, the reference to "Chloe's people" might also refer to a gathering in her home.[132] To these references, Ignatius of Antioch (ca. d. 110–30 CE) concludes his *Letter to the Smyrnaeans* with a greeting to "the house of Gavia," which may indicate a congregation is meeting in her home.[133]

Acts 12:12	συνιδών τε ἦλθεν ἐπὶ τὴν οἰκίαν τῆς Μαρίας τῆς μητρὸς Ἰωάννου τοῦ ἐπικαλουμένου Μάρκου, οὗ ἦσαν ἱκανοὶ συνηθροισμένοι καὶ προσευχόμενοι. "As soon as he [Peter] realized this, he went to the house of Mary, the mother of John whose other name was Mark, where many had gathered and were praying."
Acts 16:14–15	[14]καί τις γυνὴ ὀνόματι Λυδία, πορφυρόπωλις πόλεως Θυατείρων σεβομένη τὸν θεόν, ἤκουεν, ἧς ὁ κύριος διήνοιξεν τὴν καρδίαν προσέχειν τοῖς λαλουμένοις ὑπὸ τοῦ Παύλου. [15]ὡς δὲ ἐβαπτίσθη καὶ ὁ οἶκος αὐτῆς, παρεκάλεσεν λέγουσα· εἰ κεκρίκατέ με πιστὴν τῷ κυρίῳ εἶναι, εἰσελθόντες εἰς τὸν οἶκόν μου μένετε· καὶ παρεβιάσατο ἡμᾶς. "[14]A certain woman named Lydia, a worshipper of God, was listening to us; she was from the city of Thyatira and a dealer in purple cloth. The Lord opened her heart to listen eagerly to what was said by Paul. [15]When she and her household were baptized, she urged us, saying, 'If you have judged me to be faithful to the Lord, come and stay at my home.' And she prevailed upon us."
Colossians 4:15	ἀσπάσασθε τοὺς ἐν Λαοδικείᾳ ἀδελφοὺς καὶ Νύμφαν καὶ τὴν κατ' οἶκον αὐτῆς ἐκκλησίαν. "Give my greetings to the brothers and sisters in Laodicea and to Nympha and the church in her house."

Returning to 2 John, the question is whether the evidence is such that the "house" should be taken as shorthand for "house church." While 2 John 12 suggests it is being used as a congregating place for Christians where instruction could take place, the elder does not explicitly call it a "church." As the elder uses the term three times in 3 John (6, 9–10), he is not averse to it. Is the different terminology due to the fact that the elder considers there to be an important distinction between the "house" in 2 John and the "church" in 3 John? Or does the elder only use the term "house" instead of "church" in 2 John because he is focusing on one particular aspect: Do not receive and welcome certain persons into the physical space (i.e., "house") of the church? From 2 John, it is not clear whether the full range of activities thought to be associated with house churches took place, like regular meetings or services. Therefore, the "house" should not be considered an unambiguous reference to a "house church."[134] Nevertheless, in the elder's judgment, it occupies an important locus in his ecclesial network where lady Eclecte held a position of prominence and authority.

Conclusion

With the restoration of lady Eclecte in the address, the letter known as 2 John takes on a different complexion. It can no longer be treated within the realm of a literary fiction or semi-fiction, where an overarching metaphorical cover blurs the identity of the principal recipient. Rather, 2 John is precisely what it presents itself to be: a genuine personal letter sent between parties, who are physically separated, that addresses contemporary issues. The principal recipient is a named woman who is known to the elder and, based on the content of the letter, holds a prominent place within the Christian community where the letter is sent. She is personally known to the elder, is a trusted confidant, and is regarded as wielding enough influence and authority to help ensure that his directives are carried out. In fact, she appears to occupy a position not unlike Diotrephes in 3 John, who adversely wields his authority against the elder. In addition, this reading establishes that there is yet another prominent Christian woman within the network of the elder who is only known as the "elect sister." Like lady Eclecte, she, too, exercises a position of prominence in a Christian community within the ecclesial purview of the elder and has "children" of her own.

Postscript

The restoration of two reduplicated Greek letters to the address in 2 John 1 makes a monumental difference. When the address is expanded from εκλεκτηκυρια to εκλεκτητηκυρια, and in turn to the articulated Ἐκλέκτῃ τῇ κυρίᾳ, lady Eclecte dramatically reemerges. There is no direct evidence that the omission of the reduplicated τη was purposeful with the intent to expunge Eclecte from the letter. Given my work with ancient documents, principally papyri and inscriptions, the loss of two reduplicated letters is a common accidental omission by way of either haplography or article ellipsis (or both), depending on the circumstances of its occurrence. In a day and age when texts were written and copied out by hand, the accidental skip of two reduplicated letters is easily imagined and well documented. Though a very minor omission, it has had catastrophic consequences. It resulted in the loss of the only woman to whom a letter is addressed in the entire New Testament. Now that lady Eclecte has been restored to the letter, it offers several new avenues of research. This study has only scratched the surface. Hopefully, in the coming years, lady Eclecte will get the full and proper attention she is due. While the obscure address that 2 John was thought to possess has baffled interpreters for well over a century, so that it was presumed to contain a metaphor, when the address is correctly restored to its original form, it is simple, straightforward, and personal.

> For the simplicity on this side of complexity,
> I wouldn't give you a fig. But for the simplicity
> on the other side of complexity, for that I would
> give you anything I have.
>
> —Oliver Wendell Holmes Jr.[135]

Clemens Alexandrinus secundum translationem latinam—Adumbrationes in Epistulas canonicas

Latin text taken from *Clemens Alexandrinus. Dritter Band: Stromata Buch VII und VIII; Excerpta ex Theodoto; Eclogae propheticae; Quis dives salvetur; Fragmente.* Die griechische christliche Schriftsteller der ersten Jahrhunderte 17^{2}. Ed. O. Stählin; Rev. Ed. L. Früchtel and U. Treu. Akademie–Verlag, 1970 (1909), 215.

IV. In Epistola Iohannis Secunda

Secunda Iohannis epistola, quae ad virgines scripta est, simplicissima est. Scripta vero est ad quandam Babyloniam, "Eclectam" nomine, significat autem electionem ecclesiae sanctae. Astruit in hac epistola perfectionem fidei extare caritatem, et ut nemo dividat Iesum Christum sed unum credat Iesum Christum venisse in carne; nam qui habet filium in intellectu perceptibiliter, et patrem quoque cognoscit et magnitudinem virtutis eius sine initio temporis operantem intellegibiliter mente contuetur.

"Si quis venit ad vos," inquit, "et hanc doctrinam non portat, non suscipiatis eum in domum et ave ne dixeritis ei; qui enim dixerit ave, communicat operibus eius malignis." Tales non salutare prohibet et in hospitium suscipere; hoc enim inhumanum est, sed conquirere vel condisputare cum talibus ammonet eos qui non valent intellegibiliter divina tractare, ne per eos traducantur a doctrina veritatis, veri similibus inducti rationibus. Arbitror autem, quia et orare cum talibus non oportet, quoniam in oratione, quae fit in domo, et postquam ad orandum surgitur salutatio est, quae gaudii <est> et pacis indicium.

On the Second Epistle of John

The Second Epistle of John, which is written to virgins, is very straightforward. In fact, it was written to a certain Babylonian woman, by name Eclecte, but signifies the election of the holy church. In this epistle, he [John] establishes that the perfection of faith exists in love and that no one should divide Jesus Christ but believe in one Jesus Christ who has come in the flesh. For the one who apprehends the Son perceptibly in their intellect likewise also knows the Father, and they contemplate intelligibly the greatness of his power working without beginning in time.

It says: "If any come unto you and bring not this doctrine, receive him not into your house, neither bid him 'greetings'; for he that bids him 'greetings' is a partaker of his evil deeds (2 John 11)." He forbids us to greet such and to receive them to our hospitality. For this is not harsh in the case of a person of this sort. But he admonishes them neither to confer nor dispute with such as are not able to handle divine things with intelligence, lest through them they be seduced from the doctrine of truth, influenced by plausible reasons. Now, I think that we are not even to pray with such, because in the prayer which is made at home, after rising from prayer, the salutation of joy is also the token of peace.

NOTES

PREFACE

1. L. H. Blumell, "Petition to a Beneficiarius from Late Third Century A.D. Oxyrhynchus," *ZPE* 165 (2008): 186–90. This papyrus is now known as SB 30.17766.

CHAPTER 1: A MOST UNUSUAL CLAIM IN CLEMENT OF ALEXANDRIA

1. English translation taken from J. W. Halporn, trans. and ed., *Cassiodorus: Institutes of Divine and Secular Learning and On the Soul*, Introduction by M. Vessy, TTH 42 (Liverpool University Press, 2004), 139.
2. The bibliography on Secret Mark is immense, but most recently, see G. S. Smith and B. C. Landau, *The Secret Gospel of Mark: A Controversial Scholar, a Scandalous Gospel of Jesus, and the Fierce Debate over Its Authenticity* (Yale University Press, 2023).
3. O. Stählin, ed., *Clemens Alexandrinus. Band 1. Protrepticus und Paedagogus*, GCS 12 (J. C. Hinrichs, 1905; 2. Auflage 1936; 3. Auflage ed. U. Treu, 1972); O. Stählin, ed., *Clemens Alexandrinus. Band 2. Stromata: Buch I bis VI*, GCS 15 (J. C. Hinrichs, 1906; 2. Auflage 1939; 3. Auflage ed. L. Früchtel, zum Druck besorgt von U. Treu, 1985); O. Stählin, ed., *Clemens Alexandrinus. Band 3. Stromata: Buch VII und VIII. Excerpta ex Theodoto. Eclogae propheticae. Quis dives salvetur. Fragmente*, GCS 17 (J. C. Hinrichs, 1909; 2. Auflage L. Früchtel, zum Druck besorgt von U. Treu, 1970).
4. English titles of Clement's works are given as they appear in *The SBL Handbook of Style Second Edition: For Biblical Studies and Related Disciplines* (Scholars Press, 2014), 148. On these works, see also *CPG* 1375–79.
5. On these fragments, see Stählin, ed., *Clemens Alexandrinus. Band 3*, 195–230; *CPG* 1380–99 includes these and other attributions.
6. Grk. ὑποτυπώσεις; that is, *sketches* or *outlines*.
7. For a recent study of the fragments of Clement's *Hypotyposes*, see J. Plátová, "How Many Fragments of the *Hypotyposes* by Clement of Alexandria Do We Actually Have?" *StPatr* 79 (2017): 71–86.

8. Eusebius, *Hist. eccl.* 6.13.2, 14.1 (SC 41.104, 106): τούτοις εἰσὶν οἱ ἐπιγεγραμμένοι Ὑποτυπώσεων αὐτοῦ λόγοι, ἐν οἷς ὀνομαστὶ ὡς διδασκάλου τοῦ Πανταίνου μνημονεύει ἐκδοχάς τε αὐτοῦ γραφῶν καὶ παραδόσεις ἐκτέθειται· . . . Ἐν δὲ ταῖς Ὑποτυπώσεσιν ξυνελόντα εἰπεῖν πάσης τῆς ἐνδιαθήκου γραφῆς ἐπιτετμημένας πεποίηται διηγήσεις, μηδὲ τὰς ἀντιλεγομένας παρελθών, τὴν Ἰούδα λέγω καὶ τὰς λοιπὰς καθολικὰς ἐπιστολὰς τήν τε Βαρναβᾶ, καὶ τὴν Πέτρου λεγομένην Ἀποκάλυψιν. English translation taken from J. E. L. Oulton, trans., *Eusebius. The Ecclesiastical History*, vol. II, LCL 265 (Harvard University Press, 1932), 43, 47.
9. For the fragments of Clement's work in Eusebius's *Ecclesiastical History*, see Stählin, ed., *Band 3*, 195–202.
10. His full name is Flavius Magnus Aurelius Cassiodorus. His contemporaries referred to him as Senator, as his family belonged to a minor senatorial family, but his posterity and later Christian writers referred to him simply as Cassiodorus.
11. Cassiodorus made a name for himself early in life as a panegyrist and eventually came to work as a spokesman for the Ostrogothic rulers in Ravenna. From approximately 533–40 CE, he served as praetorian prefect of Italy, but when Ostrogothic rule collapsed in the late 530s CE with the Justinianic war of reconquest, Cassiodorus ended up in Constantinople along with other senatorial exiles.
12. In exile, he composed his famous *Commentary on the Psalms* (ca. 548 CE). On this text, see *CPL* 900.
13. Cassiodorus, *Div. Inst.* 1.8.4: In epistulis autem canonicis Clemens Alexandrinus presbyter, qui et Stromatheus vocatur, — id est, in epistula sancti Petri prima, sancti Iohannis prima et secunda, et Iacobi, — quaedam Attico sermone declaravit; ubi multa quidem suptiliter, sed aliqua incaute locutus est. quae nos ita transferri fecimus in Latinum, ut exclusis quibusdam offendiculis purificata doctrina eius securior potuisset auriri. Latin text taken from R. A. B. Mynors, ed., *Cassiodori Senatoris Institutiones* (Clarendon Press, 1937), 29. The English translation is adapted from Halporn, *Cassiodorus: Institutes of Divine and Secular Learning and On the Soul*, 128. On this text, see also *CPL* 906.

    While Cassiodorus mentions a commentary on James, in the Clementine commentaries that have come down to us in the corpus of Cassiodorus, there are only those on 1 Peter, 1 and 2 John, and Jude. It is likely that the mention of "James" was a mistake for "Jude." On this probable error, see J. Lieu, *The Second and Third Epistles of John: History and Background* (T&T Clark, 1986), 19.

    Regarding Cassiodorus's remark that he edited the commentaries of Clement by removing "some of their errors, so that his teaching can be drawn on more safely," he makes a similar remark about the works of Origen (d. ca. 253 CE): *Div. Inst.* 1.1.8. He prefaces the discussion of Origen with the statement that "when he [Origen] writes well, no one writes better; when he writes badly, no one writes worse" (ubi bene, nemo melius: ubi male, nemo peius). Cassiodorus then proceeds to report that "in the works of this same Origen, insofar as I have been able in my search to discover passages which have been spoken contrary to the rules of the Fathers, I have marked them with the sign of repudiation—'rejected'—that he may not have power to deceive a man who ought to be warned of these irregular notions by such a sign. Later writers, however, say that he ought to be avoided completely, since he subtly deceives the innocent; but if, with the Lord's help, caution is employed, his poison can do no harm." (In operibus eiusdem Origenis, quantum transiens invenire praevalui, loca quae contra regulas Patrum dicta sunt achresimi repudiatione signavi, ut decipere non praevaleat qui tali signo in pravis sensibus cavendus esse monstratur. posteriores autem in toto dicunt eum esse fugiendum, propterea quia subtiliter decipit innocentes; sed si adiutorio Domini adhibeatur cautela, nequeunt eius nocere venenosa.) Latin text from Mynors, *Cassiodori Senatoris Institutiones*, 14–15. Translation taken from L. W. Jones, *An Introduction to Divine and Human Readings by Cassiodorus Senator* (Columbia University Press, 1946), 77–78.

It is worth noting here that Photius I (ca. 810/20–93 CE), who was patriarch of Constantinople from circa. 858 to 867 CE and again from 877 to 886 CE, in his voluminous encyclopedic work *Bibliotheca,* includes a brief discussion of *Hypotyposes*, where he, like Cassiodorus, similarly claims that it contained various errors (*Cod*. 109 [89a]): κα 109 [89a]): καὶ ἔν τισι μὲν αὐτῶν ὀρθῶς δοκεῖ λέγειν, ἔν τισι δὲ παντελῶς εἰς ἀσεβεῖς καὶ μυθώδεις λόγους ἐκφέρεται. ὕλην τε γὰρ ἄχρονον καὶ ἰδέας ὡς ἀπό τινων ῥητῶν εἰσαγομένας δοξάζει, καὶ τὸν υἱὸν εἰς κτίσμα κατάγει. ἔτι δὲ μετεμψυχώσεις καὶ πολλοὺς πρὸ τοῦ Ἀδὰμ κόσμους τερατεύεται· καὶ ἐκ τοῦ Ἀδὰμ τὴν Εὔαν, οὐχ ὡς ὁ ἐκκλησιαστικὸς λόγος βούλεται, ἀλλ' αἰσχρῶς τε καὶ ἀθέως ἀποφαίνεται· μίγνυσθαί τε τοὺς ἀγγέλους γυναιξὶ καὶ παιδοποιεῖν ἐξ αὐτῶν ὀνειροπολεῖ, καὶ μὴ σαρκωθῆναι τὸν λόγον ἀλλὰ δόξαι. λόγους τε τοῦ πατρὸς δύο τερατολογῶν ἀπελέγχεται, ὧν τὸν ἥττονα τοῖς ἀνθρώποις ἐπιφανῆναι. ("In some places he [Clement] holds firmly to the correct doctrine; elsewhere he is carried away by strange and impious notions. He asserts the eternity of matter, introduces a theory of ideas from the words of Holy Scripture, and reduces the Son to a mere creature. He relates fabulous stories of transmigration of souls and of many worlds before Adam. Concerning the formation of Eve from Adam he teaches things blasphemous and scurrilous, and anti-scriptural. He imagines that the angels had intercourse with women and begot children of them, also that the Logos did not become man in reality but only in appearance. It even seems that he has a fabulous notion of two *Logoi* of the Father, of which the inferior one appeared to men.") Greek text taken from R. Henry, *Photius. Bibliothèque*, Tome II (Les Belles Lettres, 1960), 80. English translation adapted from J. Quasten, *Patrology. Vol. II: The Ante-Nicene Literature After Irenaeus* (Christian Classics, 1986), 17.

14. Latin title: *Adumbrationes Clementis Alexandrini in Epistolas Canonicas*. On the identification of Cassiodorus's *Adumbrationes* with Clement's *Hypotyposes*, see the recent discussion in D. Dainese, "Cassiodorus' *Adumbrationes*: Do They Belong to Clement's *Hypotyposeis*?" *StPatr* 79

(2017): 87–100. Dainese does not deny that Cassiodorus's *Adumbrationes* were part of Clement's *Hypotyposes*, but argues that the relationship is more nuanced than has been presented in the past and that there were likely different recensions, or editorial versions, of the work.

15. An English translation of these fragments can be found in *ANF* 2.571–77.

16. This is not to diminish Clement's exposition. He is generally a careful reader, cross-references lexically relevant scriptures, and has a clear moral component in his exegesis; but overall, there was nothing especially new or unique that could not be gleaned from his other writings. *Adumbr.* 1 Pet 5:13 (Stählin, ed., *Band 3*, 206). Concerning the story of Peter and Mark based on 1 Pet 5:13, Eusebius, *Hist. eccl.* 2.15.2 (SC 31.70–71), reports the following: "Clement quotes the story in the sixth book of *Hypotyposes*" (Κλήμης ἐν ἕκτῳ τῶν Ὑποτυπώσεων παρατέθειται τὴν ἱστορίαν). Cf. Eusebius, *Hist. eccl.* 6.14.6–7.

The first extant Christian writer to discuss Mark's association with Peter and Mark's writing of his Gospel based on Peter's stories was Papias of Hierapolis (ca. 60–130[?] CE), *Frag.* 4 (from Eusebius, *Hist. eccl.* 3.39.15) and *Test.* 3 (from Eusebius, *Hist. eccl.* 2.15.2). For the fragments and testimonia of Papias, see most recently S. C. Carlson, *Papias of Hierapolis, Exposition of Dominical Oracles: The Fragments, Testimonia, and Reception of a Second-Century Commentator*, OECT (Oxford University Press, 2021), 114–281; cf. M. W. Holmes, *The Apostolic Fathers: Greek Texts and English Translations*, 3rd ed. (Baker Academic, 2007), 732–67.

17. *Adumbr.* Jude 1 (Stählin, ed., *Band 3*, 206): Clement states that Jude was the actual brother of Jesus. At v. 9 he notes that the story of the archangel Michael disputing with the devil over the body of Moses was also found in the *Ascension of Moses* (or the *Assumption of Moses*) that is no longer extant—or at least the extant versions of this text do not contain this story. Origen also notes the *Ascension of Moses* when mentioning Jude 9 at *Princ.* 3.2.1. *Adumbr.* 1 John 1:1–2 (Stählin, ed., *Band 3*, 209–10): Clement makes the point that the Word was eternal and invokes the prologue of the Gospel of John to inform his reading of 1 John 1:1–2. Cf. Photius, *Biblio. Cod.* 109 (89a), above in note 13, where it is claimed that Clement asserted in his *Hypotyposes* that the Son was a creature.

18. 2 John is the second shortest work in the NT, after 3 John. By comparison, 1 Peter and 1 John are significantly longer, and while the Epistle of Jude is relatively short, it is about twice the length of 2 John, which is only 245 words. On this word count, see W. H. Harris, *1, 2, 3 John: Comfort and Counsel for a Church in Crisis. An Exegetical Commentary on the Letters of John*, 2nd ed. (Biblical Studies, 2009), 239.

19. It is worth noting that Clement's focus on v. 10 is typical of the handful of citations from 2 John in early Christian literature in which authors employ the verse to warn Christians against associating with heretics. See the discussion in Lieu, *The Second and Third Epistles of John*, 9.

20. While Clement's rendering of the name in Latin is Eclecta, I have used the Greek Eclecte (Ἐκλέκτη), from which the Latin form is based. For a discussion of the rendering of this name, see pp. 118, 122–23.
21. Clement's full commentary is in appendix 1. The Latin text and an accompanying English translation are provided there.
22. See note 13 above.
23. Grk. παρθένος; Lat. *virgo*.
24. The Greek and Latin (Vulg.) are identical in their employment of the term "virgin" in the New Testament: Matt 1:23; 25:1, 7, 11; Luke 1:27 (x2); Acts 21:9; 1 Cor 7:25, 28, 34, 36–38; 2 Cor 11:2; Rev 14:4.
25. The adjective "Babylonian" (Grk. Βαβυλώνιος, -α, -ον; Lat. Babylonius, -a, -um) does not appear anywhere in the New Testament.
26. The Greek and Latin (Vulg.) are identical in their employment of the term "Babylon" in the New Testament: Matt 1:11–12, 17 (x2); Acts 7:43; 1 Pet 5:13; Rev 14:8; 16:19; 17:5; 18:2, 10, 21.
27. The Latin (Vulg.) text of 1 Pet 5:13 has the same meaning as the Greek: salutat vos quae est in Babylone cumelecta et Marcus filius meus. DRV: "The church that is in Babylon, elected together with you, saluteth you. And so doth my son, Mark." Like the Greek, the Latin also does not contain the word "church" (*ecclesia*), even though translations include it.
28. That is, "church" (ἐκκλησία) or "sister" (ἀδελφή).
29. For the view that 1 Pet 5:13 might refer to a woman, see R. B. Edwards, *The Johannine Epistles* (Sheffield Academic, 1996), 27.
30. Clement's fixation on this verse in his commentary on 1 Peter (*Adumbr.* 1 Pet 5:13) shows he was well acquainted with it.
31. This is the only time this adjective appears in the New Testament. For this term, see BDAG s.v. συνεκλεκτή.
32. I cut off my investigation with the tenth century because as one goes into this century and beyond, one is well outside the domain of early/ancient Christianity and is firmly within the Middle Ages.
33. Origen, per Eusebius (*Hist. eccl.* 6.25.10; SC 41.127), mentions three letters of John but noted that not all regarded "the second and third" as genuine. Later, Dionysius of Alexandria (d. ca. 264/265 CE; Eusebius, *Hist. eccl.* 7.25.10–11; SC 41.206–07) knew of the three epistles and connected them with John the apostle but does not give any wider indication about their canonical status, even though this is part of a discussion about the authorship and status of the Book of Revelation. Eusebius (*Hist. eccl.* 3.24.17 and 25.3; SC 31.133–134) remarks that among the writings of the "New Testament," all accept 1 John, but that 2 and 3 John are among the disputed books; he reports that they may have been written by the Apostle John or by someone else with the same name. Jerome (ca. 347–419 CE), in his short vignette on the Apostle John in his *Lives of Illustrious Men*, writes that 1 John is acknowledged everywhere but that 2 and 3 John were written by a different person known as "John the Presbyter" (*Vir. ill.*

9.4–5 [TUGAL 14.13]; see also 18.3 [TUGAL 14.19]). See also the discussion of Papias of Hierapolis in Eusebius, *Hist. eccl.* 3.39.2–7, 14 (SC 31.154–56).

34. Also known as John the "Beloved," "Evangelist," "Theologian," or "Revelator."
35. For detailed discussions of "the elder," or "the presbyter," and his possible identity, including whether or not he may be identified with the apostle John, see R. E. Brown, *The Epistles of John: A New Translation with Introduction and Commentary, AB 30* (Doubleday, 1982), 646–51 and Lieu, *The Second and Third Epistles of John*, 52–64.
36. The most detailed recent discussion of the canonical status of the Johannine Epistles in the early Church can be found in chapter 1 of Lieu, *The Second and Third Epistles of John*, 5–36. Somewhat dated but still useful is H. Poggel, *Der zweite und dritte Brief des Apostels Johannes geprüft auf ihren kanonischen Charakter* (Druck und Verlag von Ferdinand Schöningh, 1896).
37. The incipit of 2 John 1 also appears in Jerome's *Lives of Illustrious Men* (*Vir. ill.* 9.5 [TUGAL 14.13]), but no commentary is provided. Jerome cites it while discussing the works of John the apostle. Jerome's original Latin version of this text is well known and believed to have been written sometime in 392/93 CE. See J. N. D. Kelly, *Jerome. His Life, Writings, and Controversies* (Harper and Row, 1975), 65. A Greek translation was also made in the late eighth or ninth century. See C. Barthold, *De viris illustribus. Berühmte Männer* (Carthusianus, 2010), 125–26. In *CPL* 616, the Greek version is assigned to the seventh century. See also the discussion in *NPNF*[2] 3.355–56. On two other occasions, Jerome also cites 2 John 1 without providing any commentary about the recipient of the letter or its content. In *Ep.* 146.1 (CSEL 36.309), Jerome cites 2 John 1, but here, he is simply making a point about the function of presbyters and says nothing about the recipient of the letter. In Jerome's *Comm. Agg.* 2 (CCSL 76A line 193), 2 John 1 is cited alongside other passages of Scripture because Jerome was making a point about election and God's people, and he cited the verse because it contained the term "elect" (*electa*). He does not comment on the passage but references it right after citing 1 Pet 5:13 because in the Latin, it also uses the word "elect" (*electa*).

    Didymus the Blind (ca. 313–98 CE) wrote a commentary on the Catholic Epistles, which is only extant in Latin. His commentary on 2 John commences with v. 6; see PL 39.1809–10 and CPG 2562.
38. On this letter, see the discussion in A. Cain, *The Letters of Jerome: Asceticism, Biblical Exegesis, and the Construction of Christian Authority in Late Antiquity* (Oxford University Press, 2009), 158–59.
39. Gen 4:19.
40. Jerome, *Ep.* 123.12 (CSEL 56.84): legimus in carminum libro: sexaginta sunt reginae et octoginta concubinae et adulescentulae, quarum non est numerus. una est columba mea, perfecta mea, una est matri suae, electa genetrici suae. ad quam scribit idem iohannes epistulam: senior electae dominae et filiis eius.

("We read in the Book of Songs: 'There are sixty queens and eighty concubines, and virgins without number. My dove, my undefiled is but one; she is the only one of her mother, she is the choice one of the one that bare her.' It is to this choice one that the same John addresses an epistle in these words: 'the elder unto the elect lady and her children.'") Latin translation derived from English translation given in *NPNF*^{2} 6.234.

41. The Greek Ἰνδικοπλεύστης means something like "sailor to India."
42. Cosmas wrote his famous *Christian Topography* after he had extensively traveled in the East as a merchant and had retired to a monastery later in life. In the section of *Christian Topography* (7.69 [SC 197.130]) where Cosmas discusses the authorship of 2 and 3 John, he notes that many in his day did not hold that John the apostle authored these letters, but believed that the true author also bore the same name and the epithet "elder."
43. The full Latin title of the work is *Complexiones in Epistulas apostolorum, Actus apostolorum et Apocalypsim Iohannis*. On this text, see *CPL* 903.
44. *Compl. 2 Ioh.* 1–3 (CCSL 98B.112): Iohannes Senior Elect<a>e Domin<a>e et Filius Eius, et quod sequitur. Iohannes senior, quoniam erat aetate prouectus, elect<a>e domin<a>e scribit ecclesiae filiis que eius, quos sacro fonte genuerat. Hos se dicit studio caritatis diligere. ("'John, the elder, to the elect lady and her children,' and what follows. 'John the elder,' since he was advanced in age, writes to the elect lady of the church and her children, whom he had begotten by the sacred font. He says that he loves them with the zeal of charity.")
45. Lieu, *The Second and Third Epistles of John*, 31 n. 93 implies that Cassiodorus took the reference to the "elect lady" as referring to the church, but this is not obvious from his brief commentary. When Cassiodorus comments on v. 4, he mentions that the children who are walking in truth are those "of the Holy Church" (*sanctae Ecclesiae*), but this does not necessarily imply that for Cassiodorus, "elect lady" equals "Holy Church."
46. On this text, its provenance, and date, see *CPL* 1123a and CCSL 108B pp. vii–xix. As noted in CCSL 108B on p. vii, it was long thought that Bede's commentary on the Catholic Epistles (*Expositio in epistolas catholicas*; ca. 708/09 CE) was the earliest Latin commentary; however, this text precedes Bede's and he utilized it in his commentary (CCSL 108B pp. xii–xvii).
47. The commentary adds a brief reference to Vul. Wis. 4:8: *Cani hominis sensus* ("The understanding of a man is gray hairs").
48. CCSL 108B.46: Electae dominae, quod non adfirmandum uel negandum est corporaliter de domina aliqua corporali dici, quod de eclaesia potius intellegendum dici.
49. CCSL 108B.46: Et natis eius. Id est, non solum seniores sed et natos fidei salutat ("'And to her children': That is, he greets not only elders but also children of faith").

50. Ps.-Hilary of Arles, *Tractatus in septem epistolas canonicas*, CCSL 108B, 109–21 (1–3 John); see also *CPL* 508.
51. CCSL 108B.119: Electa haec ecclaesia est qui scribitur epistola.
52. Bede, *In epistulas septem catholicas* (CCSL 121); see also *CPL* 1362. For an English translation of this work, see D. Hurst, ed. and trans., *Bede the Venerable: Commentary on the Seven Catholic Epistles* (Cistercian Publications, 1985).
53. Bede, *In epistulas septem catholicas* 2 Ioh. 1 (CCSL 121.329): Quidam putant hanc et sequentem epistolam non esse Iohannis apostoli sed cuiusdam presbiteri Iohannis cuius sepulchrum usque hodie monstratur in Epheso, cuius etiam Papias auditor apostolorum et Hierapoli episcopus in opusculis suis saepe meminit. Sed nunc iam generalis ecclesiae consensus habet quod has quoque epistolas Iohannes apostolus scripserit, quia re uera multam uerborum et fidei similitudinem cum prima eius epistola ostendunt et simili zelo detestantur hereticos. Seniorem autem se dicit Iohannes uel quia iam prouectus erat aetate quando has scripsit epistolas uel quia nomen senioris, id est presbiteri, etiam pontifici propter maturitatem sapientiae et grauitatis congruit. Vnde et Petrus ait: Seniores ergo qui in uobis sunt obsecro consenior et testis Christi passionum. Senior, inquit, electae dominae et natis eius quos ego diligo in ueritate, id est uero amore diligo illo uidelicet qui secundum Deum est, uel certe quos ideo diligo quia perseuerantes in ueritate considero. ("Certain persons think that this and the following letter are not by the apostle John but by a certain presbyter [named] John whose tomb is pointed out even today at Ephesus. Papias, someone who heard the apostles and was bishop of Hierapolis, even makes mention of him often in his writings. But nowadays the general consensus of the Church holds that the apostle John wrote these Letters, too, because in truth they show a great likeness in words and faith with his first Letter and condemn heretics with a like zeal. John calls himself an elder, however, either because he was already advanced in age or because the name of elder, that is, a presbyter, is also fitting for a bishop, on account of the maturity of his wisdom and his seriousness. . . . 'The elder,' he says, 'to the elect lady and her children whom I love in the truth,' that is, whom I love with a true love, one, namely, which is according to God, or at least whom I love because I regard them as persevering in the truth.") English translation taken from Hurst, *Bede the Venerable: Commentary on the Seven Catholic Epistles*, 231.
54. The Latin word *catena* literally means "chain" and is concisely defined as "a collection of quotations from early Christian writers linked together to form a commentary on a biblical writing." This definition is taken from D. C. Parker, *An Introduction to the New Testament Manuscripts and Their Texts* (Cambridge University Press, 2008), 350. For a useful overview of catena research on the New Testament, see H. A. G. Houghton and D. C. Parker, "An Introduction to Greek New Testament Commentaries with a Preliminary Checklist of

New Testament Catena Manuscripts," in *Commentaries, Catenae and Biblical Tradition*, ed. H. A. G. Houghton (Gorgias Press, 2016), 1–36.

55. Between 1838 and 1844, J. A. Cramer published an eight-volume edition of catenae on the New Testament. For his work on Acts and the Catholic Epistles, he based his edition on two manuscripts, GA 2818 and GA 307. Following the earlier work of Bernard de Montfaucon on GA 307, he described them as being based on the commentary of Chrysostom, although he acknowledged the contributions of other ancient interpreters. See J. A. Cramer, *Catenae Graecorum patrum in Novum Testamentum*, vol. III (Oxford University Press, 1838; repr. Hildesheim: Olms, 1967): iv–v. Cramer's volume (VIII) on the Catholic Epistles was not published until 1844. On the catena and manuscripts of the Catholic Epistles used by Cramer, see also G. Karo and J. H. Lietzmann, *Catenarum Graecarum Catalogus* (Nachrichten von der Königl. Gesellschaft der Wissenschaften, Philologisch-historische Klasse; Lüder Horstmann, 1902), 595–97.

56. See discussion in K. Staab, "Die griechischen Katenenkommentare zu den katholischen Briefen," *Bib* 5 (1924): 296–353, and J. H. Ropes, "The Greek Catena to the Catholic Epistles," *HTR* 19 (1926): 383–88. Two other catenae from the same collection on 2 John contain named attribution: vv. 10–11 "St. Basil (of Caesarea)" (330–79 CE) and vv. 12–13 "Severus of Antioch" (VI CE).

57. J. A. Cramer, *Catenae Graecorum patrum in Novum Testamentum*, vol. VIII (Oxford University Press, 1844; repr. Olms, 1967), 146: ἢ πρὸς ἐκκλησίαν γράφει, ἢ πρός τινα γυναῖκα διὰ τῶν εὐαγγελικῶν ἐντολῶν τὴν ἑαυτῆς οἰκίαν οἰκονομοῦσαν πνευματικῶς.

58. Cramer, *Catenae Graecorum patrum in Novum Testamentum*, 147: ταύτην γράφει τὴν ἐπιστολὴν μιᾷ τῶν δεξαμένων τὸ κήρυγμα γυναικῶν. δύο δὲ αὐτῇ παραινεῖ· ἓν μὲν τὸ ἐν ἀγάπῃ περιπατεῖν, δεύτερον δὲ τὸ ἐκτρέπεσθαι, ὡς μηδὲ τῆς προσηγορίας τοῦ χαίρειν μεταδιδόναι. The Greek from τὸ ἐκτρέπεσθαι to μεταδιδόναι is unclear, and something is surely missing. When this section of the catena is quoted by Euthymius Zigabenus (early XII CE), it is rendered differently: τὸ ἐκτρέπεσθαι τοὺς αἱρετικούς, καὶ τοσοῦτον αὐτοὺς ἐκτρέπεσθαι, ὡς μηδὲ τῆς προσηγορίας τοῦ χαίρειν μεταδιδόναι. ("To turn them away to such an extent that she does not even give the salutation 'greetings.'"). It appears that in the version of Cramer, the manuscript omitted the intervening text between ἐκτρέπεσθαι and ἐκτρέπεσθαι due to parablepsis. I have emended the text and translated it based on the necessary addition.

As an additional note on Zigabenus, while both catenae appear in his commentary on 2 John, they are separated, with the first being placed after v. 8 (followed by more commentary) and the second being placed after v. 9. See N. Kalogeras, ed., *Euthymii Zigabeni Commentarius in XIV epistolas Sancti Pauli et VII catholicas*, vol. 2 (Fratres Perri, 1877), 640–41.

59. Since the anonymous commentary simply contains πρὸς ἐκκλησίαν γράφει ("to a church") without the definite article, it could be saying that 2 John was written to a specific "church" (or congregation) as opposed to "the (universal) Church."
60. Grk. ὑπόθεσις; Lat. *argumentum*.
61. In manuscripts of 2 John, the Greek summary begins to appear in the ninth century (e.g., GA 018 [IX CE]). A form of it also occurs in a work that in 1600 Peter Felckmann wrongly attributed to Athanasius (ca. 296–373 CE), but Felckmann's seventeenth-century attribution is erroneous, as the work does not belong to Athanasius and was written centuries later (ca. VI/VII CE); see discussion on pp. 148–49 in chapter 5. It reads: ταύτην ὡς πρεσβύτερος γράφει κυρίᾳ καὶ τοῖς τέχνοις αἠτῆς. ἡ δὲ πρόφασις τῆς ἐπιστολῆς αὕτη· ὁρῶν τὰ τέκνα αὐτῆς καλῶς ἀναστρεφόμενα ἐν τῇ πίστει, καὶ πολλοὺς πλάνους περιερχομένους καὶ λέγοντας μὴ εἶναι τὴν παρουσίαν τοῦ Χριστοῦ ἐν σαρχὶ, γράφει τὴν ἐπιστολήν. ("He writes this [2 John] as an elder to a lady and her children. The letter's occasion is as follows: Seeing her children conducting themselves well in the faith and many deceivers going about and saying that Christ did not come in the flesh, he writes the letter.")

In Latin, the summary may appear in some manuscripts as early as the eighth century (?), but like the Greek, it is in the ninth century when it becomes more common. It reads: Ad sanctam feminam scribit, ut eandem dominam non dubitet litteris appellare eiusdemque filiis testimonium quod ambulent in ueritate perhibeat. ("He writes to the holy woman, so that he does not hesitate to address her as 'Lady' in letters, and that he may bear witness to her children that they walk in truth.") Latin text taken from D. de Bruyne, *Prefaces to the Latin Bible*, Introductions by P.-M. Bogaert and T. O'Loughlin, STT 19 (Brepols, 2015, reprint of 1920 edition), 256, where the list of manuscripts is also given. To the list in de Bruyne could also be added Codex Ulmensis from the ninth century since it also includes this *argumentum*; see J. Wordsworth, H. J. White, and H. F. D. Sparks, *Novum Testamentum Domini nostri Iesu Christi Latine sec. edit. S. Hieronymi ad codicum manuscriptorum fidem* 3.2 (Clarendon Press, 1949), 380.
62. GA 018 (IX CE); see C. F. Matthaei, ed., *Novum Testamentum graece et latine. Ad codd. mss. Mosquenses primum a se examinatos recensuit, varias lectiones, animadversiones criticas et inedita scholia graeca. Vol. V: SS Septem Apostolorum Epistolae Catholicae* (Ioann. Frider. Hartknochii, 1782), 152: ἐκλεκτὴν κυρίαν λέγει τὴν ἔν τινι τόπῳ ἐκκλησίαν, ὡς τὴν τοῦ κυρίου διδασκαλίαν ἀκριβῆ φυλάττουσαν. ("He [the elder] calls the 'elect lady' the church in a certain place since it keeps the exact teaching of the Lord.") Other manuscripts from later centuries will include similar marginal notes where they gloss "lady" (κυρία) with "church" (ἐκκλησία). See, for example, GA 466 (XI CE) *ad loc*, where it glosses κυρίᾳ in 2 John 1 with the marginal phrase τῇ ἐκκλησίᾳ γράφει ("he is writing to a church").
63. Ps.-Oecumenius, *Joannis Apostoli posterior/tertia epistola catholica*, PG 119.683–704. While it was once thought that Oecumenius was a bishop of

Trikka (Thessaly) in the 990s CE, it is now clear that commentaries by several different authors have been transmitted under the name of Oecumenius. The name Ps.-Oecumenius has been used because of the uncertainty of authorship.

64. Ps.-Oecumenius, *Joannis Apostoli*, PG 119.685–88.

65. Ps.-Oecumenius, *Joannis Apostoli*, PG 119.688: πρὸς δὲ γυναίκα γράφων πιστὴν, οὐδὲν ὑπεστείλατο, ὅτι ἐν χριστῷ Ἰησοῦ οὐκ ἄρρεν οὐδὲ θῆλυ οἶδε. πρός τε Γάϊον ἕνα γράφων ἔχει Παῦλον Τίτῳ τε γράφοντα καὶ Τιμοθέῳ. καὶ πρὸς Φιλήμονα δὲ ἰδιώτην. ταῦτα μὲν περὶ τῆς προγραφῆς. δείκνυται δὲ ἀπὸ τῆς ἀπαγγελίας καὶ τῆς ἄλλης τοῦ λόγου οἰκονομίας τὸ γνήσιον τῶν ἐπιστολῶν. ("Writing [2 John] to a faithful woman, he concealed nothing, for he knew that in Christ Jesus there is neither male nor female. Writing to Gaius alone he has Paul who wrote to both Titus and Timothy, and to the individual Philemon. These points concern the inscription [title]. But the true nature of the epistles can be seen from the narrative and the other arrangement of the text.")

66. Ps.-Oecumenius, *Joannis Apostoli*, PG 119.688: δύο δὲ τῇ Ἐκλεκτῇ ταύτῃ ἐπιμαρτυρεῖ, ἓν μὲν, τὸ ἐν ἀγάπῃ περιπατεῖν, ἕτερον δὲ ἐκτρέπεσθαι τοὺς αἱρετιχκοὺς. Ἐκλεκτὴν δὲ, ἢ ἀπὸ τοῦ ὀνόματος, ἢ ἀπὸ τῆς περὶ τὴν ἀρετὴν φιλοτιμίας, καλεῖ. It is worth noting that while the editor capitalizes Ἐκλεκτῇ and Ἐκλεκτὴν, the words are articulated like the adjective "elect" (ἐκλεκτή) and not the personal name Eclecte (Ἐκλέκτη).

67. As one moves beyond the tenth century into the high Middle Ages (ca. 1050–1300 CE), there are various commentaries on 2 John, but on the whole, they add relatively little to the discussion. In the first Syriac commentary by Dionysius bar Salibi (d. 1171 CE), he takes the recipient of 2 John to be an actual person and tersely states that the woman to whom the letter is addressed possessed "excellence." See J. Sedláček, trans. and ed., *Dionysii Bar Salibi Commentarii in Apocalypsim, Actus et Epistulas Catholicas*, 2 vols., CSCO 53, 60, Scriptores Syri II, 18–20 (Typographeo Reipublicae, 1909). The Syriac appears in vol. 53.163 and the Latin translation in vol. 60.128. See also N. Akçay, *The Commentary on the Acts of the Apostles, the Pauline Epistles, the Catholic Epistles, and the Apocalypse by Dionysius Jacob Bar Salibi, Metropolitan of Amid († 1171)* (Department of Syriac Studies, Syriac Orthodox Patriarchate, 2020), 564. In the *Glossa Ordinaria* commentary on 2 John printed in PL 114.703–06, which is erroneously attributed to the German cleric Walafrid Strabo (ca. 809–849 CE) but is actually a twelfth-century compilation, the commentary on the opening of 2 John is terse: The *argumentum* to the letter parallels what is found in the Latin *Codex Ulmensis* (see n. 61), and the commentary on v. 1 does not start until over halfway through the verse with the Latin phrase "non ego" (οὐκ ἐγώ). The standard version of the *Glossa* printed in 1480/81 CE includes considerably more commentary and remarkably includes the tradition, first attested by Clement, that the recipient of 2 John was a Babylonian woman named "Electa": Scribit aute(m) ad quandam babilonia(m),

que nomi(n)e p(ro)prio electa vocabat. ("He writes to a certain Babylonian, who was called by her proper name Electa.") See A. Rusch, ed., *Biblia Latina cum Glossa Ordinaria. Facsimile Reprint of the Editio Princeps Adolph Rusch of Strassburg 1480/81*, vol. IV (Brepols, 1992), at 2 John 1 (no pagination in edition). The commentary of Nicolas of Lyra (ca. 1270–1349 CE), which was printed as the *postilla* in sixteenth- and seventeenth-century editions of the *Glossa Ordinaria*, is similarly terse for 2 John 1. He takes the recipient of the letter as a woman and argues that her name was "Electa," although there is no mention of Babylon: Erat enim magna et nobilis domina, nomina Electa habens, prolem et familiam fidelem, et ministros ecclesiae sustentabat. ("For she was a great and noble lady, having the name Electa, with offspring and a faithful family, and she supported the ministers of the church.") See *Bibliorum Sacrum cum Glossa Ordinaria* (Venice, 1601), 1421.

68. Lieu, *The Second and Third Epistles of John*, 31, notes that there was some impetus for Christians to interpret the letter as addressed to a church instead of a woman since this helped to make it "catholic."
69. Ropes, "The Greek Catena to the Catholic Epistles," 388.
70. Like inscriptions (beginning titles), subscriptions (end titles), or any marginal notes.
71. ⲧⲉⲡⲓⲥⲧⲟⲗⲏ ⲛ̄ⲓⲱϩⲁⲛⲛⲏⲥ ⲉⲩⲥϩⲁⲓ̈ ⲛ̄ⲙ̄ⲡⲁⲣⲑⲉⲛⲟⲥ. On this manuscript and reading, see K. Schüssler, ed., *Biblia Coptica: Die koptischen Bibeltexte. Band 4, Lieferung 2. Das sahidische Alte und Neue Testament: Vollständiges Verzeichnis mit Standorten sa 621–672* (Harrassowitz Verlag, 2009), 115–17 (sa 648). In G. W. Horner, *The Coptic Version of the New Testament in the Southern Dialect, Vol. III: The Catholic Epistles and the Apocalypse* (Clarendon Press, 1924), 175, he first notes this subscription to 2 John but then on p. 557 states, "Before the third epistle is the heading ⲧⲉⲡⲓⲥⲧⲟⲗⲏ ⲛ̄ⲓⲱϩⲁⲛⲛⲏⲥ ⲉⲩⲥϩⲁⲓ̈ ⲛ̄ⲙ̄ⲡⲁⲣⲑⲉⲛⲟⲥ." By stating this observation, Horner was not implying that it was connected to 3 John; it was just the subscription to 2 John, although Lieu, *The Second and Third Epistles of John*, 29, n. 88, seems to suggest there is some confusion with this.
72. On Greek minuscule manuscripts, see pp. 99–100 in chapter 4. I have not found any Latin manuscripts that bear similar inscriptions. See Wordsworth, White, and Sparks, *Novum Testamentum Domini nostri Iesu Christi Latine*, 383, 386.
73. Ἰωάννου ἐπιστολὴ δεύτερα πρὸς παρθένους: GA 1838 (XI CE).
74. Ἰωάννου ἐπιστολὴ δεύτερα ἐγράφη πρὸς Πάρθους: GA 431 (XII CE). See also Ἰωάννου ἐπιστολὴ β πρὸς Πάρθους *vel sim*. in the following Greek minuscules: GA 459 GA (1092 CE); GA 325 (XI CE); GA 62 (XIV CE). These manuscripts were brought to my attention by Brown, *The Epistles of John*, 772–73, but see also B. Aland et al., eds., *Novum Testamentum Graecum: Editio Critica Maior: IV Catholic Letters. Part 1, Installment 4: The Second and Third Letter of John, The Letter of Jude* (Deutsche Bibelgesellschaft, 2005), 369. See also B. Aland

et al., eds., *Novum Testamentum Graecum: Editio Critica Maior: IV Catholic Letters*, 2nd rev. ed. (Deutsche Bibelgesellschaft, 2013), 369.

75. At this point, it occurred to me that one or the other ascriptions for 2 John could have arisen from an error; either πρὸς παρθένους ("to the virgins") was inadvertently shortened to πρὸς πάρθους ("to the Parthians"), or conversely, πρὸς πάρθους was lengthened to πρὸς παρθένους. For further discussion, see n. 82 below.

76. *Compl. 1 Ioh.* titulus (CCSL 98B.108): Iohannis ad Parthos. Elsewhere, Cassiodorus repeats this for 1 John in *Psal.* 55.235 (CCSL 97.504) and in *Div. Inst.* 1.14.1, where he states the following about the books of the New Testament: "In the New Testament: 4 Gospels, that is Matthew, Mark, Luke, John; Acts of the Apostles; Epistles of Peter to the nations, of James, of John to the Parthians; Epistles of Paul: to the Romans 1, to the Corinthians 2, to the Galatians 1, to the Philippians 1, to the Colossians 1, to the Ephesians 1, to the Thessalonians 2, to Timothy 2, to Titus 2, to Philemon 1; Apocalypse of John." (In novum — Evangelia IIII, id est, Mattheus Marcus Lucas Iohannes Actus Apostolorum Epistulae Petri ad gentes Iacobi Iohannis ad Parthos Epistulae Pauli ad Romanos I ad Corinthios II ad Galatas I ad Philippenses I ad Colosenses I ad Ephesios I ad Thessalonicenses II ad Timotheum II ad Titum II ad Philemonem I Apocalypsin Iohannis.) Latin text from Mynors, *Cassiodori Senatoris Institutiones*, 39–40.

77. Augustine, *In Ioh. Ep.* titulus (SC 75.105): In Epistolam Ioannnis ad Parthos. *Quaest. ev.* 2.39 (CCSL 44B.93): secundum hanc sententiam etiam illud dictum est a iohanne in epistula ad parthos: dilectissimi, nunc filii dei sumus et nondum apparuit quid erimus. ("According to this sentiment, even this saying was spoken by John in the Epistle to the Parthians: 'Beloved, now we are children of God, and it has not yet been revealed what we shall be.'") *Exp. Gal.* 40 (CSEL 84.111): unde et Iohannes ad Parthos dicit: scribo uobis, patres, quoniam cognouistis, quod erat ab initio. ("Hence, John also says to the Parthians: 'I write to you, fathers, because you have known Him who is from the beginning.'")

78. *Contra Varimadum* 1.5 (CCSL 90.20): Item ipse ad parthos. ("Also he [John] himself to the Parthians"), where a quote of 1 John 5:7–8 immediately follows.

79. Bede, *Ep. Cath.* prol. (CCSL 121.181): Merito Iohannis epistolae tertio loco sunt positae, quia his scripsit ipse qui de gentibus crediderunt, cum nec natura nec professione Iudaei extitissent. Denique multi scriptorum ecclesiasticorum, in quibus est sanctus Athanasius Alexandrinae praesul ecclesiae, primam eius epistolam ad Parthos scriptam esse testantur. ("Rightly were the letters of John placed third [i.e., after James and Peter], because he wrote to those who came to believe from the gentiles, since neither by race nor by belief had they been Jews. Accordingly, many church writers, among whom is Saint Athanasius, head of the church of Alexandria, assert that his first Letter was written to

the Parthians.") English translation taken from Hurst, *Bede the Venerable*, 3. Despite Bede's assertion that Athanasius of Alexandria made this claim, it is not attested in any of the extant writings of Athanasius. To explain this, one possibility could be that since Bede thought that the anonymous author of *Against Varimadus* was Athanasius (Brown, *The Epistles of John*, 772), and this text uses the inscription "to the Parthians," this might explain why Bede believed that Athanasius had held this view. Alternatively, as there is extant in Coptic, Syriac, and Armenian a letter of Athanasius to the "virgins," for which there was a Greek *vorlage*, could the Greek title πρὸς παρθένους ("to the virgins") have either been corrupted to πρὸς Πάρθους ("to the Persians") or simply misread?

80. See n. 82 below on Theodor Zahn's proposal to account for the disparate evidence.

81. In one manuscript of 1 John (GA 2492 [XIV cent. CE]), the following inscription is attested: ἐπιστολὴ πρώτη παρθένου Ἰωάννου ("First Epistle of John the virgin"). This designation is also attested in some Latin manuscripts of 1 John. See H. A. G. Houghton, *The Latin New Testament: A Guide to Its Early History, Texts, and Manuscripts* (Oxford University Press, 2016), 177. A near-exhaustive list of the titulae appearing in 1 John and 2 John can be, respectively, found in B. Aland et al., eds., *Novum Testamentum Graecum: Editio Critica Maior: IV Catholic Letters. Part 1, Installment 3: The First Letter of John*, 263, and B. Aland et al., eds., *Novum Testamentum Graecum: Editio Critica Maior: IV Catholic Letters. Part 1, Installment 4*, 369. See also second edition, Aland et al., *Novum Testamentum Graecum: Editio Critica Maior IV: Catholic Letters*, 369.

82. W. Gründstäudl, "Geistliches Evangelium und Katholische Briefe: Johanneische Intertextualität im Spiegel frühchristlicher Rezeption," in *Erzählung und Briefe im johanneischen Kreis*, ed. U. Poplutz and J. Frey, WUNT 2/420 (Mohr Siebeck: 2016), 124, similarly notes the manuscript evidence of 2 John and likewise points out that this designation is never found in manuscripts of 1 and 3 John. On p. 125, Gründstäudl raises the possibility that the designation "to the Parthians" could have been accidentally applied to 1 John in the manuscript tradition as the inscription of 2 John ("to the Parthians") could have been taken as the subscription of 1 John. To account for the confusion between the appearance of πρὸς παρθένους ("to the virgins") and πρὸς Πάρθους ("to the Parthians") in select manuscripts of 2 John, as well as the designation "to the Parthians" for 1 John by select Latin authors, Theodor Zahn made the most detailed proposal to disentangle the disparate evidence in *Forschungen zur Geschichte des neutestamentlichen Kanons und der altkirchlichen Literatur. III. Theil: Supplementum Clementinum* (Verlag von Andreas Deichert, 1884), 99–103. To summarize, he argued that either Clement or someone who was a representative of the Clementine tradition took the phrase ἡ ἐν Βαβυλῶνι συνεκλεκτή from 1 Pet 5:13 with the address ἐκλεκτῇ κυρίᾳ in

2 John 1. He then contended that the geographic designation πρὸς Πάρθους naturally arose. Over time, the tradition developed two strands: one, which preceded the Latin translation of Cassiodorus, had πρὸς Πάρθους transform into πρὸς παρθένους; and another, attested in the Latin West, transferred πρὸς Πάρθους to 1 John.

83. While Ps.-Oecumenius does not rule out the possibility that her name could be Eclecte, he also states that it might simply refer to her zeal for virtue. See n. 66 above.
84. In Jerome's treatment of 2 John in *Ep*. 123, he never states it was addressed to "virgins," but he ultimately uses 2 John to advocate for celibacy.
85. On the other hand, later Christian commentators like Cassiodorus, the anonymous author of *Against Varimadus*, Augustine, and Bede applied "to the Parthians" to 1 John. See also discussion in Lieu, *The Second and Third Epistles of John*, 28–29.
86. Here, I am in general agreement with Brown (*The Epistles of John*, 653), Lieu (*The Second and Third Epistles of John*, 66), and Gründstäudl ("Geistliches Evangelium und Katholische Briefe," 125) that Clement was influenced by 1 Pet 5:13 when he made certain contextual claims about 2 John: namely, 2 John was addressed to "a certain Babylonian woman." However, I differ regarding the extent of the influence of 1 Pet 5:13, as it does not adequately explain all of Clement's claims about the alleged addressee of 2 John 1.
87. See additional discussion on pp. 117–18 in chapter 5.
88. A third claim by Clement, but not addressed in the forgoing discussion, is Clement's assertion that the name of the recipient "signifies the election of the holy church." This is a typical Clementine hermeneutic where an allegorical reading often overlays the literal.
89. Clement's *Hypotyposes* may have been composed within a century or so of when 2 John was originally written. On the date of 2 John, see most recently J. Bernier, *Rethinking the Dates of the New Testament: The Evidence of Early Composition* (Baker Academic, 2022), 113–18, where a date for 2 John is given that ranges anywhere from ca. 60 to 100 CE based on a variety of factors.
90. I have discussed this already in L. H. Blumell, "Scripture as Artefact," in *Oxford Handbook of Early Christian Biblical Interpretation*, ed. P. Blowers and P. Martens (Oxford University Press, 2019), 7–32.
91. For example, should the letter string αλλοϲητοιμαϲται (I have used lunate sigmas) in Mark 10:40 be divided and read as ἀλλ' οἷϲ ἡτοίμαϲται (NA[28]; "but it is for those for whom it has been prepared") or as ἄλλοιϲ ἡτοίμαϲται ("for others it has been prepared")? Similarly, should the letter string οιδαμεν in Rom 7:14 be read as οἴδαμεν (NA[28]; "we know") or οἶδα μέν ("but I know")? Finally, the letter string καιομολογουμενωϲμεγαεϲτιν in 1 Tim 3:16 could be read as καὶ ὁμολογουμένωϲ μέγα ἐϲτίν (NA[28]; "without any doubt . . . is great") or καὶ ὁμολογοῦμεν ὡϲ μέγα ἐϲτίν ("and we acknowledge that . . . is great").

Examples are drawn from B. M. Metzger and B. D. Ehrman, *The Text of the New Testament: Its Transmission, Corruption, and Restoration*, 4th ed. (Oxford University Press, 2005), 22, n. 27.

92. Line length and division are unknown. I have rendered sigma with the lunate form C without any differentiation between medial (σ) and terminal (ς) forms since this is how it was written on papyri of the Roman period (i.e., 30 BCE–284 CE). Similarly, while omega (ω) was frequently rendered in the "capitalized" form as Ω on inscriptions, in papyri, it is written W. To mark the dative case in Greek, modern editions use the iota subscript (ͅ), but in ancient Greek papyri, the dative is either not marked or is done through the iota adscript (I or ι). It is only used intermittently in the first century CE, appears more regularly in the second century CE, and appears to taper off in the third century CE. I have not included the iota adscript in the diplomatic rendering of 2 John 1, although it may have been originally written. While M. Trapp, *Greek and Latin Letters: An Anthology, with Translation* (Cambridge University Press, 2003), 104–7 (no. 39), prints his Greek edition of 2 John with iota adscripts, this is conjecture.

93. See discussion on pp. 47–54 in chapter 3 for the common authorship of 2 and 3 John.

94. The adjective κυρία, derived from κυρι-ία, means "control" or "possession." Due to potential iotacism, I also briefly entertained κυρεία, from κυριεία, which means "possession" or "property rights." F. Preisigke and E. Kiessling, eds., *Wörterbuch der griechischen Papyrusurkunden, mit Einschluss der griechischen Inschriften, Aufschriften, Ostraka, Mumienschilder usw. aus Ägypten. I Band: A–K.* (pub. by author, 1925), 848, also notes the shortened spelling, but the context of 2 John 1 immediately precluded this reading.

95. That 2 John was originally written on a papyrus is evident from the first part of v. 12. See the discussion on p. 59 in chapter 3.

96. Letters written during the Ptolemaic period (ca. 323–30 BCE) through the Roman period (ca. 30 BCE–284 CE) and latter Byzantine period (ca. 284–642 CE) could be quite different in terms of format, structure, and phraseology. A discussion of the epistolary papyri, which considers these changes, appears in chapter 3.

97. In Greek, names are definite and do not require a definite article in address.

98. On this letter, see R. S. Bagnall and R. Cribiore, *Women's Letters from Ancient Egypt, 300 BC–AD 800* (University of Michigan Press, 2006), 332–33, and J. L. White, *Light from Ancient Letters* (Fortress Press, 1986), 146 (no. 94).

99. It is well attested in documentary papyri that Egyptian and other foreign names (non-Greek) are periodically undeclined. See B. Muhs, "Language Contact and Personal Names in Early Ptolemaic Egypt," in *The Language of the Papyri*, ed. T. Evans and D. Obbink (Oxford University Press, 2009), 189–97. This phenomenon is also attested in the LXX and New Testament for certain Semitic names. For example, there are several instances where Ἰάκωβος

(Jacob) is undeclined Ἰακώβ: Matt 1:2, 15–16; 8:11; 22:32; Mark 12:26; Luke 1:33; 3:34; 13:28; 20:37; John 4:5–6, 12; Acts 3:13; 7:8, 12, 14–15, 32, 46; Rom 9:13; 11:26; Heb 11:9, 20–21. The same is also the case with the name Ἀβραάμ (Abraham).

100. Even just EKLEK must be εκ + λεκ > λεγ = ἐκ + λέγω or ἐκλέγω.

101. On this letter, see a more detailed discussion on pp. 81–82 in chapter 3.

102. In papyrology (and epigraphy), the editorial siglum < > indicates that missing text has been restored by the editor since it is required. On papyrological sigla, see n. 169 in chapter 3.

103. In Greek papyri (and inscriptions), iota and eta were commonly interchanged because to many ancient writers and readers of Greek, there was little phonetic difference between the two. For example, in Codex Sinaiticus, the word "Christian" (Χριστιανός) in Acts 11:26 and 26:28 is spelled "Chrēstian" (Χρηστιανός). On the common phonetic interchange of iota and eta, see F. T. Gignac, *A Grammar of the Greek Papyri of the Roman and Byzantine Periods, Vol. I, Phonology* (Instituto Editoriale Cisalpino–La Goliardica, 1976), 235–39.

104. The term haplography literally means "writing once." It is used to describe errors where a letter string, word, or short phrase is written out twice in the original but, in the copying, is shortened and only written once due to a mistake. An English example is "an anchor or rope must be used," which becomes "an anchor rope must be used" when the "or" is dropped by a copyist owing to "anchor" ending with the same two letters. For a discussion of the haplography in SB 20.15069, see chapter 3, pp. 81–82, and the discussion in the most recent edition of this papyrus: J. M. S. Cowey et al., "Bemerkungen zu Urkunden," *ZPE* 80 (1990): 290.

105. Cf. SBLGNT and TYNGNT: ὁ πρεσβύτερος ἐκλεκτῇ κυρίᾳ.

CHAPTER 2: WHEN A LADY IS NOT A LADY: MODERN HERMENEUTICS AND THE INTERPRETATION OF 2 JOHN 1

1. The full reference is S. Brown and F. J. Moloney, *Interpreting the Gospel and Letters of John: An Introduction* (Wm. B. Eerdmans Publishing Co., 2017), 123.
2. The full reference is B. F. Westcott, *The Epistles of St. John: The Greek Text with Notes and Essays* (MacMillan and Co., 1883), 213.
3. Their work on this monumental version of the New Testament began in 1853 when they initially decided on the project.
4. B. F. Westcott and F. J. A. Hort, eds., *The New Testament in the Original Greek* (Macmillan and Co., 1881). The first edition was published on May 17, 1881. Their Greek text of the New Testament appeared in the first volume. The

second volume (published the following year), *Introduction and Appendix of Notes on Select Readings*, broached a wide variety of subjects, and arguments were set forth regarding various NT readings.

5. In the preface to the American edition, Philip Schaff heaped praise on the work. He exclaimed in Latin: *Hic habes textum omnium editionum antiquissimum et purissimum* ("Here you have the oldest and purest text of all editions"). See *The New Testament in the Original Greek*, American ed. with an Introduction by P. Schaff DD, LLD (Harper and Brothers, Franklin Square, 1881), viii.
6. On Codex Vaticanus, see discussion on pp. 101 in chapter 4.
7. Despite the critical care and overall erudition of the work, the text was immediately assailed by certain quarters when it was published because some viewed it as an assault on scripture since it presented readings that were not always "traditional." J. W. Burgon, *The Revision Revised* (John Murray, 1883), 16, vituperously contended,: "We venture to assure him, without a particle of hesitation, that ℵ B D are *three of the most scandalously corrupt copies extant*:—exhibit *the most shamefully mutilated* texts which are anywhere to be met with:—have become, by whatever process (for their history is wholly unknown), the depositories of the largest amount of *fabricated readings*, ancient *blunders*, and *intentional perversions of Truth*,—which are discoverable in any known copies of the Word of God." Italics in the original text.
8. ℵ (GA 01): ημων. A (GA 02) and B (GA 03): υμων.
9. 2 John 11 reads: ὁ λέγων γὰρ αὐτῷ χαίρειν κοινωνεῖ τοῖς ἔργοις αὐτοῦ τοῖς πονηροῖς ("For to welcome is to participate in the evil deeds of such a person"). A more literal translation of the opening of the verse is "for the one who says to him, 'greetings.'" The Latin addition at the end of the verse reads*:* ecce praedixi vobis, ut in diem Domini [nostri Jesu Christi] non confundamini ("Behold, I have foretold this to you, that ye may not be confounded in the day of [our] Lord [Jesus Christ]"). See Westcott and Hort, *The New Testament in the Original Greek*, 576.
10. In all previous studies, including that of Westcott (*The Epistles of St. John*), commentators who have discussed the letter string εκλεκτη in the context of the personal name Ἐκλέκτη have rendered it in English as "Electa." However, the proper rendering of this female name is Eclecte, which I have used throughout. When I use "Electa" in this and subsequent chapters, it will always be accompanied by quotation marks to reflect the usage of others.
11. For full reference, see n. 2 above. The publication of this commentary inaugurated the modern study of the Johannine Letters. For scholarship on the Johannine Epistles prior to the work of Westcott, see the insightful discussion in W. Smith, ed., *A Dictionary of the Bible*, 1st ed. (Little, Brown, and Company, 1863), 1.1114–16, where studies of the seventeenth through the middle of the nineteenth century are summarized and treated.

12. Westcott, *The Epistles of St. John*, 214.
13. Cf. 3 John 1 where the single name Gaius is used.
14. Westcott, *The Epistles of St. John*, 214.
15. T. G. H. James, ed., *Excavating in Egypt: The Egypt Exploration Society 1882–1982* (University of Chicago Press, 1982).
16. The full reference is A. Plummer, *The Epistles of St. John. With Notes, Introduction and Appendices*, The Cambridge Bible for Schools and Colleges (Cambridge University Press, 1886).
17. Plummer, *The Epistles of St. John*, 57.
18. Plummer, *The Epistles of St. John*, 57 and repeated at 176, where the calls the name "Electa . . . an extraordinary name."
19. Plummer also considered the reading "to the elect Kyria." While he found this option more attractive than "to the lady Electa," he noted that it was not without problems: If this were the reading, then the word ordering of this address (ἐκλεκτῇ Κυρίᾳ; "to elect Kyria") would be the opposite of what is found in 3 John 1 (Γαΐῳ τῷ ἀγαπητῷ; "to Gaius the beloved"). In this discussion, he notes in passing that the female name Kyria (Κυρία), which carries the Greek meaning "Lord (fem.)," is similar to Martha (מרתא) in Hebrew (actually it is Aramaic), which also carries the meaning "Lord." He then notes, without mentioning any names or providing any bibliographic references, that some had previously suggested the letter was "addressed to Martha of Bethany." This had been suggested previously by G. Volkmar, *Die Evangelien: oder Marcus und die Synopsis der kanonischen und ausserkanonischen Evangelien* (Fues's Verlag, 1870), 560. Somewhat earlier, A. W. Knauer, "Ueber die Ἐκλεκτὴ Κυρία, an welche der zweite Brief Johannis gerichtet ist," *ThStKr* 6 (1833): 452–58, had argued that 2 John was addressed to Mary the mother of Jesus (cf. John 19:26–27). See Plummer, *The Epistles of St. John*, 57–58.
20. Plummer, *The Epistles of St. John*, 58.
21. Plummer, *The Epistles of St. John*, 58.
22. There is a third German work (chronologically first) by H. J. Holtzmann, *Evangelium, Briefe und Offenbarung des Johannes* (J. C. B. Mohr, 1891). His analysis of 2 John is brief and totals a few pages. He tersely states that the "lady" in 2 John 1 is a metaphor for a church and does not refer to an actual woman (pp. 240–41). In 1889, an English commentary appeared by W. Alexander, *The Epistles of St. John. Twenty-One Discourses, with Greek Text, Comparative Versions, and Notes Chiefly Exegetical* (A. C. Armstrong and Son, 1889). But Alexander never broaches the question of the identity of the addressee of 2 John.
23. The full reference is H. Poggel, *Der zweite und dritte Brief des Apostels Johannes geprüft auf ihren kanonischen Charakter* (Druck und Verlag von Ferdinand Schöningh, 1896).
24. Poggel, *Der zweite und dritte Brief des Apostels Johannes*, 127–32.

25. Poggel, *Der zweite und dritte Brief des Apostels Johannes*, 130.
26. Poggel, *Der zweite und dritte Brief des Apostels Johannes*, 132.
27. The full reference is B. Weiss, *Die drei Briefe des Apostel Johannes* (Vandenhoeck und Ruprecht, 1899).
28. Weiss, *Die drei Briefe des Apostel Johannes*, 168–69.
29. Weiss, *Die drei Briefe des Apostel Johannes*, 170.
30. J. R. Harris, "The Problem of the Address in the Second Epistle of John," *Expositor*, 6th series, 3.3 (1901): 194–203.
31. See discussion on pp. 62–70 in chapter 3.
32. Harris, "The Problem of the Address in the Second Epistle of John," 196.
33. ἵνα ἀγαπῶμεν ἀλλήλους.
34. Brown, *The Epistles of John*, 652.
35. Harris, "The Problem of the Address in the Second Epistle of John," 201.
36. Harris, "The Problem of the Address in the Second Epistle of John," 201.
37. W. M. Ramsay, "Historical Commentary on the Epistles to the Corinthians," *Expositor*, 6th series, 3.5 (1901): 354–56, although Ramsay believed it was written to an actual woman: "Second John is a real letter to a lady, we entirely agree with him (p. 354)."
38. H. J. Gibbins, "The Second Epistle of St. John," *Expositor*, 6th series, 6.3 (1902): 228–36, and H. J. Gibbins, "The Problem of the Second Epistle of St. John," *Expositor*, 6th series, 12.6 (1905), 412–24.
39. Gibbins, "The Second Epistle of St. John," 229–32.
40. Gibbins, "The Second Epistle of St. John," 235.
41. Gibbins, "The Problem of the Second Epistle of St. John," 424.
42. The full reference is B. Bresky, *Das Verhältnis des zweiten Johannesbriefes zum dritten* (Aschendorff, 1906). Another German work that treated 2 John appeared the same year: J. E. Belser, *Die Briefe des heiligen Johannes* (Herdersche Verlagschandlung, 1906). On pp. 138–39, Besler briefly considers the address and claims that it metaphorically refers to a Christian community connected to the church in Ephesus.
43. Bresky, *Das Verhältnis des zweiten Johannesbriefes zum dritten*, 2–10.
44. 3 John 9: ἔγραψά τι τῇ ἐκκλησίᾳ· ἀλλ' ὁ φιλοπρωτεύων αὐτῶν Διοτρέφης οὐκ ἐπιδέχεται ἡμᾶς ("I have written something to the church, but Diotrephes, who likes to put himself first, does not welcome us").
45. See discussion on pp. 74–76 in chapter 3.
46. Bresky, *Das Verhältnis des zweiten Johannesbriefes zum dritten*, 4.
47. Bresky, *Das Verhältnis des zweiten Johannesbriefes zum dritten*, 4–5.
48. Bresky, *Das Verhältnis des zweiten Johannesbriefes zum dritten*, 7–8.
49. Bresky, *Das Verhältnis des zweiten Johannesbriefes zum dritten*, 7–8. Here, she cites Lamentations 4:2, 6, 7, 8, 10, and 22, where members of the Jewish

community are called "sons of Zion." Similarly, she mentions Baruch 4:5–29, where Jerusalem is personified as a mother.

50. The full reference is A. Deissmann, *Licht vom Osten: Das Neue Testament und die neuentdeckten Texte der hellenistisch-römischen Welt* (Verlag von J. C. B. Mohr [Paul Siebeck], 1908). First English printing: A. Deissmann, *Light from the Ancient East: The New Testament Illustrated by Recently Discovered Texts of the Graeco-Roman World*, trans. L. R. M. Strachan (Hodder and Stoughton, 1910).
51. Deissmann, *Light from the Ancient East*, 234.
52. Deissmann, *Licht vom Osten*, 106. P.Oxy. 4.744, a letter by a man named Ilarian and carrying a date corresponding with June 17, 1 BCE, begins as follows: Βεροῦτι τῇ κυρίᾳ μου ("to my lady Berous"). In another reference to 2 John 1 on p. 215, Deissmann points out how P.Fay. 119, a letter from a military veteran named Lucius Bellenus Gemellus written around 103 CE to his son, contains a greeting near the end of the letter that is analogically proximate to that found at the beginning of 2 John: ἀσπάζου Ἐπαγαθὸν καὶ τοὺς φιλοῦντες (*l.* φιλοῦντας) ἡμᾶς πρὸς ἀλήθιαν (*l.* ἀλήθειαν) ("Greet Epagathus and those who love us truly"); cf. 2 John 1: οὓς ἐγὼ ἀγαπῶ ἐν ἀληθείᾳ ("whom I love in the truth").
53. The full references are G. G. Findlay, *Fellowship in the Life Eternal: An Exposition of the Epistles of St. John* (Hodder and Stoughton, 1909); A. E. Brooke, *A Critical and Exegetical Commentary on the Johannine Epistles* (Charles Scribner's Sons, 1912).
54. On Brooke's work, see D. M. Smith, "The Epistles of John: What's New Since Brooke's ICC in 1912?" *ExpTim* 120 (2009): 373–84.
55. Findlay, *Fellowship in the Life Eternal*, 23–32.
56. Findlay, *Fellowship in the Life Eternal*, 28–30. Findlay argues that communities, cities, and kingdoms were frequently represented by the image "of a noble woman." As evidence, he cites the biblical examples of Isaiah 62:4–5, where the restored Zion is metaphorically married to God, and Revelation 17–18, where Babylon is personified as a woman. Drawing on this imagery, he returns to the "elect lady" of 2 John 1 and equates the phrase with "the Lady Church," stating that to whatever church the letter may have originally been addressed, it must have been among "the most prominent."
57. Findlay, *Fellowship in the Life Eternal*, 23.
58. See pp. 137 in chapter 5. Findlay, *Fellowship in the Life Eternal*, 23, also dismissed the reading "to the elect Kyria," noting that this was the marginal reading in the *American Standard Version* of the Bible (ASV; 1900) by arguing that the "Greek grammar protests strongly against it."
59. Brooke, *A Critical and Exegetical Commentary on the Johannine Epistles*, lxxxi.
60. Brooke, *A Critical and Exegetical Commentary on the Johannine Epistles*, lxxxi. He briefly considers the name Kyria but argues that it is doubtful since the

collocation of the wording militates against it. Citing 3 John 1, he notes that the address reads Γαΐῳ τῷ ἀγαπητῷ ("to the beloved Gaius"), where the name is given first and is then followed by an article and adjective.

61. Brooke, *A Critical and Exegetical Commentary on the Johannine Epistles*, lxxx and see also 168. Repeating the argument about the phrase της εκλεκτης in v. 13, Brooke erroneously argues that "the name Electa is almost certainly excluded by the improbability of two sisters bearing the same name."
62. C. Gore, *The Epistles of St. John* (Murray, 1920), 221.
63. J. Marty, "Contribution à l'étude des problèmes johanniques: Les petites épîtres 'II et III Jean,'" *RHR* 91 (1925): 200–11.
64. The full reference is H. H. Wendt, *Die Johannesbriefe und das johanneische Christentum* (Buchhandlung des Waiserhauses, 1925).
65. Wendt, *Die Johannesbriefe und das johanneische Christentum*, 15.
66. M. Dibelius, "Johannesbriefe," in *Religion in Geschichte und Gegenwart*, 2nd ed., ed. F. M. Schiele and L. Zscharnack (Mohr Siebeck, 1929), 3.346–49.
67. Dibelius, "Johannesbriefe," 348.
68. D. F. Büchsel, *Die Johannesbriefe*, THKNT 17 (A. Deichertsche Verlagsbuchhandlung, 1933).
69. Büchsel, *Die Johannesbriefe*, 90–95.
70. Büchsel, *Die Johannesbriefe*, 90, 94–95.
71. F. J. Dölger, "*Domina Mater Ecclesia* und die 'Herrin' im zweiten Johannesbrief," *JAC* 5 (1936): 211–17.
72. Dölger, "*Domina Mater Ecclesia* und die 'Herrin' im zweiten Johannesbrief," 214–15.
73. Tertullian, *Mart.* 1.1 (CCSL 1.3). For Tertullian's work *Ad martyras*, see CPL 1.
74. He points out that in Tertullian, the phrase is not used for the universal "Church" but rather for a local "church" and by analogy argues that in 2 John 1, κυρία is best understood as a reference to some local congregation metaphorically personified as a lady.
75. The full reference is C. H. Dodd, *The Johannine Epistles*, MNTC (Hodder and Stoughton, 1946). A year before, in 1945, R. C. H. Lenski, *The Interpretation of the Epistles of St. Peter, St. John and St. Jude* (Wartburg Press, 1945), 553–57, discusses the address in 2 John 1, but no new arguments are brought to bear, and he determines that the letter was written to a church personified as a "mistress." Interestingly, in 1939, in James Orr et al., eds., *The International Standard Bible Encyclopedia* (Eerdmans, 1939), s.v. "Elect Lady," 2.923, Robert Law argues that grammatically, it is best to read the opening address as "to the lady Electa" and notes that despite "the fact the name Eklekte has not yet been discovered," it should still be the preferred reading.
76. Dodd, *The Johannine Epistles*, 143. He similarly dismisses the reading "Kyria" but concedes that it is a better option than "Electa."

77. Dodd, *The Johannine Epistles*, 144.
78. Dodd, *The Johannine Epistles*, 144–45.
79. Dodd, *The Johannine Epistles*, 145.
80. Dodd, *The Johannine Epistles*, 145.
81. For a helpful bibliography and select overview of the study of the Johannine Letters from approximately 1900 up to 1960, see E. Haenchen, "Neuere Literatur zu den Johannesbriefen," *TRu* 26 (1960): 1–43. The overview is dominated by issues surrounding 1 John; by comparison, 2 and 3 John hardly receive any attention.
82. H. Windisch, *Die Katholischen Briefe* (Verlag J. C. B. Mohr [Paul Siebeck], 1951).
83. J. Bonsirven, *Épitres de Saint Jeạn*, VS 9 (Beauchesne, 1954).
84. J. A. Wilder, "Introduction and Exegesis of the First, Second and Third Epistles of John," in *The Interpreter's Bible*, vol. 12 (Abingdon, 1957), 207–313.
85. G. P. Lewis, *The Johannine Epistles* (Epworth, 1961), 127.
86. N. Alexander, *The Epistles of John: Introduction and Commentary*, TBC (Macmillan, 1962).
87. J. R. W. Stott, *The Epistles of John: An Introduction and Commentary* (Wm. B. Eerdmans Publishing Company, 1964).
88. R. A. Ward, *The Epistles of John and Jude: A Study Manual* (Baker Book House, 1965).
89. R. R. Williams, *The Letters of John and James* (Cambridge University Press, 1965).
90. J. W. Roberts, *The Letters of John* (R. B. Sweet, 1968).
91. The full reference is R. Schnackenburg, *Die Johannesbriefe*, HThKNT 13 (Herder, 1953; repr. 1963, 1987, 1984); English edition: R. Schnackenburg, *The Johannine Epistles: Introduction and Commentary*, trans. R. Fuller and I. Fuller (Crossroad, 1992).
92. The full reference is R. Bultmann, *Die drei Johannesbriefe*, KEK 14 (Vandenhoeck and Ruprecht, 1967); English edition: R. Bultmann, *The Johannine Epistles: A Commentary on the Johannine Epistles*, ed. R. W. Funk, trans. R. P. O'Hara et al., Hermeneia Commentary Series (Fortress Press, 1973).
93. Schnackenburg, *The Johannine Epistles*, 278. He excludes the reading "Kyria" based on the collocation of the address.
94. Schnackenburg, *The Johannine Epistles*, 278–79.
95. Bultmann, *The Johannine Epistles*, 108. For a discussion of Bultmann's approach to 2 John, see pp. 50–51, 55–56 in chapter 3.
96. Bultmann, *The Johannine Epistles*, 107. At least Bultmann recognized that in v. 13, the τῆς ἐκλεκτῆς could not be read as a name and had to be an adjective.
97. See discussion in n. 89 in chapter 5.
98. A. Ross, *The Epistles of James and John*, NICNT (Eerdmans, 1954).

99. Ross, *The Epistles of James and John*, 129–30, 227.
100. D. H. Asmussen, *Wahrheit und Liebe. Eine Einführung in die Johannesbriefe* (Im Furche-Verlag, 1957), 167.
101. W. T. Conner, *The Epistles of John*, 2nd ed. rev. (Broadman Press, 1957), 139–40.
102. E. Gaugler, *Die Johannesbriefe* (Evz-Verlag, 1964), 283.
103. For a concise overview of scholarship on the Johannine Epistles up to 1970, see R. C. Briggs, "Contemporary Study of the Johannine Epistles," *RevExp* 67 (1970): 411–22. On p. 418, his own perspective on the addressee is indicative of the broader perspective: "In II John, 'the elder,' writing to a local congregation (*kuria*, lady, refers to the church), exercises his recognized prerogative in giving warning and guidance for the church."
104. For recent bibliographies, see select chapters in J. M. Lieu and M. C. de Boer, eds., *The Oxford Handbook of Johannine Studies* (Oxford University Press, 2019), although most bibliographies are dominated by studies on the Gospel of John and then 1 John. For a helpful bibliography of German work on the Johannine Letters until 2010, see U. Schnelle, *Die Johannesbriefe* (Evangelische Verlagsanstalt, 2010), xv–xxi. For a comprehensive bibliography on scholarship through the early 1980s, see R. Brown, *The Epistles of John*, 131–46. Also useful is J. Beutler, "Die Johannesbriefe in der neuesten Literatur (1978–1985)," *ANRW* 25/5 (1988): 3773–90. See also M. Bryant, "The Johannine Epistles, 2000–2005," *Faith and Mission* 23.1 (2005): 83–89; S. E. Porter and A. K. Gabriel, *Johannine Writings and Apocalyptic: An Annotated Bibliography* (Johannine Studies 1; Brill, 2013), 217–37. Most recently, see U. C. von Wahlde, "Johannine Letters," *Oxford Bibliographies Online*, January 11, 2018, https://doi.org/10.1093/obo/9780195393361-0253.
105. During this period, only one monograph has appeared that is explicitly dedicated to 2 and 3 John: J. Lieu, *The Second and Third Epistles of John: History and Background* (T&T Clark, 1986). Similarly, there is a single commentary where 2 and 3 John occupy their own volume: H.-J. Klauck, *Der zweite und dritte Johannesbrief* EKKNT XXXIII/2 (Neukirchener Verlag, 1992).
106. F. F. Bruce, *The Epistles of John: Introduction, Exposition and Notes* (William B. Eerdmans Publishing Company, 1970).
107. J. L. Houlden, *A Commentary on the Johannine Epistles* (Harper and Row Publishers, 1974).
108. I. H. Marshall, *The Epistles of John* (William B. Eerdmans Publishing Company, 1978).
109. K. Wengst, *Der erste, zweite und dritte Brief des Johannes*, ÖTK 16 (Echter-Verlag, 1978).
110. P. Perkins, *The Johannine Epistles*, NTM 21 (Michael Glazier, 1979).
111. F. D. Howard, *1, 2, & 3 John, Jude, Revelation*, Layman's Bible Book Commentary 24 (Broadman Press, 1982).

112. P. Bonnard, *Les Épitres Johanniques* (Labor et Fides, 1983).
113. K. Grayston, *The Johannine Epistles* (William B. Eerdmans, 1984).
114. S. Smalley, *1, 2, 3 John*, WBC 51 (Word, 1984).
115. R. Kysar, *Augsburg Commentary on the New Testament. I, II, III John* (Augsburg Publishing House, 1986).
116. D. Jackman, *The Message of John's Letters: Living in the Love of God* (Inter-Varsity Press, 1988).
117. R. A. Culpepper, *The Gospel and Letters of John*, Interpreting Biblical Texts Series (Abingdon Press, 1988).
118. The full reference is R. E. Brown, *The Epistles of John: A New Translation with Introduction and Commentary*, AB 30 (Doubleday, 1982).
119. Brown, *The Epistles of John*, 651–55.
120. Brown, *The Epistles of John*, 18, 31–32, 651–52.
121. Brown, *The Epistles of John*, 652–55.
122. Brown, *The Epistles of John*, 652–53.
123. Brown, *The Epistles of John*, 652. Cf. Harris, "The Problem of the Address in the Second Epistle of John," 196–97.
124. See discussion on pp. 23–24.
125. Brown, *The Epistles of John*, 653. The full reference is F. Preisigke, ed., *Namenbuch enthaltend alle griechischen, lateinischen, ägyptischen, hebräischen, arabischen und sonstigen semitischen und nichtsemitischen Menschennamen, soweit sie in griechischen Urkunden (Papyri, Ostraka, Inschriften, Mumienschildern usw) Ägyptens sich vorfinden* (pub. by author, 1922; repr., 1967).
126. To give a noteworthy statistic, in Preisigke's *Namenbuch*, there are only about fifteen thousand names and name variants; by comparison, today, nearly forty thousand different names and name variants are attested in the papyri. This number will continue to rise as new texts are discovered and published.
127. See discussion of this name in chapter 5.
128. Brown, *The Epistles of John*, 653. This same argument also appeared in Bultmann, *The Johannine Epistles*, 107.
129. See discussion at pp. 39–40, and 138–42.
130. Brown asserts that the name Kyria "is an improvement" (over Eclecte) since it is attested in Preisigke's *Namenbuch*. However, he points out that there is still the problem of the missing article. He also considers whether it might be something like "dear lady" and refers to an unnamed woman. Brown claims that this option is unlikely as one anticipates an actual name since it seems customary for the elder to provide the name of the person being addressed, as in 3 John 1. See Brown, *The Epistles of John*, 653.
131. Brown, *The Epistles of John*, 653.
132. Brown, *The Epistles of John*, 654. See also discussion on pp. 37.
133. The full reference is Lieu, *The Second and Third Epistles of John: History and Background* (T&T Clark, 1986).

134. The full reference is J. Lieu, *The Theology of the Johannine Epistles* (Cambridge University Press, 1991).
135. The full reference is J. M. Lieu, *I, II, & III John: A Commentary* (Westminster John Knox Press, 2008).
136. Lieu, *The Second and Third Epistles of John*, 67, states that the church may have been within the "Johannine circle" but grants that this circle may have had a broader purpose.
137. Lieu, *The Theology of the Johannine Epistles*, 3; Lieu, *I, II, & III John: A Commentary*, 6; Lieu, *The Second and Third Epistles of John*, 42, 65.
138. Lieu, *The Second and Third Epistles of John*, 65 n. 41. See also Lieu, *I, II, & III John: A Commentary*, 240.
139. Lieu, *I, II, & III John: A Commentary*, 244.
140. Lieu, *The Theology of the Johannine Epistles*, 93. Her words echo those of Dodd, *The Johannine Epistles*, 145, who raised the specter of persecution as the reason for the unusual address.
141. Lieu, *The Second and Third Epistles of John*, 64.
142. Lieu, *The Second and Third Epistles of John*, 42.
143. Lieu, *The Second and Third Epistles of John*, 65. I would instead argue that using this term as a metaphor for a personified church, as Lieu does, somewhat diminishes the force of this term; rather, the full weight would be applied if it referred to an actual woman.
144. Lieu, *The Second and Third Epistles of John*, 66; Lieu, *I, II, & III John: A Commentary*, 244.
145. Lieu, *The Second and Third Epistles of John*, 66.
146. Lieu, *I, II, & III John: A Commentary*, 245.
147. Lieu, *The Second and Third Epistles of John*, 66.
148. The full reference H.-J. Klauck, *Der zweite und dritte Johannesbrief*, EKKNT 23/2 (Neukirchen Verlag, 1992).
149. For his volume on 1 John see H.-J. Klauck, *Der erste Johannesbrief*, EKKNT XXIII/1 (Neukirchen Verlag, 1991).
150. Klauck, *Der zweite und dritte Johannesbrief*, 33–38.
151. Klauck, *Der zweite und dritte Johannesbrief*, 33.
152. Klauck, *Der zweite und dritte Johannesbrief*, 33.
153. Klauck, *Der zweite und dritte Johannesbrief*, 34. Klauck articulates the name Ἐκλέκτη as Ἐκλεκτή, but this is the articulation for the adjective and not the name.
154. Klauck, *Der zweite und dritte Johannesbrief*, 34.
155. Harris, "The Problem of the Address in the Second Epistle of John," 194–203.
156. Klauck, *Der zweite und dritte Johannesbrief*, 34.
157. Klauck, *Der zweite und dritte Johannesbrief*, 34.
158. Klauck, *Der zweite und dritte Johannesbrief*, 34. On these theories, see n. 19 above.

159. Klauck, *Der zweite und dritte Johannesbrief*, 35.
160. Klauck, *Der zweite und dritte Johannesbrief*, 35–36.
161. R. W. Yarborough, *1–3 John*, BECNT (Baker Academic, 2008), 333; M. M. Thompson, *1–3 John*, The IVP New Testament Commentary Series (InterVarsity Press, 1992), 151, remarks, "The congregation to which he is writing is designated metaphorically as *the chosen lady and her children*; we would say 'the church and its members.'"
162. A notable exception I have found is the work of Edwards, *The Johannine Epistles*, 26–29, who offers a remarkably even-handed and detailed discussion of the "elect lady" and leaves all interpretive options on the table. Similarly, T. A. Bennett, *1–3 John* (William B. Eerdmans Publishing Company, 2021), 109–11, suggests that the address and letter are best understood when taken in reference to an unnamed Christian matron.
163. In some cases, one can read a modern commentary and have little or no idea of any alternate interpretation for the opening address besides the consensus reading: for example, K. Anderson and D. Keating, *James, First, Second, and Third John* (Baker Academic, 2017), 245–46; K. Jobes, *1, 2 & 3 John* (Zondervan, 2014), 255–56; G. L. Parsenius, *First, Second, and Third John* (Baker Academic, 2014), 133.
164. Westcott and Hort proposed Ἐκλέκτῃ Κυρίᾳ as a secondary reading because it made better grammatical sense but still printed ἐκλεκτῇ κυρίᾳ in their edition of 2 John.
165. The use of the term "children" in vv. 1, 4, and 13 is almost certainly metaphorical in keeping with how the word "children" is also used in 3 John 4. See discussion on pp. 165–69 in chapter 6.
166. Gibbins, "The Second Epistle of St. John," 235–36.
167. For example, in Gal 4:25–26, Paul explicitly states the subject of the metaphor ("*Hagar* is *Mount Sinai in Arabia* and corresponds to the present *Jerusalem*, . . . But the *other woman* corresponds to the *Jerusalem above*"). Italics added. Furthermore, Paul prefaces these verses by pointing out that he was speaking "allegorically" (v. 24). The "woman" of Rev 17:4 is explicitly connected with "Babylon" in v. 5, which is, in turn, revealed in v. 9 to be Rome.
168. See n. 73 above.
169. On the common authorship of 2 and 3 John, see pp. 47–54 in chapter 3.
170. See discussion on pp. 26–27.
171. On the proper meaning(s) of the adjective κυρία in the phrase τῇ κυρίᾳ πατρίδι, see discussion in L. Robert, "Les inscriptions grecques et latines de Sardes," *RAr* 7 (1936): 237–38. In IGLSyria 13.1 9008.6–7, for example, the phrase τῇ κυρίᾳ πατρίδι is properly rendered "to his honored native-city" in the *ed. pr.* See E. Littmann et al., *Syria: Publications of the Princeton University Archaeological Expeditions to Syria in 1904–5 and 1909. Div. 3: Greek and Latin Inscriptions. Sect. A: Southern Syria* (E. J. Brill, 1921), 242.

172. Brown, *The Epistles of John*, 654, cites BAG 459 (BAGD 458) as the source for this reading. While Brown mentions that it appears a handful of times in literary sources, a search of κυρία ἡ ἐκκλησία (*vel sim.*) reveals that it appears in hundreds of pre-Christian inscriptions, mainly from Attica but also other regions.
173. On this meaning, see LSJ s.v. κύριος sec. 1.5: "at Athens, κ. ἐκκλησία a *sovereign* or *principal* assembly" with references provided. See *Montanari*, s.v. κύριος sec. D: "κυρία ἐκκλησία principal assembly."
174. Aristophanes, *Ach.* 19, "when the Assembly's scheduled for a regular dawn meeting" (ὁπότ' οὔσης κυρίας ἐκκλησίας ἑωθινῆς).
175. Aristotle, *Pol.* 1282a.28: ἡ γὰρ ἐκκλησία κυρία πάντων τῶν τοιούτων ἐστὶν ("For the assembly is supreme in all such matters"). See also *Pol.* 1317b.29, 37.
176. Harpocration, *Lexicon in decem oratores Atticos*, K100: κυρία ἐκκλησία· Ὑπερείδης ἐν τῷ Κατὰ Δημέου ξενίας, εἰ γνήσιος. τίνες δὲ αἱ κύριαι ἐκκλησίαι Ἀριστοτέλης δεδήλωκεν ἐν τῇ Ἀθηναίων πολιτείᾳ λέγων: τοὺς πρυτάνεις συνάγειν τὴν βουλὴν καὶ τὸν δῆμον, τὴν μὲν βουλὴν ὁσημέραι, πλὴν ἐάν τις ἀφέσιμος ᾖ, τὸν δὲ δῆμον τετράκις τῆς πρυτανείας ἑκάστης. "προγράφουσι δὲ" φησὶ "καὶ κυρίαν ἐκκλησίαν, ἐν ᾗ δεῖ τὰς ἀρχὰς ἀποχειροτονεῖν οἳ δοκοῦσι μὴ καλῶς ἄρχειν, καὶ περὶ φυλακῆς τῆς χώρας. καὶ τὰς εἰσαγγελίας ἐν ταύτῃ τῇ ἡμέρᾳ τοὺς βουλομένους ποιεῖσθαι" φησι, καὶ τὰ ἑξῆς. ("Principal Assembly: Hypereides in *Against Demeas* for *xenia*, if it is genuine. What the principal assemblies were Aristotle has shown in the *Constitution of the Athenians*, saying that the *prytaneis* convene the council and the people, the council daily, except if it is a holiday, and the people four times each *prytany*: 'And they give prior notice,' he says, 'also of a principal assembly in which it is necessary to vote out the magistrates who seem not to be performing their magistracies well, and (to discuss) concerning the defense of the territory.' And he says that those who wish bring impeachments on that day, and so forth.") Greek text taken from J. J. Keaney, ed., *Harpocration: Lexeis of the Ten Orators* (Adolf M. Hakkert Publisher, 1991), 159–60. English translation adapted from the one given in *Topos Text* at Duke University, https://topostext.org/work/537#.
177. H.-J. Klauck, "Κυρία ἐκκλησία Bauers Wörterbuch und die Exegese des zweiten Johannesbriefes," *ZNW* 81 (1990): 135–38, also points out the problems of reading κυρία ἡ ἐκκλησία as "the lady congregation." See also Klauck, *Der zweite und dritte Johannesbrief*, 36–37.
178. F. C. Baur, "Die Johannesbriefe. Ein Beitrag zur Geschichte des Kanons," *Theologische Jahrbücher* 7 (1848): 329. More recently, see Strecker, *The Johannine Epistles*, 263.
179. For the text of 3 John 9, see n. 44 above.
180. P.-B. Smit, "A Note on the Relationship between II and III John," *BN* 123 (2004), 93–102, argues that the reference to a letter in 3 John 9 is too vague

to identify it with 2 John. Additionally, the circumstances of 2 John should not be directly used to elucidate the circumstances of 3 John.

181. P. W. Comfort, *A Commentary on the Manuscripts and Text of the New Testament* (Kregel Publications, 2015), 401.
182. E.g., 1 Cor 5:9; Eph 3:3; Col 4:16.
183. ἔγραψά τι τῇ ἐκκλησίᾳ vs. ἔγραψά ἂν τῇ ἐκκλησίᾳ. The change appears in several Greek minuscules as well as the Latin Vulgate. For a list of the Greek manuscript evidence, see B. Aland et al., eds., *Novum Testamentum Graecum: Editio Critica Maior: IV Catholic Letters. Part 1, Installment 4: The Second and Third Letter of John, The Letter of Jude*, 394. See also the second edition, B. Aland et al., eds., *Novum Testamentum Graecum: Editio Critica Maior IV: Catholic Letters*, 394.
184. See also discussion in T. K. Heckel, *Die Briefe des Jakobus, Petrus, Johannes und Judas* (Vandenhoeck and Ruprecht), 233–34.
185. Brown, *The Epistles of John*, 17, who states, "In II John 1 the audience is addressed as the *tekna* ('children') of a local church personified as a lady (see also vv. 4,13)." See also Lieu, *I, II, & III John: A Commentary*, 244.
186. κυρίᾳ καὶ τοῖς τέκνοις αὐτῆς.
187. See n. 26 above.
188. On the metaphorical use of the term "child/children" in the New Testament, see 1 Cor 4:17; Phlm 10; 1 Tim 1:2; Tit 1:4. See also discussion on pp. 165–69 in chapter 6.
189. See discussion on pp. 165–69 in chapter 6.
190. Jobes, *1, 2, & 3 John*, 256. Jobes erroneously accents the Greek name as though it is the adjective (ἐκλεκτή) and not the proper name (Ἐκλέκτη). See similar comments by Heckel, *Die Briefe des Jakobus, Petrus, Johannes und Judas*, 235.
191. See discussion on pp. 138–44 in chapter 5.
192. Regrettably, every biblical scholar, except Westcott and Hort, who renders the name Eclecte in Greek accents it incorrectly.
193. Gibbins, "The Second Epistle of St. John," 229–32, noted that since εκλεκτη in v. 1 did not have an article, it should be understood as a proper noun, although not a name.
194. Brown, *The Epistles of John*, 653; Bultmann, *The Johannine Epistles*, 107.
195. See discussion on p. 28.
196. Brown, *The Epistles of John*, 653–54. For a similar argument, see J. Painter, "The Johannine Epistles as Catholic Epistles," in *The Catholic Epistles and Apostolic Tradition*, ed. K.-W Niebuhr and R. W. Wall (Baylor University Press, 2009), 249–50, who argues that 2 John is an "encyclical letter."
197. To this example, the letter from the "Jerusalem Conference" could be added, which is included in Acts 15:23–29. The opening of this letter (v. 23) reads: οἱ ἀπόστολοι καὶ οἱ πρεσβύτεροι ἀδελφοὶ τοῖς κατὰ τὴν Ἀντιόχειαν καὶ Συρίαν καὶ Κιλικίαν ἀδελφοῖς τοῖς ἐξ ἐθνῶν χαίρειν ("The brothers, both the apostles and

the elders, to the brothers and sisters of gentile origin in Antioch and Syria and Cilicia, greetings").

198. Merely capitalizing Ἐκλέκτῃ but otherwise leaving the reading Ἐκλέκτῃ κυρίᾳ does not fully solve the problem, as the address would still remain grammatically obscure. See discussion on pp. 97–98.
199. Lieu, *The Theology of the Johannine Letters*, 93.
200. Technically, a prescript refers to a note that would appear above a letter and was typically added after the letter was written, as in the case of an annotation or docket on an official letter acknowledging its receipt. However, the term is frequently used in scholarship to refer to the opening address of a letter. When I use the term, I use it to refer to the initial address found in a letter, unless otherwise specified.

CHAPTER 3: THE ANSWER IS IN THE PAPYRI

1. J. L. Houlden, *A Commentary on the Johannine Epistles*, 139.
2. That Houlden's comments are informed by how he reads the address in 2 John 1 can be ascertained from the fact that following this statement, he immediately defaults to Bultmann's thesis that 2 John is a "derivative" work and may even be an epistolary fiction based on the nondescript address that should be understood as a metaphor.
3. See discussion in chapter 2.
4. J. Beutler, *Die Johannesbriefe* (Verlag Friedrich Pustet, 2000), 149, notes that virtually no contemporary studies think that the phrase ἐκλεκτῇ κυρίᾳ contains a personal name and that the overwhelming consensus, of which he is part, takes it as a metaphorical personification for a church.
5. The first Greek papyrus from Egypt ever published was the so-called *Charta Borgiana* in 1788 by Danish philologist Niels Iversen Schow: *Charta papyracea Graece scripta Musei Borgiani Velitris* (Rome, 1788). It was republished as SB 1.5124 (ca. 193 CE; Tebtynis). Despite the fanfare that preceded the publication of this text, which consisted of a single large papyrus containing thirteen columns of text and several smaller fragments, when it turned out to be a list of names of conscripted workers on dykes, it garnered little attention in the wider public. The next Greek papyrus to appear in print was published nearly twenty years later in 1805 and preserved a subscription list of bishops who attended the Sixth Ecumenical Council (Constantinople III) in 680/81 CE. See G. Marini, *I papiri diplomatici raccolti ed illustrati* (=P. Marini; Sacra Congregatio de Propaganda Fide, 1805), 211–12 (no. 146). It is republished in R. Riedinger, "Die Präsenz- und Subskriptionslisten des VI. oekumenischen Konzils (680/81) und der Papyrus Vind. G. 3," in *Bayerische Akademie der Wissenschaften: Philosophisch-historische* Klasse, Neue Folge 85 (Verlag Bayerische Akad. der Wiss., 1979), 24–26. Another text in P.Marini

that preserves Greek script is no. 110 (p. 170), but the text is actually Latin. It is republished as P.Ital. 1.24 (VII CE; Ravenna).

6. Vat.Gr. 2289. A. Maio, ed., *Classicorum Auctorum e Vaticanis codicibus editorum collection.* Vol. V (Rome, 1833), 600–01 (=P.Vat.Mai). The text was republished eight years later by B. Peyron, "Papiri greci del Museo di Londra e della Bibliotheca Vaticana," *Reale Accademia di Torino, Classe di Scienze Morali, Storiche e Filologiche, Memorie*, Serie II 3 (1841): 92–93. The papyrus was then republished as UPZ 1.60 by U. Wilcken in 1927. On this letter, see also White, *Light from Ancient Letters*, 66–67 (no. 35), and R. Burnet, *L'Égypte ancienne à travers les papyrus: vie quotidienne* (Flammarion [Département Pygmalion], 2003), 173–74 (no. 107). See also D. J. Thompson, *Memphis Under the Ptolemies*, 2nd ed. (Princeton University Press, 2012), 214–15.
7. U. Wilcken largely reassembled the archive and republished it in a single volume in 1927. Still, new texts periodically surface that belong to the archive, which now consists of upwards of 130 documents. For more on the archive, see G. Jennes, "Life Portraits: People in Worship," in *A Blackwell Companion to Greco-Roman and Late Antique Egypt*, ed. K. Vandorpe (John Wiley, 2019), 474–75; and B. Legras, *Les reclus grecs du Sarapieion de Memphis. Une enquête sur l'hellénisme égyptien*, Studia Hellenistica 49 (Peeters, 2011); Thompson, *Memphis under the Ptolemies*, 199–246.
8. In UPZ I p. 302, the date given for the letter is 168 BCE. More precise dates of Aug. 29, 168 BCE or Sept. 1, 179 BCE have been proposed; see TM no. 3451. It is the second of two letters written to this individual; see also UPZ 1.59: "Isias to Hephaistion."
9. According to Wilcken (UPZ I, pp. 297–99), Hephaistion had made a pilgrimage to the Serapeum in Memphis in gratitude for a triumphant return from a war. More recently, R. Merkelbach, "Zur ἐνκατοχή im Sarapeum zu Memphis," *ZPE* 103 (1994): 293–96, has argued that Hephaistion had been ill and went there to seek the healing powers of the god.
10. The English translation is slightly adapted from the one in White, *Light from Ancient Letters*, 66–67 (no. 35).
11. The letter has been assigned the TM no. 3451, https://www.trismegistos.org/tm/detail.php?tm=3451. There its wordcount is given at 193 words. For the measurements of this papyrus, see P. Canart, "Les papyri grecs de la Bibliothèque Vaticane et du Musée égyptien du Vatican. Histoire et inventaire," in *Miscellanea papyrologica*, ed. R. Pintaudi, Pap.Flor. 7 (Gonnelli, 1980), 386.
12. On this word count for 2 John, see Harris, *1, 2, 3 John*, 239.
13. Additional parallels with 3 John, including the shared use of identical epistolary clichés, could be added: 3 John 6: καλῶς ποιήσεις ("you do well"); UPZ 1.60.20: καλῶς οὖν ποιήσεις.
14. The first papyrological volume to contain letters was P.Petr. 1 nos. 25 (2), 26, 29, and 30 published in 1891. The other papyrological volumes

that began to appear in the mid to late 1880s and early 1890s featured either literary texts or other kinds of documents: for example, P.Hermias (1884; Demotic and Greek); P.CorpusRevillout 1 (1885; Demotic), P.CorpusRevillout 2 (1888; Demotic); MPER 1 (1887; Arabic, Coptic, Hebrew, Greek); MPER 2–3 (1887; Arabic, Coptic, Greek); MPER 4 (1888); P.Hawara (1889); P.Lond.Lit. (1891).

15. By 1900, only 14 papyrological volumes in print contained letters: 1891: P.Petr. 1; 1893: P.Lond. 1; P.Petr. 2; 1895: BGU 1; CPR 1; 1896: P.Grenf. 1; P.Rev. (1st ed.); 1897: P.Grenf. 2; 1898: BGU 2; P.Lond. 2; P.Oxy. 1; 1899: P.Oxy. 2; O.Wilck.; 1900: P.Fay. In these 14 volumes, I counted a little over 150 published letters. For the letters listed in these volumes, see C.-H. Kim, "Index of Greek Papyrus Letters," *Semeia* 22 (1981): 107–12.
16. If one counts documents like applications, petitions, invitations, etc., that carry "epistolary" features. On the characteristics of "proper" letters in the papyri, see useful discussion in M. Choat, *Belief and Cult in Fourth-Century Papyri*, Studia Antiqua Australiensia 1 (Brepols, 2006), 12–16.
17. For these statistics, see Brown, *The Epistles of John*, 15. In Lieu, *The Second and Third Epistles of John*, 38 n. 5, the word count 245 is given for 2 John, but for 3 John, it is 185.
18. Brown, *The Epistles of John*, 15–16, summarizes the evidence well. More recently, see Schnelle, *Die Johannesbriefe*, 5, but I am not sure why Schnelle insists in his discussion of the common authorship of 2 and 3 John that they were both composed by an elder named "John." More recently, see authorship discussion in Jobes, *1, 2, & 3 John*, 28–29.
19. English translations in the table are my own. On the parallel between 2 John 5 and 3 John 5, see discussion on pp. 145–46 in chapter 5.
20. C. Clemen, "Beiträge zum geschichtlichen Verständnis der Johannesbriefe," *ZNW* 6 (1905): 271–81. For a nineteenth-century view, see F. Schleiermacher, *Einleitung ins das Neue Testament* (G. Reimer, 1845), 399–400.
21. Clemen, "Beiträge zum geschichtlichen Verständnis der Johannesbriefe," 278. In his discussion, he considers it inconceivable that 2 John was the letter mentioned in 3 John 9.
22. A little over a decade earlier, Adolf Jülicher had not merely asserted that 2 John was the work of a forger but also claimed that 3 John was the work of a forger. According to Jülicher, a later disciple who had access to the Gospel of John and 1 John used both to create two small letters to say more about church discipline and authority. See A. Jülicher, *Einleitung in das Neue Testament*, Erster Band (Akademische Verlagsbuchhandlung von J. C. B. Mohr [Paul Siebeck], 1894), 158–60.
23. Bultmann, *Die drei Johannesbriefe*, 103.
24. Bultmann, *Die drei Johannesbriefe*, 104.
25. Bultmann, *Die drei Johannesbriefe*, 10.

26. Bultmann, *Die drei Johannesbriefe*, 104.
27. R. Bultmann, "Johannesbriefe," in *Religion in Geschichte und Gegenwart*, 3rd ed., ed. H. F. von Campenhausen et al. (Mohr Siebeck, 1959), 3.839.
28. J. Heise, *Bleiben. Menein in den Johanneischen Schriften* (Mohr, 1967), 164–70.
29. Heise, *Bleiben. Menein in den Johanneischen Schriften*, 165.
30. Heise, *Bleiben. Menein in den Johanneischen Schriften*, 166. While Heise accepted the metaphorical interpretation of ἐκλεκτῇ κυρίᾳ, he felt that the juxtaposition of the terms ἐκλεκτή and κυρία in the address did not go well together and claimed that the way the adjective ἐκλεκτή was employed in the address corresponded best with how it was used in the Pastoral Epistles and Apostolic Fathers.
31. Heise, *Bleiben. Menein in den Johanneischen Schriften*, 165, 170.
32. See E. Käsemann, "Ketzer und Zeuge: Zum johanneischen Verfasserproblem," *ZTK* 48 (1951): 292–311; a reedition was published in E. Käsemann, *Exegetische Versuche und Besinnungen*, 2 vols. (Vandenhoeck and Ruprecht, 1960), 1.168–87. According to Käsemann, the dispute between the elder and Diotrephes revolved around heresy. In his theory, the elder, not Diotrephes, was the real heretic, as he was allegedly a gnostic. Apparently, the elder propagated gnostic teachings in the Gospel of John and 1 John and was censured by Diotrephes, who was acting in his capacity as a bishop.
33. 2 John 4: ἐχάρην λίαν ὅτι εὕρηκα ἐκ τῶν τέκνων σου περιπατοῦντας ἐν ἀληθείᾳ ("I was overjoyed to find some of your children walking in the truth"); cf. 3 John 4: μειζοτέραν τούτων οὐκ ἔχω χαράν, ἵνα ἀκούω τὰ ἐμὰ τέκνα ἐν ἀληθείᾳ περιπατοῦντα ("I have no greater joy than this, to hear that my children are walking in the truth").
34. G. Schunack, *Die Briefe des Johannes* (Theologischer Verlag, 1982), 107–9.
35. Schunack, *Die Briefe des Johannes*, 108.
36. Schunack, *Die Briefe des Johannes*, 107.
37. Schunack, *Die Briefe des Johannes*, 109.
38. H. Balz, "Die Johannesbriefe" in *Die Katholischen Briefe: Die Briefe des Jakobus, Petrus, Johannes und Judas*, ed. H. Balz and W. Schrage (Vandenhoeck and Ruprecht, 1982), 156–222.
39. Balz, "Die Johannesbriefe," 158.
40. Balz, "Die Johannesbriefe," 161. 2 John 9: πᾶς ὁ προάγων καὶ μὴ μένων ἐν τῇ διδαχῇ τοῦ Χριστοῦ θεὸν οὐκ ἔχει· ὁ μένων ἐν τῇ διδαχῇ, οὗτος καὶ τὸν πατέρα καὶ τὸν υἱὸν ἔχει ("Everyone who does not abide in the teaching of Christ, but goes beyond it, does not have God; whoever abides in the teaching has both the Father and the Son"); cf. 3 John 11b: ὁ ἀγαθοποιῶν ἐκ τοῦ θεοῦ ἐστιν· ὁ κακοποιῶν οὐχ ἑώρακεν τὸν θεόν ("Whoever does good is from God; whoever does evil has not seen God").
41. Klauck, *Der zweite und dritte Johannesbrief*, 17–18.
42. Klauck, *Der zweite und dritte Johannesbrief*, 18.

43. Lieu, *I, II, and III John*, 244–45.
44. Lieu, *I, II, and III John*, 245.
45. Lieu, *I, II, and III John*, 7.
46. Jülicher, *Einleitung in das Neue Testament*, 158–60. See n. 22 above.
47. Dibelius, "Johannesbriefe," 348.
48. E. Hirsch, *Studien zum vierten Evangelium. Text, Literarkritik, Entstehungsgeschichte* (Mohr, 1936), 177–79.
49. Hirsch, *Studien zum vierten Evangelium*, 177–78.
50. Hirsch, *Studien zum vierten Evangelium*, 177.
51. R. Bergmeier, "Zum Verfasserproblem des II. und III. Johannesbriefes," *ZNW* 57 (1966): 93–100.
52. Bergmeier, "Zum Verfasserproblem des II. und III. Johannesbriefes," 99–100.
53. Bultmann, *Die drei Johannesbriefe*, 95–104.
54. Bultmann, *Die drei Johannesbriefe*, 103–4.
55. See pp. 50–51.
56. M. De Jonge, *De Brieven van Johannes* (Callenbach, 1968), 235.
57. De Jonge, *De Brieven van Johannes*, 235.
58. U. Körtner, *Papias von Hierapolis: Ein Beitrag zur Geschichte des frühen Christentums* (Vandenhoeck and Ruprecht, 1983).
59. Körtner, *Papias von Hierapolis*, 198–202. Körtner rejects the idea that the "John the elder" mentioned by Papias is the author of 2 and 3 John. He argues instead that the two letters are pseudonymous and that the author was trying to pass them off as letters of "John the elder."
60. Körtner, *Papias von Hierapolis*, 199.
61. Körtner, *Papias von Hierapolis*, 199.
62. Körtner, *Papias von Hierapolis*, 199–200. Like Jülicher, Dibelius, and Hirsch, Körtner also claimed that 3 John was a literary fiction. Despite the overtly personal nature of the letter, he raises the possibility that the names used in 3 John are merely pseudonyms conscripted by the writer to address contemporary issues. For example, he speculates whether the name Gaius was used in the letter since it was so common in antiquity.
63. Beutler, *Die Johannesbriefe*, 144–45.
64. Beutler, *Die Johannesbriefe*, 145.
65. Lieu, *I, II, & III John*, 6.
66. Lieu, *I, II, & III John*, 240–41.
67. Lieu, *I, II, & III John*, 265.
68. Lieu is the only one to mention the epistolary papyri in her discussion of 2 John. See discussion on p. 59.
69. J. R. Harris, "The Problem of the Address in the Second Epistle of John," 194–203.
70. B. Bresky, *Das Verhältnis des zweiten Johannesbriefes zum dritten*. See pp. 23–24 in chapter 2.

71. A. Deissmann, *Licht vom Osten: Das Neue Testament und die neuentdeckten Texte der hellenistisch-römischen Welt*. See pp. 24–25 in chapter 2.
72. Marty, "Contribution à l'étude des problèmes johanniques: Les petites épîtres 'II et III Jean,'" 208, n. 5.
73. R. W. Funk, "The Form and Structure of II and III John," *JBL* 86 (1967): 424–30.
74. Funk, "The Form and Structure of II and III John," 424. When his study appeared, about one thousand epistolary papyri were available in published form. See Kim, "Index of Greek Papyrus Letters," 107–12.
75. Funk, "The Form and Structure of II and III John," 426, states, "It would thus appear that the ἐχάρην λίαν periods in II and III John are the functional equivalents of the εὐχαριστῶ thanksgiving periods, well-known from Paul and elsewhere." This is not the case; in 2 and 3 John, ἐχάρην λίαν functions in a distinctly different way than εὐχαριστῶ in Paul. In 2 and 3 John, ἐχάρην λίαν is used (see discussion at pp. 64–65) to express joy at the receipt of good news, whereas εὐχαριστῶ is used to give thanks to God. See P. Arzt-Grabner, "Paul's Letter Thanksgiving," in *Paul and the Ancient Letter Form*, ed. S. E. Porter and S. A. Adams (Brill, 2010), 129–58.
76. Funk, "The Form and Structure of II and III John," 424.
77. Here, it probably goes without saying, but a genuine letter (i.e., one sent to address a historically present situation to an actual recipient who was physically removed from the sender) can still seek to impose an ecclesiastical agenda.
78. U. C. von Wahlde, *The Gospel and Letters of John. Volume 3: Commentary on the Three Johannine Letters* (William B. Eerdmans, 2010), 402–8, contains an appendix on how 2 and 3 John contain the formal elements of the "Greek Letter," but he does not cite a single papyrus although the examples he cites are clearly based on conclusions derived directly from the epistolary papyri. Similarly, in Jobes, *1, 2, & 3 John*, 282, 290–91, 335, she mentions a handful of papyri in her treatment of 3 John but not in 2 John. In P. Arzt-Grabner, *Letters and Letter Writing*, Papyri and the New Testament 2 (Brill Schöningh, 2023), he does a masterful job with the epistolary papyri and generally comparing them, where appropriate, with letters in the New Testament. However, no sustained comparison of 2 John and the epistolary papyri exists.
79. Lieu, *The Second and Third Epistles of John*, 37–51.
80. In Lieu's most recent treatment of 3 John (*I, II, & III John*), she includes a handful of papyrological references (pp. 265–83). However, there are no such references in her treatment of 2 John.
81. Lieu, *The Second and Third Epistles of John*, 50.
82. Lieu, *The Second and Third Epistles of John*, 51.
83. Lieu, *I, II, & III John*, 239.
84. The Chinese invented an early paper form during the Eastern Han period ca. 25–225 CE. It was not until the eighth century that it really spread into

the Islamic world and became more widespread in the Mediterranean. In the LDAB, the earliest text written on paper is BKU 3.2 396 (TM 243980) from the sixth century; it preserves recipes for pharmaceutical products and is written in Greek and Latin. The earliest text on paper in the HGV is SB 26.16820 from the late eighth or ninth century. It contains a division table.

85. Pliny, *NH* 13.74–83. See also N. Lewis, *Papyrus in Classical Antiquity* (Clarendon, 1974), 34–69.

86. Ps.-Demetrius, *Eloc.* 223: ἐπεὶ δὲ καὶ ὁ ἐπιστολικὸς χαρακτὴρ δεῖται ἰσχνότητος, καὶ περὶ αὐτοῦ λέξομεν. Ἀρτέμων μὲν οὖν ὁ τὰς Ἀριστοτέλους ἀναγράψας ἐπιστολάς φησιν, ὅτι δεῖ ἐν τῷ αὐτῷ τρόπῳ διάλογόν τε γράφειν καὶ ἐπιστολάς· εἶναι γὰρ τὴν ἐπιστολὴν οἷον τὸ ἕτερον μέρος τοῦ διαλόγου ("We will next discuss the style for letters, since that too should be plain. Artemon, the editor of Aristotle's Letters, says that a letter should be written in the same manner as a dialogue; the letter, he says, is like one of the two sides to a dialogue."). Greek text and translation taken from D. C. Innes, ed. and trans., *Demetrius: On Style*, LCL 199 (Harvard University Press, 1999), 476–79.

87. R. Richards, *Paul and First-Century Letter Writing: Secretaries, Composition and Collection* (InterVarsity, 2004), 163, notes that the average Roman-era papyrus letter was about 87 words, but his statistics are questionable. On the general brevity of the epistolary papyri, see also Arzt-Grabner, *Letters and Letter Writing*, 8–11. He notes that the longest extant letter preserved on papyrus is P.Ammon 1.3 (ca. 324–30 CE; sent from Alexandria to Panopolis). It was at least six columns in length, and the extant text contains 1,514 words. According to Arzt-Grabner, its length can be compared to Paul's letter to the Galatians. On the other end of the spectrum, he notes O.Claud. 1.151 (II CE), where the complete letter from start to finish consists of a mere 25 words.

88. These statistics are taken from O. Roller, *Das Formular der paulinischen Briefe: Ein Beitrag zur Lehre vom antike Briefe*, BWANT 58 (W. Kohlhammer, 1933), 360–61 statistics for Cicero; 362 statistics for Pliny; 362–63 statistics for Cornelius Fronto.

89. See n. 18 in chapter 1. After 2 and 3 John, the next shortest letter in the New Testament is Philemon, with 335 words, followed by Jude, with 461 words. By comparison, 1 John has 2,141 words and is about ten times as long as either 2 or 3 John.

90. For comparison, UPZ 1.60, mentioned at the start of this chapter and containing just under two hundred words, was written on a single sheet of papyrus measuring 32.9 x 18.2 cm. See n. 11 above. The typical papyrus roll could measure up to 15 meters in length and generally ranged from 22 to 38 cm in height. Depending on the kind of document, the width of the papyrus might vary. See W. Johnson, *Bookrolls and Scribes in Oxyrhynchus* (University of Toronto Press, 2004), 143–52.

91. On Ptolemaic letters, see R. Buzon, "Die Briefe der Ptolemäerzeit: Ihre Struktur und ihre Formeln" (PhD diss., Ruprecht-Karl-Universität Heidelberg, 1984). See also J. L. White, "The Greek Documentary Letter Tradition Third Century B.C.E. to Third Century C.E.," *Semeia* 22 (1981): 89–106.
92. G. Tibiletti, *Le lettere private nei papiri greci del III e IV secolo d.C.: Tra paganesimo e cristianesimo* (Vita e Pensiero, 1979).
93. For the kinds of changes epistolary papyri underwent in the third and fourth centuries CE, see discussion in J.-L. Fournet, "Esquisse d'une anatomie de la lettre antique tardive d'après les papyrus," in *Correspondances. Documents pour l'histoire de l'Antiquité tardive. Actes du colloque international Université Charles-de-Gaulle - Lille 3, 20–22 novembre 2003*, ed. R. Delmaire, J. Desmulliez, and P.-L. Gatier (Maison De L'orient, 2009), 23–66. Accompanying the literary changes, the layout of the letters on the papyrus also changed. Until the third century, it was common for letters to be written on sheets of papyrus where the height of the sheet was greater than the width and for the letter to have a vertically rectangular shape. However, in the latter part of the third century, there was a shift, and the height tended to be less than the length, so the letters had a distinct horizontally rectangular shape.
94. On a reasonable range of dates for the composition of 2 John, see n. 89 in chapter 1.
95. See n. 200 in chapter 2.
96. On the different types of letters found among the papyri, F. X. J. Exler, *The Form of the Ancient Greek Letter: A Study in Greek Epistolography* (Catholic University of America, 1923), 23, posited four general categories: familiar letters, business letters, petitions/applications, and official letters. For Exler, familial letters were those between relatives and friends but also included letters that used language that suggested familiarity between the sender and the addressee. Business letters dealt with commercial or even legal matters but took the form of a letter. Petitions/applications were those letters where the sender requested redress and were typically addressed to an official. Finally, official letters were those written or received by officials and represented administrative communication.
97. Arzt-Grabner, *Letters and Letter Writing*, 74–77; H.-J. Klauck, *Ancient Letters and the New Testament: A Guide to Context and Exegesis* (Baylor University Press, 2006), 17–18; White, *Light from Ancient Letters*, 198–200.
98. In epistolary correspondence from the fifth century BCE onward, when the verb χαίρω started to appear regularly in epistolary address, it came to be written in the prescript as the infinitive χαίρειν. Without the accompaniment of a finite verb, which causes natural grammatical problems, Greek grammarians argued that a λέγει ought to be understood as operative even if it was not written in the address. Thus, such greetings are to be understood as follows: "A says (λέγει) to B χαίρειν (to rejoice)" or "to feel greeted"—therefore, "A to

B, greetings." See discussion in P. Ceccarelli, *Ancient Greek Letter Writing: A Cultural History (600–150 BC)* (Oxford University Press, 2013), 89–99.

99. P.Fay. 109.1 (I CE; Euhemeria, Arsinoite).

100. The initial health wish is attested in over seven hundred epistolary papyri; see D. Nachtergaele, *The Formulaic Language of the Greek Private Papyrus Letters* (Trismegistos, 2023), 121. See also P. Arzt, "The 'Epistolary Introductory Thanksgiving' in the Papyri and in Paul," *NovT* 36 (1994): 38–44.

    Seneca (ca. 4 BCE–65 CE) describes this initial health wish in Latin letters: "The old Romans had a custom which survived even into my lifetime. They would add to the opening words of a letter: 'If you are well, it is well; I also am well.'" Seneca, *Ep.* 15.1: *si vales, bene est, ego valeo.* Latin text and translation is taken from R. M. Gummere, trans., *Seneca. Epistles, Volume I: 1–65*, LCL 75 (Harvard University Press, 1917), 94–95. However, whereas the Latin health wish *si vales, bene est, ego valeo* became so fixed that it was often just abbreviated *SVBEEV*, the Greek counterpart attested in the epistolary papyri had considerable variation. See Exler, *The Form of the Ancient Greek Letter*, 106.

101. πρὸ μὲν πάντων εὔχομαί σε ὑγιαίνειν. Nachtergaele, *The Formulaic Language of the Greek Private Papyrus Letters*, 149–70, for the formula πρὸ πάντων εὔχομαί σε ὑγιαίνειν *vel sim.*

102. For example, BGU 2.632.3–5 (II CE): πρὸ μὲν πάντων εὔχομαί σε ὑγιαίνειν, καἰγὼ (*l.* καὶ ἐγὼ) γὰρ αὐτὸς ὑγιαίν[ω] ("Before all else, I pray that you are well; I myself am also well"); W.Chr. 480.2–6 (II CE): πρὸ μὲν πάντων εὔχομαί σε ὑγιαίνειν καὶ διὰ παντὸς ἐρωμένον (*l.* ἐρρωμένον) εὐτυχεῖν μετὰ τῆς ἀδελφῆς μου καὶ τῆς θυγατρὸς αὐτῆς καὶ τοῦ ἀδελφοῦ μου ("Before all else, I pray that you are well and that you may prosper in continual health, together with my sister and her sister and my brother"); SB 28.16995.2–5 (I/II CE): εἰ ἔρρωσαι σύ τε καὶ Πρώταρχος καὶ οὓς αἱρεῖ, εἴη ἂν ὡς [ἐ]γὼ βούλομαι, καὶ αὐτοὶ δὲ ὑγιαίνομεν ("If you and Protrachus are well, and those whom you choose, then it would be as I want, and we ourselves are well").

103. Nachtergaele, *The Formulaic Language of the Greek Private Papyrus Letters*, 121, notes that these formulae hardly appear in letters from the fifth century onward.

104. G. Geraci, "Ricerche sul Proskynema," *Aeg* 51 (1971): 3–211.

105. A few examples include BGU 3.843.1–5 (I/II CE): Τακάλι[ς] Σερήνῳ τῷ ἀδ[ελφῷ] πλεῖστα χαίρειν. πρὸ μὲμ (*l.* μὲν) πά[ν]των εὔχομαί σε ὑγιαίνειν καὶ [τὸ] προσκύνημά σου ποιῶ παρὰ [τῷ] κυρίῳ Σαράπιδι ("Takalis to Serenus her brother, very many greetings. Before all else I pray that you are well and I make obeisance on your behalf before the lord Sarapis"); P.Mich. 8.490.1–5 (II CE): Ἀπολλινᾶρις Ταησίῳ τῇ μητρὶ πολλὰ χαίρειν. πρὸ παντὸς ἔρρωσό μοι ὑγιαίνουσα τὸ προσκύνημά σου ποιῶν παρὰ πᾶσι τοῖς θεοῖς ("Apollinaris to Thaesion, his mother, many greetings. Before all else I wish you good health and make obeisance on your behalf to all the gods"); P.Fay. 130 (II/III CE): Μύσθης

Σεραπάμμωνι τ[ῷ] ἀδελφῷ πλεῖστα χαίρειν. πρὸ μὲν πάντων εὔχομαί σε ὑγιαίνιν (*l.* ὑγιαίνειν) καὶ τ[ὸ] προσκύνημά σου ποιῶ κατ' ἑκάστην ἡμέραν παρὰ τοι (*l.* τοῖς) ἐνθά[δ]ε θεοῖς. ("Mysthes to Serapammon his brother, very many greetings. Before all else, I pray that you are well and I make obeisance on your behalf every day to the gods here").

106. The *proskynesis* formula might contain a generic obeisance to a "god" or "the gods," or oftimes deities like "Sarapis" or "Isis" are specifically invoked. Nachtergaele, *The Formulaic Language of the Greek Private Papyrus Letters*, 202–11. It is believed that the formula disappeared in the fourth and fifth centuries CE due to the rise of Christianity, but it appears that there were even cases of a Christianized *proskynesis* to the "Lord God" (Κυρίῳ Θεῷ). See M. Depauw, *The Demotic Letter. A Study of Epistolographic Scribal Traditions Against Their Intra- and Intercultural Background*, Demotische Studien 14 (Gisela Zauzich Verlag, 2006), 180, and Choat, *Belief and Cult in Fourth-Century Papyri*, 94–96.
107. Ps.-Demetrius in *Epistolary Types* gives twenty-one reasons for writing a letter. See A. J. Malherbe, *Ancient Epistolary Theorists* (Scholars Press, 1988), 30–41.
108. J. L. White, "New Testament Epistolary Literature in the Framework of Ancient Epistolography," *ANRW* 25/2 (1984): 1736.
109. P. Parsons, "Background: The Papyrus Letter," *Didactica classica Gandensia* 20 (1980): 10.
110. Parsons, "Background: The Papyrus Letter," 7–8.
111. Nachtergaele, *The Formulaic Language of the Greek Private Papyrus Letters*, 240–50. Periodically, the valediction was expanded to "I pray you farewell" (ἐρρῶσθαί σε εὔχομαι) and expresses a more endearing touch. Though prayers for the health of the addressee may sound uniquely Christian, as with the health formula where εὔχομαι ("I pray") was also employed, such terminology is found in all kinds of contexts and was used in non-Christian and Christian letters.
112. H. Koskenniemi, *Studien zur Idee und Phraseologie des griechischen Briefes bis 400 n. Chr.* (Akateeminen Kirjakauppa; Otto Harrassowitz, 1956), 151.
113. In the New Testament, only three letters employ the infinitive χαίρειν as the salutation: Jas 1:1 and two embedded letters in Acts at 15:23 and 23:26. In the epistolary papyri, sometimes χαίρειν was intensified in the address. In letters where the sender wanted to enthusiastically greet the addressee, the sender might add πολύς, -η, -ον ("many" or "much") or the superlative πλεῖστος, -η, -ον ("very many" or "most"), which in these situations carried an adverbial function and always appeared as πολλά or πλεῖστα: "A [to] B πολλὰ χαίρειν ('many greetings')" or "A [to] B πλεῖστα χαίρειν ('very many greetings')." On the adverbial use of these adjectives with comparable examples, see LSJ s.v. πλεῖστος. For a listing of letters that employ πολλὰ χαίρειν or πλεῖστα χαίρειν, see Exler, *The Form of the Ancient Greek Letter*, 27–29. The intensifier πολλά appears in the prescript of about 150 epistolary papyri dated between the first

century BCE and the fifth/sixth century CE. In contrast, the use of πλεῖστα is more common, with almost 400 attestations between the first century BCE and the fourth/fifth century CE. See Nachtergaele, *The Formulaic Language of the Greek Private Papyrus Letters*, 55. She further notes on the same page, "The two intensifiers had the same evolution and they existed next to each other: they are not linked to different regions of Egypt."

114. After χαίρειν, the next most common salutation was εὖ πράττειν ("be well"), which was preferred by Plato and Epicurus (Diogenes Laertius, *Lives* 3.61 [Plato], 10.14 [Epicurus]). Other salutations are also attested. In P.Oxy. 1.115, a second-century CE letter of condolence sent by a woman named Eirene to a couple who had presumably lost a loved one, the opening address is: Εἰρήνη Ταοννώφρει καὶ Φίλωνι εὐψυχεῖν ("Eirene to Taonnophris and Philon, be of good courage"). The use of εὐψυχεῖν, which appears in epitaphs bidding farewell to the deceased, was surely chosen as the verb of salutation due to the context. Similarly, in another letter of condolence from the same period, εὐθυμεῖν ("to be of good cheer") is used in the address (P.Hamb. 4.254.1 [early II CE]).

115. Exler, *The Form of the Ancient Greek Letter*, 56, 64. These typically tend to be official letters.

116. χάρις ὑμῖν καὶ εἰρήνη. 1 Thess. 1:1.

117. χάρις ὑμῖν καὶ εἰρήνη ἀπὸ θεοῦ πατρὸς ἡμῶν καὶ κυρίου Ἰησοῦ Χριστοῦ. Rom 1:7; 1 Cor 1:3; 2 Cor 1:2; Gal 1:3; Phil 1:2; Phlm 3.

118. ἔσται μεθ᾽ ἡμῶν χάρις ἔλεος εἰρήνη παρὰ θεοῦ πατρὸς καὶ παρὰ Ἰησοῦ Χριστοῦ τοῦ υἱοῦ τοῦ πατρὸς ἐν ἀληθείᾳ καὶ ἀγάπῃ.

119. Bultmann, *Die drei Johannesbriefe*, 103, even notes that 2 John contains all three parts of the epistolary prescript: superscript, adscript, and salutation.

120. 3 John 2: ἀγαπητέ, περὶ πάντων εὔχομαί σε εὐοδοῦσθαι καὶ ὑγιαίνειν, καθὼς εὐοδοῦταί σου ἡ ψυχή ("Beloved, I pray that all may go well with you and that you may be in good health, just as it is well with your soul"). 3 John is the only New Testament letter containing a health wish for the recipient. In epistolary papyri, the prepositional opening of the health wish is most often πρὸ μὲν πάντων ("before everything") or is periodically διὰ παντὸς ("continually"). However, 3 John's περὶ πάντων ("concerning all") might be attested once: BGU 3.885.1–2 (ca. 76 CE): Θεόκτιστ[ος Ἀπολ(λωνίῳ) τῷ φιλτάτῳ χαίρειν.] περὶ πάντω[ν εὔχομαί σε ὑγιαίνειν] ("Theoctistus to his dearest Apollonius, greetings. Concerning all things I pray that you are well"). In the epistolary papyri, the phrase περὶ πάντων most often appears in requests to the addressee to make all things in a particular situation known to the sender: for example, SB 10.10529 Fr A.22–24 (I/II CE): ἐὰν εὕρῃς εὐκερίαν (*l.* εὐκαιρίαν), γράψις (*l.* γράψεις) μοι ἀσφαλῶς περὶ πάντων ("If you find an opportunity, assuredly write to me about everything"). Similarly, 3 John's use of εὐοδοῦσθαι ("to go well" or "to prosper") only occurs in one letter: P.Oxy. 14.1680.3–5 (III/IV CE): καὶ ε[ὔχομ]αι τῷ θεῷ ὁλοκληρεῖν σε καὶ εὐοδο[ῦ]σθαι καὶ ὑγιαινοτι (*l.* ὑγιαίνο(ν)) σε ἀπολαβεῖν ἐν τοῖς

ἰδίοις ("And I pray to god that you are whole and that you prosper and that we receive you home in good health"). As in 3 John 2, it was not unusual to have more than one complimentary verb in a health wish: O.Krok. 2.231.2 (98–117 CE): [πρὸ μὲν πάντων ε]ὔχομαί σε ἰσχύιν (*l.* ἰσχύειν) καὶ ὑγ<ι>αίνειν ("Before everything I pray that you are strong and well"); Chr.Wilck.480.2–6 (II CE): πρὸ μὲν πάντων εὔχομαί σε ὑγιαίνειν καὶ διὰ παντὸς ἐρωμένον (*l.* ἐρρωμένον) εὐτυχεῖν μετὰ τῆς ἀδελφῆς μου καὶ τῆς θυγατρὸς αὐτῆς καὶ τοῦ ἀδελφοῦ μου ("Before everything I pray you are well and continually happen to be strong with my sister and her daughter and my brother"); CPR 7.55.2–3 (II CE): πρὸ μ̣ὲ̣[ν] τῶν ὅλ̣ω̣ν εὔχομαί σ̣ε̣ ὑγιαίνειν κ̣α̣[ὶ] τ̣ὰ̣ μ̣ε[γ]ά̣[λ]α π̣ράττ̣ε̣ιν. ("Before everything I pray you are well and the best things happen"); P.Mich. 8.510.2–3 (late II CE): πρὸ [μὲν] πάν[τ]ων εὔχομ[αί σε ὑγ]ι̣έ̣ν̣[ι]ν̣ (*l.* ὑγιαίνειν) καὶ [εὐτ]υ̣χῖ̣ν̣ (*l.* εὐτυχεῖν) ("Before everything I pray that you are well and happy").

121. White, *Light from Ancient Letters*, 201.
122. Klauck, *Ancient Letters and the New Testament*, 33.
123. The examples provided in the table are not exhaustive.
124. White, "New Testament Epistolary Literature in the Framework of Ancient Epistolography," 1736.
125. The examples provided in the table are not exhaustive. The translation in the NRSVue of "dear lady" is too strong; "lady" is sufficient.
126. The opening of the body in this letter begins with a request using σε ἠρώτησα (ll. 3–4) and then a few lines later it is followed up with the present request.
127. Ἀπίων Ἐπιμάχῳ τῶι πατρὶ καὶ κυρίῳ πλεῖστα χαίρειν.
128. ἐρωτῶ σε οὖν, κύριέ μου πάτηρ (*l.* πάτερ).
129. It is also worth noting that 3 John 5 does the same thing (see also 3 John 11). As in 2 John 5 with κυρία, 3 John 5 defaults to the title used in v. 1 ἀγαπητός ("beloved") when a form of request is being made.
130. There is only one extant example in the epistolary papyri where the reflexive pronoun follows βλέπε as in 2 John 8: W.Chr. 60.24–26 (41 CE): καὶ σὺ βλέπε σατὸν (*l.* σεαυτὸν) ἀπὸ τῶν Ἰουδαίων ("and guard yourself from the Jews").
131. The examples provided in the table are not exhaustive.
132. 3 John 14 employs similar language. The desire of "the elder" in 2 John 12 and 3 John 14 to speak with the recipients of the letters "face to face" (lit. "mouth to mouth" [στόμα πρὸς στόμα]) contains a similar expression to what appears in LXX Jer 39:4 [32:4]: καὶ λαλήσει στόμα αὐτοῦ πρὸς στόμα αὐτοῦ ("and his mouth shall speak to his mouth"). This idiom is not attested in the epistolary papyri. Instead, the idiom for "face to face" seems to have been predominantly κατὰ πρόσωπον: P.Lond. 2.479.1–7 (pp. 255–56; III CE): Τιθ̣ιό̣εις Ε̣ἰ̣ρηνίω[ν]ι τῷ φιλτάτ̣[ῳ] χαίρε̣[ιν]. πρὸ μὲν πάντων εὔχομαι [σ]ε ὑγιαίνειν πανοικησίᾳ. ἐβ̣ουλόμην μὲν ἐγὼ ἐλθεῖν εἵν̣α̣ (l. ἵνα) σοι κατὰ [π]ρόσωπον διηγήσομαι ("Tithoes to the dearest Eirenion, greetings. Before all else, I pray that you are healthy with your whole household. I want to come so that I can tell you face to face").

133. J. L. White, "Epistolary Formulas and Cliches in Greek Papyrus Letters," *SBLSP* 2 (1978): 307.
134. In addition to the examples provided, see the following similar examples where ἐλπίζω is used: BGU 1.249.13–14 (ca. 75/76 CE); O.Did. 349.4–5 (ca. 77–96 CE); P.Amh. 2.131.5–8 (=P.Sarap. 80; II CE).
135. Cf. 3 John 14: ἐλπίζω δὲ εὐθέως σε ἰδεῖν ("instead I hope to see you soon").
136. The examples provided in the table are not exhaustive.
137. See discussion on p. 63.
138. This number jumps to over 2,300 if you include letters from other periods. See p. 61.
139. Nachtergaele, *The Formulaic Language of the Greek Private Papyrus Letters*, 311.
140. Exler, *The Form of the Ancient Greek Letter*, 62. See also F. Ziemann, "De epistularum Graecarum formulis sollemnibus quaestiones selectae" (PhD diss., Halle, 1910), 253.
141. Nachtergaele, *The Formulaic Language of the Greek Private Papyrus Letters*, 278.
142. When it is used fictively, it can be done to express solidarity and/or equality with the addressee. See discussion on pp. 166–67 in chapter 6.
143. Bagnall and Cribiore, *Women's Letters from Ancient Egypt*, 85–86.
144. In order of attestation, the next most used kinship terms of address include πατήρ ("father"), ὑίος ("son"), μήτηρ ("mother"), θυγάτηρ ("daughter"), and σύμβιος ("spouse"). Nachtergaele, *The Formulaic Language of the Greek Private Papyrus Letters*, 278–79, provides statistics.
145. The most common of these titles are adjectives that appear in the superlative form and are φίλτατος, -η ("most dear" or "dearest"), τιμιώτατος, -η ("most honored" or "most esteemed"), and γλυκύτατος, -η ("sweetest"). Regarding the use of φίλτατος and τιμιώτατος, they do not generally appear to have been exceptionally intimate titles of address. They often may have been employed merely for politeness or flattery, as they periodically appear in letters where a subordinate addresses a superior. See H. Koskenniemi, *Studien zur Idee und Phraseologie des griechischen Briefes bis 400 n. Chr.*, 98–103. On the other hand, the use of γλυκύτατος appears more intimate and seems to have been used between persons with a close connection, like members of the same family or between husband and wife. See Koskenniemi, *Studien zur Idee und Phraseologie des griechischen Briefes bis 400 n. Chr.*, 103. These epithets might appear independently, being the only modifier of the addressee's name, or be compounded with kinship terminology. As with the previous kinship and familial titles discussed, when these are employed, the word order remains the same.
146. See Nachtergaele, *The Formulaic Language of the Greek Private Papyrus Letters*, 285, who notes nearly four hundred attestations of these titles in epistolary address.
147. Seneca reports that *domine* ("sir") was such a standard greeting that it was the customary greeting for people whose name one had forgotten (Seneca, *Ep.* 3.1): Itaque si proprio illo verbo quasi publico usus es et sic illum amicum vocasti,

quomodo omnes candidatos bonos viros dicimus, quomodo obvios, si nomen non succurrit, dominos salutamus, hac abierit ("Now if you used this word of ours in the popular sense, and called him 'friend' in the same way in which we speak of all candidates for election as 'honourable gentlemen,' and as we greet all men whom we meet casually, if their names slip us for the moment, with the salutation, 'my dear sir,'—so be it"). The translation is taken from Gummere, trans., *Seneca. Epistles, Volume I: Epistles 1–65*, 11.

148. E. Dickey, *Greek Forms of Address: From Herodotus to Lucian*, OCM (Clarendon Press, 1996), 101.
149. E. Dickey, "Κύριε, Δέσποτα, Domine: Greek Politeness in the Roman Empire," *JHS* 121 (2001): 9.
150. Nachtergaele, *The Formulaic Language of the Greek Private Papyrus Letters*, 34, n. 4.
151. On potential reasons for this epistolary change, see Fournet, "Esquisse d'une anatomie de la lettre antique tardive d'après les papyrus," 43.
152. Bresky, *Das Verhältnis des zweiten Johannesbriefes zum dritten*, 3–4. Nearly eighty years after Bresky's flawed study, it was still cited approvingly by Brown (*The Epistles of John*, 652) as a "detailed study" of the phrase ἐκλεκτῇ κυρίᾳ.
153. Despite this fact, several modern studies perpetuate the claim that if the phrase εκλεκτη κυρια were to contain a personal name, the most likely candidate would be Κυρία (Kyria). See discussion on pp. 144–49 in chapter 5.
154. 2 John 1: οὓς ἐγὼ ἀγαπῶ ἐν ἀληθείᾳ; 3 John 1: ὃν ἐγὼ ἀγαπῶ ἐν ἀληθείᾳ.
155. See nn. 163 and 166 below.
156. *Aegyptische Urkunden aus den Königlichen Museen zu Berlin III* (Weidmannsche Buchhandlung, 1903), 170–71. The TM no. for this letter is 28097. It is presently housed in the *Ägyptisches Museum und Papyrussammlung* in Berlin and has the inventory no. P. 7104.
157. This famous letter has been the subject of various editions and minor studies: Sel.Pap. 1.120; J. G. Winter, *Life and Letters in the Papyri* (University of Michigan Press, 1933), 106; H. Ljungvik, "Zum Markusevangelium 6, 14," *ZNTW* 33 (1934): 90–92; White, *Light from Ancient Letter*, 181–82 (no. 114); R. Bieringer, "Reconcile Yourselves to God. An Unusual Interpretation of 2 Corinthians 5:20 in its Context," in *Jesus, Paul, and Early Christianity: Studies in Honour of Henk Jan De Jonge*, NovTSup 130, ed. R. Buitenwerf, H. W. Hollander, and J. Tromp (Brill, 2008), 20–21; J. Muir, *Life and Letters in the Ancient Greek World*, Routledge Monographs in Classical Studies (Routledge, 2009), 33–34; R. N. Longenecker, *Introducing Romans: Critical Issues in Paul's Most Famous Letter* (Wm. B. Eerdmans, 2011), 218; L. L. Welborn, *An End to Enmity: Paul and the "Wrongdoer" of Second Corinthians*, BZNW 185 (De Gruyter, 2011), 449.
158. Accordingly, for a time, the letter was simply referred to as a "Letter of a Prodigal Son." Deissmann, *Licht vom Osten*, 123–27 (no. 11). Deissmann

was the first to point out the parallels with the Parable of the Prodigal Son (p. 124).

159. E. G. Turner, ed., *Catalogue of Greek and Latin Papyri and Ostraca in the Possession of the University of Aberdeen*, Aberdeen Univ. Studies 116 (The University Press, 1939).

160. For a helpful overview of this village, see R. S. Bagnall and D. Rathbone, eds., *Egypt: From Alexander to the Early Christians* (The J. Paul Getty Museum, 2004), 131–37.

161. I was working as part of the BYU Egypt Excavation in a predominantly Roman and Byzantine cemetery.

162. The fragment was subsequently published as L. H. Blumell, E. Cole, and W. Wendrich, "Another Letter from Antonius Longus to His Mother Nilous," *BASP* 55 (2018): 45–57.

163. Though numerous examples can be given, two will be cited. The three letters written by a certain Ammonius to Aphrodisius in the Aphrodisius archive (ca. 38–40 CE; Arsinoite nome) contain identical prescripts: P.Ryl. 2.229–31. Likewise, in the five letters written by Claudius Terentianus to his father, Claudius Tiberianus, and dated to the early second century CE, the epistolary prescript is basically the same, as the only differences are the absence of a modifier in one letter and the switching of order of modifiers in another letter: P.Mich. 8.476–80.

164. For example, in the archive of Asclepiades that dates to the end of the first century (ca. 29–23 BCE) and comes from Bousiris in the Heracleopolite Nome, there are eleven private letters, and all but one, which is likely a draft, are addressed to Asclepiades. See A. Sarri, *Material Aspects of Letter Writing in the Graeco-Roman World: 500 BC–AD 300* (De Gruyter, 2018), 251.

165. On the letters in this archive, see A. Sarri, *Material Aspects of Letter Writing in the Graeco-Roman World*, 257 and https://www.trismegistos.org/arch/archives/pdf/149.pdf.

166. Other examples can be marshaled. A notable example of Christian correspondence where the sender employs the same epistolary prescript in multiple letters to different recipients is in the Dossier of Sotas, bishop of Oxyrhynchus, in the middle of the third century CE. The prescripts are identical in three letters of recommendation from this dossier to different recipients. The prescript of PSI 2.208 reads: χαῖρε ἐν κ(υρί)ῳ, ἀγαπητὲ [ἄδ]ελφε Πέτρε, Σώτ̣[ας] σε προσαγορεύω ("Greetings in the Lord, beloved brother Peter, I Sotas salute you"). In PSI IX 1041 it reads: χαῖρε ἐν κ(υρί)ῳ, ἀγαπητὲ ἄδελφε Παῦλε, Σώτας σε προσαγορ(εύω) ("Greetings in the Lord, beloved brother Paul, I Sotas salute you"). In P.Alex. 29, where the name of the sender is partly lost in a lacuna, the name Sotas can be safely restored due to the extant prescript: [χ]α̣ίρε ἐ̣[ν κ(υρί)ῳ ἀγα]πητὲ ἄδελφε Μάξιμε, Σ]ώ̣τ̣ας σὲ προσαγορεύωι (*l.* προσαγορεύω) ("Greetings in the Lord, beloved brother Maximus, I Sotas salute you").

167. G. A. Gerhard, ed., *Veröffentlichungen aus den badischen Papyrus-Sammlungen. Vol. VI: Griechische Papyri* (C. Winter, 1938), no. 171.
168. Cowey et al., "Bemerkungen zu Urkunden," 290.
169. On the so-called Leiden system used in both papyrology and epigraphy, see U. Wilcken, "Das Leydener Klammersystem," *APF* 10 (1932): 211–12. For updates, see S. Dow, *Conventions in Editing: A Suggested Reformulation of the Leiden System*, GRBS Study Aids 2 (Duke University Press, 1969). While this system documents and corrects mistakes, it is also used to treat other textual problems that appear (e.g., damage to the text or loss of text due to various external factors).
170. Here are a few examples where definite articles are erroneously omitted, albeit not in the opening address of a letter: UPZ 2.180a.50.4–5 (113 BCE); P.Gen. (2) 1.4.1–2 (ca. 87 CE); P.Oxy. 40.2908.2 (270/71 CE); O.Deiss. 67.1–2 (III CE); Chr.Wilck. 131.13–14 (IV CE).
171. There is a third epistolary example, but it is only a partial loss of an article: SB 18.14042.1 (late III BCE): Ἀπολλοφάνης Φίβει τ<ῷ> αδελφῷ χαίρειν ("Apollophanes to his brother Phib, greetings").
172. Here it is worth reiterating a well-known papyrological dictum: The first edition is rarely the final edition.
173. As a title of epistolary address, υἱός is well attested. It is proper for it to be fronted with an article when it follows the name: SB 10.10529 (I/II CE): Ἀσκλᾶς Ἀσκληπιάδη τῷ υἱῷ χαίρειν ("Asclas to his son Asclepiades, greetings"); P.Bodl. 1.157.1–2 (II CE): Σοηροῦς Χαιράτι τῷ υἱῷ πλεῖστα χαίρειν ("Souerous to Chairas his son, very many greetings"). Numerous other examples could be provided.
174. The article should be present as in P.Oxy. 61.4127.1–3 (IV): Πτολεμαῖος Θωνίῳ τῷ ἀγαπητῷ ἀδελφῷ ἐν κ(υρί)ῳ χαίρειν ("Ptolemy to Thonius his beloved brother, in the Lord greetings").
175. For the date of this letter, see discussion in D. Hagedorn, "Bemerkungen zu Urkunden," *ZPE* 151 (2005): 127–28.
176. The writer also forgot the second tau in the word.
177. I use the lunate sigma (ϲ) here because this is how sigma appears in the epistolary papyri and other documentary and literary texts. The use of the medial sigma (σ) and terminal sigma (ς) already implies some kind of interpretation because they presuppose where a word ends.
178. R. L. Plummer and E. R. Elledge, *1–3 John: Exegetical Guide to the Greek New Testament* (B&H Academic, 2024), 158; H. W. Bateman IV and A. C. Peer, *John's Letters: An Exegetical Guide for Preaching and Teaching* (Kregel, 2018), 346; M. M. Culy, *1, 2, 3 John: A Handbook on the Greek Text* (Baylor University Press, 2004), 141–42; D. B. Wallace, *Greek Grammar Beyond the Basics: An Exegetical Syntax of the New Testament* (Zondervan, 1996), 309–11. BDAG s.v. κυρία notes that making εκλεκτη "a proper noun"—which would include

a proper name—"and κυρ. an adj. has little to recommend it." But no evidence is invoked in support of this bald assertion.

CHAPTER 4: THE READING IS EVEN IN SOME MANUSCRIPTS

1. Yarborough, *1–3 John*, 5.
2. παρὰ Ἰησοῦ Χριστοῦ vs. παρὰ Κυρίου Ἰησοῦ Χριστοῦ; the latter reading is first attested by a corrector to ℵ (GA 01).
3. ἃ εἰργασάμεθα vs. ἃ εἰργάσασθε; the former reading is attested in B (GA 03), while the latter reading in ℵ (GA 01), A (GA 02), and GA 0232^{vid}. The NA^{28} prints the former reading.
4. ἡ χαρὰ ἡμῶν vs. ἡ χαρὰ ὑμῶν; the former reading appears in ℵ (GA 01), while the latter appears in A (GA 02) and B (GA 03). NA^{28} prints the former reading in the text, while the latter is printed in the notes.
5. Variants of a secondary level where the correct reading appears secure include the following: (v. 9) "in the teaching" (ἐν τῇ διδαχῇ) attested in ℵ (GA 01), A (GA 02), and B (GA 03) versus "in the teaching of Christ" (ἐν τῇ διδαχῇ τοῦ Χριστοῦ) attested in GA 041. In this verse, the phrase "in the teaching of Christ" (ἐν τῇ διδαχῇ τοῦ Χριστοῦ) is securely attested in the first half of the verse, but the issue that is raised is whether it is repeated in the second half of the verse. An unusual addition at the end of v. 11 in several Latin manuscripts of 2 John adds a whole sentence to the verse. However, few, if any, regard the variant as evincing an original or early reading; see n. 9 in chapter 2. At the end of the letter in v. 13, many minuscules read ἀμήν ("amen"), but it is widely thought to be a liturgical addition.
6. The textual apparatus in the ECM for 2 John readily bears this out.
7. In 2 John, only vv. 1 and 10 contain no textual notes in NA^{28}.
8. P. Gurry, "The Number of Variants in the Greek New Testament: A Proposed Estimate," *NTS* 62 (2016): 113. See pp. 118–21 of the article for estimates given by other scholars.
9. The ECM lists three man uscripts that contain this variant; I am at five manuscripts and counting. On these manuscripts, see the discussion on pp. 104–09.
10. Technically, a printed Greek version of the New Testament appeared in 1514 in the Complutensian Polyglot Bible, but it was not circulated until after the Old Testament portion was completed (ca. 1517), and it received the imprimatur of the pope. It was not bound and published until 1522. See n. 13 below.
11. The full title is: D. Erasmus, ed., *Novum Instrumentum omne, diligenter ad Erasmo Roterodamo recognitum et emendatum, non solum ad graecam veritatem, verum etiam ad multorum utriusque linguae codicum, eorumque veterum simul et emendatorum fidem, postremo adprobatissimorum autorum citationem, emendationem, et interpretationem, praecipue, Origenis, Chrysostomi, Cyrilli, Vulgarii, Hieronymi, Cypriani, Ambrosii, Hilarii, Augustini, una cum Annotationibus,*

quae lectorem doceant, quid qua ratione mutatum sit. Quisquis igitur amas veram theologiam, lege, cognosce, ac diende judica. Neque statim offendere, si quid mutatum offenderis, sed expende, num in melius mutatum sit. Apud inclytam Germaniae Basilaeam (Johann Froben, 1516).

12. When Erasmus worked on his edition of the Greek New Testament in Basil, Switzerland, he relied on two manuscripts for the text of 2 John: GA 1 (XII CE) and GA 2815 (XII CE). Erasmus's subsequent two editions, printed in 1519 and 1522 under the title *Novum Testamentmum Omne*, kept the same printing, although the fourth (1527) and fifth editions (1536) printed κυρίᾳ without the *diaeresis* (*trema*).

Traditionally, a *diaeresis* (*trema*), two dots placed above a letter (e.g., ϊ or ϋ), appeared over either iota or upsilon to make a "distinction" (διαίρεσις) between one vowel and another. See E. G. Turner, *Greek Manuscripts of the Ancient World*, rev. ed. by P. Parsons, Bulletin Supplement Institute of Classical Studies 46 (University of London Institute of Classical Studies, 1987), 10–11.

13. The Complutensian Polyglot Bible was the first printed polyglot Bible and appeared in six volumes: vols. 1–4 cover the Old Testament, vol. 5 the New Testament, vol. 6 contains various dictionaries and study aids. The fifth volume on the New Testament was printed in 1514 but was not distributed until 1522: J. L. de Stunica [Diego Lopez de Zuñiga] et al., eds., *Novum Testamentum Grece et Latine in Academia Complutensi Noviter Impressum* being the fifth volume of *Biblia Sacra Polyglotta, complectentia Vetus Testamentum Hebraico, Graeco, et Latino Idiomate; Novum Testamentum Graecum et Latinum; et Vocabularum Hebraicum et Chaldaicum Veteris Testamenti, cum Grammatica Hebraica, nec non Dictionario Graeco; Studio, Opera, et Impensis Cardinalis Francisce Ximenes de Cisneros*, Industria Arnaldi Gulielmi de Brocaric artis impressorie magistri (Compluti [Alcala], 1514, 1515, 1517).

14. S. de Colines, ed., *he kaine diatheke. En leutetia ton paresion, para Simoni to Kolinaio, dekembriou menos deuteron phthinontos, etei apo tes theogonias a. ph. l. d.* [Romanized Greek] (pub. by author, 1534).

15. R. Estienne, ed., *Novum Testamentum Graece* (ex officiana Roberti Stephani Typographi Typis Regiis, 1546; 2nd ed., 1549).

16. R. Estienne, ed., *Novum Testamentum Graece* (ex officiana Roberti Stephani Typographi Typis Regiis, 1550).

17. Estienne, *Novum Testamentum Graece* (1550), ad loc.: ταύτην ὡς πρεσβύτερος γράφει κυρίᾳ καὶ τοῖς τέχνοις αήτῆς. ἡ δὲ πρόφασις τῆς ἐπιστολῆς αὕτη. ὁρῶν τὰ τέκνα αὐτῆς καλῶς ἀναστρεφόμενα ἐν τῇ πίστει, καὶ πολλοὺς πλάνους περιερχομένους, καὶ λέγοντας μὴ εἶναι τὴν παρουσίαν τοῦ Χριστοῦ ἐν σαρχὶ, γράφει τὴν ἐπιστολήν ("He writes this [2 John] as an Elder to a lady and her children. The occasion of the letter is as follows: seeing her children conducting themselves well in the faith and many deceivers going about and saying that Christ did not come in the flesh, he writes the letter"). For this *argumentum*, see also n. 61 in chapter 1. On the other hand, he may have also been influenced by the *Glossia*

Ordinaria, which mentions a lady named "Electa" in connection with 2 John 1; see n. 67 in chapter 1.

18. R. Estienne, ed., *Novum Testamentum Graece* (ex officiana Roberti Stephani Typographi Typis Regiis, 1551).
19. T. Beza, ed., *Novum Testamentum, cum versione Latina veteri, et nova Theodori Bezae* (Fuggeri Typographus, 1565).
20. Beza, *Novum Testamentum*, ad loc.: Non nulli Electae nomen proprium esse volunt quod non probo. Dicedum enim fuisset κυρίᾳ Ἐκλεκτῇ, dominae Electae. Considering the foregoing discussion of the epistolary papyri and the address appearing in 3 John 1, it should be clear that Beza's reasoning for rejecting the reading based on collocation is patently wrong.
21. Of these editions, only four (1565, 1582, 1588–89, and 1598) were independent, as all others were simply reprints.
22. Their last name is sometimes rendered as Elzevier. The first edition was actually printed by Isaac Elzevir (1596–1651), the younger brother of Abraham and nephew of Bonaventure: [I. Elzevir], *Novum Testamentum Graece*, Lugduni Batavorum (Ex officina Elzeviriana, 1624). The second edition was printed by Abraham and Bonaventure but edited by Jeremias Hoelzlin (1583–1644): J. Hoelzlin, ed., *Novum Testamentum Graece*, Lugduni Batavorum (Ex officina Elzeviriana, 1633). The oft-cited preface to this edition (see n. 23 below) was written by Daniel Heinsius (1580–1655). See discussion in H. J. de Jonge, "Jeremias Hoelzlin: Editor of the 'Textus Receptus' Printed by the Elzevirs Leiden 1633,' in *Miscellanea Neotestamentica*, vol. 1, ed. T. Baarda, A. F. J. Klijn, and W. C. VanUnnik (Brill, 1978), 105–28.
23. In the preface to the second edition, it is boasted by Daniel Heinesius that the reader has "the text now received by all, in which we give nothing changed or corrupted," from which arose the designation "Received Text." For translation and discussion, see Metzger and Ehrman, *The Text of the New Testament*, 152. As all three Elzevir editions were rather bald since they contained no apparatus or marginalia, there was no discussion of the reading ἐκλεκτῇ κυρίᾳ.
24. On his life, see S. Lee, ed., *Dictionary of National Biography: Wordsworth–Zuylestein*, vol. 63 (Smith, Elder, 1900), 385–86.
25. This information is derived from *The Amsterdam Database of New Testament Conjectural Emendation*, https://ntvmr.uni-muenster.de/nt-conjectures. The manuscript is referenced as follows: "Secundae stricturae Patricii Junii," shelf mark UBA III C 20 e add. Library of the University of Amsterdam, to be dated approximately 1642.
26. Rom 14:14; 16:2, 8, 11–13, 22; 1 Cor 1:31; 4:17; 7:22, 39; 9:1–2; 11:11; 15:58; 16:19; 2 Cor 2:12; 10:17; Gal 5:10; Eph 2:21; 4:1, 17; 5:8; 6:1, 10, 21; Phil 1:14; 2:19, 24, 29; 3:1; 4:1–2, 4, 10; Col 3:18, 20; 4:7, 17; 1 Thess 3:8; 4:1; 5:12; 2 Thess 3:4, 12; Philm 1:16, 20. Outside of Paul's letters, it also appears once, in Rev 14:13.

27. Junius, *Secundae stricturae*, 3: ἐν κυρίῳ, ut de ecclesia intelligatur, forte de uno 7 Asiaticarum, quarum mentio in Apocalypsi; non autem de singulari aliqua persona. atque ita vers ("'In the Lord:' so that it may be understood about the church, perhaps about one of the seven Asian [churches], which are mentioned in the Apocalypse; but not about any particular person").
28. J. J. Greisbach's second edition of his *Novum Testamentum Graece*, published in 1806, neutrally mentions the conjecture in the apparatus. A few years later, G. C. Knapp's 1813 edition of his *Novum Testamentum Graece* similarly noted the conjecture.
29. H. Grotius, *Annotationes in Novum Testamentum denuo emendatius editae*, P. H. de Groot, ed., 9 vols. (Zuidema, 1826–1834). On this work, see most recently D. van Miert, *The Emancipation of Biblical Philology in the Dutch Republic, 1590–1670* (Oxford University Press, 2018), 133–69.
30. The articulation for the name is not Ἐκλεκτῇ as this is the articulation for the adjective; the articulation for the name is instead Ἐκλέκτῃ.
31. Grotius, *Annotationes in Novum Testamentum denuo emendatius editae*, 8.207.
32. Grotius, *Annotationes in Novum Testamentum denuo emendatius editae*, 207: "At hic omnino una indicator persona, ut videmus infra 13. Et ἐκλεκτῇ puto fuisse nomen proprium."
33. Grotius, *Annotationes in Novum Testamentum denuo emendatius editae*, 211: "Pro τῆς ἐκλεκτῆς alii libri sine articulo habent ἐκλεκτῆς, alii vero Εὐδέκτης, quod verum puto, ut sit nomen proprium, sicut Ἐκλεκτὴ ("Regarding τῆς ἐκλεκτῆς, some books have it without the article as ἐκλεκτῆς, while others have Εὐδέκτης. I believe it to be true, that it is a proper name, just as Ἐκλεκτὴ"). While Grotius claims that some manuscripts preserved the reading Εὐδέκτης, I have not found this reading in a single Greek manuscript. Additionally, I have been unable to find any other attestation of this name in Greek. C. Reineccius, ed., *Biblia Sacra quadrilinguia Novi Testamenti Graeci cum versionibus Syriaca, Graeca vulgari, Latina et Germanica* (Sumtibus Haeredum Lanckisianorum, 1713), 844, mentions the reading Emention and cites Grotius. This is undoubtedly a conjectural emendation on the part of Grotius. The closest attested Greek name I have found is the masculine name Εὐδέκτας (Eudectas); see LGPN V1-52784 (223/22 BCE; Crete).
34. B. Walton, ed., *Biblia Sacra Polyglotta, complectentia Textus Originalis, Hebraicum cum Pentateucho Samaritano, Chaldaicum, Graecum, Versionumque antiquarum Samaritanae, Graecae LXXII. Interpretum, Chaldaicae, Syriacae, Arabicae, Aethiopicae, Vulgatae Latinae, quicquid comparari potetat, &c.* Edidit Brianus Walton, S.T.D., 6 vols. (imprimebat Thomas Roycroft, 1654, 1655, 1656, 1657).
35. The first volume appeared in 1654, followed by the second and third in 1655 and 1656, respectively. The last three volumes all appeared in 1657.

36. In places, Walton compared the Greek text of Estienne with readings found in Codex Alexandrinus. In the supplementary sixth volume, which contained an apparatus, he also included readings from Codex Bezae, Claromontanus, and various other manuscripts. In vol. 6, Walton noted some alternate readings in 2 John but none for v. 1.
37. Walton, *Biblia Sacra Polyglotta*, vol. 5, ad loc., Latin translation given: "A Seniore electa & domine & filius eius."
38. The best edition of 2 John in Ethiopic can be found in S. Uhlig and H. Maehlum, eds., *Novum Testamentum Aethiopice: Die Gefangenschaftsbriefe, Äthiopistische Forschungen*, Band 33 (Franz Steiner Verlag Stuttgart, 1993). There, the Ethiopic translates to: "From an/the elder to an elect and a lady and her children." The Ethiopic conjunction wa- appears before "lady": wa-la-'əgzə't ("and for a/the lady"). This is also the current reading in modern Ethiopic editions.
39. Walton, *Biblia Sacra Polyglotta*, vol. 5 ad loc., the Latin translation of the Syriac is given as: "Senior electae Kyriae & filiis eius."
40. In D. King, J. E. Walters, and G. A. Kiraz, eds. and trans., *Hebrews and the General Catholic Epistles According to the Syriac Peshitta Version, with English Translation*, Surath Ktobh (Gorgias Press, 2016), xxvii, the following is noted: "The Syriac translator has transliterated the word for 'lady' (κυρίᾳ), perhaps mistaking it for a proper name like Quriya." See also translation and discussion on p. 151 of that text. In the commentary on 2 John by Dionysios bar Ṣalibi (d. 1171 CE), he understands κυρία as "lady"; see J. Sedláček, trans. and ed., *Dionysii Bar Salibi Commentarii in Apocalypsim, Actus et Epistulas Catholicas*, CSCO 53.163 (Syriac text) and CSCO 60.128 (Latin translation).
41. More is said about the rendering Kyria (or Cyria) on pp. 144–49 in chapter 5.
42. J. Fell, ed., *Novi Testamenti Libri Omnes. Accesserunt Parallela Scripturae Loca, necnon variantes Lectiones ex plus 100 MSS. Codicibus et antiquis versionibus collectae* (e Theatro Sheldoniano, 1675).
43. Fell claimed in the title to have included variant readings from over 100 manuscripts, and some variants were noted in the apparatus at the bottom of each page. However, the manuscripts he consulted made little impact on his printed edition.
44. J. Mill, ed., *H KAINH DIAΘHKH. Novum Testamentum Graecum, cum lectionibus variantibus MSS. Exemplarium, Versionem, Editionum, SS. Patrum et Scriptorum Ecclesiasticorum, et in easdem notis*, Studio et labore Joannis Millii, S.T.P. (e Theatro Sheldoniano, 1707).
45. The edition also includes a lengthy preface that broaches the history of the textual transmission of the Greek New Testament.
46. Mill, *H KAINH DIAΘHKH*, ad loc.

47. G. von Maestricht, ed., *H KAINH DIAΘHKH. Novum Testamentum, post priores Steph. Curcellaei et D.D. Oxoniensium labores. Cum Prolegomenis G.D.T.M. et notis in fine adjectis* (ex officina Wetsteniana, 1711).
48. A second revised edition of Maestricht's edition was published in 1735 by J. J. Wettstein. The reading in 2 John 1 remained ἐκλεκτῇ κυρίᾳ.
49. The full reference is D. Mace, trans. and ed., *The New Testament in Greek and English, Containing the Original Text Corrected from the Authority of the most Authentic Manuscripts: And a New Version Formed agreeably to the Illustrations of the Most Learned Commentators and Critics: with Notes and Various Readings, and a Copious Alphabetical Index*, 2 vols. (1729).
50. For an appraisement of Mace's text-critical changes in the New Testament, see E. J. Epp, "Critical Editions of the New Testament, and the Development of Text-Critical Methods: From Erasmus to Griesbach (1516–1807)," in *The New Cambridge History of the Bible: From 1450 to1750*, ed. E. Cameron (Cambridge University Press, 2016), 126.
51. Mace, trans. and ed., *The New Testament in Greek and English*, ad loc.
52. J. A. Bengel, ed., *H KAINH DIAΘHKH. Novum Testamentum Graecum ita adornatum ut Textus probatarum editionem medullam, Margo variantium lectionum in suas classes distributarum locorumque parallelorum delectum, apparatus subjunctus criseos sacrae Millianae praesertim compendium limam supplementum ac fractum exhibeat, inserviente J.A.B Edente Jo. Albert Bengel*, 4 vols. (1734). On the "new era" under Bengel, see Epp, "Critical Editions of the New Testament, and the Development of Text-Critical Methods: From Erasmus to Griesbach," 127.
53. Bengel, *H KAINH DIAΘKH*, ad loc. He notes no variants for 2 John 1, although he notes other textual variants in the letter.
54. J. A. Bengel, *Gnomon Novi Testamenti, in quo, ex nativa Verborum Vi Simplicitas, Profunditas, Concinnitas, et Salubritas sensuum coelestium, indicatur* (Sumtibus Ac Typis IO. Henr. Philippi Schrammii, 1742).
55. Bengel, *Gnomon Novi Testamenti*, 1069. A discussion of this passages appears on pp. 147–49 in chapter 5.
56. See n. 40 above.
57. P. D. Burk, ed., *Joannis Alberti Bengelii Apparatus Criticus ad Novum Testamentum, criseos sacrae compendium, limam, supplementum, ac fructum exhibens. Cura Philippi Davidis Burkii* (Sumtibus IO. Georgii Cottae, 1763), 929: "V. I κυρία, nomen proprium, V. 5" ("V. 1, κυρία, proper name, V. 5"). On pp. 482–83, the same notes on 2 John appear as are found in the 1734 Greek New Testament.
58. E. Harwood, ed., *H KAINH ΔIAΘKH. The New Testament, collated with the most approved manuscripts; with select notes in English, critical and explanatory, and references to those authors who have best illustrated the sacred writings. To which are added, a Catalogue of the principal Editions of the Greek*

Testament; and a List of the most esteemed Commentators and critics, 2 vols. (J. D. Cornish, 1776). A second edition appeared in 1784, and the reading remained the same.

59. G. C. Knapp, ed., *Novum Testamentum Greece recognorit atque insiagioris lectionum varietatis et argumentorunm notitiam snubjunxit* (Halle, 1797).
60. J. Wesley, *Explanatory Notes upon the New Testament* (William Bowyer, 1755). It underwent four subsequent editions before 1800.
61. Wesley, *Explanatory Notes upon the New Testament*, ad loc.
62. J. J. Wettstein, ed., *Novum Testamentum Graecum editionis receptae, cum Lectionibus Variantibus Codicum MSS., Editionum aliarum, Versionum et Patrum, necnon Commentario pleniore ex Scriptoribus veteribus, Hebraeis, Graecis, et Latinis, historiam et vim verborum illustrante*, 2 vols. (Ex officina Dommeriana, 1751, 1752).
63. Wettstein, *Novum Testamentum Graecum editionis receptae*, ad loc.
64. J. J. Griesbach, ed., *Libri Historici Novi Testamenti, Graece, Pars I. sistens Synopsin Evangeliorum Matthaei, Marci, et Lucae. Textum ad fidem Codd. Versionum et Patrum emendavit et lectionis varietatem adjecit Jo. Jac. Griesbach* (Curt, 1774). It was followed the next year by J. J. Griesbach, ed., *Libri Historici Novi Testamenti, Graece, Pars II. sistens Evangelium Johannis et Acta Apostolorum* (Curt, 1775), and *Epistolae N.T. et Apoc.* (Curt, 1775). These were then reprinted as J. J. Griesbach, ed., *Novum Testamentum Graece, Textum ad fidem Codicum Versionem et Patrum recensuit et Lectionis Variatatem adjecit D. Jo. Jac. Griesbach* (Curt, 1777).
65. J. J. Griesbach, ed., *Novum Testamentum Graece, Textum ad fidem Codicum Versionem et Patrum recensuit et Lectionis Variatatem adjecit D. Jo. Jac. Griesbach* (Apud Jo. Jac. Curtii Haeredes, 1796 and 1806).
66. Griesbach, *Novum Testamentum Graece*, ad loc. Griesbach cites the first manuscript containing this reading as "31" and the other as "73."
67. J. J. Griesbach, ed., *Novum Testamentum Graece. Ex Recensione Jo. Jac. Griesbachii, cum selecta Lectionis Varietate*, 2 vols. (Sumtibus G. J. Göschen, 1805, 1807).
68. Griesbach, *Novum Testamentum Graece. Ex Recensione Jo. Jac. Griesbachii, cum selecta Lectionis Varietate*, ad loc.
69. Several later editions of his Greek New Testament were subsequently issued by various printers after his death. These were primarily based on his second edition of the Greek New Testament and therefore rendered the opening address in 2 John 1 as ἐκλεκτῇ κυρίᾳ.
70. K. Lachmann, ed., *Novum Testamentum Graece, ex recensione Caroli Lachmanni* (Apud Black, Young et Young, 1831).
71. C. Tischendorf, ed., *Novum Testamentum Graece, ad antiquissimos testes denuo recensuit apparatum criticum omni studio perfectum apposuit commentationem isagogicam praetexuit Constantinus Tischendorf, editio octava critica maior*, 2

vols. (J. C. Hinrichs, 1869 [vol. 1], 1872 [vol 2]). Vol. 2 contains Acts through Revelation.

72. Tischendorf, *Novum Testamentum Graece,* ad loc.

73. S. P. Tregelles, ed., *The Greek New Testament, edited from ancient authorities; with the various readings of all the ancient MSS., the ancient versions, and earlier ecclesiastical writers (to Eusebius inclusive); together with the Latin version of Jerome, from the Codex Amiatinus of the sixth century* (Samuel Bagster and Sons, 1857–72). It was published in six parts; "Part III," published in 1865, contained "Acts and the Catholic Epistles."

74. Tregelles, *The Greek New Testament*, ad loc.

75. See p. 17–18 in chapter 2.

76. R. F. Weymouth, ed., *The Resultant Greek Testament: Exhibiting the text in which the majority of modern editors are agreed, and containing the readings of Stephens (1550), Lachmann, Tregelles, Tischendorf, Lightfoot, Ellicott, Alford, Weiss, The Bale Edition (1880), Westcott and Hort, and the Revision Committee* (Elliot Stock, 1892). Weymouth translated this text, and it was a published posthumously in 1903 as *The New Testament in Modern Speech* (Pilgrim Press, 1903; rev. 1924).

77. In his *The New Testament in Modern Speech,* he rendered the passage: "The elder to the elect lady."

78. Weymouth, *The Resultant Greek Testament*, ad loc.: "ἐκλεκτῇ] Ἐκλ. ςWHm: JElz κυρίᾳ] Κυρ. LnTiBWHm" = "ἐκλεκτῇ] Ἐκλ(εκτῇ) (οὕτω)ς W(estcott) H(ort) m(arginal reading): (King)J(ames Version [reading is presumed to underlie)] Elz(evir) κυρίᾳ] Κυρ(ίᾳ) L(achman)n Ti(schendorf) B(ale Edition) W(estcott)H(ort) m(arginal reading)."

79. B. Weiss, ed., *Das Neue Testament. Textkritische Untersuchungen und Textherstellung,* 3 vols. (Hinrichs, 1894 [Acts, Catholic Epistles, Revelation]; 1896 [Pauline Epistles]; 1900 [Gospels]).

80. Weiss, *Das Neue Testament,* ad loc.

81. E. Nestle, ed., *Novum Testamentum Graece cum apparatu critico ex editionibus et libris manuscriptis collecto* (Privilegierte Württembergische Bibelanstalt, 1898).

82. Nestle, *Novum Testamentum Graece,* ad loc.: "*1* h Εκλεκτη | hT Κυρια."

83. 2nd ed. 1899; 3rd ed. 1901; 4th ed. 1903; 5th ed. 1904; 6th ed. 1906; 7th ed. 1908; 8th ed. 1910; 9th ed. 1912. Beginning in the 3rd ed. of 1901, Weymouth's text was removed, and Weiss's readings were fully included throughout the New Testament (not just for Acts to Revelation), as he had recently published his critical text of the Gospels in 1900. See n. 79 above.

84. K. Aland et al., *Novum Testamentum Graece post Eberhard Nestle et Erwin Nestle communiter ediderunt Kurt Aland, Matthew Black, Carlo M. Martini, Bruce M. Metzger, Allen Wikgren; apparatum criticum recensuerunt et editionem novis curis elaboraverunt Kurt Aland et Barbara Aland una cum Instituto studiorum textus Novi Testamenti Monasteriensi* (Deutsche Bibelgesellschaft, 1979).

85. K. Aland, M. Black, B. Metzger, A. Wikren, and C. Martini, eds., *The Greek New Testament*. 3rd ed. (United Bible Societies, 1975; corrected printing, 1983). In the corrected printing in 1983, the punctuation was changed to match the Nestle-Aland^{26}.
86. Readings of seven critical editions, Tischendorf, Westcott and Hort, von Soden, Vogels, Merk, Bover, and Nestle^{25}, were collated in an appendix at the end of the edition. But there is no reference to any discussion of 2 John 1.
87. In every printed edition, the name properly articulated Ἐκλέκτῃ has been improperly articled as the adjective Ἐκλεκτῇ but with the capitalization of the first letter signifying it is to be taken as a name.
88. See discussion on pp. 74–76 of chapter 3 and pp. 144–49 in chapter 5.
89. When Westcott and Hort decided to proffer Ἐκλέκτῃ Κυρίᾳ as an alternative, taking it as a double name, at least they solved the grammatical problem. Nonetheless, the use of an odd double name in a letter like 2 John would undoubtedly be "strange," as they admit. See discussion on pp. 17–18 in chapter 2.
90. These fragments once belonged to a larger page from a codex, and all that remains on them are a few verses. There is general agreement that $\mathfrak{P}^{52}$ (=P.Ryl. Gr. 3.457), a papyrus fragment containing John 18:31–33 on one side and 18:37–38 on the other, dates to the second century CE and is among the earliest remains of the New Testament. It is believed that $\mathfrak{P}^{104}$ (=P. Oxy. 64.4404), a fragment preserving a portion of Matt 21, and $\mathfrak{P}^{90}$ (=P. Oxy. 50.3523), a piece that preserves a portion of John 18–19, also date to the second century. For a discussion of early Christian textual remains, see Blumell, "Scripture as Artefact," 7–32.
91. Notable Christian papyri that preserve extended text and probably date to the third century include: $\mathfrak{P}^{45}$ (=P. Chester Beatty I), which preserves sections from Matthew, Mark, Luke, John, and Acts; $\mathfrak{P}^{46}$ (=P. Chester Beatty II + P.Mich. inv. 6238), which preserves most of Paul's Letters except for the Pastorals; $\mathfrak{P}^{47}$ (=P. Chester Beatty III), which preserves a large section of Revelation on multiple sheets; $\mathfrak{P}^{66}$ (=P. Bodmer II), which preserves much of the Gospel of John; $\mathfrak{P}^{72}$ (=P. Bodmer VII–VIII), which includes the Epistles of Jude and 1 and 2 Peter; $\mathfrak{P}^{75}$ (=P. Bodmer XIV–XV), which includes extensive portions of the Gospels of Luke and John; $\mathfrak{P}^{115}$ (=P.Oxy. 66.4499), which preserves large sections of Revelation.
92. For general discussion of early Christian literary remains in Egypt, see R. S. Bagnall, *Early Christian Books in Egypt* (Princeton University Press, 2009).
93. For a comprehensive list of the manuscript evidence, see K. Aland with M. Welte, B. Köster and K. Junack, eds., *Kurzgefasste Liste der griechischen Handschriften des Neuen Testaments*, 2nd ed. (Walter de Gruyter, 1994). Updates are now online and can be found at the *Institut für Neutestamentliche Textforschung* (INTF) at the University of Münster, https://www.uni-muenster

.de/INTF/. For an updated bibliography on New Testament manuscripts, see J. K. Elliott, *A Bibliography of Greek New Testament Manuscripts*, 3rd ed., NovTSup 160 (Brill, 2015). The general categorization here follows that given in Parker, *An Introduction to the New Testament Manuscripts and Their Texts*, 35.

94. For a generally useful introduction, presentation, and assessment of these papyri with transcriptions and notes (nos. 1–139 except nos. 73–74), see P. W. Comfort and D. P. Barrett, *The Text of the Earliest New Testament Greek Manuscripts*, 2 vols., 3rd ed. (Kregel Academic, 2019). However, the dates proposed by Comfort and Barrett are, in many cases, far too early. On the dating of early Christian manuscripts, see especially P. Orsini and W. Clarysse, "Early New Testament Manuscripts and Their Dates: A Critique of Theological Paleography," *ETL* 88 (2012): 443–74.
95. For a useful overview of the Greek majuscule evidence, see D. C. Parker, "The Majuscule Manuscripts of the New Testament," in *The Text of the New Testament in Contemporary Research: Essays on the Status Quaestionis*, 2nd ed., ed. B. D. Ehrman and M. W. Holmes, NTTSD 42 (Brill, 2013), 41–68.
96. Three majuscules are written on paper: GA 0287 (IX CE), GA 0290 (IX CE), and 0295 (IX CE).
97. For a useful overview of the Greek minuscule evidence, see B. Aland and K. Wachtel, "The Greek Minuscules of the New Testament," in *The Text of the New Testament in Contemporary Research: Essays on the Status Quaestionis*, 2nd ed., ed. B. D. Ehrman and M. W. Holmes, NTTSD 42 (Brill, 2013), 69–91.
98. K. Aland and B. Aland, *The Text of the New Testament: An Introduction to the Critical Editions and to the Theory and Practice of Modern Textual Criticism*, trans. E. F. Rhodes, 2nd ed. (William B. Eerdmans Publishing Company, 1995), 81. The oldest dated minuscule manuscript is the manuscript of the Uspenski Gospels (GA 461), which carries a date of 835 CE.
99. For a discussion of these types of evidence for New Testament textual criticism, see chapters 13–16 (pp. 351–460) in B. D. Ehrman and M. W. Holmes, eds., *The Text of the New Testament in Contemporary Research: Essays on the Status Quaestionis*, 2nd ed., NTTSD 42 (Brill, 2013).
100. For a useful overview of Greek New Testament lectionaries, see C. Osburn, "The Greek Lectionaries of the New Testament," in *The Text of the New Testament in Contemporary Research: Essays on the Status Quaestionis*, 2nd ed., ed. B. D. Ehrman and M. W. Holmes, NTTSD 42 (Brill, 2013), 93–113.
101. R. Kasser, ed., *Papyrus Bodmer XVII: Actes des Apôtres, Epîtres de Jacques, Pierre, Jean et Jude* (Bibliothèque Bodmer, 1961).
102. Kasser, *Papyrus Bodmer XVII*, 261. 2 John 1 appears on p. 255 of the manuscript.
103. I have used lunate sigmas in the transcription, as did Kasser.

104. On the first line, λ is clearly visible, and as the fragment is broken off at the bottom left leg of the lambda, there are no traces of any letter before it. However, to the right of the bottom leg of the lambda, the lower part of the lunate epsilon is visible. Therefore, the transcription here should properly be rendered εκ]λε̣ [κ. This is a minor point in that it does not change an overall reading but important because it more accurately reflects the text visible on the papyrus. In line 2, I would read τ]οις, as the omicron is clear, but I cannot see any traces of the vertical of the tau. I see nothing different from what Kasser printed on line 3. On line 5, I am not sure why Kasser puts eighteen dots after θεια, as he is not implying that eighteen letters follow the first four.
105. For example, when I edited 𝔓[141] (=P.Oxy. 85.5478) with B. W. Griffin, two fragments from Luke attesting 2:32–34, 40–42 and 24:22–28, 30–38, the second fragment was a thin vertical strip from somewhere in the middle of the column attesting anywhere from one to seven letters. Trying to reconstruct the missing text on either side was educated guesswork.
106. A couple of additional items deserve mention here. Some might retort that if an extra τη is inserted in line 2, then it throws the alignment of the first two lines off, as the sigma of line 2 is no longer under the lambda in line 1 but would be distinctly to the right of it. To this, I would say the following: (1) In Kasser's transcription, the sigma is slightly to the left of the lambda on the previous line, but in the image, the sigma is actually a little to the right; (2) in a transcription that includes spacing, the addition of τη would be more pronounced since it would take up four letter spaces instead of two. To clarify, in the rendering εκλεκτη τη κυρια, the τη requires four letter spaces (the space before and after the article in addition to the two letters), but in a diplomatic rendering εκλεκτητηκυρια, it just occupies two. Therefore, in a diplomatic transcription, even with sixteen letters, the alignment in line 2 still works.

Another relevant item I would mention is the periodic debates over whether a *nomen sacrum* appears in a lacuna or whether the word is written *scriptio plene*. This is most contested in the famous 𝔓[52] containing John 18:31–33 on one side and 18:37–38 on the other. Given the fragment's early date, some have wondered whether it evinces *nomina sacra*. The name Jesus (Ἰησοῦς) appears in vv. 32 and 33, but in both instances, the papyrus is broken off where the name would occur. The debate is whether in v. 32 it is rendered Ἰησοῦ or ιηυ and in v. 33 Ἰησοῦν or ιηυ. The consensus is that one ultimately does not know. Despite arguments about the number of letters in a line and alignment, as the difference is two letters in v. 32 and three letters in v. 33, it is still too slight to make any definitive argument one way or the other.
107. See also the discussion of GA 1243 on pp. 104–06, which has a text remarkably similar to that in 𝔓[74] and contains the longer reading εκλεκτη τη κυρια.

108. Also known as B, GA 03, and Vat. gr. 1209. For a comprehensive introduction to Codex Vaticanus, see the chapters in Patrick Andrist, ed., *Le manuscrit B de la Bible (Vaticanus graecus 1209): Introduction au fac-similé, Actes du Colloque de Genève (11 juin 2001), Contributions supplémentaires*, HTB 7 (Éditions du Zèbre, 2009). For a concise introduction, see J. N. Birdsall, "The Codex Vaticanus: Its History and Significance," in *The Bible as Book: The Transmission of the Greek Text*, ed. S. McKendrick and O. A. O'Sullivan (The British Library, 2003), 33–41. For the reception of Codex Vaticanus up to the time of Westcott and Hort, see A.-T. Yi, *From Erasmus to Maius: The History of Codex Vaticanus in New Testament Textual Scholarship*, ANTF 58 (De Gruyter, 2024). For the date of Codex Vaticanus, see discussion in G. Cavallo, *Ricerche sulla maiuscola biblica* (Le Monnier, 1967), 55–59, who suggests it was copied in the middle of the fourth century.
109. For the New Testament, Codex Vaticanus contains the four Gospels, followed by Acts and the Catholic Epistles, the Pauline Epistles, and then the manuscript is lost after Heb 11:4.
110. For an online image, see https://digi.vatlib.it/view/MSS_Vat.gr.1209.
111. The initial omicron at the beginning of the verse is written in a distinctly larger font with decorative elements and is positioned at the top of the margin between the left and middle columns. Sigmas take the lunate form and have been reproduced accordingly in the transcription. Between the second ε and κ in εκλεκτη, I have noted the line break with " |".
112. Also known as ℵ or as GA 01. See the useful discussion on this Bible in D. C. Parker, *Codex Sinaiticus: The Story of the World's Oldest Bible* (British Library, 2010). Cavallo, *Ricerche sulla maiuscola biblica*, 55, suggests that it was copied about ten years after Vaticanus ca. 360 CE, although such a dating is incredibly specific.
113. In 1844, von Tischendorf visited the monastery and received as a gift 43 leaves from the codex. In 1853 he made no new discoveries but did obtain additional small fragments. In 1859 he procured all 347 remaining leaves of the codex.
114. After Herm. *Mand.* 4.3, the codex is lost, so we do not know if it contained any additional texts.
115. For an online image, see https://codexsinaiticus.org/en/.
116. The initial omicron protrudes into the left margin marking off the opening of 2 John with ekthesis, but the omicron is written with the same font as the rest of the text and does not possess any additional adornment.
117. Also known as A or as GA 02. Compared to Vaticanus and Sinaiticus, there are relatively few overarching studies of this Bible. See W. A. Smith, *A Study of the Gospels in Codex Alexandrinus: Codicology, Palaeography, and Scribal Hands*, NTTSD 48 (Brill, 2014), 7–101, where the first two chapters provide a detailed history and overview of this Bible.

118. C. G. Woide, ed., *Novum Testamentum Graecum e codice ms. alexandrine, qui Londini in Bibliotheca Musei Britannici asservatur* (J. Nichols, 1786).
119. B. H. Cowper, *Codex Alexandrinus. Η ΚΑΙΝΗ ΔΙΑΘΗΚΗ. Novum Testamentum Graece ex Antiquissimo Codice Alexandrine a C. G. Woide olim descriptum* (D. Nutt, et Williams and Norgate, 1860), ad loc.
120. The first line of text is written with red ink, while the second is written with black. The initial omega is written in a larger font and extends into the margin. For an image, see https://manuscripts.csntm.org/manuscript/View/GA_02?OSIS=2John.1. The sign "±" is a more recent papyrological convention to indicate that in a lacuna, there are "plus or minus" letters missing. Here, "±3" means that the lacuna could be filled by anywhere from two to four letters.
121. Cowper, *Codex Alexandrinus*, ad loc.
122. It may be noted that Codex Ephraemi Rescriptus (C or GA 04), dated to the fifth century, does not contain 2 John but only parts of 1 and 3 John. Codex Bezae Cantabrigiensis (D or GA 05), dated to the late fourth or fifth century, only preserves the last three verses of 3 John in Latin.
123. For the New Testament contents of the manuscript, see description in NA[28] p. 803. The manuscript is Vat. gr. 2061. Images of this manuscript can be found at https://digi.vatlib.it/view/MSS_Vat.gr.2061.pt.A. The codex contains a total of 316 folios with the text of the New Testament scattered across folios 198–308.
124. A useful description of the New Testament text of the codex can be found in D. E. Heath, "A Transcription and Description of Manuscript Vatican 2601 (Gregory 048)" (PhD diss., Michigan State University, 1965), 2–10; see also discussion in P. Orsini, *Manoscritti in maiuscola biblica. Materiali per un aggiornamento* (Edizioni dell'Università degli studi di Cassino, 2005), 152–54.
125. The lone transcription of the New Testament text of 2 John in GA 048 appears in Heath, "A Transcription and Description of Manuscript Vatican 2601," 211. According to the transcription, the text of 2 John 1 does not become legible until the μονος αλλα κτλ that is past the address. While I think Heath's transcription could be improved, having looked at a digital image of the page on which 2 John 1 appears, I could not make much headway and was unable to securely make a reading in the address.
126. In the *ed. pr.*, P.Ant. I p. 24, the text is dated to the third century by C. H. Roberts. More recent assessments of the piece have placed it in the fifth century; see M. J. Kruger, "The Date and Content of P. Antinoopolis 12 (0232)," *NTS* 58 (2012): 245–71, and Orsini and Clarysse, "Early New Testament Manuscripts and Their Dates," 472.
127. P.Ant. 1.12, pp. 24–26.
128. Due to the pagination, Roberts thought the sheet belonged to a codex that carried the "Johannine writings" and that the Gospel, Revelation, and 1 John all preceded 2 John. More recently, Kruger, "The Date and Content of P. Antinoopolis 12 (0232)," 264–69, has argued that it is most likely that the

other Catholic Epistles preceded 2 John, and given the extra space based on the pagination, Hebrews may have potentially been included.

129. P.Ant. 1, p. 25.
130. W. L. Richards, *The Classification of the Greek Manuscripts of the Johannine Epistles*, SBLDS 35 (Scholars, 1977), 13.
131. This manuscript carries the St. Catherine's lib. no. gr. 0262. The codex is made of parchment and contains 281 leaves in one column per page. Images of the complete manuscript are available through the website at the Library of Congress: https://www.loc.gov/item/00271079321-ms/.
132. Aland and Aland, *The Text of the New Testament*, 159–63, 332–37.
133. Aland and Aland, *The Text of the New Testament*, 159.
134. Aland and Aland, *The Text of the New Testament*, 159.
135. Aland and Aland, *The Text of the New Testament*, 161.
136. M. M. Carder, "A Caesarean Text in the Catholic Epistles," *NTS* 16 (1969): 258.
137. Carder, "A Caesarean Text in the Catholic Epistles," 258, n. 2.
138. Carder, "A Caesarean Text in the Catholic Epistles," 258.
139. The full reference is K. Wachtel, *Der byzantinische Text der katholischen Briefe: Eine Untersuchung zur Entstehung der Koine des Neuen Testaments*, ANTF 24 (Walter de Gruyter, 1995).
140. Wachtel, *Der byzantinische Text der katholischen Briefe*, 55, 458.
141. In Richards's study, in 2 John, only v. 1 and v. 10 receive no textual discussion. See Richards, *The Classification of the Greek Manuscripts of the Johannine Epistles*, 265–73.
142. Richards, *The Classification of the Greek Manuscripts of the Johannine Epistles*, 139.
143. Richards, *The Classification of the Greek Manuscripts of the Johannine Epistles*, 285.
144. Richards, *The Classification of the Greek Manuscripts of the Johannine Epistles*, 285.
145. The manuscript carries the shelf no. Urb. Gr. 3. It is written with one column per page, and images of it can be found at https://digi.vatlib.it/view/MSS_Urb.gr.3.
146. Aland and Aland, *The Text of the New Testament*, 161.
147. R. B. Waltz, *The Encyclopedia of New Testament Textual Criticism: Last Preliminary Edition* (pub. by author, 2013), 1097–98.
148. This codex comprises 131 leaves and is written with one column per page. In Richards's study of the classification of the Johannine epistles, he includes GA 330 among the 81 manuscripts he surveys. Examining the text of its Johannine Letters, he classifies it as a "B^1" manuscript that preserves a predominantly "Byzantine" text. He also notes that the percentage of agreement it shares with the extant text of $\mathfrak{P}^{74}$ is 42.9 percent.

See Richards, *The Classification of the Greek Manuscripts of the Johannine Epistles*, 152–53, 285.

149. Waltz, *The Encyclopedia of New Testament Textual Criticism*, 1098.
150. This manuscript carries the St. Catherine's lib. no. gr. 1342, fol. 1–178. Images of the complete manuscript are available through the website at the Library of Congress: https://www.loc.gov/item/0027107699A-ms/.
151. The manuscript is made of paper and contains 178 leaves with two columns of text per page.
152. Aland and Aland, *The Text of the New Testament*, 159, 162.
153. Wachtel, *Der byzantinische Text der katholischen Briefe*, 55, 458.
154. Waltz, *The Encyclopedia of New Testament Textual Criticism*, 1087.
155. Waltz, *The Encyclopedia of New Testament Textual Criticism*, 1085.
156. Waltz, *The Encyclopedia of New Testament Textual Criticism*, 840.
157. The manuscript has only been the subject of a single book-length treatment by J. R. Harris, *The Origin of the Leicester Codex of the New Testament* (C. J. Clay and Sons, 1887). On this manuscript, see also an article by M. R. James, "The Scribe of the Leicester Codex," *JTS* 5 (1904): 445–47. Most recently, a dissertation has been devoted explicitly to this manuscript and its textual profile; see M. Burks, "The Text of the Leicester Codex: A Quantitative Analysis of GA 69" (PhD diss., New Orleans Baptist Theological Seminary, 2023).
158. GA 69 is missing the following: Matt 1:1–18:15, Acts 10:45–14:17, Jude 7–25, and Rev 19:10–22:21. Historically, this codex has been referred to as *Codex Leicestriensis*. It consists of 213 leaves, of which 91 leaves are parchment, and 122 are paper. Images of the complete manuscript are available at https://manuscripts.csntm.org/manuscript/View/GA_69.
159. Aland and Aland, *The Text of the New Testament*, 159, 162. On the other hand, they have assigned the text of the Pauline Epistles it contains to "Category III."
160. Carder, "A Caesarean Text in the Catholic Epistles?," 252. Her comments are largely echoed by B. M. Metzger, *Manuscripts of the Greek Bible: An Introduction to Greek Paleography* (Oxford University Press, 1981), 138, who notes of the text in the Gospels in this codex that it "is most remarkable.... the type of text which it contains has been identified as Caesarean, resembling, in the Gospels, that used by Origen and Eusebius."
161. M. M. Carder, "An Enquiry into the Textual Transmission of the Catholic Epistles" (ThD diss., Victoria University, 1968), 90–115. To this she also adds GA 1739.
162. Richards, *The Classification of the Greek Manuscripts of the Johannine Epistles*, 203–06. Richards also notes about GA 69 (p. 285) that it had a 42.9 percent agreement in the Johannine Epistles with 𝔓[74].
163. Burks, "The Text of the Leicester Codex: A Quantitative Analysis of GA 69," 77–80. Here Burks notes, using quantitative analysis, that GA 1243

shares a 66.20 percent agreement with the text in GA 69 in the Catholic Epistles. In total, Burks compares the text of GA 69 in the Catholic Letters with fifty others (p. 7), and the level of agreement with GA 1243 is not in the top quarter.

164. B. F. Westcott and F. J. A. Hort, eds., *The New Testament in the Original Greek: Introduction and Appendix* (Harper and Brothers, 1882).
165. Westcott and Hort, *Introduction and Appendix*, 77 (§105).
166. B. H. Streeter, *The Four Gospels: A Study of Origins, Treating of the Manuscript Tradition, Sources, Authorship, and Dates* (Macmillan, 1924), 50.
167. The bibliography on Origen is immense, but for a recent work that considers Origen and his works from a variety of perspectives, see R. E. Heine and K. J. Torjesen, eds., *The Oxford Handbook of Origen* (Oxford University Press, 2022).
168. At the Fifth Ecumenical Council of Constantinople in 553 CE, the "Origenists" were anathematized. See Cyril of Scythopolis, "*Life of Sabbas*, 198.20–199.9," in *Kyrillos von Skythopolis*, ed. E. Schwartz, TU 49.2 (J. C. Hinrichs, 1939). While the official proceedings of the Council of Constantinople make no mention of the condemnation of the "Origenists," it has been the consensus in scholarship since the time of F. Diekamp that the bishops who met at this council condemned the Origenists before its formal opening. See F. Diekamp, *Die origenistischen Streitigkeiten im sechsten Jahrhundert und das fünfte allgemeine Concil* (Aschendorff, 1899). See also R. Price, trans., *The Acts of the Council of Constantinople of 553: With Related Texts on the Three Chapters Controversy*, TTH 53 (Liverpool University Press, 2009), 2.270–81. On the Canons of 553 CE against the Origenists, see *ACO* 4.1 pp. 248–49. At the Lateran Council of 649 CE, Origen was posthumously condemned as a heretic. See *ACO2* 1.379–84. See also R. Price, trans., with P. Booth and C. Cubitt, *The Acts of the Lateran Synod of 649*, TTH 61 (Liverpool University Press, 2014), 381–82.
169. In the first column was written the Hebrew text, in the second column a Greek transliteration, and in the following four columns, respectively, the texts of Aquila, Symmachus, the Septuagint, and Theodotian.
170. Origen, *Comm. Matt.*15.14 (GCS, Or. 10.388): παρὰ τοῖς Ἑβδομήκοντα διὰ τὴν τῶν ἀντιγράφων διαφωνίαν.
171. For a discussion of some of these, see B. D. Ehrman, "Heracleon, Origen, and the Text of the Fourth Gospel," *VC* 47 (1993): 105–18; S. Brock, "Origen's Aims as a Textual Critic of the Old Testament," *StPatr* 10 (1970): 215–18; B. M. Metzger, "Explicit References in the Works of Origen to Variant Readings in New Testament Manuscripts," in *Biblical and Patristic Studies in Memory of Robert Pierce Casey*, ed. J. N. Birdsall and R. W. Thomson (Herder, 1963), 78–95; F. Pack, "Origen's Evaluation of Textual Variants in the Greek Bible," *ResQ* 4 (1960): 139–46; K. W. Kim, "Codices 1582, 1739, and Origen," *JBL* 69 (1950): 167–75; M.-J. Lagrange, "Origène, la critique textuelle et la tradition topographique," *RB* 4 (1895): 501–24.

172. Eusebius, *Hist. eccl.* 6.36.1–2 states that Origen was over sixty when he composed his *Commentary on Matthew* (and *Contra Celsum*). Perhaps it was composed sometime in the mid- to late 240s or 250s.
173. Origen, *Comm. Matt.* 12.15 (GCS, Or. 10.103): κατά τινα τῶν ἀντιγράφων.
174. Origen, *Comm. Matt.* 13.14 (GCS, Or. 10.213–14): κατὰ μέν τινα τῶν ἀντιγράφων· ἐν ἐκείνῃ τῇ ὥρᾳ προσῆλθον οἱ μαθηταὶ τῷ Ἰησοῦ, κατὰ δὲ ἄλλα· ἐν ἐκείνῃ τῇ ἡμέρᾳ ("according to some of the copies: 'in that hour the disciples came to Jesus,' but according to others: 'in that day'").
175. Origen, *Comm. Matt.* 15.14 (GCS, Or. 10.387–88): ὅτι μήποτε τὸ ἀγαπήσεις τὸν πλησίον σου ὡς ἑαυτὸν . . . ἀλλ᾽ ὑπό τινος τὴν ἀκρίβειαν μὴ νοήσαντος τῶν λεγομένων προστεθεῖσθαι . . . νυνὶ δὲ δῆλον ὅτι πολλὴ γέγονεν ἡ τῶν ἀντιγράφων διαφορά, εἴτε ἀπὸ ῥᾳθυμίας τινῶν γραφέων, εἴτε ἀπὸ τόλμης τινῶν μοχθηρᾶς <εἴτε ἀπὸ ἀμελούντων> τῆς διορθώσεως τῶν γραφομένων, εἴτε καὶ ἀπὸ τῶν τὰ ἑαυτοῖς δοκοῦντα ἐν τῇ διορθώσει <ἢ> προστιθέντων ἢ ἀφαιρούντων. Emended text supplemented from Latin translation that is provided in parallel column with the Greek text.
176. Origen, *Comm. Matt.* 16.19; *Comm. ser. Matt.* 43, 117, 118.
177. Origen, *Comm. ser. Matt.* 117 (GCS, Or. 11.255–56): In multis exemplaribus non continetur quod Barabbas etiam dicebatur, et forsitan recte, ut ne nomen Iesu conveniat alicui iniquorum. In tanta enim multitudine scripturarum neminem scimus Iesum peccatorem, sicut in aliis nominibus invenimus iustorum ut eiusdem nominis inveniantur esse etiam iniqui, utputa Iudas apostolus zelotes et Iudas patriarcha item et Machabaeus Iudas omnes laudabiles, sed et Iudas proditor; et in Genesi inveniuntur eiusdem nominis esse filii Seth et filii Cain, sicut Enoch et Lamech et Mathusalem. Non autem conveniebat esse tale aliquid et in nomine Iesu. English translation adapted from R. E. Heine, trans., *The Commentary of Origen on the Gospel of St Matthew*, vol. 2, OECT (Oxford University Press, 2018), 734–35.
178. Though Origen focuses his attention on the inclusion of the name "Jesus" at Matt 27:17, this is also an issue in v. 16, where "Barabbas" is first introduced in Matthew.
179. At present, no papyrus attests Matt 27:17 (16); the only papyrus that attests anything from Matt 27 is $\mathfrak{P}^{105}$ (=P.Oxy. 64.4406; V/VI cent. CE) attesting 27:62–64. Here, Vaticanus reads: τίνα θέλετε ἀπολύσω ὑμῖν τὸν Βαραββᾶν ἢ Ἰησοῦν; Sinaiticus and Alexandrinus read: τίνα θέλετε ἀπολύσω ὑμῖν Βαραββᾶν ἢ Ἰησοῦν.
180. Codex Bezae reads: τίνα θέλετε ὑμῖν ἀπολύσω Βαραββᾶν ἢ Ἰησοῦν; Codex Washingtonianus reads: τίνα θέλετε ἀπολύσω ὑμῖν Βαραββᾶν ἢ Ἰησοῦν.
181. Also known by the siglum Θ or as GA 038. There, Matt 27:17 reads: τίνα θέλετε τῶν δύο ἀπολύσω ὑμῖν Ἰησοῦν Βαραββᾶν ἢ Ἰησοῦν.
182. Notably, manuscripts GA 1 (XII CE), GA 118 (XIII CE), and GA 1582 (X CE).
183. In GA 700, the reading is "Jesus Barabbas," but a later scribe tried to expunge the reading "Jesus."

184. In this edition, the Greek text was taken from UBS[3] (1975). It was included, albeit in brackets, in UBS[1] published in 1966.
185. Metzger, *Textual Commentary on the Greek New Testament*, 68.
186. Principal committee members of UBS[3] were Kurt Aland, Matthew Black, Carlo Maria Martini, Bruce Metzger, and Allen Wikgren.
187. For example, in GA 466 (XI CE), a minuscule manuscript that contains the Apostolos and the Pauline Letters, above the word κυρια in 2 John 1, there is a siglum that directs the reader to the margin, where the following gloss is given: τῇ ἐκκλησίᾳ γράφει ("He writes to a church").
188. See n. 175 above.
189. See pp.14–15 in chapter 1 and discussion on pp. 81–84 in chapter 3.
190. Most notably, J. R. Royse, *Scribal Habits in Early Greek New Testament Papyri*, NTTSD 36 (Brill, 2008), esp. 705–36; J. R. Royse, "Scribal Tendencies in the Transmission of the Text of the New Testament," in *The Text of the New Testament in Contemporary Research: Essays on the Status Quaestionis*, 2nd ed., ed. B. D. Ehrman and M. W. Holmes, NTTSD 42 (Brill, 2013), 461–78.
191. Royse, "Scribal Tendencies in the Transmission of the Text of the New Testament," 461.
192. On these papyri, see n. 91 above.
193. Royse, *Scribal Habits in Early Greek New Testament Papyri*, 718.
194. Royse, *Scribal Habits in Early Greek New Testament Papyri*, 709–20.
195. P. M. Head, "The Habits of New Testament Copyists: Singular Readings in the Early Fragmentary Papyri of John," *Bib* 85 (2004): 399–408, and "Observations on Early Papyri of the Synoptic Gospels, Especially on the 'Scribal Habits,'" *Bib* 71 (1990): 240–47.
196. A. Wilson, "Scribal Habits and the New Testament Text," in *Digging for the Truth: Collected Essays Regarding the Byzantine Text of the Greek New Testament—A Festschrift in Honor of Maurice A. Robinson*, ed. M. Billington and P. Streitenberger (FYM, 2014), 21–39.
197. Studies on the tendencies of the scribes of Codex Vaticanus and Sinaiticus have shown that they also had a propensity to omit text. See Royse, *Scribal Habits in Early Greek New Testament Papyri*, 726–28; D. Jongkind, *Scribal Habits of Codex Sinaiticus*, TS 3rd series, vol. 5 (Gorgias Press, 2007), 151–53; P. Malik, "The Earliest Corrections in Codex Sinaiticus: A Test Case from the Gospel of Mark," *BASP* 50 (2013): 207–54, who notes a number of cases of omission.

CHAPTER 5: IS ECLECTE EVEN A NAME? ONOMASTICS, INSCRIPTIONS, AND THE ORDER OF THINGS

1. G. G. Findlay, *Fellowship in the Life Eternal: An Exposition in the Epistles of St. John*, 23. In Findlay's transliteration of the name "Eklekté," he mistakenly accented it as an adjective and not a proper name, which would be "Eklékte."

With the accent on the ultima, it is signaling that it is the adjective (ἐκλεκτή) and when it is on the penultima, that it is the personal name (Ἐκλέκτη).

2. Findlay, *Fellowship in the Life Eternal*, 23–32.
3. *Ghostname* is a term used in papyrology for the false reading of a name into a text where it does not occur, and the name is otherwise unattested in onomastic lexica or other papyri. Such "names" have arisen where editors have misread the Greek, mistakenly taken a toponym or an occupation for a personal name, or erroneously conflated a title and a name. On this phenomenon, see Trismegistos Ghostnames, www.trismegistos.org/ghostnames/.
4. Yarbrough, *1–3 John*, 333.
5. Brown, *The Epistles of John*, 653; see pp. 30–31 in chapter 2.
6. D. W. Burdick, *The Letters of John the Apostle: An In-Depth Commentary* (Moody Press, 1985), 415. As Burdick provides no references to any of these "studies," one is at a loss to know which of them he has in mind.
7. Klauck, *Der zweite und dritte Johannesbrief*, 34.
8. For a discussion of these two claims, see pp. 10–11 in chapter 1.
9. Foreign names appearing in Greek (i.e., Egyptian, Semitic, etc.) do not follow this general classification.
10. On the name Νικόδημος (Nicodemus), see *DELG* 726 s.v. νίκη.
11. On the name Στέφανος, see *DELG* 1018 s.v. στέφω. On the name Ἀρίστιος, see S. Minon et al., eds., *Lexonyme: Dictionnaire étymologique et sémantique des anthroponymes grecs antiques, vol. 1 (A–E)*, Hautes Études du monde gréco-romain 63 (Librairie Droz, 2023), 158 s.v. Ἀρίστιος.
12. I have used lunate sigmas "C" in this inscription.
13. The constellation Corona was also called Στέφανος, but the little context provided in the inscription excludes this reading.
14. In the case of short inscriptions or fragmentary texts, issues of context are made considerably more difficult.
15. While the name Gaius is widely attested as a Latin praenomen (from Caius), it came to be used as a personal name in Greek. On the Greek usage of the Latin name Gaius, see H. Solin, "Latin Cognomina in the Greek East," in *The Greek East in the Roman Context: Proceedings of a Colloquium Organised by the Finnish Institute at Athens; May 21 and 22, 1999*, ed. O. Salomies, Papers and monographs of the Finnish Institute at Athens 7 (Bookstore Tiedekirja, 2001), 195.
16. On these names, see Minon et al., *Lexonyme: Dictionnaire étymologique et sémantique des anthroponymes grecs antiques*, 18 s.v. Ἄγαθος and Ἀγάθη.
17. The etymological root of these anthroponyms is the Greek verb ἐκλέγω (ἐκ+ λέγω), "to pick out" or "single out."
18. Simple adjectives of the second declension ending in -τος are oxytone (i.e., ἐκλεκτός), but proper names of the second declension ending in -τος retract the accent (i.e., Ἔκλεκτος). Adjectives of the first declension ending in -τη are

oxytone (ἐκλεκτή), but proper names in the first declension ending in -τη are paroxytone (i.e. Ἐκλέκτη). For these rules of accentuation, see H. W. Chandler, *A Practical Introduction to Greek Accentuation*, 2nd rev. ed. (Clarendon Press, 1881; repr. 1983), §127, 185, 325.

19. To derive these approximate statistics, I have used the numbers and name lists provided in R. Bauckham, *Jesus and the Eyewitnesses: The Gospels as Eyewitness Testimony* (William B. Eerdmans, 2006), 56–66, and J. W. Welch and J. F. Hall, *Charting the New Testament* (Foundation for Ancient Research and Mormon Studies, 2002), §16–1.
20. These approximate statistics are derived from the name index in LCL 265, pp. 483–91, which also lists toponyms and certain proper nouns.
21. The TLG is the largest repository of ancient and medieval Greek literature. Its stated purpose is to digitize every extant Greek text from the eighth century BCE until the fall of Byzantium in 1453 CE. For the database, see https://stephanus.tlg.uci.edu.
22. Herodian 1.16.5 and 1.17.2; Dio Cassius 72.4.6 and 73.1.1. The same Eclectus is also mentioned in the later fragments of John of Antioch (VII CE): *Fr.Hist.*, 121.
23. For this database, see https://www.brepols.net/series/LLT-O.
24. SHA, *Comm.* 15.2; *Pert.* 4.5 and 11.11. The SHA (*Scriptores Historiae Augustae*) is a collection of Latin biographies on the emperors from 117 to 284 CE.
25. The two papyri that form this day-book record payments of *syntaximon* (συντάξιμον) in Philadelphia from roughly July 1 to August 27, 33 CE, are P.Corn. 21 and P.Princ. 1.2. Between the two papyri, which can be joined, portions of nineteen extant columns are preserved. On these two papyri, see A. E. Hanson, "P. Princeton I 11 and P. Cornell 21v," *ZPE* 37 (1980): 241–48.
26. Thus far, the series has published eight volumes covering regions spanning Anatolia to Italy and Sicily. A ninth volume covering Syria, Arabia, and the Middle East will soon be published. Two additional volumes covering the onomastic evidence from Egypt have just begun. See https://www.lgpn.ox.ac.uk.
27. This data can be readily found on the Trismegistos portal: https://www.trismegistos.org. However, one needs a paid subscription, or institutional subscription, to gain full access.
28. T. Ilan, *Lexicon of Jewish Names in Late Antiquity. Part I: Palestine 330 BCE–200 CE* (Mohr Siebeck, 2002); T. Ilan, *Lexicon of Jewish Names in Late Antiquity. Part II: Palestine 200–600 CE* (Mohr Siebeck, 2012).
29. The database can be found at http://www.manfredclauss.de.
30. Heikki Solin's collection of Greek personal names in both Greek and Latin is a helpful supplement to the EDCS for the onomastic evidence from Rome. It attests over ten thousand named persons from Rome preserved in the epigraphic record and frequently provides additional data. See H. Solin, *Die griechischen Personennamen in Rom. Ein Namenbuch. Zweite, völlig neu*

bearbeitete Auflage, Corpus Inscriptionum Latinarum: Auctarium, Series Nova 2, 3 vols. (Walter de Gruyter, 2003).

31. For this name, see TM Nam 9228.
32. The interchange of κ and γ in ancient Greek texts is well attested, and this phonetic interchange is discussed in Gignac, *A Grammar of the Greek Papyri of the Roman and Byzantine Periods. Vol. I, Phonology*, 77–80.
33. Minon et al., *Lexonyme: Dictionnaire étymologique et sémantique des anthroponymes grecs antiques*, s.v. Ἔκλεκτος.
34. Minon et al., *Lexonyme: Dictionnaire étymologique et sémantique des anthroponymes grecs antiques*, s.v. Ἐκλέκτη.
35. This inscription is principally known as CIL 6.8827 (=CLE 162); EDCS 18700402. The date of the inscription to the middle of the first century is certain given the reference to Claudia Octavia, who was put to death by Nero on June 2, 62 CE. On this inscription, see the discussion in M.-Th. Raepsaet-Charlier, *Prosopographie des femmes de l'ordre sénatorial (Ier–IIe siècles)* (Peeters, 1987), 223–24 (no. 246 [3]), and C. F. Martinez, *Poesía epigráfica latina I. introducción, traducción y notas* (Gredos, 1998), 146 (no. 162).
36. For example, ICUR 5.14205 (II CE; Rome).
37. First published in G. Binazzi, "Orso, Cassiano e Apollinare. Appunti sulla diffusione dei culti al seguito milizie," *Romanobarbarica* 9 (1986–87): 6.
38. I have only included the main memorial section of the inscription that contains the reference to Eclecte. The inscription continues for another four lines and includes a reference to a Tiberius Claudius Atticus, who is described as a brother.
39. While this inscription could give the impression that there are three parents, Gaius is the *praenomen* of the father Doryphorus and highlights the lineage.
40. On this irregular Latin form of the dative case of the name Eclecte, see Solin, *Die griechischen Personennamen in Rom*, 976.
41. First published in S. Greggi, "La documentazione epigrafica dell'antica *Nomentum*," *Annali Associazione Nomentana di Storia e Archeologia* 8 (2007): 61 (no. 78).
42. First published in M. R. Ambrogio et al., "Via Portuense, localita Pozzo Pantaleo. Indagini archeologiche per l'allargamento della sede stradale (Municipio XI)," *Bullettino della Commissione Archeologica Comunale di Roma* 117 (2016): 390.
43. On this irregular dative form of the name Eclecte, see n. 40 above.
44. Solin, *Die griechischen Personennamen in Rom*, 976.
45. The use of midpoints to separate words is a convention traditionally found in Latin texts. See L. Keppie, *Understanding Roman Inscriptions* (The Johns Hopkins Press, 1991), 21.

46. For the Greek invocation Θεοῖς Καταχθονίοις *vel sim.*, the parallel of the Latin *Dis Manibus* ("to the spirits of the departed"), see the discussion in SEG 50.1055, which includes examples.
47. For a discussion of the epitaphs from Lipara, see SEG 53.1010. Lipara is one of the Aeolian Islands north of Sicily.
48. The "|" sign separating the word indicates a line break. It was customary in Greek epitaphs that consisted of a single name to inscribe the name in the genitive case, signifying possession for the person being commemorated. Thus, "(The gravestone) of / belonging to NN."
49. See n. 32 above.
50. Σαραπάδι > Σαραπιάδι; χαίρεν > χαίρειν.
51. For comparison, the masculine counterpart Ἔκλεκτος/Eclectus has nearly eighty attestations among literary texts, papyri, and inscriptions.
52. By contrast, the masculine name Eclectus is attested all over the Mediterranean world.
53. See discussion of the name in Solin, *Die griechischen Personennamen in Rom*, 976–77.
54. D. Booms, *Latin Inscriptions* (The British Museum Press: 2016), 16–19.
55. In Mark 6:22, the earliest reading is "his [i.e., Antipas] daughter Herodias" (τῆς θυγατρὸς αὐτοῦ Ἡρῳδιάδος) and suggests that Antipas's wife was named Herodias as well as their daughter. In Matt 14:6, she is referred to as the unnamed "daughter of Herodias" (ἡ θυγάτηρ τῆς Ἡρῳδιάδος). Here, I count two persons named Herodias, mother and daughter.
56. Eve: 2 Cor 11:3; 1 Tim 2:13; Hagar: Gal 4:24–25; Rachel: Matt 2:18; Rahab: Matt 1:5; Heb 11:31; Jas 2:25; Rebekah: Rom 9:10–12; Ruth: Matt 1:5; Sarah: Rom 4:19, 9:9; 1 Pet 3:6; Tamar: Matt 1:3. Along the same lines, I have also excluded the name Candace (Κανδάκη) appearing in Acts 8:27 since it is a title and not a personal name.
57. Under the name Hannah.
58. There are many more attestations of this female name, but they refer to the same group of women, Ptolemaic queens bearing the name Berenice (I–IV).
59. There is one attestation of this name in the papyri in P.IFAO 3.41 col. 2.11 (III CE), but apparently it refers to a male, so the name may have been unisex. However, the reading is not completely certain.
60. There were many more attestations of the name Drusilla, but they referred to the same person, Julia Drusilla the sister of Caligula.
61. Under the name Elisheba.
62. See n. 68 below.
63. The one Lydia mentioned in the LJN is to a fictitious woman in a later apocryphal Christian source; see LJN 1.321–22.
64. Only attestation of this name is the one in 2 Tim 1:5. The name is unisex, and the masculine Lois (Λῶις) is attested a handful of times; see TM Nam 10235.

65. There are six attestations of this name, but they are all for males since it was a unisex name.
66. Statistics for this name are based on the spelling Νύμφα/Nympha, appearing in the New Testament, and the alternative spelling Νύμφη/Nymphe.
67. On the spread of biblical names like Mary in late antiquity, see L. H. Blumell, *Lettered Christians: Christians, Letters, and Late Antique Oxyrhynchus* (Brill, 2012), 249, 269–70.
68. The etymology of the name, according to BDB, p. 33, could be "Baal exalts (?)" or "Baal is husband to (?)." In *HALOT*, vol. 1 p. 39, the possible meaning given for the name is "where is the prince." While the name Jezebel appears in a single Greek inscription, it is a homiletic inscription of the V/VI CE that refers to the Jezebel of the Old Testament. See SEG 53.899: πάλιν ἡ Ἡρωδιὰς μαίνεται, | πάλιν ὀρχεῖται, ἄρα μιμεῖ|ται τὴν Ἰεζαβελ τὴν τῶν | προφητῶν φονεύτριαν ("Once again Herodias rages, once again she dances, thus she imitates Jezebel, the murderer of the prophets"). Note here that Herodias refers not to a contemporary person but to the Herodias who appears in the New Testament (Matt 14:3–10; Mark 6:17–29).
69. Rev. 2:20: ἀφεῖς τὴν γυναῖκα Ἰεζάβελ.
70. BDAG s.v. Λωΐς.
71. The name appears to be based on the Greek comparative adjective λωΐων (in both masc. and fem.), which means "more favorable, better." See *EDC* 1.883 and *DELG* s.v. λωΐων. Alternatively, the Macedonian month Λῷος might also be a possibility.
72. BDAG s.v. Δάμαρις.
73. CIL 8.21653 (EDCS 26800888) and ICUR 7.20054 (EDCS 33000086). Given the paucity of the name, some have speculated whether it is a variant of Δαμαλίς, a Greek unisex name. However, this name is still relatively rare, with fewer than twenty attestations.
74. The name appears in Greek in IGUR 2.574. For the other attestation of the name in a Greek inscription, where it refers to Herod Antipas's wife or daughter, see n. 68 above. When it appears in Latin in CIL 2.384 (EDCS 50000160), it refers to the wife of Herod. The other attestation is in A. E. Gordon, *Album of Dated Latin Inscriptions. Rome and the Neighborhood. Vol. I: Text* (University of California Press, 1958), no. 51 (=EDCS 11800845) and refers to a different woman bearing the name.
75. Horace, *Carm.* 1.8.1; 1.13.1; 1.25.8; 3.9.6; Martial, *Epig.* 11.21.
76. The full reference is G. Kaibel, ed., *Inscriptiones Graecae, XIV. Inscriptiones Siciliae et Italiae, additis Galliae, Hispaniae, Britanniae, Germaniae inscriptionibus* (Georg Reimer, 1890).
77. W. Froehner, *Les inscriptions grecques* (C. de Mourgues, 1865), 280 (no. 203).
78. G. Manilli, *Villa Borghese fuori di Porta Pinciana* (Grignani, 1650), 94.
79. W. Pape and G. E. Benseler, *Handwörterbuch der griechischen Sprache. 3.1: Wörterbuch der griechischen Eigennamen: A–K* (Friedrich Vieweg and Sohn,

1863), s.v. Ἐκλέκτη. In Pape's 1850 edition, *Handwörterbuch der griechischen Sprache: Wörterbuch der griechischen Eigennamen* (Friedrich Vieweg and Sohn, 1850), the name is not included, although the masculine counterpart, Ἔκλεκτος, appears.

80. J. C. von Orelli, *Inscriptionum Latinarum Selectarum Amplissima Collectio*, 3 vols. (Orelli, Fuesslini et Sociorum, 1828, rev. 1856), 3.6579.
81. See chapter 2, pp. 39–40. 2 John 13: ἀσπάζεταί σε τὰ τέκνα τῆς ἀδελφῆς σου τῆς ἐκλεκτῆς ("The children of your elect sister send you their greetings").
82. See discussion on pp. 168–69 in chapter 6.
83. In the papyri, we occasionally find instances of two siblings bearing the same name. From the prescript of BGU 1.332 (II/III CE), it is evident that two brothers bore the name Ptolemy: Σεραπιὰς τοῖς τέκνοις Πτολεμαίῳ καὶ Ἀπολιναρίᾳ καὶ Πτολεμαίῳ πλεῖστα χαίρειν ("Serapias to her children Ptolemy and Apolinaria and Ptolemy, very many greetings").
84. While Raymond Brown never adduced this flawed argument, he is the only commentator to note that in 2 John 1, there is curiously an article missing; he correctly noted that in 2 John 13, the της εκλεκτης could only be an adjective. To "solve" the unusualness of the missing article before the first εκλεκτη, he posited that the letter was an "encyclical" intended for many congregations —"to *an* elect lady" and not "to *the* elect lady" (emphasis added). See discussion on pp. 40 in chapter 2.
85. This greeting also appears in 3 John 15. On this concluding greeting formula, see, most recently, Arzt-Grabner, *Letters and Letter Writing*, 163–70.
86. If it were a proper name, based on the present collocation of this greeting in 2 John 13, one would instead expect τῆς ἀδελφῆς σου Ἐκλέκτης ("of your sister Eclecte") without the definite article fronting εκλεκτης.
87. Bultmann, *Die drei Johannesbriefe*, 103–04.
88. Lieu, *The Second and Third Epistles of John*, 65 n. 65. In Lieu, *I, II, & III John*, 240, she makes a similar claim without providing additional reasoning.
89. The adjective ἐκελκτός, -ά, -όν does not otherwise appear in the Johannine corpus outside of a variant reading attested in some manuscripts of John 1:34. NA[28] John 1:34: κἀγὼ ἑώρακα καὶ μεμαρτύρηκα ὅτι οὗτός ἐστιν ὁ υἱὸς τοῦ θεοῦ ("And I myself have seen and have testified that this is the Son of God"). The variant reading is ὁ ἐκλεκτὸς τοῦ θεοῦ ("the chosen one of God") and first appears in 𝔓[5vid] (=P.Oxy. II 208 [fol. I r.7]; II/III CE), then ℵ* and some other later manuscripts.
90. The kind of pun that would exist here would be an *equivoque* (i.e., where the same word was used in two different ways).
91. One of the earliest and most famous nominal puns comes from Book 9 of the *Odyssey*, where Odysseus and his men are captives of the cyclops Polyphemus. To escape, Odysseus devises a shrewd plan whereby he first informs Polyphemus that his name is Outis (Οὖτις), which in Greek means "nobody." After stabbing Polyphemus in the eye during the escape, the cyclops begins crying out, "Outis

is killing me" (Οὖτις με κτείνει), but none of the other cyclopes in the area comes to Polyphemus's rescue because they hear "nobody is killing me" and assume that he must be suffering from a divine affliction rather than an attack by a mortal (Homer, *Od.* 9.366, 369, 408, 455,460). Here, the pun is clearly for comic effect, although it advances the mission of Odysseus, the protagonist. See also Aristophanes, *Av.* 813–16, for a play on Σπάρτη and σπάρτη. In Aristotle, *Rhet.* 2.23.28 (1440b), names directly based on adjectives or nouns are punned (i.e., Θρασύβουλος and θρασύβουλος—"Thrasybulus" is a "man bold in counsel"; Θρασύμαχος and θρασύμαχος—"Thrasymachus" is a man "bold in battle"; Πῶλος and πῶλος—"Polus" is a "colt"; Δράκων and δράκων—"Draco" and "dragon"). For the general use of word plays and puns with names in Greek literature, see K. E. Apostolakis, "Proper Names, Nicknames, Epithets: Aspects of Comic Language in Middle Comedy," in *The Play of Language in Ancient Greek Comedy: Comic Discourse and Linguistic Artifices of Humour, from Aristophanes to Menander*, ed. K. E. Apostolakis and I. M. Konstantakos, Trends in Classics - Supplementary Volumes, 154 (De Gruyter, 2024), 311–45. See also C. J. Fordyce, "Puns on Names in Greek," *CJ* 28 (1932): 44–46, and E. S. McCartney, "Puns and Plays on Proper Names," *CJ* 14 (1919): 343–58.

92. M. P. J. Dillon, "A Homeric Pun from Abu Simbel (*Meiggs & Lewis* 7a)," *ZPE* 118 (1997): 128–30. See also discussion in R. S. Bagnall, *Everyday Writing in the Graeco-Roman East* (University of California Press, 2011), 7–26.
93. For one of the many plays on names appearing in the Old Testament, see Ruth 1:20.
94. BDAG s.v. Πέτρος, where it is noted that πέτρος is equivalent to a "stone." In *Montanari*, s.v. πέτρος, it is noted that it is similar to λίθος.
95. BDAG s.v. πέτρα, where it gives the first meaning as "bedrock or massive rock foundations."
96. For recent discussions of this pun, see M. Bockmuehl, *Simon Peter in Scripture and Memory: The New Testament Apostle in the Early Church* (Baker Academic, 2012), 72–74, and R. T. France, *The Gospel of Matthew*, NICNT (Wm. B. Eerdmans, 2007), 621.
97. *Montanari*, s.v. ὀνήσιμος.
98. On the predominantly servile nature of this name, see Solin, *Die griechischen Personennamen in Rom*, 986, 993. See also BDAG s.v. Ὀνήσιμος.
99. On this play, see discussion in BDAG s.v. ἄχρηστος. Some commentators have alleged iterations of a secondary play where ἄχρηστος sounded like ἄχριστος, whose established meaning is "unanointed" but here could connote "without Christ." Thus, one was "useless" if they were "without Christ." Whether this more elaborate play was ever intended remains to be established, but later Christians like Justin (ca. 100–65 CE), Athenagorus (ca. 130–90 CE), and Tertullian (ca. 160–220 CE) explicitly played on the meanings of χριστιανός ("Christian") and χρηστός ("excellent"). See Justin, Apol. *1 Apol.* 1.4.1; Athenagorus, *Leg.* 2; Tertullian, *Apol.* 3.5.

100. For example, P.Fouad 85 (VI/VII CE). For a discussion of the puns on names in this letter, see J.-L. Fournet, "Les lettres privées de l'Égypte gréco-romaine: limites et malentendus," in *La correspondance privée dans la Méditerranée antique: sociétés en miroir*, ed. M. Dana, Scripta Antiqua 168 (Ausonius, 2023), 41–42.
101. *Montanari*, s.v. βαρύς.
102. At present, it has fewer than fifteen attestations in published papyri.
103. P.Oxy. 56.3858: "For this very reason I have written to you with my request to you, so as to not weigh (you) down (l. 10) by coming to you, for I know that you are busy" (δι' αὐτὸ̣ τοῦτο ἔγραψά σοι, ἀξ̣ιῶν σε, ἵνα μὴ ἐπιβαρήσω τοῦ ἐλθεῖν πρὸς σέ, εἰδώς σου τὴν ἀσχολία(ν)). In the *ed. pr.*, the pun on the name was missed, but it is discussed in L. H. Blumell and T. A. Wayment, *Christian Oxyrhynchus: Texts, Documents, and Sources (Second Through Fourth Centuries)* (Baylor University Press, 2015), 569–70.
104. Cf. the pun on the name Irenaeus in Eusebius, *Hist. eccl.* 5.24.18 (SC 41.71): "And Irenaeus, who deserved his name, making an *eirenicon* in this way, gave exhortations of this kind for the peace of the church and served as its ambassador" (καὶ ὁ μὲν Εἰρηναῖος φερώνυμός τις ὢν τῇ προσηγορίᾳ αὐτῷ τε τῷ τρόπῳ εἰρηνοποιός, τοιαῦτα ὑπὲρ τῆς τῶν ἐκκλησιῶν εἰρήνης παρεκάλει τε καὶ ἐπρέσβευεν).
105. A close relationship can already be detected in other parts of the letter, like the end of v. 1, where "love" is extended to Eclecte, or in v. 12, where the elder can expect to come and speak with her "face to face."
106. B. M. Metzger, *Textual Commentary on the Greek New Testament*, 719.
107. Brown, *The Epistles of John*, 653.
108. Plummer and Elledge, *1–3 John: Exegetical Guide to the Greek New Testament*, 158. But see also Dodd, *The Johannine Epistles*, 143.
109. TLB 2 John 1: "*From:* John, the old Elder of the church. *To:* That dear woman Cyria." I find many of the renderings in 2 John from the TLB egregious. Frequently, they do not reflect what is actually in the Greek text.
110. T. A. Wayment, *The New Testament. A Translation for Latter-day Saints*, rev. ed. (Greg Kofford Books, 2022), ad loc.
111. BDAG s.v. κυρία.
112. Preisigke, *Namenbuch*, see n. 125 in chapter 2 for complete bibliographic reference. H. W. Beyer and H. Lietzmann, eds., *Die jüdische Katakombe der Villa Torlonia in Rom* (Walter de Gruyter and Co., 1930).
113. Preisigke, *Namenbuch*, s.v. (col. 188): "Κυρία, w. Oxy. III. VI. Soc. III. (Soc. III = PSI 3.175.6 [A.D. 462])."
114. See TM Nam 10038.
115. In the LGPN database, there are thirty-seven attestations of the name, with the earliest appearing in the first century BCE.
116. *CIRB* 315.4–5 (late I BCE / early I CE; Pantikapaion [N. Black Sea]): τὴν τροφίμην Κυρίαν ("the mistress Kyria"); SEG 46.2012.c1 (before 70 CE;

Jerusalem): Κυρία ἡ καὶ Κυρίλ(λ)η ("Kyria also known as Kyrilla"); SEG 46.2012.c12 (before 70 CE; Jerusalem): Κυρία ("Kyria"); E. L. Hicks, "Inscriptions from Western Cilicia," *JHS* 12 (1891): 264 (no. 50; 50–100 CE; Diokaisareia): Κυρία Λεωνίδου ("Kyria daughter of Leonides"); Heberdey-Wilhelm, *Reisen in Kilikien* 50.9–10 (I CE; Rhosos): Κυρίας Μί[κ]κης ("Kyria Mikke"); SEG 60.1664.3–4 (116 CE; Qatna): Κυρία ("Kyria"); SEG 67.1045.3 (Imperial Period; Phrygia): Κυρίᾳ μητρὶ ("for [their] mother Kyria"); IGB 4.1925b.c9 (117–38 CE; Serdica): Κυρία γ[υ]νὴ ("Kyria [his] wife"); *MIA* 178.4 (II/III CE; Pantikapaion [N. Black Sea]): Κυρία ("Kyria").

117. Ammianus Marcellinus 29.5.
118. See pp. 66–67 in chapter 3.
119. Ἀπίων Ἐπιμάχῳ τῶι πατρὶ καὶ κυρίῳ πλεῖστα χαίρειν.
120. ἐρωτῶ σε οὖν, κύριέ μου πάτηρ (*l.* πάτερ).
121. Γαΐῳ τῷ ἀγαπητῷ . . . ἀγαπητέ, πιστὸν ποιεῖς.
122. κυρίᾳ . . . καὶ νῦν ἐρωτῶ σε, κυρία.
123. This list is not exhaustive. A number of other examples could have been provided like BGU 3.814 (III CE) or O.Lund 17 (III/IV CE).
124. Brown, *The Johannine Epistles*, 653.
125. D. E. Hiebert, *The Epistles of John* (Bob Jones University Press, 1988), 282–83; D. L. Akin, *The New American Commentary Volume 38: 1, 2, 3 John* (Broadman and Holman Publishers, 2001), 220; P. W. Comfort and W. C. Hawley, *1–3 John*, Cornerstone Biblical Commentary (Tyndale House, 2007), 385; W. H. Harris III, *1, 2, 3, John: Comfort and Counsel for a Church in Crisis. An Exegetical Commentary on the Letters of John*, 2nd ed. (Biblical Studies, 2009), 241.
126. NET 2 John 1 ad loc.
127. The best study for the import of Athanasius in fourth-century Christianity is still T. D. Barnes, *Athanasius and Constantius: Theology and Politics in the Constantinian Empire* (Harvard University Press, 2001).
128. See chapter 4, pp. 92–93.
129. For full bibliographic references, see nn. 52 and 54 in chapter 4.
130. Bengel, *Gnomon Novi Testamenti*, 1069.
131. CPG 2249; MPG 28.283–438.
132. P. Felckmann, ed., *Operum sancti patris nostri Athanasii archiepiscopi Alexandrini, t. II* (1600), 61–136.
133. B. de Montfaucon, *Athanasii archiepiacopi Alexandrini opera omnia*, 3 vols. (1698), 3.124–25. Montfaucon's preface and edition were reprinted in MPG 28.281–438.
134. Today, it is believed that the *Synopsis scripturae sacrae* is likely a composite work. See T. Zahn, "Die sogenannte Synopsis des Athanasius," in *Geschichte des neutestamentlichen Kanons Zweiter Band: Urkunden und Belege zum ersten un dritten Band* (A. Deichert'sche, 1890), 302–18; G. Dorival, "L'apport des

Synopses transmises sous le nom d'Athanase et de Jean Chrysostome à la question du Corpus Littéraire de la Bible?," in *Qu'est-ce qu'un Corpus Littéraire? Recherches sur le corpus biblique et les corpus patristiques*, ed. G. Dorival (Peeters, 2005), 53–93; see also F. Barone, "Pour une édition critique de la *Synopsis Scripturae Sacrae* du Pseudo-Jean Chrysostome," *RevPhil* 83 (2009): 7–19.

135. CPG 2249.
136. Felckmann, ed., *Operum sancti patris nostri Athanasii archiepiscopi Alexandrini*, 123.
137. Montfaucon, *Athanasii archiepiacopi Alexandrini opera omnia*, 3.190.
138. Bengel, *Gnomon Novi Testamenti*, 1069.
139. Burk, *Joannis Alberti Bengelii Apparatus Criticus ad Novum Testamentum*, 929.

CHAPTER 6: REREADING 2 JOHN: THE ELDER, THE LADY, HER CHILDREN, AND A HOUSE

1. S. K. Stowers, *Letter Writing in Greco-Roman Antiquity* (The Westminster Press, 1986), 47.
2. That 2 John was written on a papyrus, see discussion on pp. 59–60 in chapter 3. In 2 John 12, "the elder" states that he has written the letter with "ink" using the underlying Greek term μέλας, which means "black." The "black" inks of the Roman period tend to fade over two millennia, so they now have a dark-brown hue.
3. Hypothetically, of course, even if the two letters (2 John and 3 John) contained distinctly different handwriting, they could still stem from the same "elder." The use of scribes and secretaries is widely attested in ancient letter writing. There are various examples where a collection of letters from the same author has distinctly different scripts. For example, there is the dossier of a woman named Isidora from the second half of the first century BCE (ca. 28 BCE), which contains four letters: BGU 4.1204–07. Numbers 1205 and 1206 are written in one hand, while numbers 1204 and 1207 are written in another that is distinctly different. In the Archive of Lucius Bellienus Gemellus, from the late first century CE, there are five letters from Lucius: P.Fay. 110–11, 114–15, 117. P.Fay 110 is written in a hand distinctly different from the others. Another example occurs in the Paniscus Archive from the end of the third century CE. In this collection, there are six letters written by Paniscus to his wife: P.Mich. 3.214, 216–20. Numbers 214 and 220 are written in a different hand than the other four.
4. See n. 34 in chapter 5.
5. See n. 31 in chapter 5.
6. See discussion on pp. 81–83 in chapter 3.
7. See discussion on pp. 112–13 in chapter 4.
8. See discussion on pp. 97–98 in chapter 4.

9. On the personal name Presbyterus, see TM Nam 27717 that it is both late and rare.
10. Papias in Eusebius, *Hist. eccl.* 3.39.4, 7 (SC 31.154–55). Most recently, see discussion in Carlson, *Papias of Hierapolis, Exposition of Dominical Oracles*, 38–39. Cf. Jobes, *Letters to the Church*, 406.
11. Lengthy discussions surrounding the possible identity of "the elder" can be found in Brown, *The Johannine Epistles*, 646–51, and in Lieu, *The Second and Third Epistles of John*, 52–64.
12. See BDAG s.v. πρεσβύτερος.
13. For this usage in the papyri, see G. Schmelz, *Kirchliche Amtstäger im spätantiken Ägypten nach den Aussagen der griechischen und koptischen Papyri und Ostraka* (K. G. Saur 2002), 4.
14. Vul. 2 John 1: senior electae dominae.
15. Philo, *Opif.* 105: ὁ δ' ἰατρὸς Ἱπποκράτης ἡλικίας ἑπτὰ εἶναί φησι, παιδίου, παιδός, μειρακίου, νεανίσκου, ἀνδρός, πρεσβύτου, γέροντος, ταύτας δὲ μετρεῖσθαι μὲν ἑβδομάσιν, οὐ μὴν ταῖς κατὰ τὸ ἑξῆς. . . . ἀνὴρ δ' ἄχρις ἑνὸς δέοντος ἐτέων πεντήκοντα, ἐς τὰ ἑπτάκις ἑπτά· πρεσβύτης δ' ἄχρι πεντήκοντα ἕξ, ἐς τὰ ἑπτάκις ὀκτώ· τὸ δ' ἐντεῦθεν γέρων ("Hippocrates the physician states that there are seven ages: little boy, the boy, the lad, the young man, the man, the elderly man, the old man, and that these ages are measured by multiples of seven though not in regular succession. . . . a man until forty-nine, until seven times seven; an elderly man until fifty-six, up to seven times eight; after that an old man"). Greek text and English translation taken from F. H. Colson and G. H. Whitaker, trans., *Philo*, vol. I, LCL 226 (Harvard University Press, 1929), 85, 87.
16. Irenaeus, *Haer.* 2.22.4 (SC 294.220): Omnes enim uenit per semetipsum saluare: omnes, inquam, qui per eum renascuntur in Deum, infantes et paruulos et pueros et iuuenes et seniors ("For he [Jesus] came to save all through means of himself: all, I say, who are reborn through him to God—infants, little ones, children, youths, and the elderly").
17. D. Lake, "Elder (NT)," in *The Zondervan Encyclopedia of the Bible*, vol. 2, ed. M. C. Tenney and M. Silva (Zondervan, 2009), 290–91.
18. W. Otto, *Priester und Tempel im hellenistischen Ägypten: Ein beitrag zur kulturgeschichte des hellenismus*, 2 vols. (B. G. Teubner, 1905–1908; repr. Rome, 1971), 1.47–48.
19. That is, πρεσβύτεροι (τῆς) κώμης. On this office, see A. Tomsin, "Étude sur les πρεσβύτεροι des villages de la χώρα égyptienne," *Bulletin de la Classe des Lettres et Politiques de l'Academie Royale de Belgique*, 5th series, 38 (1952): 95–130, 467–532.
20. For example, Gen 18:12; 19:4, 31, 33–34; 24:1.
21. For example, Gen 24:2; 50:7; Exod 19:7; Deut 31:9. See also *GELS* s.v. πρεσβύτερος.

22. Matt 15:2; 16:21; 21:23; 26:3, 47, 57; 27:1, 3, 12, 20, 41; 28:12; Mark 7:3, 5; 8:31; 11:27; 14:43, 53; 15:1; Luke 7:3; 9:22; 20:1; 22:52; John 8:9. The sole exception is Luke 15:25, where it used to refer to an "elder" brother.
23. Acts 4:5, 8, 23; 6:12;23:14; 24:1; 25:15. At Acts 2:17, it is used with respect to age but is quoting Joel 2:28 (3:1).
24. χειροτονήσαντες . . . κατ' ἐκκλησίαν πρεσβυτέρους. See also Acts 20:17–18.
25. Acts 15:23: οἱ ἀπόστολοι καὶ οἱ πρεσβύτεροι ἀδελφοὶτοῖς κατὰ τὴν Ἀντιόχειαν καὶ Συρίαν καὶ Κιλικίαν ἀδελφοῖς τοῖς ἐξ ἐθνῶν χαίρειν ("The brothers, both the apostles and the elders, to the brothers and sisters of gentile origin in Antioch and Syria and Cilicia, greetings").
26. In 1 Tim 5:1–2, it is used to denote age—elderly men and women—but in 1 Tim 5:17, 19 and Tit 1:5, it refers to leadership within the church. Paul uses πρεσβύτης to describe himself as an "elderly man" to Philemon (Phlm. 9). Rev 4:4, 10; 5:5–6, 8, 11, 14; 7:11, 13; 11:16; 14:3; 19:4.
27. Jas 5:14 mentions "elders of the church" who anoint the sick and bless them; in Heb 11:2, it is used of "ancestors"; 1 Pet 5:1 mentions "elders" in the context of leadership, and its author also mentions himself among them: συμπρεσβύτερος ("fellow-elder"). See also 1 Pet 5:5.
28. Papias of Hierapolis in Eusebius, *Hist. eccl.* 3.39.3–4 (SC 31.154): οὐκ ὀκνήσω δέ σοι καὶ ὅσα ποτὲ παρὰ τῶν πρεσβυτέρων καλῶς ἔμαθον καὶ καλῶς ἐμνημόνευσα, συγκατατάξαι ταῖς ἑρμηνείαις, διαβεβαιούμενος ὑπὲρ αὐτῶν ἀλήθειαν. . . . εἰ δέ που καὶ παρηκολουθηκώς τις τοῖς πρεσβυτέροις ἔλθοι, τοὺς τῶν πρεσβυτέρων ἀνέκρινον λόγους, τί Ἀνδρέας ἢ τί Πέτρος εἶπεν ἢ τί Φίλιππος ἢ τί Θωμᾶς ἢ Ἰάκωβος ἢ τί Ἰωάννης ἢ Ματθαῖος ἤ τις ἕτερος τῶν τοῦ κυρίου μαθητῶν ἅ τε Ἀριστίων καὶ ὁ πρεσβύτερος Ἰωάννης, τοῦ κυρίου μαθηταί, λέγουσιν ("And I shall not hesitate to append to the interpretations all that I ever learnt well from the elders and remember well, for of their truth I am confident. . . . but if ever anyone came who had followed the elders, I inquired into the words of the elders, what Andrew or Peter or Philip or Thomas or James or John or Matthew, or any other of the Lord's disciples, had said, and what Aristion and the elder John, the Lord's disciples, were saying"). Translation slightly adapted from K. Lake, trans., *Eusebius. The Ecclesiastical History*, vol. I, LCL 153 (Harvard University Press, 1926), 291, 293.
29. Irenaeus, *Haer.* 5.36 (SC 153.458): Presbyteri Apostolorum discipuli; see also *Haer.* 5.33.3 (SC 153.414–15).
30. P. R. Jones, "The Missional Role of Ο ΠΡΕΣΒΥΤΕΡΟΣ," in *Communities in Dispute: Current Scholarship on the Johannine Epistles*, ed. R. A. Culpepper and P. N. Anderson (SBL Press, 2014), 141.
31. Jones, "The Missional Role of Ο ΠΡΕΣΒΥΤΕΡΟΣ," 144, describes the title "elder" in 2 John as carrying a "church-leader" meaning.
32. On these documents, see discussion in T. Gagos and P. J. Sijpesteijn, "Towards an Explanation of the Typology of the So-Called 'Orders to Arrest,'" *BASP*

33 (1996): 77–97; H.-J. Drexhage, "Zu den Überstellungsbefehlen aus dem römischen Agypten (1.–3. Jahrhundert n.Chr.)," in *Migratio et Commutatio. Studien zur Alten Geschichte und deren Nachleben Thomas Pekáry dargebracht*, ed. H.-J. Drexhage and J. Sünskes (Scripta Mercaturae Verlag, 1989), 102–18; U. Hagedorn, "Das Formular der Überstellungsbefehle im römischen Ägypten," *BASP* 16 (1979): 61–74.

33. While they were traditionally called "Orders to Arrest," they do not use a verb or an expression that translates as "arrest."
34. In both Ptolemaic and Roman Egypt, the *strategus* served as the military and civil governor of a nome within Egypt.
35. [ὁ] στρ̣ατηγὸς πρεσβ(υτέροις) καὶ ἀρχεφ(όδῳ) Κ̣αινῆς̣ κτλ. On the restoration of the definite article ὁ at the beginning of the summons and other corrections for the first line, see D. Hagedorn, "Entsprach der Monat Domitianos in Ägypten dem Phaophi oder dem Hathyr?," *ZPE* 159 (2007): 265.
36. ὁ στρατηγὸς νομοφύλακι κ[αὶ ἀρχεφόδῳ] κώμης Νάουεος (*l.* Νάουεως) κτλ. Additional examples could be given: e.g., P.Mich. 10.590 (III/IV).
37. Drexhage, "Zu den Überstellungsbefehlen aus dem römischen Agypten (1.–3. Jahrhundert n.Chr.)," 103–5.
38. Lieu, *The Theology of the Johannine Letters*, 8.
39. ὁ πατὴρ Ἀδάμα[ι] χαίρειν.
40. P.Tebt. 3.1.752.2–9: μὴ ὀκνήσῃς τοῦ εἰς οἶκον ἀποστεῖλαι ὡς ἔσχε̣ τὰ καθ' αὐτούς, ποῖά τινά ἐστιν, καὶ π[ε]ρὶ τοῦ ἐμφανίσαι τὸ φρόνιμον, ἵνα μὴ ἀναβαίνω περὶ τῶν αὐτῶν ("Do not delay to send to the house how things are with them, what kind they are, and to exhibit good sense, so that I shall not have to come up about these matters").
41. ὁ πατὴρ Ἀμμωνίωι καὶ τοῖς ἐν οἴκῳ πᾶσι χαίρειν.
42. BGU 6.1296.24–24: περὶ μὲν τῶν ἄ[λ]λων οὐκέτι οὐθέν σοι γράφω̣.
43. ὁ πατὴρ Ἑστιείωι χαίρειν καὶ ἐρρῶσθαι.
44. There is another letter where the sender only identifies with the title ὁ πατήρ, but it contains a different prescript, as it dates to the third or fourth century CE: P.Oxy. 1.123.1: κυρίῳ μου υἱῷ Διονυσοθέωνι ὁ πατὴρ χαίρειν ("To my lord son, Dionysotheon, [from] your father, greetings").
45. ἡ μήτηρ Ἀσκλᾶτι χαίρε[ιν] καὶ διὰ παντὸς ὑγιαίν[ειν] καθάπερ εὔχομαι.
46. P.Rein. 2.118.1–2: κυρίᾳ μου μητρὶ ἡ θυγάτηρ χαίριν (*l.* χαίρειν) ("To my lady mother, [from] your daughter, greetings").
47. P.Rein. 2.118.11–17: ἀσπάζομε (*l.* ἀσπάζομαι) τὰς ἀδελφάς μου καὶ τὰ πεζα (*l.* παιδία) αὐουτῶν (*l.* αὐτῶν). ἀσπάζοντέ (*l.* ἀσπάζονται) σε τὰ π̣[ε]ζα (*l.* παιδία) μου.
48. D. F. Watson, "A Rhetorical Analysis of 2 John According to Greco-Roman Convention," *NTS* 35 (1989): 107–9, classifies 2 John as a paraenetic letter.
49. Quintilian, *Inst.* 3.8.13: Valet autem in consiliis auctoritas plurimum. Nam et prudentissimus esse haberique et optimus debet qui sententiae suae de utilibus

atque honestis credere omnes velit. Latin text and English translation taken from D. A. Russell, trans. and ed., *Quintilian. The Orator's Education*, vol. 2, LCL 125 (Harvard University Press, 2002), 122–23.

50. In the Septuagint, where it occurs a handful of times, it is principally used to distinguish a female slave or servant from a "mistress" or free woman: LXX Ps. 122:2 (123:2): ἰδοὺ ὡς ὀφθαλμοὶ δούλων εἰς χεῖρας τῶν κυρίων αὐτῶν, ὡς ὀφθαλμοὶ παιδίσκης εἰς χεῖρας τῆς κυρίας αὐτῆς ("As the eyes of servants look to the hand of their master, as the eyes of a maid to the hand of her mistress"). The same kind of contrast appears in Gen 16:4, 8–9 between Sara and Hagar and in Prov 24:58 (30:23) and Isa 24:2. See also 1 Kgs 17:17 and 2 Kgs 5:3. When it appears in Isa 40:10, it means "power." The same distinction often occurs in various pseudepigraphical texts of the Old Testament where biblical stories are recast: T. Ab. 3.10; Jos. Asen. 4.14. In early Christian literature outside of the New Testament, it appears principally in the *Shepherd of Hermas*, where it is used as a title of respect but also to refer to Greek goddesses, just as "lord" (κύριος) can be used to refer to Greek gods (Irenaeus, *Adv. Haer.* 1.18.1).

51. Epictetus, *Ench.* 40: αἱ γυναῖκες εὐθὺς ἀπὸ τεσσαρεσκαίδεκα ἐτῶν ὑπὸ τῶν ἀνδρῶν κυρίαι καλοῦνται. For commentary on this passage, see Dickey, *Greek Forms of Address: From Herodotus to Lucian*, 101.

52. Though rare, it is even used as a title for a daughter ("lady daughter"), but this evidence is late in epistolary addresses. SB 14.11437.1–3 (IV/V CE): τῇ κυρίᾳ μου θυγατρὶ Σουσάννᾳ Μαρτύριος ὁ σὸς πατήρ ("To my lady daughter Susanna, [from] your father, Matryrius"). See also SB 14.11538 (V ? CE). The title does appear much earlier with "daughter" in the valedictory "greetings" at the end of a letter: BGU 16.2617.6–7 (July 11, 7 BCE): [ἄσπ]άζου τὰς κυρίας μου θυγατρες (*l.* θυγατέρας) Τρυφᾶν καὶ Ἄρτεμιν ("Greet my lady daughters Trypha and Artemis"); P.Mich. 3.33 (297 CE): ἀσπάζομε (*l.* ἀσπάζομαι) τὴν κυρίαν μου θυγατέραν Ἡλιοδώραν ("I greet my lady daughter Heliodora").

53. See pp. 73 in chapter 3.

54. John Chrysostom, *Ep. Olymp.* 6.1.53 (SC 13bis.130): καὶ ἡ κυρία μου Σαβινιανὴ ἡ διάκονος ("And my lady Sabiniana, the deaconess"). See also discussion in L. Dinneen, *Titles of Address in Christian Greek Epistolography to 527 A.D.* (The Catholic University of America, 1929), 78.

55. That is, *Quaestiones Romanae.*

56. Plutarch, *Quaest. rom.* 30 (271E): ὅπου σὺ Γάιος, ἐγὼ Γαΐα ("Where you are Gaius, there am I Gaia"). The Latin is "Ubi tu Gaius, ego Gaia." On this phrase, see discussion in K. H. Hersch, *The Roman Wedding: Ritual Meaning in Antiquity* (Cambridge University Press, 2010), 187–90.

57. Plutarch, *Quaest. rom.* 30 (271E): ὅπου σὺ κύριος καὶ οἰκοδεσπότης, καὶ ἐγὼ κυρία καὶ οἰκοδέσποινα.

58. On the use of the title "mistress" (οἰκοδέσποινα), see discussion in C. Osiek and M. Y. MacDonald, with J. H. Tulloch, *A Woman's Place: House Churches in Earliest Christianity* (Fortress Press, 2006), 150–52.
59. Matt 3:17; 12:18; 17:5; Mark 1:11; 9:7; 12:6; Luke 3:22; 20:13; Acts 15:25; Rom 1:7; 11:28; 12:19; 16:5, 8–9, 12; 1 Cor 4:14, 17; 10:14; 15:58; 2 Cor 7:1; 12:19; Eph 5:1; 6:21; Phil 2:12; 4:1; Col 1:7; 4:7, 9, 14; 1 Th 2:8; 1 Tim 6:2; 2 Tim 1:2; Phlm 1:1, 16; Heb 6:9; Jas 1:16, 19; 2:5; 1 Pet 2:11; 4:12; 2 Pet 1:17; 3:1, 8, 14–15, 17; 1 John 2:7; 3:2, 21; 4:1, 7, 11; 3 John 1:1–2, 5, 11; Jude 1:3, 17, 20.
60. On these meanings, see discussion in BDAG s.v. ἀγαπητός, ή, όν. For a comprehensive lexical treatment, see J. A. L. Lee, *A History of New Testament Lexicography*, Studies in Biblical Greek 8 (Peter Lang, 2003), 193–211.
61. As an epistolary title, it is often coupled with familial language to accentuate a bond between the sender and the recipient. In 3 John, Gaius is designated with the familial title "child," although this does not appear in the address (3 John 3–4; see discussion on pp. 167–69). "Brothers" (ἀδελφοί) are mentioned in 3 John 3, 5, and 10 but without the epithet "beloved." On the use of this adjective and familial language, see A. M. Nobbs, "Beloved Brothers in the New Testament and Early Christian World," in *The New Testament in Its First Century Setting: Essays on Context and Background in Honour of B. W. Winter on His 65th Birthday*, ed. P. J. Williams et al. (Eerdmans, 2004), 143–50; cf. *NewDocs* 4.250–55.
62. On Christian letters of recommendation in the papyri, see T. M. Teeter, "Letters of Recommendation or Letters of Peace?" *APF* 3 (1997): 954–60; T. M. Teeter, "Christian Letters of Recommendation in the Papyrus Record," *Patristic and Byzantine Review* 9 (1990): 59–69; *NewDocs* 8.169–72; K. Treu, "Christliche Empfehlungs-Schemabriefe auf Papyrus," in *Zetesis. Album Amicorum Door Vrienden en Collega's Aangeboden Aan Prof. Dr. E. de Strycker Ter Gelegenheid Van Zijn 65e Verjaardag*, ed. Émile De Strycker (Boekhandel, 1973), 629–36.
63. Treu, "Christliche Empfehlungs-Schemabriefe auf Papyrus," 634.
64. The nine letters include P.Alex. 29 (mid III CE), P.Oxy. 8.1162 (III/IV CE), P.Oxy. 36.2785 (mid III CE), P.Oxy. 56.3857 (IV CE), PSI 3.208 (mid III CE), PSI 9.1041 (mid III CE), SB 3.7269 (IV CE), SB 10.10255 (=PSI 15.1560; III/IV CE), and SB 16.12304 (III/IV CE). The only other early letter where the title "beloved" appears is P.Oxy. 14.1680 (III/IV CE), but it is only evinced in the epistolary address at the end of the letter on the back: [τῷ κυρίῳ] καὶ ἀγαπητῷ πατρὶ Ἀπόλλωνι [-c. ?-] ("to my lord and beloved father Apollonius").
65. On this reading, see discussion on 3 John in A. Malherbe, *Social Aspects of Early Christianity*, 2nd ed. (Fortress Press, 1983), 105–6.
66. 3 John 12: Δημητρίῳ μεμαρτύρηται ὑπὸ πάντων καὶ ὑπὸ αὐτῆς τῆς ἀληθείας· καὶ ἡμεῖς δὲ μαρτυροῦμεν, καὶ οἶδας ὅτι ἡ μαρτυρία ἡμῶν ἀληθής ἐστιν.
67. 2 John 1 and 12 and 3 John 1 and 14.

68. In Phlm 2, some later manuscripts (D[2] [GA 05], K [GA 018], L [GA 020], Ψ [GA 044], etc.) read Ἀπφίᾳ τῇ ἀγαπητῇ ("to our beloved Aphia"), whereas the earlier texts (א [GA 01] and A [GA 02]) read Ἀπφίᾳ τῇ ἀδελφῇ ("to our sister Aphia"). The later change from ἀδελφή to ἀγαπητή is most likely explained as a scribal harmonization since Philemon is addressed as "beloved" (i.e., Φιλήμονι τῷ ἀγαπητῷ) in the first verse.
69. It was previously published as SB 3.7243.
70. SB 3.7243 (IV): [κυρίᾳ μ]ου ἀγαπητῇ [ἀ]δελφῇ [Διδύμη καὶ] αἱ ἀδελφαὶ ἐν κ(υρί)ῳ χαίριν (*l.* χαίρειν). In the *ed. pr.*, the letter was thought to open with [Σοφιάτι μ]ου κτλ. On the present reading, see Bagnall and Cribiore, *Women's Letters from Ancient Egypt*, 196–97.
71. P.Nepheros 18.1–4: κυρίῳ μου ἀδελφῷ Εὐδαίμωνι καὶ τῇ ἀγαπητῇ ἀδελφῇ μου Ἀπίᾳ συμβιος (*l.* συμβίῳ) σου Ταουὰκ' ἐν κ(υρί)ῳ χέρειν (*l.* χαίρειν). See discussion on this letter in Bagnall and Cribiore, *Women's Letters from Ancient Egypt*, 207–08.
72. In the New Testament, a high concentration of the title "beloved" appears in Romans 16, where Paul uses it in valedictory greetings. Three times it is used for men and once for a woman who seems to have been especially dear to Paul because of how she is described. Rom 16:12: ἀσπάσασθε Περσίδα τὴν ἀγαπητήν, ἥτις πολλὰ ἐκοπίασεν ἐν κυρίῳ ("Greet the beloved Persis, who has worked hard in the Lord"). Cf. Rom 16:5: ἀσπάσασθε Ἐπαίνετον τὸν ἀγαπητόν μου ("Greet my beloved Epaenetus"); Rom 16:8: ἀσπάσασθε Ἀμπλιᾶτον τὸν ἀγαπητόν μου ἐν κυρίῳ ("Greet Ampliatus, my beloved in the Lord"); Rom 16:9: ἀσπάσασθε . . . καὶ Στάχυν τὸν ἀγαπητόν μου ("Greet . . . and my beloved Stachys").
73. E.g., Matt 23:8; John 19:26–27; 1 Cor 4:14; 2 Cor 6:13; Gal 4:19; Heb 2:11. See also P. Arzt-Grabner, "'Brothers' and 'Sisters' in Documentary Papyri and in Early Christianity," *RivB* 50 (2002): 202, who notes the following of the familial term "brother" in the New Testament: "Out of 343 references for ἀδελφός in the New Testament more than 260 have to be interpreted in a metaphorical sense."
74. Matt 12:50: ὅστις γὰρ ἂν ποιήσῃ τὸ θέλημα τοῦ πατρός μου τοῦ ἐν οὐρανοῖς αὐτός μου ἀδελφὸς καὶ ἀδελφὴ καὶ μήτηρ ἐστίν.
75. E.g., Luke 1:59–60, 62, 67; Acts 23:16; 2 Tim 1:5.
76. E.g., Jas 2:15.
77. Bagnall and Cribiore, *Women's Letters from Ancient Egypt*, 85–86.
78. E. Dickey, "Literal and Extended Use of Kinship Terms in Documentary Papyri," *Mnemosyne* 57 (2004): 131–76.
79. Dickey, "Literal and Extended Use of Kinship Terms in Documentary Papyri," 173.
80. Dickey, "Literal and Extended Use of Kinship Terms in Documentary Papyri," 165.

81. Dickey, "Literal and Extended Use of Kinship Terms in Documentary Papyri," 165–66.
82. Poggel, *Der zweite und dritte Brief des Apostels Johannes*, 127–32.
83. 3 John 3: ἐχάρην γὰρ λίαν ἐρχομένων ἀδελφῶν καὶ μαρτυρούντων σου τῇ ἀληθείᾳ, καθὼς σὺ ἐν ἀληθείᾳ περιπατεῖς ("For I was overjoyed when some brothers and sisters arrived and testified to your faithfulness to the truth, how you walk in the truth").
84. 3 John 4: μειζοτέραν τούτων οὐκ ἔχω χαράν, ἵνα ἀκούω τὰ ἐμὰ τέκνα ἐν ἀληθείᾳ περιπατοῦντα.
85. The elder's usage appears similar to Paul's, where he calls his disciples "children": 1 Cor 4:14, 17.
86. ἐχάρην λίαν ὅτι εὕρηκα ἐκ τῶν τέκνων σου περιπατοῦντας ἐν ἀληθείᾳ.
87. In 2 John 4, when the elder says "some of your children," the most straightforward interpretation of the partitive expression is that the elder is only speaking about those "children" he has recently met and is not implying that other children of Eclecte are necessarily "walking in error" and have fallen away. Here, I disagree with the reading espoused by Smalley, *1, 2, 3 John*, 310–11. Smalley's view is shared by Brooke, *A Critical and Exegetical Commentary on the Johannine Epistles*, 172.
88. J. Painter, *1, 2, and 3 John*, SPS 18 (The Liturgical Press, 2002), 340, notes that v. 4 implies "the lady seems to have many children."
89. ἀσπάζεταί σε τὰ τέκνα τῆς ἀδελφῆς σου τῆς ἐκλεκτῆς. This verse has been discussed at length in chapters 2 (pp. 39–40) and 5 (pp. 138–42) regarding how best to take the phrase της εκλεκτης—as an adjective or a proper name. The former is clearly the correct reading: τῆς ἐκλεκτῆς.
90. πιστὸν ποιεῖς ὃ ἐὰν ἐργάσῃ εἰς τοὺς ἀδελφοὺς καὶ τοῦτο ξένους.
91. οὔτε αὐτὸς ἐπιδέχεται τοὺς ἀδελφοὺς καὶ τοὺς βουλομένους κωλύει.
92. Note that the elder never says "your brothers" to Gaius but simply calls them "brothers."
93. See discussion on pp. 142–44 in chapter 5.
94. 2 John 5–6. At the end of v. 4, the elder mentions "the Father" (ὁ πατήρ), which is the antecedent of "his" in 2 John 6. In 2 John 3, the elder mentions "God the Father" and then Jesus Christ as the "son of the Father" (παρὰ θεοῦ πατρὸς καὶ παρὰ Ἰησοῦ Χριστοῦ τοῦ υἱοῦ τοῦ πατρός).
95. 2 John 7: ὅτι πολλοὶ πλάνοι ἐξῆλθον εἰς τὸν κόσμον, οἱ μὴ ὁμολογοῦντες Ἰησοῦν Χριστὸν ἐρχόμενον ἐν σαρκί· οὗτός ἐστιν ὁ πλάνος καὶ ὁ ἀντίχριστος.
96. D. R. Streett, *They Went Out from Us: The Identity of the Opponents in First John*, BZNW 177 (Walter de Gruyter, 2011), 6–111. Though Streett focuses on the opponents of 1 John, he sees them as the same as those mentioned in 2 John.
97. [9]πᾶς ὁ προάγων καὶ μὴ μένων ἐν τῇ διδαχῇ τοῦ Χριστοῦ θεὸν οὐκ ἔχει· ὁ μένων ἐν τῇ διδαχῇ, οὗτος καὶ τὸν πατέρα καὶ τὸν υἱὸν ἔχει. [10]εἴ τις ἔρχεται πρὸς ὑμᾶς καὶ

ταύτην τὴν διδαχὴν οὐ φέρει, μὴ λαμβάνετε αὐτὸν εἰς οἰκίαν καὶ χαίρειν αὐτῷ μὴ λέγετε· [11]ὁ λέγων γὰρ αὐτῷ χαίρειν κοινωνεῖ τοῖς ἔργοις αὐτοῦ τοῖς πονηροῖς.

98. In this verse, there is much discussion surrounding the precise meaning of the verb προάγω ("to go beyond"). Streett, *They Went Out from Us*, 349–53, offers a good summary; see also Jobes, *1, 2, & 3 John*, 270–71. Some later manuscripts preserve the reading "turn aside / transgress" (παραβαίνω).

99. E.g., Streett, *They Went Out from Us*, 356–57, who states (p. 356) that "these visitors appear to be itinerant teachers or prophets." He is not alone in this view.

100. *Did* 11:3–4 is often cited in these discussions where Christians are exhorted, "in accordance with the rule of the gospel," to receive "every apostle who comes to you" and welcome them into their home and provide them with lodging ([3]κατὰ τὸ δόγμα τοῦ εὐαγγελίου οὕτως ποιήσατε. [4]πᾶς δὲ ἀπόστολος ἐρχόμενος πρὸς ὑμᾶς δεχθήτω ὡς κύριος.). Other passages like Matt 10:40–42, where Jesus gives a general entreaty to receive and host a traveling "prophet" or a "righteous person," are also often cited. See also Mark 9:37; Luke 10:16; John 13:20; Rom 12:13; Heb 13:2.

101. 2 John 4 and 12.

102. 3 John 3 and 14.

103. 3 John 12.

104. 2 John 12 and 3 John 14.

105. See discussion in L. H. Blumell, "Christians on the Move in Late Antique Oxyrhynchus," in *Travel and Religion in Antiquity*, ed. P. Harland, Studies in Christianity and Judaism / Études sur le christianisme et le judaïsme 21 (Wilfred Laurier University Press, 2011), 235–54, and in Blumell, *Lettered Christians*, 89–162.

106. This term appears over eighty times in the New Testament: Matt 2:11; 5:15; 7:24–27; 8:6, 14; 9:10, 23, 28; 10:12–14; 12:25, 29; 13:1, 36, 57; 17:25; 19:29; 24:17, 43; 26:6; Mark 1:29; 2:15; 3:25, 27; 6:4, 10; 7:24; 9:33; 10:10, 29–30; 12:40; 13:15, 34–35; 14:3; Luke 4:38; 5:29; 6:48–49; 7:6, 37, 44; 8:27, 51; 9:4; 10:5, 7; 15:8, 25; 17:31; 18:29; 20:47; 22:10–11, 54; John 4:53; 8:35; 11:31; 12:3; 14:2; Acts 4:34; 9:11, 17; 10:6, 17, 32; 11:11; 12:12; 16:32; 17:5; 18:7; 1 Cor 11:22; 16:15; 2 Cor 5:1; Phil 4:22; 1 Tim 5:13; 2 Tim 2:20; 3:6; 2 John 1:10.

107. According to BDAG s.v. οἰκία, the principal meaning is "a structure used as a dwelling, house." A secondary meaning is also given: "social unit within a dwelling, household, family." One of the most detailed explorations of the meaning of the related terms οἰκία ("house") and οἶκος ("house") can be found in H.-J. Klauck, *Hausgemeinde und Hauskirche im frühen Christentum*, SBS 103 (Katholisches Bibelwerk, 1981). Klauck argues that both terms, οἰκία and οἶκος, can (1) carry a narrow meaning of "house" in the literal sense (i.e., an inhabited edifice) as well as (2) carry an extended meaning, denoting a family or clan. In his 1981 monograph, Klauck believes that οἶκος more often denotes an actual "house" and that οἰκία tends more often to carry the extended meaning of "household" or "family," but

in his 1994 treatment of 2 John 10 in *Der zweite und dritte Johannesbrief*, 65–66, Klauck states that he favors the reading of "house" in the literal sense.

108. For an insightful treatment of the physical landscapes of houses serving as early Christian meeting places, see J. Cianca, *Sacred Ritual, Profane Space: The Roman House as Early Christian Meeting Place*, Studies in Christianity and Judaism (McGill-Queen's University Press, 2018).
109. There is nothing especially unusual about female home ownership in the first or second century CE. In the papyri of Roman Egypt, there are numerous examples of females owning houses, either in whole or in part. For a useful discussion of such evidence, see D. Hobson, "Women as Property Owners in Roman Egypt," *TAPA* 113 (1983): 311–21.
110. 2 John 12: πολλὰ ἔχων ὑμῖν γράφειν οὐκ ἐβουλήθην διὰ χάρτου καὶ μέλανος, ἀλλ' ἐλπίζω γενέσθαι πρὸς ὑμᾶς καὶ στόμα πρὸς στόμα λαλῆσαι.
111. The kinds of activities that might be imaged to have taken place when the elder arrived may be conveyed by an episode portrayed in Acts 20:7–12. While visiting disciples at a residence in Troas on his way back to Jerusalem, Paul and others stayed for a period; during such time, they fellowshipped, shared meals, and met "on the first day of the week," and Paul provided the local disciples with instruction and exhortation before departing.
112. 2 John 13.
113. See n. 89 above.
114. Painter, *1, 2, and 3 John*, 340, 357.
115. A. Verhoogt, "Dictating Letters in Greek and Roman Egypt from a Comparative Perspective," University of Michigan, https://sites.lsa.umich.edu/wp-content/uploads/sites/235/2015/02/dictating1.pdf.
116. The ecclesial network of 2 John includes three loci; if 3 John is included, at least two more loci are included: Gaius and Diotrephes. A third might be added depending on the reference in 3 John 10 to "those who want to do so" (τοὺς βουλομένους).
117. Brown, *The Johannine Epistles*, 52–53.
118. 2 John 9 could lend some weight to this view, as "the elder" states that these people do not "abide" (μένω; lit. "remain") in the prescribed teaching about Christ. One reading is that they formerly "abided" ("remained") in the teaching (i.e., were within) but have left and are now outside.
119. [11]εἰς ἣν δ' ἂν πόλιν ἢ κώμην εἰσέλθητε, ἐξετάσατε τίς ἐν αὐτῇ ἄξιός ἐστιν· κἀκεῖ μείνατε ἕως ἂν ἐξέλθητε. [12]εἰσερχόμενοι δὲ εἰς τὴν οἰκίαν ἀσπάσασθε αὐτήν· [13]καὶ ἐὰν μὲν ᾖ ἡ οἰκία ἀξία, ἐλθάτω ἡ εἰρήνη ὑμῶν ἐπ' αὐτήν, ἐὰν δὲ μὴ ᾖ ἀξία, ἡ εἰρήνη ὑμῶν πρὸς ὑμᾶς ἐπιστραφήτω.
120. See appendix 1.
121. B. J. Malina, "The Received View and What It Cannot Do: III John and Hospitality," *Semeia* 35 (1986): 171–89, has some good discussion as it relates to 3 John and, to a lesser extent, 2 John. At times, however, the article is a little excessive.

122. Specifically see Rom 12:13 and Heb 13:2. See also Matt 5:42.
123. Malina, "The Received View and What It Cannot Do," 181.
124. Osiek, MacDonald, with Tulloch, *A Woman's Place: House Churches in Earliest Christianity*, 246–49.
125. E. Adams, *The Earliest Christian Meeting Places: Almost Exclusively Houses?*, LNTS 450 (Bloomsbury, 2013), argues that there were other places early Christians congregated but does not deny that the home was a prominent place of Christian gatherings.
126. Rom 16: 3, 5: ἀσπάσασθε Πρίσκαν καὶ Ἀκύλαν . . . καὶ τὴν κατ' οἶκον αὐτῶν ἐκκλησίαν.
127. R. W. Gehring, *The House Church and Mission: The Importance of Household Structures in Early Christianity* (Hendrickson, 2004), 155–59, discusses the meaning of this phrase.
128. 1 Cor 16:19: ἀσπάζεται ὑμᾶς ἐν κυρίῳ πολλὰ Ἀκύλας καὶ Πρίσκα σὺν τῇ κατ' οἶκον αὐτῶν ἐκκλησίᾳ.
129. Col 4:15: ἀσπάσασθε τοὺς ἐν Λαοδικείᾳ ἀδελφοὺς καὶ Νύμφαν καὶ τὴν κατ' οἶκον αὐτῆς ἐκκλησίαν.
130. Phlm. 1–2: [1]Παῦλος δέσμιος Χριστοῦ Ἰησοῦ καὶ Τιμόθεος ὁ ἀδελφὸς Φιλήμονι τῷ ἀγαπητῷ καὶ συνεργῷ ἡμῶν [2]καὶ Ἀπφίᾳ τῇ ἀδελφῇ καὶ Ἀρχίππῳ τῷ συστρατιώτῃ ἡμῶν καὶ τῇ κατ' οἶκόν σου ἐκκλησίᾳ.
131. The accusative form of the name that appears in Col 4:15 is νυμφαν; if it is articulated Νυμφᾶν with the circumflex, it is the masculine name Nymphas, but if it is instead accented Νύμφαν, it becomes the feminine Nympha. On top of this, in some manuscripts, the possessive pronoun is the masculine "his" (αὐτοῦ), whereas in others, it is the feminine "her" (αὐτῆς).
132. Osiek, MacDonald, with Tulloch, *A Woman's Place: House Churches in Earliest Christianity*, 9–10, 12, 14, 217, discusses how the reference can be taken.
133. Ignatius, *Smyrn.* 13.2: ἀσπάζομαι τὸν οἶκον Γαουΐας, ἣν εὔχομαι ἑδρᾶσθαι πίστει καὶ ἀγάπῃ σαρκικῇ τε καὶ πνευματικῇ ("I greet the house of Gavia, and I pray that she may be grounded in faith and love both physically and spiritually"). Some manuscripts read Ταουΐα ("Tavia"), and this is often how this female name is cited in English discussions of this passage. At present, the Greek form of the female name Ταουΐα is unattested elsewhere. On the other hand, Γαουΐα is attested elsewhere. See LGPN s.v. Γαουΐα.
134. Adams, *The Earliest Christian Meeting Places*, 43, questions whether the "house" in 2 John is a "house church," although he recognizes it can be read against such a background. I am in general agreement with his caution about automatically assuming it is a house church; where I disagree is that it is clear from 2 John that certain functions like gatherings and teaching/preaching did occur at the house.

135. Quote taken from J. McDargh, "The Paradigm-Shifting Research of Ana-María Rizzuto: Origins, Strategy, Reception, and Horizon," in *Ana-María Rizzuto and the Psychoanalysis of Religion: The Road to the Living God*, ed. M. J. Reineke and D. M. Goodman (Lexington Books, 2017), 14. While the quote is ascribed to Oliver Wendell Holmes Jr. (1841–1935), others ascribe it to his father, Oliver Wendell Holmes Sr. (1809–1894).

WORKS CITED

Adams, E. *The Earliest Christian Meeting Places: Almost Exclusively Houses?* The Library of New Testament Studies 450. Bloomsbury, 2013.

Akçay, N. *The Commentary on the Acts of the Apostles, the Pauline Epistles, the Catholic Epistles, and the Apocalypse by Dionysius Jacob Bar Salibi, Metropolitan of Amid († 1171).* Department of Syriac Studies, Syriac Orthodox Patriarchate, 2020.

Akin, D. L. *The New American Commentary Volume 38: 1, 2, 3 John*. Nashville: Broadman and Holman Publishers, 2001.

Aland, B., K. Aland, G. Mink, H. Strutwolf, and K. Wachtel, eds. *Novum Testamentum Graecum: Editio Critica Maior: IV Catholic Letters. Part 1, Installment 4: The Second and Third Letter of John, The Letter of Jude.* Deutsche Bibelgesellschaft, 2005.

Aland, B., K. Aland, G. Mink, H. Strutwolf, and K. Wachtel, eds. *Novum Testamentum Graecum: Editio Critica Maior: IV Catholic Letters. Part 1: Text.* 2nd rev. ed. Deutsche Bibelgesellschaft, 2013.

Aland, B., K. Aland, G. Mink, and K. Wachtel, eds. *Novum Testamentum Graecum: Editio Critica Maior: IV Catholic Letters. Part 1, Installment 3: The First Letter of John*. Deutsche Bibelgesellschaft, 2003.

Aland, B., and K. Wachtel. "The Greek Minuscules of the New Testament." In *The Text of the New Testament in Contemporary Research: Essays on the Status Quaestionis.* 2nd ed, edited by B. D. Ehrman and M. W. Holmes. New Testament Tools, Studies, and Documents 42. Brill, 2013.

Aland, K., and B. Aland. *The Text of the New Testament: An Introduction to the Critical Editions and to the Theory and Practice of Modern Textual Criticism.* 2nd ed. Translated by E. F. Rhodes. Eerdmans, 1995.

Aland, K., M. Black, C. Martini, B. Metzger, and A. Wikgren, eds. *The Greek New Testament*. 3rd ed. United Bible Societies, 1975. Corrected printing, 1983.

Aland, K., M. Black, C. M. Martini, B. M. Metzger, and A. Wikgren, eds. *Novum Testamentum Graece. Post Eberhard Nestle et Erwin Nestle communiter ediderunt Kurt Aland, Matthew Black, Carlo M. Martini, Bruce M. Metzger, Allen Wikgren; apparatum criticum recensuerunt et editionem novis curis elaboraverunt Kurt Aland et Barbara Aland una cum Instituto studiorum textus Novi Testamenti Monasteriensi (Westphalia).* 26th ed. Deutsche Bibelgesellschaft, 1979.

Aland, K., with M. Welte, B. Köster, and K. Junack, eds. *Kurzgefasste Liste der griechischen Handschriften des Neuen Testaments.* 2nd ed. Walter de Gruyter, 1994.

Alexander, N. *The Epistles of John: Introduction and Commentary*. Torch Bible Commentaries. Macmillan, 1962.

Alexander, W. *The Epistles of St. John. Twenty-One Discourses, with Greek Text, Comparative Versions, and Notes Chiefly Exegetical.* New York: A. C. Armstrong & Son, 1889.

Ambrogio, M. R., C. Ariosto, L. Cianfriglia, S. Mazzotta, and V. Zubboli. "Via Portuense, località Pozzo Pantaleo. Indagini archeologiche per l'allargamento della sede stradale (Municipio XI)." *Bullettino della Commissione Archeologica Comunale di Roma* 117 (2016): 385–392.

Anderson, K., and D. Keating. *James, First, Second, and Third John.* Baker Academic, 2017.

Andrist, P., ed. *Le manuscrit B de la Bible (Vaticanus graecus 1209): Introduction au fac-similé, Actes du Colloque de Genève (11 juin 2001), Contributions supplémentaires.* Histoire du Texte Biblique 7. Éditions du Zèbre, 2009.

Apostolakis, K. E. "Proper Names, Nicknames, Epithets: Aspects of Comic Language in Middle Comedy." In *The Play of Language in Ancient Greek Comedy: Comic Discourse and Linguistic Artifices of Humour, from Aristophanes to Menander*, edited by K. E. Apostolakis and I. M. Konstantakos. Trends in Classics—Supplementary Volumes, 154. Berlin: Walter de Gruyter, 2024.

Arzt, P. "The 'Epistolary Introductory Thanksgiving' in the Papyri and in Paul." *Novum Testamentum* 36 (1994): 29–46.

Arzt-Grabner, P. "'Brothers' and 'Sisters' in Documentary Papyri and in Early Christianity." *Rivista biblica italiana* 50 (2002): 185–204.

———. *Letters and Letter Writing.* Papyri and the New Testament 2. Brill Schöningh, 2023.

———. "Paul's Letter Thanksgiving." In *Paul and the Ancient Letter Form*, edited by S. E. Porter and S. A. Adams. Brill, 2010.

Asmussen, H. D. *Wahrheit und Liebe. Eine Einführung in die Johannesbriefe.* Im Furche-Verlag, 1957.

Bagnall, R. S. *Early Christian Books in Egypt.* Princeton University Press, 2009.

———. *Everyday Writing in the Graeco-Roman East.* University of California Press, 2011.

Bagnall, R. S., and R. Cribiore. *Women's Letters from Ancient Egypt, 300 BC–AD 800.* University of Michigan Press, 2006.

Bagnall, R. S., and D. Rathbone, eds. *Egypt: From Alexander to the Early Christians.* The J. Paul Getty Museum, 2004.

Balz, H. "Die Johannesbriefe." In *Die Katholischen Briefe: Die Briefe des Jakobus, Petrus, Johannes und Judas*, edited by H. Balz and W. Schrage. Vandenhoeck and Ruprecht, 1982.

Barnes, T. D. *Athanasius and Constantius: Theology and Politics in the Constantinian Empire.* Harvard University Press, 2001.

Barone, F. "Pour une édition critique de la Synopsis Scripturae Sacrae du Pseudo-Jean Chrysostome." *Revue de philologie* 83 (2009): 7–19.

Bateman, H. W., IV, and A. C. Peer. *John's Letters: An Exegetical Guide for Preaching and Teaching.* Kregel, 2018.

Bauckham, R. *Jesus and the Eyewitnesses: The Gospels as Eyewitness Testimony.* Eerdmans, 2006.

Baur, F. C. "Die Johannesbriefe. Ein Beitrag zur Geschichte des Kanons." *Theologische Jahrbücher* 7 (1848): 293–337.

Belser, J. E. *Die Briefe des heiligen Johannes.* Herdersche Verlagschandlung, 1906.

Bengel, J. A., ed. *Joannis Bengelii Gnomon Novi Testamenti, in quo, ex nativa Verborum Vi Simplicitas, Profunditas, Concinnitas, et Salubritas sensuum coelestium, indicatur.* Tübingen, 1742.

———. *Novum Testamentum Graecum ita adornatum ut Textus probatarum editionem medullam, Margo variantium lectionum in suas classes distributarum locorumque parallelorum delectum, apparatus subjunctus criseos sacrae Millianae praesertim compendium limam supplementum ac fractum exhibeat, inserviente J.A.B. Edente Jo. Albert Bengel.* 4 Vols. Tübingen, 1734.

Bennett, T. A. *1–3 John.* Eerdmans, 2021.

Bergmeier, R. "Zum Verfasserproblem des II. und III. Johannesbriefes." *Zeitschrift fur die neutestamentliche Wissenschaft und die Kunde der alteren Kirche* 57 (1966): 93–100.

Bernier, J. *Rethinking the Dates of the New Testament: The Evidence of Early Composition.* Baker Academic, 2022.

Beutler, J. *Die Johannesbriefe.* Verlag Friedrich Pustet, 2000.

———. "Die Johannesbriefe in der neuesten Literatur (1978–1985)." *Aufstieg und Niedergang der romischen Welt* 25/5 (1988): 3773–3790.

Beyer, H. W., and H. Lietzmann, eds. *Die jüdische Katakombe der Villa Torlonia in Rom.* Walter de Gruyter., 1930.

Beza, T., ed. *Novum Testamentum, cum Versione Latina Veteri, et Nova Theodori Bezae.* Geneva, 1565.

Bieringer, R. "Reconcile Yourselves to God. An Unusual Interpretation of 2 Corinthians 5:20 in its Context." In *Jesus, Paul, and Early Christianity: Studies in Honour of Henk Jan De Jonge*, edited by R. Buitenwerf, H. W. Hollander and J. Tromp. Brill, 2008.

Binazzi, G. "Orso, Cassiano e Apollinare. Appunti sulla diffusione dei culti al seguito milizie." *Romanobarbarica* 9 (1986–87): 5–24.

Birdsall, J. N. "The Codex Vaticanus: Its History and Significance." In *The Bible as Book: The Transmission of the Greek Text*, edited by S. McKendrick and O. A. O'Sullivan. The British Library, 2003.

Blumell, L. H. "Christians on the Move in Late Antique Oxyrhynchus." In *Travel and Religion in Antiquity*, edited by P. Harland. Studies in Christianity and Judaism/Études sur le christianisme et le judaïsme 21. Wilfred Laurier University Press, 2011.

———. *Lettered Christians: Christians, Letters, and Late Antique Oxyrhynchus*. New Testament Tools, Studies, and Documents 39. Brill, 2012.

———. "Petition to a *Beneficiarius* from Late Third Century A.D. Oxyrhynchus." *Zeitschrift für Papyrologie und Epigraphik* 165 (2008): 186–190.

———. "Scripture as Artefact." In *The Oxford Handbook of Early Christian Biblical Interpretation*, edited by P. Blowers and P. Martens. Oxford University Press, 2019.

Blumell, L. H., E. Cole, and W. Wendrich. "Another Letter from Antonius Longus to his Mother Nilous." *Bulletin of the American Society of Papyrologists* 55 (2018): 45–57.

Blumell, L. H., and T. A. Wayment. *Christian Oxyrhynchus: Texts, Documents, and Sources (Second Through Fourth Centuries)*. Baylor University Press, 2015.

Bockmuehl, M. *Simon Peter in Scripture and Memory: The New Testament Apostle in the Early Church*. Baker Academic, 2012.

Bonnard, P. *Les Épitres Johanniques*. Labor et Fides, 1983.

Bonsirven, J. *Épitres de Saint Jean*. Verbum Salutis 9. Beauchesne, 1954.

Booms, D. *Latin Inscriptions*. The British Museum Press, 2016.

Bresky, B. *Das Verhältnis des zweiten Johannesbriefes zum dritten*. Aschendorff, 1906.

Briggs, R. C. "Contemporary Study of the Johannine Epistles." *Review and Expositor* 67 (1970): 411–422.

Brock, S. "Origen's Aims as a Textual Critic of the Old Testament." *Studia Patristica* 10 (1970): 215–218.

Brooke, A. E. *A Critical and Exegetical Commentary on the Johannine Epistles*. Charles Scribner's Sons, 1912.

Brown, R. E. *The Epistles of John: A New Translation with Introduction and Commentary*. Anchor Bible 30. Doubleday, 1982.

Brown, S., and F. J. Moloney. *Interpreting the Gospel and Letters of John: An Introduction*. Eerdmans, 2017.

Bruce, F. F. *The Epistles of John: Introduction, Exposition and Notes*. Eerdmans, 1970.

Bryant, M. "The Johannine Epistles, 2000–2005." *Faith and Mission* 23, no. 1 (2005): 83–89.

Büchsel, D. F. *Die Johannesbriefe*. A. Deichertsche Verlagsbuchhandlung, 1933.

Bultmann, R. *Die drei Johannesbriefe*. Kritisch-exegetischer Kommentar über das Neue Testament 14. Vandenhoeck & Ruprecht, 1967.

———. "Johannesbriefe." In *Religion in Geschichte und Gegenwart*. Vol. 3. 3rd ed., edited by H. F. von Campenhausen, E. Dinkler, G. Gloege, K. E. Løgstrup, and K. Galling. . Mohr Siebeck, 1959.

———. *The Johannine Epistles: A Commentary on the Johannine Epistles*. Edited by R. Funk. Translated by R. P. O'Hara, with L. C. McGaughy and R. W. Funk. Hermeneia Commentary Series. Fortress, 1973.

Burdick, D. W. *The Letters of John the Apostle: An In-Depth Commentary*. Moody Press, 1985.

Burgon, J. W. *The Revision Revised*. London: John Murray, 1883.
Burk, P. D., ed. *Joannis Alberti Bengelii Apparatus Criticus ad Novum Testamentum, criseos sacrae compendium, limam, supplementum, ac fructum exhibens*. Tübingen, 1763.
Burks, M. "The Text of the Leicester Codex: A Quantitative Analysis of GA 69." PhD diss., New Orleans Baptist Theological Seminary, 2023.
Burnet, R. *L'Égypte ancienne à travers les papyrus: vie quotidienne*. Flammarion [Département Pygmalion], 2003.
Buzon, R. "Die Briefe der Ptolemäerzeit: Ihre Struktur und ihre Formeln." PhD diss., Ruprecht-Karl-Universität Heidelberg, 1984.
Cain, A. *The Letters of Jerome: Asceticism, Biblical Exegesis, and the Construction of Christian Authority in Late Antiquity*. Oxford University Press, 2009.
Canart, P. "Les papyri grecs de la Bibliothèque Vaticane et du Musée égyptien du Vatican. Histoire et inventaire." In *Miscellanea Papyrologica*, edited by R. Pintaudi. Papyrologica Florentina 7. Gonnelli, 1980.
Carder, M. M. "A Caesarean Text in the Catholic Epistles?" *New Testament Studies* 16 (1970): 252–270.
———. "An Enquiry into the Textual Transmission of the Catholic Epistles." ThD diss., Victoria University, 1968.
Carlson, S. C. *Papias of Hierapolis, Exposition of Dominical Oracles: The Fragments, Testimonia, and Reception of a Second-Century Commentator*. OECT. Oxford University Press, 2021.
Cavallo, G. *Ricerche sulla maiuscola biblica*. Le Monnier, 1967.
Ceccarelli, P. *Ancient Greek Letter Writing: A Cultural History (600–150 BC)*. Oxford University Press, 2013.
Chandler, H. W. *A Practical Introduction to Greek Accentuation*. 2nd rev. ed. Oxford: At the Clarendon Press, 1881. Aristide D. Caratzas, 1983.
Choat, M. *Belief and Cult in Fourth-Century Papyri*. Brepols, 2006.
Cianca, J. *Sacred Ritual, Profane Space: The Roman House as Early Christian Meeting Place*. Studies in Christianity and Judaism. McGill-Queen's University Press, 2018.
Clemen, C. "Beiträge zum geschichtlichen Verständnis der Johannesbriefe." *Zeitschrift fur die neutestamentliche Wissenschaft und die Kunde der alteren Kirche* 6 (1905): 271–281.
Colines, S. de., ed. *He Kaine Diatheke*. En Leutetia ton Paresion: para Simoni to Kolinaio, 1534.
Colson, F. H., and G. H. Whitaker, trans. *Philo*. Vol. I. Loeb Classical Library 226. Harvard University Press, 1929.
Comfort, P. W. *A Commentary on the Manuscripts and Text of the New Testament*. Kregel, 2015.
Comfort, P. W., and D. P. Barrett. *The Text of the Earliest New Testament Greek Manuscripts*. 2 Vols., 3rd ed. Kregel Academic, 2019.

Comfort, P. W., and W. C. Hawley. *1–3 John, Cornerstone Biblical Commentary*. Tyndale House Publishers, 2007.

Conner, W. T. *The Epistles of John*. 2nd ed. rev. Broadman, 1957.

Cowey, J. M. S., R. Duttenhöfer, A. Kolb, M. Richter, and P. Schubert. "Bemerkungen zu Urkunden." *Zeitschrift für Papyrologie und Epigraphik* 80 (1990): 289–293.

Cowper, B. H. *Codex Alexandrinus. Novum Testamentum Graece ex Antiquissimo Codice Alexandrino a C. G. Woide olim descriptum*. London: D. Nutt, et Williams & Norgate, 1860.

Cramer, J. A., ed. *Catenae Graecorum patrum in Novum Testamentum*. Vol. III. Oxford: Oxford University Press, 1838. Reprint, Olms, 1967.

———. ed. *Catenae Graecorum patrum in Novum Testamentum*. Vol. VIII. Oxford: Oxford University Press, 1844. Reprint, Olms, 1967.

Culpepper, R. A. *The Gospel and Letters of John*. Interpreting Biblical Texts Series. Abingdon, 1988.

Culy, M. M. *1, 2, 3 John: A Handbook on the Greek Text*. Baylor University Press, 2004.

Dainese, D. "Cassiodorus' *Adumbrationes*: Do They Belong to Clement's Hypotyposeis?" *Studia Patristica* 79 (2017): 87–100.

De Bruyne, D. *Prefaces to the Latin Bible*. Introductions by P.-M. Bogaert and T. O'Loughlin. Studia Traditionis Theologiae 19. Brepols, 2015; Reprint of 1920th ed.

Deissmann, A. *Licht vom Osten: Das Neue Testament und die neuentdeckten Texte der hellenistisch-römischen Welt*. J. C. B. Mohr [Paul Siebeck], 1908.

———. *Light from the Ancient East: The New Testament Illustrated by Recently Discovered Texts of the Graeco-Roman World*. Translated by L. R. M. Strachan. Hodder & Stoughton, 1910.

De Jonge, H. J. "Jeremias Hoelzlin: Editor of the 'Textus Receptus' Printed by the Elzevirs Leiden 1633." In *Miscellanea Neotestamentica*, edited by T. Baarda, A. F. J. Klijn, and W. C. VanUnnik. Brill, 1978.

De Jonge, M. *De Brieven van Johannes*. Nijkerk: Callenbach, 1968.

Depauw, M. *The Demotic Letter. A Study of Epistolographic Scribal Traditions against their Intra- and Intercultural Background*. Demotische Studien 14. Gisela Zauzich Verlag, 2006.

Dibelius, M. "Johannesbriefe." In *Religion in Geschichte und Gegenwart*. Vol. 3. 2nd ed., edited by F. M. Schiele and L. Zscharnack. Mohr Siebeck, 1929.

Dickey, E. *Greek Forms of Address: From Herodotus to Lucian*. Oxford Classical Monographs. Clarendon Press, 1996.

———. "Κύριε, Δέσποτα, Domine: Greek Politeness in the Roman Empire." *Journal of Hellenic Studies* 121 (2001): 1–11.

———. "Literal and Extended Use of Kinship Terms in Documentary Papyri." *Mnemosyne* 57 (2004): 131–176.

Diekamp, F. *Die origenistischen Streitigkeiten im sechsten Jahrhundert und das fünfte allgemeine Concil*. Münster: Aschendorff, 1899.

Dillon, M. P. J. "A Homeric Pun from Abu Simbel (*Meiggs & Lewis* 7a)." *Zeitschrift für Papyrologie und Epigraphik* 118 (1997): 128–130.

Dinneen, L. *Titles of Address in Christian Greek Epistolography to 527 A.D.* The Catholic University of America, 1929.

Dodd, C. H. *The Johannine Epistles*. Moffatt New Testament Commentary. Hodder & Stoughton, 1946.

Dölger, F. J. "*Domina Mater Ecclesia* und die 'Herrin' im zweiten Johannesbrief." *Jahrbuch für Antike und Christentum* 5 (1936): 211–217.

Dorival, G. "*L'apport des Synopses transmises sous le nom d'Athanase et de Jean Chrysostome à la question du Corpus Littéraire de la Bible?*" In *Qu'est-ce qu'un Corpus Littéraire? Recherches sur le corpus biblique et les corpus patristiques*, edited by G. Dorival. Peeters, 2005.

Dow, S. *Conventions in Editing: A Suggested Reformulation of the Leiden System*. Greek, Roman and Byzantine Scholarly Aids 2. Duke University Press, 1969.

Drexhage, H.-J. "Zu den Überstellungsbefehlen aus dem römischen Agypten (1.–3. Jahrhundert n.Chr.)." In *Migratio et Commutatio. Studien zur Alten Geschichte und deren Nachleben Thomas Pekáry dargebracht*. edited by H.-J. Drexhage and J. Sünskes. Scripta Mercaturae Verlag, 1989.

Edwards, R. B. *The Johannine Epistles*. New Testament Guides. Sheffield Academic Press, 1996.

Ehrman, B. D. "Heracleon, Origen, and the Text of the Fourth Gospel." *Vigiliae Christianae* 47 (1993): 105–118.

Ehrman, B. D., and M. W. Holmes, eds. *The Text of the New Testament in Contemporary Research: Essays on the Status Quaestionis*. 2nd ed. New Testament Tools, Studies, and Documents 42. Brill, 2013.

Elliott, J. K. *A Bibliography of Greek New Testament Manuscripts*. 3rd ed. Supplements to Novum Testamentum 160. Leiden; Boston: Brill, 2015.

Elzevir, I., ed. *Novum Testamentum Graece*. Lugduni Batavorum (Leiden): Ex Officina Elzeviriana, 1624.

Epp, E. J. "Critical Editions of the New Testament, and the Development of Text-Critical Methods: From Erasmus to Griesbach (1516–1807)." In *The New Cambridge History of the Bible: From 1450–1750*, edited by E. Cameron. Cambridge University Press, 2016.

Erasmus, D., ed. *Novum Instrumentum omne, diligenter ad Erasmo Roterodamo recognitum et emendatum, non solum ad graecam veritatem, verum etiam ad multorum utriusque linguae codicum, eorumque veterum simul et emendatorum fidem, postremo adprobatissimorum autorum citationem, emendationem, et interpretationem, praecipue, Origenis, Chrysostomi, Cyrilli, Vulgarii, Hieronymi, Cypriani, Ambrosii, Hilarii, Augustini, una cum Annotationibus, quae lectorem doceant, quid qua ratione mutatum sit. Quisquis igitur amas veram theologiam, lege, cognosce, ac deinde judica. Neque statim offendere, si quid mutatum offenderis, sed expende, num in melius mutatum sit*. Basel: Johann Froben, 1516.

———. ed. *Novum Testamentum Omne*. 2nd ed. Basel: Johann Froben, 1519.

———. ed. *Novum Testamentum Omne*. 3rd ed. Basel: Johann Froben, 1522.

Estienne, R., ed. *Novum Testamentum Graece*. Lutetiae: Ex Officina Roberti Stephani Typographi Typis Regiis, 1549.

———. ed. *Novum Testamentum Graece*. Lutetiae: Ex Officina Roberti Stephani Typographi Typis Regiis, 1550.

———. ed. *Novum Testamentum Graece*. Lutetiae: Ex Officina Roberti Stephani Typographi Typis Regiis, 1551.

Exler, F. X. J. *The Form of the Ancient Greek Letter: A Study in Greek Epistolography*. Catholic University of America, 1923.

Felckmann, P. *Operum sancti patris nostri Athanasii archiepiscopi Alexandrini*. Tome II. Heidelberg, 1600.

Fell, J., ed. *Novi Testamenti Libri Omnes. Accesserunt Parallela Scripturae Loca, necnon Variantes Lectiones ex plus 100 MSS. Codicibus et antiquis versionibus collectae*. Oxonii: E Theatro Sheldoniano, 1675.

Findlay, G. G. *Fellowship in the Life Eternal: An Exposition of the Epistles of St. John*. Hodder & Stoughton, 1909.

Fordyce, C. J. "Puns on Names in Greek." *Classical Journal* 28 (1932): 44–46.

Fournet, J.-L. "Esquisse d'une anatomie de la lettre antique tardive d'après les papyrus." In *Correspondances. Documents pour l'histoire de l'Antiquité tardive. Actes du colloque international Université Charles-de-Gaulle - Lille 3, 20–22 novembre 2003*, edited by R. Delmaire, J. Desmulliez, and P.-L. Gatier. Maison De L'Orient de la Méditerranée, 2009.

———. "Les lettres privées de l'Égypte gréco-romaine: limites et malentendus." In *La correspondance privée dans la Méditerranée antique: sociétés en miroir*, edited by M. Dana. Scripta Antiqua 168. Ausonius, 2023.

France, R. T. *The Gospel of Matthew*. New International Commentary on the New Testament. Eerdmans, 2007.

Froehner, W. *Les inscriptions grecques*. Paris: C. de Mourgues, 1865.

Funk, R. W. "The Form and Structure of II and III John." *Journal of Biblical Literature* 86 (1967): 424–430.

Gagos, T., and P. J. Sijpesteijn. "Towards an Explanation of the Typology of the So-Called 'Orders to Arrest'." *Bulletin of the American Society of Papyrologists* 33 (1996): 77–97.

Gaugler, E. *Die Johannesbriefe*. Evz-Verlag, 1964.

Gehring, R. W. *The House Church and Mission: The Importance of Household Structures in Early Christianity*. Hendrickson Publishers, 2004.

Geraci, G. "Ricerche sul Proskynema." *Aegyptus* 51 (1971): 3–211.

Gerhard, G. A., ed. *Veröffentlichungen aus den badischen Papyrus-Sammlungen. Vol. VI: Griechische Papyri*. C. Winter, 1938.

Gibbins, H. J. "The Problem of the Second Epistle of St. John." *The Expositor*, 6th series, 12, no. 6 (1905): 412–424.

———. "The Second Epistle of St. John." *The Expositor*, 6th series, 6, no. 3 (1902): 228–236.

Gignac, F. T. *A Grammar of the Greek Papyri of the Roman and Byzantine Periods, Vol. I, Phonology*. Instituto Editoriale Cisalpino – La Goliardica, 1976.

Gordon, A. E. *Album of Dated Latin Inscriptions. Rome and the Neighborhood. Vol. I: Text*. University of California Press, 1958.

Gore, C. *The Epistles of St. John*. Murray, 1920.

Grayston, K. *The Johannine Epistles*. Eerdmans, 1984.

Greggi, S. "La documentazione epigrafica dell'antica Nomentum." *Annali Associazione Nomentana di Storia e Archeologia* 8 (2007): 22–46.

Griesbach, J. J., ed. *Epistolae N.T. et Apocalypsis*. Halle: Curt, 1775.

———. *Libri Historici Novi Testamenti, Graece, Pars I. Sistens Synopsin Evangeliorum Matthaei, Marci, et Lucae. Textum ad fidem Codd. Versionum et Patrum emendavit et lectionis varietatem adjecit*. Halle: Curt, 1774.

———.*Libri Historici Novi Testamenti, Graece, Pars II. Sistens Evangelium Johannis et Acta Apostolorum*. Halle: Curt, 1775.

———.*Novum Testamentum Graece*. 2nd ed. 2 Vols. Halle: Schwickert, 1806.

———. *Novum Testamentum Graece. Ex Recensione Jo. Jac. Griesbachii, cum selecta Lectionis Varietate*. 2 Vols. Lipsiae, 1805, 1807.

———.*Novum Testamentum Graece, Textum ad fidem Codicum Versionum et Patrum recensuit et Lectionis Variatatem adjecit*. Halle: Curt, 1777.

———.*Novum Testamentum Graece, Textum ad fidem Codicum Versionum et Patrum recensuit et Lectionis Variatatem adjecit*. London, 1796; Halle, 1806.

Grotius, H. *Annotationes in Novum Testamentum*. 9 Vols. Edited by P. Henricus de Groot. Groningen: Zuidema, 1826–1834.

Gründstäudl, W. "Geistliches Evangelium und Katholische Briefe: Johanneische Intertextualität im Spiegel frühchristlicher Rezeption." In *Erzählung und Briefe im johanneischen Kreis*, Edited by U. Poplutz and J. Fre. Wissenschaftliche Untersuchungen zum Neuen Testament 2/420. Mohr Siebeck, 2016.

Gummere, R. M., trans. *Seneca. Epistles, Vol. I: Epistles 1–65*. Loeb Classical Library 75. Harvard University Press, 1917.

Gurry, P. "The Number of Variants in the Greek New Testament: A Proposed Estimate." *New Testament Studies* 62 (2016): 97–121.

Haenchen, E. "Neuere Literatur zu den Johannesbriefen." *Theologishe Rundschau* 26 (1960): 1–43.

Hagedorn, D. "Bemerkungen zu Urkunden." *Zeitschrift für Papyrologie und Epigraphik* 151 (2005): 127–128.

———. "Entsprach der Monat Domitianos in Ägypten dem Phaophi oder dem Hathyr?" *Zeitschrift für Papyrologie und Epigraphik* 159 (2007): 261–266.

Hagedorn, U. "Das Formular der Überstellungsbefehle im römischen Ägypten." *Bulletin of the American Society of Papyrologists* 16 (1979): 61–74.

Halporn, J. W., trans. and ed. *Cassiodorus: Institutes of Divine and Secular Learning and On the Soul*. Introduction by M. Vessy. Texts Translated for Historians 42. Liverpool University Press, 2004.

Hanson, A. E. "P. Princeton I 11 and P. Cornell 21v." *Zeitschrift für Papyrologie und Epigraphik* 37 (1980): 241–248.

Harris, J. R. *The Origin of the Leicester Codex of the New Testament*. London: C. J. Clay & Sons, 1887.

———. "The Problem of the Address in the Second Epistle of John." *The Expositor*, 6th series, 3, no. 3 (1901): 194–203.

Harris, W. H., III. *1, 2, 3 John: Comfort and Counsel for a Church in Crisis. An Exegetical Commentary on the Letters of John*. 2nd ed. Biblical Studies Press, 2009.

Harwood, E., ed. *The New Testament, Collated with the Most Approved Manuscripts; with Select Notes in English, Critical and Explanatory, and References to Those Authors Who Have Best Illustrated the Sacred Writings. To Which Are Added, a Catalogue of the Principal Editions of the Greek Testament; and a List of the Most Esteemed Commentators and Critics.* 2 Vols. London: J. D. Cornish, 1776.

Head, P. M. "The Habits of New Testament Copyists: Singular Readings in the Early Fragmentary Papyri of John." *Biblica* 85 (2004): 399–408.

———. "Observations on Early Papyri of the Synoptic Gospels, Especially on the 'Scribal Habits.'" *Biblica* 71 (1990): 240–247.

Heath, D. E. "A Transcription and Description of Manuscript Vatican 2601 (Gregory 048)." PhD diss., Michigan State University, 1965.

Heberdey, R., and A. Wilhelm. *Reisen in Kilikien*. Denkschriften der Kaiserlichen Akademie der Wissenschaften in Wien, philosophisch-historische Klasse 44.6. Vienna: Alfred Hölder, 1896.

Heckel, T. K. *Die Briefe des Jakobus, Petrus, Johannes und Judas*. Vandenhoeck & Ruprecht, 1990.

Heine, R. E., trans. *The Commentary of Origen on the Gospel of St. Matthew*. Vol. 2. Oxford Early Christian Texts. Oxford University Press, 2018.

Heine, R. E., and K. J. Torjesen, eds. *The Oxford Handbook of Origen*. Oxford University Press, 2022.

Heise, J. *Bleiben. Menein in den Johanneischen Schriften*. Mohr, 1967.

Henry, R., ed. *Photius. Bibliothèque, Tome II*. Les Belles Lettres, 1960.

Hersch, K. H. *The Roman Wedding: Ritual Meaning in Antiquity*. Cambridge University Press, 2010.

Hicks, E. L. "Inscriptions from Western Cilicia." *Journal of Hellenic Studies* 12 (1891): 225–273.

Hiebert, D. E. *The Epistles of John*. Bob Jones University Press, 1988.

Hirsch, E. *Studien zum vierten Evangelium. Text, Literarkritik, Entstehungsgeschichte*. Mohr, 1936.

Hobson, D. "Women as Property Owners in Roman Egypt." *Transactions of the American Philological Association* 113 (1983): 311–321.

Hoelzlin, J., ed. *Novum Testamentum Graece*. Lugduni Batavorum (Leiden): Ex officina Elzeviriana, 1633.

Holmes, M. W. *The Apostolic Fathers: Greek Texts and English Translations.* 3rd ed. Baker Academic, 2007.

Holtzmann, H. J. *Evangelium, Briefe und Offenbarung des Johannes.* 3rd ed. J. C. B. Mohr (Paul Siebeck), 1912.

Horner, G. W., ed. *The Coptic Version of the New Testament in the Southern Dialect, Vol. III: The Catholic Epistles and the Apocalypse.* At the Clarendon Press, 1924.

Houghton, H. A. G. *The Latin New Testament: A Guide to Its Early History, Texts, and Manuscripts.* Oxford University Press, 2016.

Houghton, H. A.G., and D. C. Parker. "An Introduction to Greek New Testament Commentaries with a Preliminary Checklist of New Testament Catena Manuscripts." In *Commentaries, Catenae and Biblical Tradition*, edited by H. A. G. Houghton. Gorgias Press, 2016.

Houlden, J. L. *A Commentary on the Johannine Epistles.* Harper & Row, 1974.

Howard, F. D. *1, 2, & 3 John, Jude, Revelation*. Layman's Bible Book Commentary 24. Broadman, 1982.

Hurst, D., ed. and trans. *Bede the Venerable: Commentary on the Seven Catholic Epistles.* Cistercian Studies Series 82. Cistercian Publications, 1985.

Ilan, T. *Lexicon of Jewish Names in Late Antiquity. Part I: Palestine 330 BCE–200 CE.* Mohr Siebeck, 2002.

———. *Lexicon of Jewish Names in Late Antiquity. Part II: Palestine 200–600 CE.* Mohr Siebeck, 2012.

Innes, D. C., ed. and trans. *Demetrius: On Style.* Loeb Classical Library 199. Harvard University Press, 1999.

Jackman, D. *The Message of John's Letters: Living in the Love of God.* Inter-Varsity, 1988.

James, M. R. "The Scribe of the Leicester Codex." *Journal of Theological Studies* 5 (1904): 445–447.

James, T. G. H., ed. *Excavating in Egypt: The Egypt Exploration Society 1882–1982.* University of Chicago Press, 1982.

Jastrow, M. A. *Dictionary of the Targumim, the Talmud Babli and Yerushalmi, and the Midrashic Literature.* 2nd ed. G. P. Putnam's Sons, 1903.

Jennes, G. "Life Portraits: People in Worship." In *A Blackwell Companion to Greco-Roman and Late Antique Egypt*, edited by K. Vandorpe. John Wiley & Sons, 2019.

Jobes, K. H. *1, 2, & 3 John.* Exegetical Commentary on the New Testament. Zondervan, 2014.

Johnson, W. *Bookrolls and Scribes in Oxyrhynchus.* University of Toronto Press, 2004.

Jones, L. W. *An Introduction to Divine and Human Readings by Cassiodorus Senator.* Columbia University Press, 1946.

Jones, P. R. "The Missional Role of Ο ΠΡΕΣΒΥΤΕΡΟΣ." In *Communities in Dispute: Current Scholarship on the Johannine Epistles*, edited by R. A. Culpepper and P. N. Anderson. SBL Press, 2014.

Jongkind, D. *Scribal Habits of Codex Sinaiticus*. Texts and Studies 3rd series, Vol. 5. Gorgias Press, 2007.

Jülicher, A. *Einleitung in das Neue Testament*. Erster Band. Freiburg: Akademische Verlagsbuchhandlung von J. C. B. Mohr [Paul Siebeck], 1894.

Junius, P. *Secundae Stricturae*. UBA III C 20 e add, 1642.

Kaibel, G., ed. *Inscriptiones Graecae, XIV. Inscriptiones Siciliae et Italiae, additis Galliae, Hispaniae, Britanniae, Germaniae inscriptionibus*. Berlin, 1890.

Kalogeras, N., ed. *Euthymii Zigabeni Commentarius in XIV Epistolas Sancti Pauli et VII Catholicas*. Vol. 2. Athens: Fratres Perri, 1877.

Karo, G., and J. H. Lietzmann. *Catenarum Graecarum Catalogus. Nachrichten von der Königl. Gesellschaft der Wissenschaften, Philologisch-historische Klasse*. Lüder Horstmann, 1902.

Käsemann, E. *Exegetische Versuche und Besinnungen*. Erster Band. Vandenhoeck & Ruprecht, 1960.

———. "Ketzer und Zeuge: Zum johanneischen Verfasserproblem." *Zeitschrift für Theologie und Kirche* 48 (1951): 292–311.

Kasser, R., ed. *Papyrus Bodmer XVII: Actes des Apôtres, Epîtres de Jacques, Pierre, Jean et Jude*. Bibliothèque Bodmer, 1961.

Keaney, J. J., ed. *Harpocration: Lexeis of the Ten Orators*. Adolf M. Hakkert, 1991.

Kelly, J. N. D. *Jerome: His Life, Writings, and Controversies*. Harper & Row, 1975.

Keppie, L. *Understanding Roman Inscriptions*. The Johns Hopkins Press, 1991.

Kim, C.-H. "Index of Greek Papyrus Letters." *Semeia* 22 (1981): 107–112.

Kim, K. W. "Codices 1582, 1739, and Origen." *Journal of Biblical Literature* 69 (1950): 167–175.

King, D., J. E. Walters, and G. A. Kiraz, eds. and trans. *Hebrews and the General Catholic Epistles According to the Syriac Peshitta Version, with English Translation*. Surath Ktobh. Gorgias Press, 2016.

Klauck, H.-J. *Ancient Letters and the New Testament: A Guide to Context and Exegesis*. Baylor University Press, 2006.

———. *Der erste Johannesbrief*. Evangelisch-katholischer Kommentar zum Neuen Testament XXIII/1. Neukirchen Verlag, 1991.

———. *Der zweite und dritte Johannesbrief*. Evangelisch-katholischer Kommentar zum Neuen Testament XXIII/2. Neukirchener Verlag, 1992.

———. *Hausgemeinde und Hauskirche im frühen Christentum*. Stuttgarter Bibelstudien 103. Katholisches Bibelwerk, 1981.

———. "Κυρία ἐκκλησία Bauers Wörterbuch und die Exegese des zweiten Johannesbriefes." *Zeitschrift fur die neutestamentliche Wissenschaft und die Kunde der alteren Kirche* 81 (1990): 135–138.

Knapp, G. C., ed. *Novum Testamentum Graece recognorit atque insignioris lectionum varietatis et argumentorum notitiam subjunxit*. Halle, 1797.

Knauer, A. W. "Ueber die Ἐκλεκτῇ Κυρίᾳ, an welche der zweite Brief Johannis gerichtet ist." *Theologische Studien und Kritiken* 6 (1833): 452–458.

Körtner, U. *Papias von Hierapolis: Ein Beitrag zur Geschichte des frühen Christentums.* Vandenhoeck & Ruprecht, 1983.

Koskenniemi H. *Studien zur Idee und Phraseologie des griechischen Briefes bis 400 n. Chr.* Akateeminen Kirjakauppa, 1956.

Kruger, M. J. "The Date and Content of P. Antinoopolis 12 (0232)." *New Testament Studies* 58 (2012): 254–271.

Kysar, R. *Augsburg Commentary on the New Testament: I, II, III John.* Augsburg, 1986.

Lachmann, K., ed. *Novum Testamentum Graece, ex recensione Caroli Lachmanni.* Berolini, 1831.

Lagrange, M.-J. "Origène, la critique textuelle et la tradition topographique." *Revue biblique* 4 (1895): 501–524.

Lake, D. "Elder (NT)." In *The Zondervan Encyclopedia of the Bible.* Vol. 2, edited by M. C. Tenney and M. Silva. Zondervan, 2009.

Lake, K., trans. *Eusebius. The Ecclesiastical History Books 1–5.* Vol. I. Loeb Classical Library 153. Harvard University Press, 1926.

Lee, J. A. L. *A History of New Testament Lexicography.* Studies in Biblical Greek 8. Peter Lang, 2003.

Lee, S., ed. *Dictionary of National Biography: Wordsworth—Zuylestein.* Vol. 63. Smith, Elder, 1900.

Legras, B. *Les reclus grecs du Sarapieion de Memphis. Une enquete sur l'hellenisme egyptien.* Studia Hellenistica 49. Peeters, 2011.

Lenski, R. C. H. *The Interpretation of the Epistles of St. Peter, St. John, and St. Jude.* Wartburg Press, 1945.

Lewis, G. P. *The Johannine Epistles.* Epworth, 1961.

Lewis, N. *Papyrus in Classical Antiquity.* Clarendon Press, 1974.

Lieu, J. *I, II, and III John: A Commentary.* Westminster John Knox Press, 2008.

———. *The Second and Third Epistles of John: History and Background.* T & T Clark, 1986.

———. *The Theology of the Johannine Epistles.* Cambridge University Press, 1991.

Lieu, J. M., and M. C. de Boer, eds. *The Oxford Handbook of Johannine Studies.* Oxford University Press, 2019.

Littmann, E., D. Magie Jr., and D. R. Stuart. *Syria: Publications of the Princeton University Archaeological Expeditions to Syria in 1904–5 and 1909. Division 3: Greek and Latin Inscriptions. Section A: Southern Syria.* Brill, 1921.

Ljungvik, H. "Zum Markusevangelium 6, 14." *Zeitschrift für die neutestamentliche Wissenschaft* 33 (1934): 90–92.

Llewelyn, S. "The εἰς (τὴν) οἰκίαν Formula and the Delivery of Letters to Third Persons or to Their Property." *Zeitschrift für Papyrologie und Epigraphik* 101 (1994): 71–78.

Longenecker, R. N. *Introducing Romans: Critical Issues in Paul's Most Famous Letter.* Eerdmans, 2011.

Mace, D. *The New Testament in Greek and English, Containing the Original Text Corrected from the Authority of the Most Authentic Manuscripts: And a New Version Formed Agreeably to the Illustrations of the Most Learned Commentators and Critics: With Notes and Various Readings, and a Copious Alphabetical Index.* 2 Vols. London, 1729.

Maio, A., ed. *Classicorum Auctorum e Vaticanis codicibus editorum collection.* Vol. V. Rome, 1833.

Malherbe, A. J. *Social Aspects of Early Christianity.* 2nd ed. Fortress Press, 1983.

———. *Ancient Epistolary Theorists.* Scholars Press, 1988.

Malik, P. "The Earliest Corrections in Codex Sinaiticus: A Test Case from the Gospel of Mark." *Bulletin of the American Society of Papyrologists* 50 (2013): 207–254.

Malina, B. J. "The Received View and What It Cannot Do: III John and Hospitality." *Semeia* 35 (1986): 171–189.

Manilli, G. *Villa Borghese fuori di Porta Pinciana.* Rome: Grignani, 1650.

Marini, G. *I papiri diplomatici raccolti ed illustrati.* Rome: Sacra Congregatio de Propaganda Fide, 1805.

Marshall, I. H. *The Epistles of John.* Eerdmans, 1978.

Martinez, C. F. *Poesía epigráfica latina I. introducción, traducción y notas.* Gredos, 1998.

Marty, J. "Contribution à l'étude des problèmes johanniques: Les petites épîtres 'II et III Jean.'" *Revue de l'histoire des religions* 91 (1925): 200–211.

Matthaei, C. F., ed. *Novum Testamentum graece et latine. Ad codd. mss. Mosquenses primum a se examinatos recensuit, varias lectiones, animadversiones criticas et inedita scholia graeca. Vol. V: SS Septem Apostolorum Epistolae Catholicae.* Riga: Ioann. Frider. Hartknochii, 1782.

McCartney, E. S. "Puns and Plays on Proper Names." *Classical Journal* 14 (1919): 343–358.

McDargh, J. "The Paradigm-Shifting Research of Ana-María Rizzuto: Origins, Strategy, Reception, and Horizon." In *Ana-María Rizzuto and the Psychoanalysis of Religion: The Road to the Living God*, edited by M. J. Reineke and D. M. Goodman. Lexington Books, 2017.

Merkelbach, R. "Zur ἐνκατοχή im Sarapeum zu Memphis." *Zeitschrift für Papyrologie und Epigraphik* 103 (1994): 293–296.

Metzger, B. M. "Explicit References in the Works of Origen to Variant Readings in New Testament Manuscripts." In *Pages in Biblical and Patristic Studies in Memory of Robert Pierce Casey*, edited by J. N. Birdsall and R. W. Thomson. Herder, 1963.

———. *Manuscripts of the Greek Bible: An Introduction to Greek Paleography.* Oxford University Press, 1981.

———. *A Textual Commentary on the Greek New Testament.* 2nd ed. Deutsche Bibelgesellschaft, 1994.

Metzger, B. M., and Ehrman, B. D. *The Text of the New Testament: Its Transmission, Corruption, and Restoration*. 4th ed. Oxford University Press, 2005.

Mill, J., ed., *Η ΚΑΙΝΗ ΔΙΑΘΗΚΗ. Novum Testamentum Graecum, cum lectionibus variantibus MSS. Exemplarium, Versionem, Editionum, SS. Patrum et Scriptorum Ecclesiasticorum, et in easdem notis*, Studio et labore Joannis Millii, S.T.P. Oxonii: e Theatro Sheldoniano, 1707.

Minon, S., G. Genevrois, E. N. Izquierdo, F. Réveilhac, and J.-C. Chuat, eds., *Lexonyme: Dictionnaire etymologique et semantique des anthroponymes grecs antiques, vol. 1 (A–E)*. Hautes etudes du monde gréco-romain 63. Librairie Droz, 2023.

Montanari, F. *The Brill Dictionary of Ancient Greek*. Brill, 2015.

Montfaucon, B. de. *Athanasii archiepiacopi Alexandrini opera omnia*. Vol. 3. Paris, 1698.

Muhs, B. "Language Contact and Personal Names in Early Ptolemaic Egypt." In *The Language of Papyri*, edited by T. Evans and D. Obbink. Oxford University Press, 2010.

Muir, J. *Life and Letters in the Ancient Greek World*. Routledge Monographs in Classical Studies. Routledge, 2009.

Mynors, R. A. B., ed. *Cassiodori Senatoris Institutiones*. Clarendon Press, 1937.

Nachtergaele, D. *The Formulaic Language of the Greek Private Papyrus Letters*. Trismegistos, 2023.

Nestle, E., ed. *Novum Testamentum Graece cum apparatu critico ex editionibus et libris manuscriptis collecto*. Stuttgart: Privilegierte Württembergische Bibelanstalt, 1898.

Nobbs, A. M. "Beloved Brothers in the New Testament and Early Christian World." In *The New Testament in Its First Century Setting: Essays on Context and Background in Honour of B. W. Winter on His 65 Birthday*, edited by P. J. Williams, A. D. Clark, P. M. Head, and D. Instone-Brewer. Eerdmans, 2004.

Orelli, J. C. von. *Inscriptionum Latinarum Selectarum Amplissima Collectio*. 3 Vols. Turici: Orelli, Fuesslini et Sociorum, 1828; rev. 1856.

Orr, J., J. L. Nuelsen, E. Y. Mullins, M. O. Evans, and M. G. Kyle, eds. *The International Standard Bible Encyclopedia*. 5 Vols. Eerdmans, 1939.

Orsini, P. *Manoscritti in maiuscola biblica: Materiali per un aggiornamento*. Edizioni dell'Università degli Studi di Cassino, 2005.

Orsini, P., and W. Clarysse. "Early New Testament Manuscripts and Their Dates: A Critique of Theological Paleography." *Ephemerides Theologicae Lovanienses* 88 (2012): 443–474.

Osburn, C. D. "The Greek Lectionaries of the New Testament." In *The Text of the New Testament in Contemporary Research: Essays on the Status Quaestionis*. 2nd ed., edited by B. D. Ehrman and M. W. Holmes. New Testament Tools, Studies, and Documents 42. Leiden and Boston: Brill, 2013.

Osiek C., and M. Y. MacDonald, with J. H. Tulloch. *A Woman's Place: House Churches in Earliest Christianity.* Fortress Press, 2006.

Otto, W. *Priester und Tempel im hellenistischen Ägypten: Ein beitrag zur kulturgeschichte des hellenismus.* 2 Vols. B. G. Teubner, 1905–1908; Reprint, Rome, 1971.

Oulton, J. E. L., trans. *Eusebius. Ecclesiastical History Books 6–10.* Vol. II. Loeb Classical Library 265. Harvard University Press, 1932.

Pack, F. "Origen's Evaluation of Textual Variants in the Greek Bible." *Restoration Quarterly* 4 (1960): 139–146.

Painter, J. *1, 2, and 3 John.* Sacra Pagina Series 18. The Liturgical Press, 2002.

———. "The Johannine Epistles as Catholic Epistles." In *The Catholic Epistles and Apostolic Tradition*, edited by K.-W. Niebuhr and R. W. Wall. Baylor University Press, 2009.

Pape, W. *Handwörterbuch der griechischen Sprache: Wörterbuch der griechischen Eigennamen Band 3.* Braunschweig: Friedrich Vieweg & Sohn, 1850.

Pape, W., and G. E. Benseler. *Handwörterbuch der griechischen Sprache. 3.1: Wörterbuch der griechischen Eigennamen: A–K.* Braunschweig: Friedrich Vieweg & Sohn, 1863.

Parker, D. C. *An Introduction to the New Testament Manuscripts and Their Texts.* Cambridge University Press, 2008.

———. *Codex Sinaiticus: The Story of the World's Oldest Bible.* British Library, 2010.

———. "The Majuscule Manuscripts of the New Testament." In *The Text of the New Testament in Contemporary Research: Essays on the Status Quaestionis.* 2nd ed., edited by B. D. Ehrman and M. W. Holmes. New Testament Tools, Studies, and Documents 42. Brill, 2013.

Parsenius, G. L. *First, Second, and Third John.* Baker Academic, 2014.

Parsons, P. "Background: The Papyrus Letter." *Didactica classica Gandensia* 20 (1980): 3–19.

Perkins, P. *The Johannine Epistles.* New Testament Message 21. Michael Glazier, 1979.

Peyron, B. "Papiri greci del Museo di Londra e della Bibliotheca Vaticana." *Reale Accademia di Torino, Classe di Scienze Morali, Storiche e Filologiche, Memorie* Serie II 3 (1841): 1–112.

Plátová, J. "How Many Fragments of the Hypotyposes by Clement of Alexandria Do We Actually Have?" *Studia Patristica* 79 (2017): 71–86.

Plummer, A. *The Epistles of St. John. With Notes, Introduction and Appendices.* The Cambridge Bible for Schools and Colleges. Cambridge: Cambridge University Press, 1886.

Plummer, R. L., and E. R. Elledge. *1–3 John: Exegetical Guide to the Greek New Testament.* B&H Academic, 2024.

Poggel, H. *Der zweite und dritte Brief des Apostels Johannes geprüft auf ihren kanonischen Charakter.* Paderborn: Druck und Verlag von Ferdinand Schöningh, 1896.

Poplutz, U., and J. Frey, eds. *Erzählung und Briefe im johanneischen Kreis.* Wissenschaftliche Untersuchungen zum Neuen Testament 2/420. Mohr Siebeck, 2016.

Porter, S. E., and A. K. Gabriel. *Johannine Writings and Apocalyptic: An Annotated Bibliography.* Johannine Studies 1. Brill, 2013.

Preisigke, F., ed. *Namenbuch enthaltend alle griechischen, lateinischen, ägyptischen, hebräischen, arabischen und sonstigen semitischen und nichtsemitischen Menschennamen, soweit sie in griechischen Urkunden (Papyri, Ostraka, Inschriften, Mumienschildern usw.) Ägyptens sich vorfinden.* Published by the author, 1922; Reprint, Amsterdam, 1967.

Preisigke, F., and E. Kiessling, eds. *Wörterbuch der griechischen Papyrusurkunden, mit Einschluss der griechischen Inschriften, Aufschriften, Ostraka, Mumienschilder usw. aus Ägypten. I Band: A–K.* Published by the author, 1925.

Price, R., trans. *The Acts of the Council of Constantinople of 553: With Related Texts on the Three Chapters Controversy.* Texts Translated for Historians 53. Liverpool University Press, 2009.

Price, R., trans., with P. Booth, and C. Cubitt. *The Acts of the Lateran Synod of 649.* Texts Translated for Historians 61. Liverpool University Press, 2014.

Quasten, J. *Patrology. Vol. II: The Ante-Nicene Literature after Irenaeus.* Christian Classics, 1986.

Raepsaet-Charlier, M.-T. *Prosopographie des femmes de l'ordre sénatorial (Ier–IIe siècles).* Peeters, 1987.

Ramsay, W. M. "Historical Commentary on the Epistles to the Corinthians." *The Expositor,* 6th series, 3.5 (1901): 343–360.

Reineccius, C., ed. *Biblia Sacra quadrilinguia Novi Testamenti Graeci cum versionibus Syriaca, Graeca vulgari, Latina et Germanica.* Leipzig: Gleditsch, 1713.

Richards, W. L. *The Classification of the Greek Manuscripts of the Johannine Epistles.* Society of Biblical Literature Dissertation Series 35. Scholars Press, 1977.

Richards, E. R. *Paul and First-Century Letter Writing: Secretaries, Composition and Collection.* InterVarsity Press, 2004.

Riedinger, R. "Die Präsenz- und Subskriptionslisten des VI. oekumenischen Konzils (680/81) und der Papyrus Vind. G. 3." In *Bayerische Akademie der Wissenschaften: Philosophisch-historische Klasse. Neue Folge 85.* Verlag Bayerische Akad. der Wiss., 1979.

Robert, L. "Les inscriptions grecques et latines de Sardes." *Revue archéologique* 7 (1936): 237–238.

Roberts, J. W. *The Letters of John.* R. B. Sweet, 1968.

Roller, O. *Das Formular der paulinischen Briefe: Ein Beitrag zur Lehre vom antike Briefe.* Beihefte zur Wissenschaft vom Alten und Neuen Testament 58. W. Kohlhammer Verlag, 1933.

Ropes, J. H. "The Greek Catena to the Catholic Epistles." *Harvard Theological Review* 19 (1926): 383–388.

Ross, A. *The Epistles of James and John*. New International Commentary on the New Testament. Eerdmans, 1954.

Royse, J. R. *Scribal Habits in Early Greek New Testament Papyri*. New Testament Tools, Studies, and Documents 36. Brill, 2008.

———. "Scribal Tendencies in the Transmission of the Text of the New Testament." In *The Text of the New Testament in Contemporary Research: Essays on the Status Quaestionis*. 2nd ed., edited by B. D. Ehrman and M. W. Holmes. New Testament Tools, Studies, and Documents 42. Brill, 2013.

Rusch, A., ed. *Biblia Latina cum Glossa Ordinaria. Facsimile Reprint of the Editio Princeps Adolph Rusch of Strassburg 1480/81*. Vol. 4. Brepols, 1992.

Russell, D. A., ed. and trans. *Quintilian. The Orator's Education*. Vol. 2. Loeb Classical Library 125. Harvard University Press, 2002.

Sarri, A. *Material Aspects of Letter Writing in the Graeco-Roman World: 500 BC–AD 300*. De Gruyter, 2018.

Schleiermacher, F. *Einleitung ins Neue Testament*. Berlin: G. Reimer, 1845.

Schlüssler, K., ed. *Biblia Coptica: Die koptischen Bibeltexte. Band 4, Lieferung 2. Das Sahidische Alte und Neue Testament: Vollständiges Verzeichnis mit Standorten sa 621–672*. Harrassowitz Verlag, 2009.

Schmelz, G. *Kirchliche Amtstäger im spätantiken Ägypten nach den Aussagen der griechischen und koptischen Papyri und Ostraka*. K. G. Saur, 2002.

Schnackenburg, R. *Die Johannesbriefe*. Herders Theologischer Kommentar zum Neuen Testment 13. Herder, 1953; Reprint, 1963, 1977, 1984.

———. *The Johannine Epistles: Introduction and Commentary*. Translated by R. Fuller and I. Fuller. Crossroad, 1992.

Schnelle, U. *Die Johannesbriefe*. Evangelische Verlagsanstalt, 2010.

Schow, N. I., *Charta papyracea Graece scripta Musei Borgiani Velitris*. Rome, 1788.

Schunack, G. *Die Briefe des Johannes*. Theologischer Verlag, 1982.

Schwartz, E., ed. *Kyrillos von Skythopolis*. J. C. Hinrichs Verlag, 1939.

Sedláček, J., trans. and ed. *Dionysii Bar Salibi Commentarii in Apocalypsim, Actus et Epistulas Catholicas*. 2 Vols. Corpus Scriptorum Christianorum Orientalium 53 and 60; Scriptores Syri II, 18–20. Typographeo Reipublicae, 1909.

Smalley, S. *1, 2, 3 John*. World Biblical Commentary 51. Word, 1984.

Smit, P.-B. "A Note on the Relationship between II and III John." *Biblische Notizen* 123 (2004): 93–102.

Smith, W., ed. *A Dictionary of the Bible*. 1st ed. Boston: Little, Brown, and Company, 1863.

Smith, D. M. "The Epistles of John: What's New Since Brooke's ICC in 1912?" *Expository Times* 120, no.8 (2009): 373–384.

Smith, G. S., and B. C. Landau, *The Secret Gospel of Mark: A Controversial Scholar, a Scandalous Gospel of Jesus, and the Fierce Debate over Its Authenticity*. Yale University Press, 2023.

Smith, W. A. *A Study of the Gospels in Codex Alexandrinus: Codicology, Palaeography, and Scribal Hands*. New Testament Tools, Studies, and Documents 48. Brill, 2014.

Solin, H. "Latin Cognomina in the Greek East." In *The Greek East in the Roman Context: Proceedings of a Colloquium Organised by the Finnish Institute at Athens; May 21 and 22, 1999*, edited by O. Salomies. Papers and Monographs of the Finnish Institute at Athens 7. Bookstore Tiedekirja, 2001.

———. *Die griechischen Personennamen in Rom. Ein Namenbuch. Zweite, völlig neu bearbeitete Auflage*. Corpus Inscriptionum Latinarum: Auctarium, Series Nova, 2. 3 Vols. Walter de Gruyter, 2003.

Staab, K. "Die griechischen Katenenkommentare zu den katholischen Briefe." *Biblica* 5 (1924): 296–353.

Stählin, O., ed. *Clemens Alexandrinus. Band 1. Protrepticus und Paedagogus*. Die griechischen christlichen Schriftsteller der ersten [drei] Jahrhunderte 12. J. C. Hinrichs, 1905; 2. Auflage 1936; 3. Auflage ed. U. Treu, 1972.

———. ed. *Clemens Alexandrinus. Band 2. Stromata: Buch I bis VI*. Die griechischen christlichen Schriftsteller der ersten [drei] Jahrhunderte 15. J. C. Hinrichs, 1906; 2. Auflage 1939; 3. Auflage ed. L. Früchtel, zum Druck besorgt von U. Treu, 1985.

———. ed. *Clemens Alexandrinus. Band 3. Stromata: Buch VII und VIII. Excerpta ex Theodoto. Eclogae propheticae. Quis dives salvetur. Fragmente*. Die griechischen christlichen Schriftsteller der ersten [drei] Jahrhunderte 17. J. C. Hinrichs, 1909; 2. Auflage ed. L. Früchtel, zum Druck besorgt von U. Treu, 1970.

Stott, J. R. W. *The Epistles of John: An Introduction and Commentary*. Eerdmans, 1964.

Stowers, S. K. *Letter Writing in Greco-Roman Antiquity*. The Westminster Press, 1986.

Streeter, B. H. *The Four Gospels: A Study of Origins, Treating of the Manuscript Tradition, Sources, Authorship, & Dates*. Macmillan and Co., 1924.

Streett, D. R. *They went out from us: The Identity of the Opponents in First John*. Beihefte zur Zeitschrift für die neutestamentliche Wissenschaft 177. Berlin; New York; Walter de Gruyter GmbH & Co. KG, 2011.

Stunica, J. L. de [Diego Lopez de Zuñiga], D. Ducas, and H. N. de Toledo, et al., eds. *Novum Testamentum Grece et Latine in Academia Complutensi Noviter Impressum*. 5th volume of *Biblia Sacra Polyglotta*. Compluti [Alcalá]: Industria Arnaldi Gulielmi de Brocaric, 1514–1517.

Teeter, T. M. "Christian Letters of Recommendation in the Papyrus Record." *The Patristic & Byzantine Review* 9 (1990): 59–69.

———. "Letters of Recommendation or Letters of Peace?" *Archiv für Papyrusforschung und verwandte Gebiete* 3 (1997): 954–960.

Thompson, D. J. *Memphis under the Ptolemies*. 2nd ed. Princeton University Press, 2012.

Thompson, M. M. *1–3 John*. The IVP New Testament Commentary Series. InterVarsity Press, 1992.

Tibiletti, G. *Le lettere private nei papiri greci del III e IV secolo d.C.: Tra paganesimo e cristianesimo*. Vita e Pensiero, 1979.

Tischendorf, C., ed. *Novum Testamentum Graece, ad antiquissimos testes denuo recensuit apparatum criticum omni studio perfectum apposuit commentationem isagogicam praetexuit Constantinus Tischendorf, editio octava critica maior.* Leipzig: J. C. Hinrichs, 1869 (Vol. 1), 1872 (Vol. 2).

Tomsin, A. "Étude sur les πρεσβύτεροι des villages de la χώρα égyptienne." *Bulletin de la Classe des Lettres et Politiques de l'Academie Royale de Belgique*, 5th series, 38 (1952): 95–130, 467–532.

Trapp, M. *Greek and Latin Letters: An Anthology, with Translation.* Cambridge University Press, 2003.

Tregelles, S. P., ed. *The Greek New Testament, edited from ancient authorities; with the various readings of all the ancient MSS., the ancient versions, and earlier ecclesiastical writers (to Eusebius inclusive); together with the Latin version of Jerome, from the Codex Amiatinus of the sixth century.* London: Samuel Bagster & Sons, 1857–1872.

Treu, K. "Christliche Empfehlungs-Schemabriefe auf Papyrus." In *Zetesis. Album Amicorum Door Vrienden en Collega's Aangeboden Aan Prof. Dr. E. de Strycker Ter Gelegenheid Van Zijn 65e*, edited by E. de Strycker. Boekhandel, 1973.

Turner, E. G., ed. *Catalogue of Greek and Latin Papyri and Ostraca in the Possession of the University of Aberdeen.* Aberdeen University Studies 116. The University Press, 1939.

———. *Greek Manuscripts of the Ancient World.* Revised edition by P. Parsons. Bulletin Supplement Institute of Classical Studies 46. University of London Institute of Classical Studies, 1987.

Uhlig, S., and H. Maehlum, eds. *Novum Testamentum Aethiopice: Die Gefangenschaftsbriefe.* Äthiopistische Forschungen. Band 33. Franz Steiner, 1993.

Van Miert, D. *The Emancipation of Biblical Philology in the Dutch Republic, 1590–1670.* Oxford University Press, 2018.

Verhoogt, A. "Dictating Letters in Greek and Roman Egypt from a Comparative Perspective." https://sites.lsa.umich.edu/wp-content/uploads/sites/235/2015/02/dictating1.pdf.

Volkmar, G. *Die Evangelien: oder Marcus und die Synopsis der kanonischen und ausserkanonischen Evangelien.* Leipzig: Fues's Verlag, 1870.

Von Maestricht, G., ed. *H KAINH DIAΘHKH. Novum Testamentum, post priores Steph. Curcellaei et D.D. Oxoniensium labores. Cum Prolegomenis G.D.T.M. et notis in fine adjectis.* Amstelodami: Ex Officina Wetsteniana, 1711.

Von Wahlde, U. C. *The Gospel and Letters of John. Volume 3: Commentary on the Three Johannine Letters.* Eerdmans, 2010.

———. "Johannine Letters." *Oxford Bibliographies Online.* January 11, 2018. https://doi.org/10.1093/obo/9780195393361-0253.

Wachtel, K. *Der byzantinische Text der katholischen Briefe: Eine Untersuchung zur Entstehung der Koine des Neuen Testaments.* Arbeiten zur neutestamentlichen Textforschung 24. Walter de Gruyter, 1995.

Wallace, D. B. *Greek Grammar Beyond the Basics: An Exegetical Syntax of the New Testament*. Zondervan, 1996.

Walton, B., ed. *Biblia Sacra Polyglotta, complectentia Textus Originalis, Hebraicum cum Pentateucho Samaritano, Chaldaicum, Graecum, Versionumque antiquarum Samaritanae, Graecae LXXII. Interpretum, Chaldaicae, Syriacae, Arabicae, Aethiopicae, Vulgatae Latinae, quicquid comparari potetat, &c.* 5 Vols. Londini: Imprimebat Thomas Roycroft, 1654–1657.

———. ed. *Biblia Sacra Polyglotta*. Vol. 5. Londini: Imprimebat Thomas Roycroft, 1657.

Waltz, R. B. *The Encyclopedia of New Testament Textual Criticism: Last Preliminary Edition*. 2013.

Ward, R. A. *The Epistles of John and Jude: A Study Manual*. Baker Book House, 1965.

Watson, D. F. "A Rhetorical Analysis of 2 John According to Greco-Roman Convention." *New Testament Studies* 35 (1989): 104–130.

Wayment, T. A. *The New Testament. A Translation for Latter-Day Saints*. Rev. ed. Greg Kofford Books, 2022.

Weiss, Bernhard, ed. *Das Neue Testament. Textkritische Untersuchungen und Textherstellung*. 3 Vols. Leipzig: Hinrichs, 1894 (Acts, Catholic Epistles, Revelation); 1896 (Pauline Epistles); 1900 (Gospels).

———. *Die drei Briefe des Apostel Johannes*. Göttingen: Vandenhoeck und Ruprecht, 1899.

Welborn, L. L. *An End to Enmity: Paul and the "Wrongdoer" of Second Corinthians*. Beihefte zur Zeitschrift für die neutestamentliche Wissenschaft 185. De Gruyter, 2011.

Welch, J. W., and J. F. Hall. *Charting the New Testament*. Foundation for Ancient Research and Mormon Studies, 2002.

Wendt, H. *Die Johannesbriefe und das johanneische* Christentum. Buchhandlung des Waiserhauses, 1925.

Wengst, K. *Der erste, zweite und dritte Brief des Johannes*. Ökumenischer Taschenbuch-Kommentar 16. Echter-Verlag, 1978.

Wesley, J. *Explanatory Notes Upon The New Testament*. London: William Bowyer, 1755.

Westcott, B. F. *The Epistles of St. John: The Greek Text with Notes and Essays*. London: Macmillan, 1883.

Westcott, B. F., and F. J. A. Hort, eds. *The New Testament in the Original Greek*. Cambridge and London: Macmillan, 1881.

———. eds. *The New Testament in the Original Greek*. American ed. With an Introduction by P. Schaff. New York: Harper and Brothers, Franklin Square, 1881.

———. eds. *The New Testament in the Original Greek: Introduction and Appendix*. New York: Harper & Brothers, 1882.

Wettstein, J. J., ed. *Novum Testamentum*. Amstelodami: Ex Officina Wetsteniana, 1735.

———. ed. *Novum Testamentum Graecum editionis receptae, cum Lectionibus Variantibus Codicum MSS., Editionum aliarum, Versionum et Patrum, necnon Commentario pleniore ex Scriptoribus veteribus, Hebraeis, Graecis, et Latinis, historiam et vim verborum illustrante.* 2 Vols. Amstelaedami, 1751–1752.

Weymouth, R. F., ed. *The Resultant Greek Testament: Exhibiting the Text in Which the Majority of Modern Editors Are Agreed, and Containing the Readings of Stephens (1550), Lachmann, Tregelles, Tischendorf, Lightfoot, Ellicott, Alford, Weiss, The Bale Edition (1880), Westcott and Hort, and the Revision Committee.* London: Elliot Stock, 1892.

———. *The New Testament in Modern Speech.* Pilgrim Press, 1903; rev. 1924.

White, J. L. "Epistolary Formulas and Cliches in Greek Papyrus Letters." *Society of Biblical Literature Seminar Papers* 2 (1978): 289–319.

———. "The Greek Documentary Letter Tradition Third Century B.C.E. to Third Century C.E." *Semeia* 22 (1981): 89–106.

———. "New Testament Epistolary Literature in the Framework of Ancient Epistolography." *Aufstieg und Niedergang der romischen Welt* 25/2 (1984): 1730–1757.

———. *Light from Ancient Letters.* Fortress Press, 1986.

Wilcken, U. "Das Leydener Klammersystem." *Archiv für Papyrusforschung und verwandte Gebiete* 10 (1932): 211–212.

Wilder, J. A. "Introduction and Exegesis of the First, Second and Third Epistles of John." In *The Interpreter's Bible.* Vol. 12., edited by George A. Buttrick. Abingdon, 1957.

Williams, R. R. *The Letters of John and James.* Cambridge University Press, 1965.

Wilson, A. "Scribal Habits and the New Testament Text." In *Digging for the Truth: Collected Essays Regarding the Byzantine Text of the Greek New Testament – A Festschrift in Honor of Maurice A. Robinson*, edited by M. Billington and P. Streitenberger. Focus Your Mission, 2014.

Windisch, H. *Die Katholischen Briefe.* Verlag J. C. B. Mohr (Paul Siebeck), 1951.

Winter, G. *Life and Letters in the Papyri.* University of Michigan Press, 1933.

Woide, C. G., ed. *Novum Testamentum Graecum e codice ms. alexandrino, qui Londini in Bibliotheca Musei Britannici asservatur.* London: J. Nichols, 1786.

Wordsworth, J., H. J. White, and H. F. D. Sparks. *Novum Testamentum Domini nostri Iesu Christi Latine sec. edit. S. Hieronymi ad codicum manuscriptorum fidem* 3.2. Clarendon Press, 1949.

Yarborough, R. W. *1–3 John.* Baker Exegetical Commentary on the New Testament. Grand Baker Academic, 2008.

Yi, A.-T. *From Erasmus to Maius: The History of Codex Vaticanus in New Testament Textual Scholarship.* Arbeiten zur neutestamentlichen Textforschung 58. De Gruyter, 2024.

Zahn, T. *Forschungen zur Geschichte des neutestamentlichen Kanons und der altkirchlichen Literatur. III. Theil: Supplementum Clementinum.* Erlangen: Verlag von Andreas Deichert, 1884.

———. "Die sogenannte Synopsis des Athanasius." In *Geschichte des neutestamentlichen Kanons. Zweiter Band: Urkunden und Belege zum ersten un dritten Band.* Erste Hälfte. Erlangen and Leipzig: A. Deichert'sche, 1890.

Ziemann, F. "De epistularum Graecarum formulis sollemnibus quaestiones selectae." PhD diss., Halle, 1910.

INDICES

Index of Ancient Authors

Index of Inscriptions, Manuscripts, and Papyri

Index of Modern Authors (1881 to present)

Index of Biblical References

Subject Index